A
SOCIAL AND ECONOMIC
HISTORY OF
THE NEAR EAST
IN
THE MIDDLE AGES

A
SOCIAL AND ECONOMIC HISTORY OF THE NEAR EAST IN THE MIDDLE AGES

✳

E. Ashtor

UNIVERSITY OF CALIFORNIA PRESS
Berkeley, Los Angeles, London

University of California Press
Berkeley and Los Angeles, California

ISBN: 0-520-02962-3

Library of Congress catalog card no. 74-29800
Printed in Great Britain

Published under the auspices of the
Gustav E. von Grunebaum Centre for Near Eastern Studies
University of California, Los Angeles

Contents

Maps

Graphs

Preface

A bibliophile interested in the history of the Moslem East could easily fill a large library. Many great scholars who had a profound knowledge of Oriental languages have indeed written voluminous works on Arabic civilisation and the vicissitudes of the Caliphate. What justification is there for a new book on this subject? The purpose of the present book is very different from most learned treatises to be found in Western libraries.

The scholars who have hitherto undertaken research into the history of the Near East in the middle ages have had recourse to the rich historical literature of the Arabs and the Persians which provides copious materials for Oriental history. But, alas, the old Oriental writers tell the story of the aristocracy: their books are focused on the courts of the princes and on the achievements of their armies. The Orientalists themselves, with few exceptions, have always been mainly interested in the spiritual life of the Moslems, in Islam and in Arabic literature. So many texts which indeed refer to social and economic life have been overlooked or misunderstood by scholars to whom these problems meant nothing. But very often such texts, e.g. reports on revolutionary movements, are obscure, contradictory and incomplete, so that it is very difficult to harmonise them or to see the wood for the trees. All the scholars who have written on Moslem civilisation have dwelt on the great progress made by the Arabs in the days of the caliphs, but they have omitted to show why there was later a technological stand-still and what the consequences of it were. The risings of the lower strata of society are described as riots, but probably some of them had far-reaching aims.

This book aims to show that the Near East was in the middle ages not at all a static, unchanging society. On the contrary, the attempt will be made to disclose momentous changes in the social framework of the Near Eastern population and to delineate great social movements. It will be argued that even in the Near East the bourgeois played a great role in political history and that there were strong revolutionary movements, though different from those known to Western history. To narrate once more the story of the Turkish sultans and to discuss the achievements of Arab and Persian poets and philosophers is no part of the book's intention. In this it will be quite distinct from the numerous reference books available in the Western world.

Trying to sum up various essays and my own research in an overall synthesis of the social and economic development of the Near East in the course of nine hundred years is bold, if not rash. But even if it will only serve as a challenge for further research, it will have fulfilled an important task.

Some conjectures and conclusions may prove to be mistaken, but the author can honestly say that he has drawn them from the sources. This book is based on the study of many Arabic chronicles, not a few of them still unpublished and hidden in the great libraries of London and Oxford. A great number of Judaeo-Arabic geniza documents have been used, as have numerous documents in the archives of Venice and other towns of Italy which traded with the Near East in the middle ages. These latter documents were unknown to Heyd, when he wrote his excellent History of Levantine trade in the middle ages. It goes without saying that printed documents have not been neglected, so far as they were known to the author.

To a certain extent the present book summarises the results of the author's published research. The findings have been often corrected and modified, and new materials have been added to them. As far as possible the author has abstained from polemics, as this book is meant for the general reader, not as a scholarly treatise. For the same reason quite often European translations of Oriental sources have been quoted.

In submitting his results to the reader, the author asks for the indulgence generally shown to an attempt at research in a field hitherto very much neglected.

Zurich, October 1972   E. Ashtor

CHAPTER I

The Kingdom of the Arabs

The Orientalists have dealt with the origins of Islam, elucidating the Christian and Jewish influences on Mohammed. They have tried to explain the victories of the Arabs, who conquered almost the whole of the Near East and defeated within a decade the experienced armies of Persia and Byzantium. Sociologists have elaborated theories about the factors which brought about the emigration of Bedouin tribes from Arabia and their settlement in other countries.

The interest of the economic historian will be focused on the effects of the Moslem conquests on the economy of the Near East and on social conditions in the countries ruled by Mohammed's successors ever since.

Did the conquest of these countries by the Arabs bring about a social upheaval, or were the armies of occupation rather superimposed on the old strata of society? Did the conquest result in a change of the social system? Were the Arabs within a short time absorbed by the autochthonous society, as had been the fate of so many invaders?

a) *The settlement of the Arabs*

Students of history have always been impressed by the vigour of the Arab conquerors and above all by the exceptional rapidity of their advance.

In a first wave of conquests, lasting from 633 to 656, they subdued Syria, Babylonia, Persia and Egypt. The fate of Palestine and Syria was sealed by the battle on the river Yarmuk in 636, that of Babylonia by that of al-Kadisiyya in 637. In the years 638–40 the Arabs took the fortified towns which still offered resistance in Palestine, overran Upper Mesopotamia and invaded Khuzistan, the province of Persia bordering on south-eastern Babylonia. The conquest of Egypt begun in 639 was complete in 642, when the capital, Alexandria, surrendered. Thereupon the victorious Arabs penetrated into the countries east of

Babylonia and west of Egypt. The last great Persian army was defeated in the battle of Nihawend in 642, and in the following years the Moslems conquered most provinces of Media and Adherbeidjan. There followed the conquest of Fars and Khurasan, so that in 651 the Oxus was reached. All this was achieved by expeditionary forces of limited size. The Arabs who invaded Irak in 633 were no more than 2–3,000, and in the decisive battle of al-Kadisiyya they numbered no more than 6–7,000. In the battle on the Yarmuk the number of the Arabs probably did not exceed 25,000. The conquest of Persia was achieved by 35–40,000. Egypt was first invaded by 4,000 men, who were later reinforced by 6,000 more. While the numbers of the Persian and Byzantine armies should not be overestimated either, they were certainly superior to those of the Arabs.[1] Nor did the Arabs use weapons unknown by their enemies. On the other hand, they encountered armies which were well trained and whose commanders distinguished themselves by great strategic skill.

The great military achievements of the Arabs have rightly been explained by the exhaustion of both the Persian and the Byzantine empires, which had been at war with each other for twenty-five years. The two empires were also weakened by internal dissensions, the Persian empire by feudal disintegration, and the Byzantine empire by the strife between the Eastern churches. The contest between the orthodoxy upheld by the Byzantine emperor and the Monophysites became identified in Egypt and in Syria with the antagonism between the Greek rulers and the indigenous populations. So the inhabitants of these countries did not regard the Arab invaders as enemies, but welcomed them as liberators, or at least remained neutral. Two famous Orientalists, the Italian Leone Principe di Caetani, and the German C. H. Becker, considered the Moslem conquests to be mainly the consequence of the economic conditions in the Arabian peninsula. According to Caetani they were brought about by climatic changes which had begun many centuries before. The aridity of Arabia had been growing during long ages. Where once great streams had flowed and glaciers had covered the slopes of the mountains there were now deserts and steppes which could not feed an ever-increasing population. The discrepancy between the worsening conditions and the increase of the population had resulted in periodical migratory movements. The first of these began about 5000 B.C. After 3800 B.C. emigration from Arabia gathered such force that the Sumerian civilisation in Mesopotamia was semitised. About 2500 B.C. a true Arab dynasty, that of

Hammurabi, sprang up in Babylonia. There followed the migratory movements of the Aramaeans and that of the Chaldaeans which engendered the dynasty of Nebuchadnezzar. That shortage of grazing land and food through increasing desiccation drove the Bedouins to a policy of military expansion was also the opinion of C. H. Becker. The Arab conquests were not the realisation of ideas conceived by the Moslem leaders. On the contrary, the roving Arab tribes on the borders of Babylonia began the invasion and later applied for help to the Moslem leaders at Medina. Becker admitted, however, that Islam supplied the essential unity and the central power. Although hunger and avarice were the driving forces, the new religion was the rallying factor.[2]

New research has substantiated the ideas of Caetani and Becker. In a series recently published by Altheim-Stiehl, a group of scholars has collected and discussed much informative material on the expansion of the Arabs into the lands of the Fertile Crescent and in other regions of the Near East before Islam. They have shown that the immigration of the Arabs in Syria came to an apogee in Seleucid times. It was then that the old Edessa was founded by an Arab tribe. Edessa was an Arab kingdom in the second half of the second century B.C. Even in some regions of Upper Mesopotamia, such as the district of Sindjar, Arabs were in control in the first two centuries B.C. At the same time Arab tribesmen founded a kingdom in Mesene, east of the lower Tigris, a state which flourished for about 300 years. In Transjordan Arab tribes were to be found at the time of the campaigns of Antiochus III against Egypt in 218–7 B.C. The Ituraeans, an Arab people, built a kingdom in Central Syria in the first century B.C. Since the Swiss traveller J.-L. Burckhardt discovered the ruins of Petra in 1812, our knowledge of the kingdom of the Nabataeans has steadily increased. It is now known that this Arab people occupied the south of Transjordan at the beginning of the sixth century B.C., and later built a rich and strong state in Palestine and Southern Syria. Another Arab tribe which penetrated Syria were the Safaites, who settled east and south-east of Damascus. They left in these regions many thousands of Arabic inscriptions which date from the first century B.C. to the beginning of the fourth century A.D.

Of all the principalities which Arab tribes founded before Islam in the lands of the Fertile Crescent, the strongest was the kingdom of Palmyra, by the middle of the third century the greatest power in the Near East. Arab immigration in the Fertile Crescent went on under the

reign of the later Roman and the Byzantine emperors, and in the fifth
century Upper Mesopotamia was called by Syriac writers Bet Arbaye –
the Land of the Arabs. In the south-western borderland of Babylonia
the Lakhmids had founded, with the help of the Persian kings, the
kingdom of al-Hira, a buffer state, destined to defend the Persian
dominions against the Byzantines. From the middle of the fourth to
the middle of the sixth century the kings of al-Hira were in control of
the region between the Euphrates and the fertile provinces of Central
Syria. The Byzantines, on the other hand, created a similar Arab buffer
state, the principality of the Ghassanids, who ruled over the Hauran,
Phoenicia, Northern Transjordan and Palestine. Egypt too had a
numerous Arab population long before the Moslem conquests.
According to Herodotus, its eastern provinces were called Arabia in the
fifth century B.C.

So when the Moslems invaded the lands of the Fertile Crescent and
Egypt they found everywhere large numbers of Arabs, most of them
nomads or only half-sedentary. Several Arab tribes were living on the
banks of the Euphrates, the North Arabian tribes of the Banu Taghlib,
Tamim, Numair, Idjl and Rabia. The Banu Iyad were in control of
al-Anbar and the surrounding district. Many of the Arab tribesmen
had become peasants, as is borne out by old and reliable texts. al-Hira
was a relatively big Arab town, numbering about 50,000 inhabitants.[3]
In short, the Moslem conquests were a new stage in a series of migratory
movements. Economic necessity was the main driving force. When the
perennial nomadic aggression was set in motion partly by a religious
impulse it became an overwhelming power to which the old eastern
empires succumbed.

In order to estimate the impact of the Moslem conquests and the
role which the Arabs were to play in the social framework of the old
Near Eastern societies, one would like to know the numbers of the
conquerors who settled in the conquered countries.

A. Müller has concluded that in the year 636 the total of the Arab
forces outside Arabia was perhaps 80,000. In the days of the caliph
Uthman (644–56) the Moslem armies, from Eastern Persia to Carthage,
numbered according to him, 250–300,000 men. The accounts which
the Arabic historians give of the battle of Siffin in 657 would be in
keeping with these estimates. For the old Arabic authors say that for
this decisive battle in the first civil war in the Moslem empire 150,000
men were mobilised. But all these figures are probably exaggerated.
The Egyptian historian al-Makrizi, on the other hand, found in one of

his sources that in the days of the caliph Muawiya (661–80) there were 40,000 Arabs in Egypt. However, the number of the Arabs increased steadily. According to the conjecture of H. Lammens in about 720 they numbered in Syria 200,000 altogether, against a total of four million inhabitants. Other scholars are inclined to suppose that the number of the Arabs was much greater, amounting to 300–400,000, whereas the total of Syria's population was smaller.[4] However that may have been, the Arabs, the newcomers together with those coming earlier, were in the period subsequent to the conquests a small minority everywhere.

But invaders who settle in the conquered countries are always minorities. So it is far more important to establish the social stratification of the new rulers of the Near East. A mere glance at the old Arabic sources is enough to bring home to the reader that the Arab conquests resulted in considerable changes in the composition of Near Eastern populations. A part of the Arab tribes who lived in Syria before the conquest and had embraced Christianity would not accept Moslem rule, and left for Byzantium. Old Arabic authors relate that Djabala b. al-Aiham, the prince of the Banu Ghassan, went to Asia Minor with 30,000 men. The exodus of Greek-speaking town-dwellers must have been massive. Byzantine officials and traders, and also natives of Syria and Egypt who had been brought up in the Greek culture and were faithful to Orthodox Christianity, could not bear living under the rule of people whom they regarded as pure barbarians. So many thousands of the inhabitants of the coastal towns of Syria and Phoenicia went to Byzantium. al-Baladhuri says that this happened in the towns of Sidon, Beirut, Byblos, Arka and Tripoli. The same happened in Alexandria. An Arab author of the ninth century narrates that 200,000 inhabitants of this town emigrated to Byzantium. Although this number must be greatly exaggerated, it points to the fact that the exodus of the Greeks was a sizable phenomenon. But also agriculturalists who were imbued with Byzantine culture abandoned their old homes. An old Arab historian speaks about the emigration of the inhabitants of the small towns of Balis and Kasirin in Northern Syria. Certainly we are not mistaken when supposing that they were landlords of estates in the surrounding districts. In Babylonia too there was probably a similar phenomenon: many Persians left the country during the Arab invasion and subsequently. But it goes without saying that not all Greeks and Persians abandoned their towns and villages. An Arab author, writing in the second half of the ninth century, says that the big villages on the route from Baghdad to Kufa were in his days inhabited by Persians and Arabs.[5]

The Moslem rulers were aware of the consequences which must follow the exodus of the Greeks and the Persians, and tried to check the decline of the abandoned towns by the settlement of other town-dwellers. They brought Persians and Jews to the towns of Syria and Palestine which had been abandoned by their former inhabitants. According to al-Yakubi, who wrote in the ninth century, the Persians were a sizable group in the populations of the provinces of Damascus, Jordan and Palestine. There were many Persians in the towns of Baalbek and Arka, while Jews were settled in Tripoli, which had been abandoned by the Greek population.[6]

The great majority of the people who settled in the lands conquered by the Moslems were, however, Arab Bedouin. It is true that some of the sources of data concerning the Arab tribes under the reign of the caliphs belong to the second half of the ninth century, a period when the distribution of the Arabs over the countries of the Near East had changed to a certain extent. We are probably not mistaken, however, in supposing that a great part of the Arab tribes mentioned there had been living in the same regions since the Moslem conquests.

Among the Arabs who settled in Southern Irak almost all the tribes of Northern and Southern Arabia were represented. There were Kais, Tamim and Bakr b. Wail, all of them hailing from Northern Arabia, and clans of Asad, Hamdan, Kudaa, Madhhidj and other South Arabians. On the banks of the Euphrates there were numerous clans of Kais, while Upper Mesopotamia was divided between Mudar, Bakr and Rabia, all of them Northern Arabians. But also the Banu Ukail, Numair and Habib played a great role in this region. Most of these tribesmen led the life of nomads, as had done their ancestors in the Arabian peninsula, though others had gone over to a half-settled life.

The Arab tribes who lived in Syria before the Moslem conquest were mostly South Arabians, and even after the conquest these clans still represented an important sector of the Arab population. Kalbites lived in the oasis of Tadmor, Tayy, Kinda, Himyar, Kalb and Hamdan in the province of Hims, Bahra in the districts surrounding Hamath. Yemenites were also to be found near Kafrtab and Lattakia, Kinda in the districts of Shaizar and Antartus. In the neighbourhood of Damascus there were Ghassan, Kudaa, Kalb and Lakhm, besides Rabia from Northern Arabia. In Palestine there were many clans of Lakhm, Djudham and Kinda. But in the wake of the Arab invasion many North

Arabian clans came to Syria and spread all over the country. Kaisites lived in the districts surrounding Damascus, in the Hauran, the Bathaniyya, the Golan, near Jericho and in Southern Palestine. However, the South Arabian tribes were also joined by newcomers, such as the Amila who gave their name to a great part of Galilee. So the Arab population of Syria and Palestine was a very chequered one.

The successive waves of Arab immigrants who settled in the conquered countries brought to Egypt also a variegated population of Bedouin tribesmen. After the conquest many Yemenites had settled in Egypt and later other groups of Southern Arabs joined them. In the year 673 Ziyad, the mighty viceroy of Irak, transplanted numerous clans of Kudaa, Tudjib, Lakhm and Djudham to Egypt. But there were in Egypt also Himyar, Madhhidj, Ghutaif, Walan, Maafir, Khaulan and other South Arabians. Later, in the days of the caliph Hisham, there began a systematic settlement of North Arabian clans. According to Arabic sources, upon the request of the governor of Egypt, the caliph sent him in the year 727 3,000 Kaisites. They were settled in the northeastern province called al-Hauf, south of Tinnis and east of Bilbais. The government obliged them to engage in agriculture, but they had also the monopoly of transporting Egyptian grains to the shores of the Red Sea, whence it was sent to the Hidjaz. In the middle of the eighth century new clans of Kaisites, who had heard about the good fortune of their brethren, joined them. Meanwhile the Arabs had begun to spread over the countryside and to settle everywhere in the villages. Before long they imposed their language on most provinces of Egypt. That was undoubtedly the consequence of the slow but steady spontaneous immigration of Bedouins who lived from cattle breeding and exchanged their products against those of the native peasants. The Arab tribesmen pitched their tents on the border of the cultivated land, on both sides of the Nile valley, and advanced slowly to the south. The scale of the Bedouin immigration is indicated by the fact that its surplus was sufficient to scatter Arab nomads in the eastern Sudan.[7]

b) *Bedouinisation and acculturation*

The settlement of the Arabs in the conquered countries had two important consequences for social and economic life. There began two phenomena which look at the first glance contradictory, but are in fact two sides of the same process, i.e. the clash of the Arabs with the autochthonous population. In fact, the Arab invaders split into two great sectors, whose attitudes towards the autochthonous population and their civilisation were very different. The tribesmen proved to be a very harmful factor in the economic life of the fertile regions of the Near East whose mainstay was agriculture. On the other hand, the Arabs who went over to settled life came under the influence of the old Oriental civilisations which were alive in the autochthonous populations, and in course of time a recombination of different civilisations ensued. The result was the birth of a splendid Arab syncretism. This new Arabic civilisation came into being in the Moslem towns where the inhabitants' way of life was quite different from and opposed to that of their Bedouin ancestors.

Some Arabs who had been husbandmen in their old fatherland founded villages in the lands of the Fertile Crescent and elsewhere. There were also nomads who changed their way of life and became peasants. This happened, for instance, in Southern Lebanon, where Arab tribesmen went over to a sedentary life. But there can be no doubt that the number of these Bedouin was rather limited. The caliphal government had indeed no interest in their becoming husbandmen, since Arabs paid less in taxes than the native peasants. So these were protected by the government, which did its best to prevent encroachment on their property by the Arab tribes. Furthermore, the first caliphs cherished the idea of keeping the Arab warriors as a caste apart. Becoming peasants, they probably believed, the Arabs would lose their military qualities. Nevertheless it happened that Arab warriors left the camp-towns and settled in villages where they engaged in agriculture. But settlement in the countryside did not always prove a success. Quite often it was a failure and the Arabs returned to the nomadic way of life.[8]

Thus a great part of the Arabs who had left Arabia for the lands of the Fertile Crescent and for other regions remained Bedouins. The number of nomadic tribes roving in the conquered countries must have increased considerably, since the overwhelming majority of the conquering armies consisted of Bedouins. As most of these Bedouin warriors had no experience of settled life and had a rather negative attitude towards husbandry, their presence must have been more than detrimental to agricultural activities in many regions. Progressive bedouinisation became a major phenomenon in the economic and social life of the lands of the Fertile Crescent and of other Moslem countries. This was all the more serious as sedentary life had probably been declining in many regions of the Near East a long time before the

Moslem conquests. The districts south of the part of the limes stretching from Constantine (in Northern Syria) to Nisibis had been the land of the nomads already in the fifth and sixth centuries A.D.

The migrations of the Bedouins wrought havoc on the agricultural activities of the settled population in various ways. The overgrazing of goats and camels, a typical feature of Bedouin life, had a devastating effect on natural vegetation. Areas of land which had formerly been cultivated were abandoned. Pasture land increased at the expense of arable fields. When the former inhabitants, experienced peasants, had left, Bedouins began to engage in agriculture, but in their own primitive way. Small holdings of land were tilled artificially, yielded a modest crop and were then abandoned for some years. Often the Bedouins committed acts of robbery, carrying away the sheep flocks of the peasants or causing damage in other ways. Arabic geographers, writing in the tenth century, were aware of the connection between the encroachment of the Bedouins and the decline of agriculture.

The open plains and deforested hills were much more exposed to the disastrous consequences of the Bedouin intrusion, whereas mountains and wooded regions were relatively safe. As these latter regions did not provide the Bedouins with suitable pasture for their sheep and camels, they steered clear of them. Cold regions were also spared the ravages of the Bedouins. Even marshy land was an obstacle to their migrations, although to a lesser extent than mountainous regions. In the swamp land of Southern Irak, for example, remnants of old autochthonous populations could maintain themselves. But the highlands became the refuges of the sedentary populations. The mountainous ranges in Syria are the best example of this phenomenon. All the highlands, from the north to the south, became refuges where dissident religious groups could withstand the onslaught of the Moslems. So the Djabal Ansariyya became the land of the Alauites, the Lebanon that of the Maronites, the mountainous regions of southern Lebanon the retreat of the Druses and the Metwalis. In the course of the long centuries of Moslem rule, the distribution of these sects over the various parts of the mountain ranges has changed, but it is an undeniable fact that they served as havens of refuge from the beginnings of the Moslem period. It was not till the ninth century that Arab tribes penetrated into this region, and most of them went over to sedentary life. The concentration and growing density of the settled population in the mountainous regions and other refuges sometimes had very detrimental consequences for their agriculture. The remnants of the woods were cut down, and the fertile slopes were no longer sufficient to nourish the increasing population.

However, not all the mountainous regions of the Near East were spared the intrusion of the Bedouins. The heights of Transjordan and even parts of the Hauran were overrun by the Arab tribes. The population of the oases succumbed to them almost completely and became wholly dependent upon them. Either the Bedouins supplanted the old inhabitants, or these were obliged to adapt their activities to the needs and wishes of the Bedouins. The fate of the oasis of Palmyra is an example of this phenomenon. The regions where agriculture was carried on without artificial irrigation were particularly exposed to the incursions of the Bedouins. On the other hand, in the districts neighbouring the towns agriculture could successfully resist.[9] Bedouinisation in the Near East was a phenomenon particularly perceptible in the later middle ages, but it began very soon after the Arab conquests. It was the outcome of the immigration of nomadic tribes which continued to be the mainstay of the various dynasties ruling over this part of the world, a class which led a largely independent life, recklessly exploiting the sedentary population.

A great part of the regiments which formed the invading Arab armies was however prevented from maintaining the Bedouin way of life. For the caliphal government settled them, together with their families, in big camp-towns, the so-called amsar. At the beginning these camps were destined to serve as abodes for the intervals between campaigns, but in course of time they became permanent settlements and developed into large towns. As many non-Arabs from the surrounding districts and even from distant regions flocked to these camp-towns, where there was plenty of work, the population became a mixed one, half Arab and half non-Arab. So the amsar were the foci of cultural fusion.

In Irak, as Babylonia was called after the Arab conquest, there were two big camp-towns, Basra and Kufa, both of them founded in the year 638. Basra was destined to accommodate strong forces controlling the approaches to Irak from the south and the routes to the south-western provinces of Persia. It was populated mainly by people hailing from Eastern Arabia. Kufa, not far from the western bank of the Euphrates, had a mixed population of Arabs from the north and the south of the peninsula. In Syria al-Djabiya was at the beginning of the Moslem period the main camp of the Arab army. It had been the principal residence of the Ghassanids, the Arab princes who had ruled before the Moslem conquests over Southern Syria and Transjordan. It lay in the Golan, a day's journey south-east of Damascus. After the conquest of Syria the caliph Omar came there and held the Day of al-Djabiya, famous in Moslem history as the great diet where the foundations of the caliphate were laid. But later, when the Arabs began the invasions of Asia Minor, the camp of Dabik, north of Aleppo, became their headquarters. For several reasons al-Djabiya did not develop into a big town, as did Basra and Kufa. In fact, many Arabs who had come to Syria and Palestine with the invading armies or subsequently, settled in the old towns, where many houses were left empty after the exodus of the Greek Christians. Another big camp was in the village of Emmaus, in the plain of Judaea at the foot of the mountains. In Egypt the Arab camp before Babylon, the old Byzantine fortress, became a big town. It kept the name which it was given by the Egyptians – Fostat, which means a camp surrounded by a ditch.

The records embodied in the writings of the old Arabic authors enable us to follow step by step the transformation of the camps into real towns and their role in the development of Arabic civilisation. At the beginning Basra and Kufa were no more than agglomerations of huts made of rushes. Later these simple cabins were replaced by tents aligned in long rows, and finally, in about 670, houses of baked bricks were built. Basra was also enclosed by a rampart of dried earth and a ditch. The changes in the inner organisation of the amsar are characteristic of the adaptation of the Arab invaders to town life. Kufa was after its foundation divided into asba, seven districts each populated mainly by people belonging to one confederation of tribes. Basra was divided into five quarters, called accordingly akhmas. Later, in 670, the asba of Kufa were replaced by four districts which no longer had any connection with particular tribes. So camps which began as rallying points of warriors became towns.

It is worthwhile to stress the role which the Yemenites played in the development of the amsar. In contradistinction to the Arabs from Central and Northern Arabia most Yemenites had some experience or knowledge of town life. Some had been living, before their emigration from Arabia, in urban settlements, and others had been in more or less close touch with them. Thanks to their tradition of urban life, the Yemenites could more easily adapt themselves to the necessities of town life in the conquered countries, and so they became in some way the protagonists of urbanisation. That they played this role is borne out by texts referring to their appointment to high-ranking municipal posts and by other records. Settlers belonging to various Yemenite tribes took the lead in the urbanisation of Kufa, South Arabians were prominent in the first stages of the development of Fostat, and even the Arabian populations of Damascus and Jerusalem were in the period after the conquest almost exclusively Yemenite colonies. People who had become accustomed to town life in Basra, Kufa and other amsar played a great role in the development of Arab town life in other agglomerations. Arab geographers of the caliphal period relate that Arabs from Basra settled later in Mosul and, further, that Arabs from Mosul went to live in other towns of Upper Mesopotamia.[10]

Owing to the immigration of many non-Arabs in the amsar, the Arabs came there in close contact with the autochthonous civilisation. The symbiosis of non-Arabs and Arabs in the towns and mainly in the amsar resulted in the latter's acculturation and gave birth to the Arabic civilisation. That was a long and sometimes painful process, which may be traced by the modern historian who has a sociological outlook.

It is clear *a priori* that the settlement of the Arabs amidst populations which had inherited the millenary tradition of the old Oriental civilisation would result in their adaptation to other ways of life and to recombination of the different cultural traditions. That was the destiny of all conquerors who settled in civilised countries. But the question is to what extent the conquerors accepted the civilisation of the autochthonous populations. Which tradition, the Arab or the non-Arab, was to become the primary factor in the syncretic civilisation that developed?

As in all similar cases, the Arabs were torn by contradictory motives. They were attracted by the civilised way of life which was offered them by the Persians, Syrians and Egyptians. They soon became aware of the fact that the customs and institutions of these non-Arab populations were superior to those of their Bedouin ancestors. On the other hand, they longed for the freedom of the steppes and deserts of the Arabian peninsula. They suffered from the narrowness and closeness of life in the town, and believed that it made them ill, whereas life in the desert was healthy. The simple food of the Bedouins seemed to them incomparably preferable to that of the townspeople. The education given by the Bedouins to their children was considered much more suitable for the sons of free men than that of the townsfolk. The men of the rank and file who were settled in the big camp-towns insisted that they should have pasture land, where they could go in the spring with their horses and live with their herds of sheep (rabi wa-laban). Arabs belonging to the higher strata of society much preferred to live, as far as possible, in the countryside, and if possible on the edge of the desert. There they built for themselves castles, the so-called badiyas, or adapted for that purpose old Roman fortresses. But, characteristically enough, they installed baths there – a Greek fashion. So the life of the first Arab generations after the conquests was the bi-culturism of a transition period.

The numerical predominance of Bedouins or descendants of Bedouins in the amsar operated against acculturation. The strong influence of the noble families of the old Arab tribes, the buyutat, was another factor which was bound to slow down the adaptation of the Arabs to the ancient Oriental civilisations. The experience of town life which the Yemenites brought with them, on the other hand, rendered acculturation easier.

Whereas these factors more or less balanced each other, intermarriage and imitation caused the Arabs progressively to succumb to the strong influence of the autochthonous civilisations. The autochthonous tradition predominated in modes of food, dress and furniture. But a thorough study of the way of life adopted by the Arabs shows that it did not reflect a donor-receiver relation. The upper strata of Arab society were more inclined to take over the fashions of the old autochthonous civilisations, while the lower, poorer classes stuck to the old Arab customs. The rich and high-ranking Arabs would use beds, but the poor would sleep on the floor like their Bedouin ancestors. The rich ate on tables like ours, the poor from dishes put on Bedouin tables of leather. It appears from inventories of dowries dating from the period of the Crusades that couples belonging to the lower strata of society still slept on mattresses. They had no beds.[11]

Whereas the autochthonous tradition prevailed in matters of material civilisation, the Arabs gave to the new syncretical civilisation their language and their religion. It goes without saying that these two elements almost outweighed all that other traditions bequeathed to the Moslem civilisation. In fact, the Arabic language, the koiné, which became the vehicle of the brilliant new culture, came into being in the amsar, where people of all Arab tribes lived together.

It was, however, a long time before the Arabic language was commonly used for written documents and for literary expression. According to the prevailing tradition it was the caliph Abdalmalik (685–705) who made Arabic the official language of the administration, replacing the Persian and Greek languages which had been used before.

There are however contradictory accounts of the great change, indicating probably that the reform was a gradual one and that it was not undertaken at the same time in all Moslem countries. In Egypt Arabic was introduced in 706, whereas it had already become the official language in Irak in 699. But one would be mistaken in believing that from these dates Arabic alone was used. Arabic became one of the languages used, the others being retained for a very long time.

At the same time as Arabic became the official language of the new Moslem empire, the Arabs began to use it for literary expression. They had long had their own poetry, but in the middle of the eighth century, a hundred years after their settlement in the lands of the Fertile Crescent, they began also to write works on Arabic philology and on history.

That the birth of the Arabic civilisation was a typical recombination of different cultural traditions is clearly shown by the development of Moslem law, which resulted from the adaptation by the Arabs of Byzantine and Persian administrative and judicial practice to their specific needs and their religious ideas. As a result of the fusion, Byzantine and Persian institutions were transformed into Moslem. The *piae causae* became the wakf, an institution considered as typically Moslem. The *agoranomos* was transformed into the muhtasib (chief of market-police) whom the Moslems reckoned as holder of a religious post. But also principles of juridical argumentation, norms and even terms were taken over from Persian, Byzantine and Jewish casuistry. In the middle of the eighth century the Arabs began also to write the first books on law.

Before long the fusion of the cultural traditions was so complete that Arabs began to identify themselves with the historical heritage of their new countries and to glorify their achievements.[12]

c) *Arabs and non-Arabs: social tension*

The caliph Omar, Mohammed's second successor and the real founder of the Moslem empire, conceived the idea of a state consisting of a dominant Arab military class, and working classes, to which would belong the native non-Arabs and non-Moslems. The Arabs would live apart and be maintained by taxes paid by the subjects of the Moslem state. Every Arab would get from the Treasury a pension, the so-called ata. That was the basic idea of the régime of which Omar laid the foundations.

He was not far-sighted, for he did not take into consideration that the non-Arab subjects would progressively become Moslem and that consequently a state built on religious principles would eventually be incapable of preserving the privileges of the ruling nation. His failure to realise that the non-Arab converts would claim the same rights as the Arab Moslems was a fatal error which later caused revolts and civil wars, resulting in much bloodshed. But four generations of Arabs enjoyed the privileges which the régime of Omar bestowed upon them. The descendants of poor Bedouin became the ruling class of a great empire, a kind of rich military aristocracy. The antagonism between these Arab warriors and the non-Arab working classes was from the outset the major problem of the caliphate.

The lowest rate of the ata was, at the beginning of Moslem rule, $1\frac{2}{3}$, $2\frac{1}{12}$ or $2\frac{1}{2}$ dinars a month, but most Arab soldiers got from 4 to 8 dinars. The veterans who had served in the armies invading Syria and Irak even got double this latter sum. In the second half of the seventh and the first half of the eighth century the majority of the Syrian regiments had apparently a monthly wage of 8 dinars, the warriors belonging to some tribes even 16 dinars. The ata of the army in Irak was however lower. There an Arab soldier received no more than 2–4 dinars a month. In order to estimate the economic and social standing which such a wage guaranteed to an Arab warrior, one should compare it with the income of a skilled craftsman or with the pay of the Byzantine military. Probably one is not mistaken in concluding from the rather fragmentary records from the early Moslem period that military pay amounted to double the average income of a highly qualified craftsman. The Byzantine soldier (private), on the other hand, got, at the same time, no more than $1\frac{1}{2}$ nomisma (the same as a dinar) a month. This sum was equal to the income of a qualified worker in the most developed provinces of Byzantium.[13] In other words, the Moslem régime was from the beginning, in economic terms, the rule of a military aristocracy.

But the wealth of the Arab military, in the golden prime of Moslem rule, derived also from the warrior's share in the booty. Even allowing for a great deal of exaggeration in the accounts of the old Arabic writers, one must conclude that fabulous amounts of money and enormous treasures were distributed among the warriors who took part in the wars of conquest. According to the Arabic sources, the booty taken at Ctesiphon was estimated at 900 m dirhams, the share of every Arab warrior amounting to 12,000. After a successful campaign in North Africa, undertaken by the general Abdallah b. Abi Sarh, every Arab horseman got 3,000 mithkal (4.46 grammes) of gold.

It goes without saying that those who held high posts had many opportunities to enrich themselves, and some of them became indeed very rich. Mughira b. Shuba, the ill-famed governor of Kufa and Basra, was only one of them. Governors and even caliphs engaged in various speculations, withholding the pay due to the military or hoarding great quantities of wheat, so that the prices should rise, and hindering others from selling their grain. In fact, several of the high-ranking companions of the Moslem prophet and the Arab governors were great merchants. It seems, however, that the estates they acquired in various ways yielded them even greater sums and were the main source of their great riches.

Their riches enabled the Arab chieftains to lead a luxurious life. In the amsar, the camp-towns, and in their tents in the countryside, the chiefs of the tribes lived in great luxury. The contrast between the lower classes of society and the 'nobles', the ashraf, must have been very great. This contrast too became from that time a characteristic feature of the Moslem world and even of those civilisations which have succeeded to it and inherited its social framework. Arabic writers referring to the early Moslem period mention the noble families in the amsar, the al-Mahaliba in Basra, the Masamia, chiefs of the Bakr in Kufa, the Djarudiya, chiefs of the Abdalkais in the same town, the Ashaitha, chiefs of the Kinda. All these passages point to the great influence in the amsar of the noble families. Seldom does one find in the old Arabic sources details about the riches of these families, but undoubtedly they were very rich. They had a great income from their estates and lived together with many slaves, servants and clients. The number of the slaves must have been considerable, since the supply from the African slave-markets was always sufficient. The slaves were occupied in various services, as servants and as assistants in workshops, while the women were concubines.[14]

Most Arabic authors of the middle ages did not dwell on the economic state of the different classes or on that of individuals. But some of them collected data on this subject, no doubt expecting them to arouse curiosity and amusement though for the modern scholar they are materials illustrating the glaring contrast between the riches of the upper strata and the misery of the lower strata of the caliphal society. Let us quote some of these passages.

The third successor of Mohammed, the caliph Uthman (644–56) is said to have left estates worth 100,000 or even 200,000 dinars. Further, he left with his treasurer, in cash, 150,000 dinars and a million dirhams. The riches of Abdarrahman b. Auf, a close friend of Mohammed, were proverbial. He left ingots of gold to the value of 400,000 dinars. He was a great merchant and also possessed large estates. Talha b. Ubaid-allah, one of the earliest converts to Islam and one of those to whom Mohammed promised a place in Paradise, was the proprietor of many estates in Irak and in Transjordan. He left, according to some authorities, 200,000 dinars and 2,200,000 dirhams. These figures refer to the money in cash. The estates and the merchandise which he left amounted to 30 m dirhams. The crops of his estates in Irak alone yielded him every year 100,000 dirhams – and all this without ever holding a post in the Moslem government. Abdallah, the son of the caliph Omar, was a very rich man too. He could well afford to be generous and was known to make a single gift of alms amounting to 20,000 or 30,000 dirhams. Abbas, an uncle of Mohammed, was very wealthy and well known as a usurer. His activities were denounced by Mohammed publicly, but like so many other companions of his he did not neglect this world for the sake of the other. al-Zubair b. al-Awwam, called 'the Apostle', was also one of the early converts to Islam and took part in all Mohammed's battles. He loved luxury and obtained from Mohammed the permission to wear silken garments, which are forbidden by Moslem law. The value of the property he left was estimated at 35.2 or even at 52 m dirhams. He had indeed houses and even whole quarters in Medina, Basra, Kufa, Fostat and Alexandria. As one reads in the Arabic sources that he also left claims, one must conclude that he also engaged in commerce. Whence the riches of Zaid b. Thabit had been derived is not very difficult to guess. He had been the secretary of Mohammed and recorded his revelations. After the Prophet's death he was entrusted with the government of Medina and accompanied Omar on his journey to Syria. After the battle on the Yarmuk he distributed the booty and later he was finance minister of the caliph Uthman. The Arabic authors narrate that he left estates and merchandise worth 100,000 dinars and beside these many big ingots of gold which had to be divided by hoes. Yala b. Murra (or Munya), a companion of Mohammed, left 50,000 dinars in cash, claims and plots of land whose value was 300,000 dinars. One should stress the fact that this man held not at all a high rank in the hierarchy of the new Moslem state. Khabbab b. al-Aratt, who had been once a poor craftsman, left 40,000 dirhams, al-Mikdad b. Amr b. Thalaba, known as al-Mikdad 'the Black', was one of the first Moslems. He could afford to build a splendid house in the vicinity of Medina. Sad b. Abi Wakkas, who had won the battle of al-Kadisiyya, did not die a poor man either. He too had built a fashionable house in al-Akik, a country-seat near Medina,where many other rich people had built their houses. All these data refer to the first Moslem generation. With all the reserve due to Oriental exaggeration, they leave no doubt as to the legendary riches amassed by the companions of Mohammed. Needless to say that the high-ranking Moslems of the following generations, the governors and generals, followed in their footsteps. What the Arabic historian at-Tabari says about Khalid al-Kasri, governor of Irak (724-38), sheds a bright light on their situation. He had brought under cultivation virgin land and acquired estates so that he had a yearly income of 20 m dirhams.

The wealth and luxury of the rich, it goes without saying, aroused envy and bitterness among the poor. The rank and file asked whence these riches had come and felt themselves cheated by the distribution of the booty. A poet expressed their disappointment in concise verses:

> We set out with them for battle and with them we return from the field,
> But they have riches, we do not.[15]

Although the impact of Mohammed's preaching was tremendous and Islam had become a very important factor in the social and political life of a great part of the world, the worldliness of the upper strata of the Moslem society was a phenomenon characteristic of the new caliphal empire. Surely it was not by chance that the Umayyads, a family of rich merchants from Mecca, who had vigorously opposed Mohammed, supplanted his companions and became the first dynasty of caliphs. Placed at the apex of the social pyramid of the new empire, they represented Arab nationalism, rather than Moslem zeal. They built a state which should realise the aspirations of the Arabs for rule over other peoples. The caliphate of the Umayyads was a true Arab kingdom. Their reign brought the Arabs great military achievements, but internal dissensions, caused by the contradictions upon which their régime was founded, necessarily brought about its fall within a period of no more than 90 years.

The Umayyad power was founded by Muawiya (661-80), who had been governor of Syria, and from that time Syria was the seat of the government. The Umayyads kept the tradition of the old tribal kings of Arabia, and the great Arab tribes who had come thence to Syria were their mainstay. These tribes had come into contact with the Arabs who lived in Syria before the Moslem conquests and had become acquainted with the Byzantine civilisation. So dynastic rule was an institution familiar to the Syrian Arabs, and in contradistinction to the first four caliphs the Umayyads could bequeath the throne to their descendants.

The rule of the Umayyads, however, encountered from the outset bitter enmity from several sides. The supporters of the family of Ali, the son-in-law of Mohammed, did not waive the claims of his descendants on the caliphate, but plotted against the government and even rose in open revolt. There was also a strong party of faithful Moslems who distrusted the Umayyads, criticised their secularity and considered them to be usurpers. After the death of Muawiya, Abdallah b. az-Zubair, the son of an old companion of the Moslem prophet, rose in Medina as a rival caliph, and there followed a civil war which lasted thirteen years. Finally another branch of the Umayyad family succeeded in quelling the revolt. The great caliph Abdalmalik (685–705) once more cemented the cracks. But the Arabs of Irak, where Ali had resided, could not acquiesce in the shift of the point of gravity of the caliphate to Syria, and in the year 700 the Iraki general Abdarrahman b. al-Ashath, at the head of a great army, revolted against the Umayyads and refused to surrender, though the caliph had already defeated him and offered his soldiers the same pay as that of the Syrian army.

The days of Muawiya, Abdalmalik and the latter's son and successor al-Walid I (705–15) were the apogee of Arab power. In successive waves of conquest the armies of the caliphs enlarged the boundaries of the Moslem empire until it stretched from the valley of the Indus to the shores of the Atlantic Ocean and from the banks of the Jaxartes to the edges of the Sahara.

Under the reign of Muawiya, the Moslem armies for the first time crossed the Oxus and invaded Bukhara. At the same time the Arabs overran all the countries of North Africa as far as the Atlantic Ocean. They did not, however, succeed in holding this vast region permanently, and when the great general Ukba b. Nafi was defeated and killed in a battle against the Berbers in 683, they were forced to retreat to Barca. Nor were the expeditions against the Byzantines successful. From the year 663 the Arabs began to make expeditions every year into Asia Minor, and in 672 they even laid siege on Constantinople. For seven years the capital of Byzantium was beleaguered, but the great effort made by the Moslems ended in failure. It was the technological superiority of the Byzantines which tipped the scales. The ravages made by Greek fire, then used by the Byzantines for the first time, compelled the Arabs to retreat.

When the great civil war came to an end in 693, there began a new wave of conquests. Hassan b. an-Numan led the Arabs to new victories in North Africa which resulted in the final conquest of Tunisia. The wars of conquest were continued under the reign of the caliph al-Walid I. The Arab armies finally conquered the whole of North Africa, and in 711 they crossed the Strait of Gibraltar and subdued Spain. In the East, Kutaiba b. Muslim conquered Transoxiana and Ferghana and got as far as Kashghar, the borderland of China. At the same time an Arab expeditionary force established Moslem rule in the valley of the Indus. The Arabs also suffered setbacks, however. New onslaughts on Byzantium, such as the siege of Constantinople in 716-7, failed again and several expeditions beyond the Pyrenees into the kingdom of the Franks ended in disaster. Nevertheless, the Umayyads had become the rulers of an empire extending over three continents and containing apparently inexhaustible resources.

But the Arab tribes which were the backbone of the empire's power were also the factor which sapped it. They stuck to the old tribal principles – unconditional faithfulness, mutual help and, first of all, revenge for the injuries done to brethren and ancestors. The obligation to side with clansmen was the foremost duty of the Arab. In course of time the antagonism between the two great confederations of tribes, the North Arabian Kaisites and the South Arabian Yemenites, became the main factor in political life. That was a new phenomenon, which had not existed in Arabia before Islam. It developed in Syria, where the Yemenite tribes who had lived in the country from a remote period suffered from the encroachment of the Kaisites, who came thither in the wake of the invading Moslem armies. Muawiya's son and successor, Yazid I (680-3), was considered by the Kaisites to be the protector of the Yemenites, and after his death they supported Abdallah b. az-Zubair, the rival anti-Umayyad caliph. The battle of Mardj Rahit in 684, where they fought against the caliph Marwan I and were utterly defeated, poisoned the relations between the Arab tribes for a long time to come. The later Umayyad caliphs were drawn into the rivalry either by their maternal relationship or by the advisers who surrounded them. Some of them sided indeed with one of the rival group, others were looked on as partisans even when they were not. Under Yazid II (720-

4) the Kaisites had the upper hand; in the days of Hisham (724-43) the Yemenites were in control in Irak and in the neighbouring provinces; under al-Walid II (743-4) the Kaisites were once more in control, but under Yazid III (744) the Yemenites triumphed again. From Syria and Irak the long feud between the Kais and Yemen spread throughout all the countries where Arabs lived, to Persia in the East, to North Africa and Spain in the West. Mutual hatred increased and tribal particularism began to smother loyalty to the dynasty.[16]

Another grave problem of the Umayyad caliphate was the question of the mawali, the non-Arabs who had embraced Islam. The number of the converts to Islam grew steadily, even without a strong Moslem mission. The desire to belong to the ruling religion and to be regarded as a member of the ruling caste was a very strong incentive. According to the theocratic principle, upon which the Moslem state was founded, the status of a subject ought to be fixed by the religion. But in fact the non-Arab converts became 'mawali', clients of Arab tribes, without obtaining the full rights of citizens. They participated in military expeditions and fought valiantly against the heathen, but were not entered on the pay-roll, the diwan, they either had a meagre share in the booty or none at all, and – worst of all – they had to pay the poll tax, considered a token of inferiority. When the caliphal government distributed crown lands to meritorious Moslems, the mawali, who were often more pious than the Arabs, clamoured to share the lands with their fellows. But their demands were rejected.[17] There were other kinds of discrimination. Often the Arabs fought on horseback, the mawali as foot-soldiers. Sometimes they were obliged to pray in separate mosques. They were given nicknames by the proud and overbearing Arabs. On the other hand, they were conscious of their high cultural standards, their numerical strength and their economic importance for the Moslem empire. Some groups of the mawali were descendants of the Persian knights and others too had noble status.[18] Those descended from the peasantry were for a long time really persecuted. When, upon embracing Islam, they had left the villages and come to the town, they were forcibly sent back. That was the practice of al-Hadjdjadj, the famous viceroy of Irak under Abdalmalik and al-Walid I. The pious caliph Omar II (717-20) tried to solve this problem and gave orders to leave them in the towns. But it seems that after his death the old practice was once more put into operation. So the mawali became a disruptive force, ready to lend their arms to any rebel against the Umayyad dynasty.

d) *Social revolts*

The great cleavage between the upper and the lower strata of society, the contrast between the preaching of Mohammed and the rule of the Umayyad plutocracy, the contradiction between theocratic principles and administrative practice and the concentration of great numbers of second-class citizens, the mawali, in the big towns – all these problems meant that there were in the Umayyad caliphate really pre-revolutionary conditions. Discontent was widespread, and there were many groups which plotted against the caliphs of Damascus, eagerly looking for a propitious moment for open revolt.

Besides casual and isolated insurrections there were two main streams of opposition and rebellion, that of the Khawaridj and that of the mawali. Both of them produced dangerous revolts and finally brought about the downfall of the Umayyad caliphate.

The Khawaridj were both a sect and a social revolutionary movement or, more correctly, a sect of dissenters which aroused a great revolutionary movement. It had begun in 658 when some pious supporters of Ali, who fought the first civil war of Islam against Muawiya, opposed the idea of arbitration and held that the sword should decide. They were the champions of a true theocracy, but also staunch democrats, for they contended that any pious Moslem could hold the post of caliph. In the Arab society of those days, imbued with conservative ideas of patriarchal rule by noble chieftains (though not necessarily sons of former chieftains), this was a truly revolutionary principle. To claim the right of every Persian and Negro of becoming caliph, as did the Khawaridj, must have been shocking to most Arabs. They maintained also that a caliph who had transgressed the law of Islam had forfeited his right to hold the post and must be deposed. That too was a principle totally contradicting the Islamic doctrine. For according to the teachings of the Moslem doctors one must obey the caliph and his governors even when they are sinners. As long as they do not command transgression of the Koranic law, a true Moslem is bound to obey the authorities.

It is not difficult to understand that a movement like this, proclaiming the quality of races, appealed strongly to many people who were not satisfied with the régime of the Umayyads. The Khawaridj belonged indeed to very different strata. Many of them were true proletarians, others were disappointed intellectuals. Among them there were Arab tribesmen and mawali. In consequence they were not a compact group, and even their tenets were such that they engendered dissension among themselves. On the other hand, they were desperate radicals, people who would never give in, who would succeed or fight to the end.

Basra, the metropolis of Southern Irak, was a hotbed of Khawaridj discontent. Nowhere, indeed, was there in Umayyad times any place in the Near East where social antagonism was so strong. So began in 670 the long series of great Khawaridj revolts in Basra. About ten years later a Kharidjite leader in Basra, Abu Bilal Mirdas b. Udayya, left the town and started a revolt in the neighbouring province of Khuzistan. Although the number of his followers was very small, they defeated an army sent against them, only to be crushed by a second expeditionary force.

The most daring and tenacious Kharidjite rebel was Nafi b. al-Azrak. He was a true proletarian, the son of a manumitted blacksmith of Greek origin. According to his tenets a Kharidjite ought to not acquiesce in the rule of other Moslems. Moreover, the latter, being mortal sinners, should be exterminated together with their wives and their children. That was the principle they called istirad. So the permanent revolution and the merciless murder of their adversaries became the slogan of this group of Khawaridj. Nafi b. al-Azrak rose in the year 684 and fell a year later, but his followers and disciples continued the fight. Small groups of bold horsemen, experts in the tactics of hit and run, carried out a series of raids. They would appear somewhere, attack the government troops, set fire to the houses of peaceful citizens, and before reinforcements had come they were away. After Nafi b. al-Azrak another capable commander, Katari b. al-Fudjaa, led the Khawaridj to many victories. His troops terrorised the districts between Basra and Khuzistan and succeeded in sacking several towns, such as al-Madain. When they were defeated they disappeared, reorganised their forces and came back to renew their attacks. When the great civil war was over and al-Hadjdjadj had become governor of Irak in 694, he entrusted the general al-Muhallab with the task of suppressing the Azrakites. For five years they resisted his forces, but were already hard pressed when dissension broke out within their camps. The Arabs fell out with the mawali. So even these inveterate democrats could not overcome their prejudice against the non-Arabs. It was the nemesis of Arab nationalism. In the year 699 Katari was killed and the remnants of his army were exterminated.

Before this revolt was quelled another Kharidjite group rose in Western Irak. Its first leader was Salih b. Musarrih, and after his death

Shabib b. Yazid took over the leadership of these insurgents, who also belonged to the radical wing of the Khawaridj. Most of them were tribesmen like himself, many of them Shaibanites who had some time before emigrated from the banks of the lower Euphrates to Upper Mesopotamia. Shabib's revolt was a typical guerrilla war. He was at once everywhere and nowhere. He defeated the generals of al-Hadjdjadj and sometimes conquered a town, but without holding it for long. He was slain in 697.

At the same time the Khawaridj revolted also in other parts of the caliphal empire. In 685 they rose in Southern Arabia and succeeded in imposing their rule successively on various provinces of the region. In close alliance with strong Bedouin tribes they conquered also the Yamama, Hadramaut and the town of Taif. But in 692 even this movement was put down. From time to time there were other Kharidjite revolts, most of which were quelled within a short time. In the middle of the eighth century, however, when the Umayyad caliphate was already tottering, the subversive activities of the Khawaridj were one of the disruptive forces which shook the foundations of the régime and plunged it into anarchy.

Beside the Azrakites there were less radical groups of Khawaridj. Such a group was the so-called Sufriyya, founded by Abdallah b. as-Saffar (the son of the coppersmith), a man of proletarian origin. These Khawaridj opposed the istirad, but nevertheless became involved in the movement of Salih b. Musarrih. They carried on an intense propaganda, in both the eastern and western parts of the Moslem empire.

A third branch of the Khawaridj was the Ibadiyya, whose centre was Basra. For a long time they tried to avoid bloodshed and to arrive at their goals by peaceful ways. They condemned the terroristic activities of the radical Azrakites, and their leader Abdallah b. Ibad entered upon friendly relations with the heads of the caliphal government. In the first two decades of the eighth century they adopted a rather quietist attitude, hoping to win over to their ideas the Umayyad government itself. But later, under the leadership of Abu Ubaida Muslim, they embarked on revolutionary activities on a very large scale. They established seminaries in Basra where missionaries were trained. Then they sent teams of these Khawaridj doctors to all parts of the Moslem world in order to rouse revolt. In Basra an Ibadi shadow-government was set up.

These activities had a great success at the middle of the eighth century. The Ibadites rebelled in Oman and at the same time they established their rule in Tripolitania. Both regions remained centres of Ibadi missions and also of independent Ibadi states for a long time to come.[19]

So the moderate wing of the Khawaridj had much more success than the radicals. The principles of the Azrakites were indeed such that they could hardly make a foundation for a durable commonwealth. Their tenets could not fail to provoke splits within the movement itself. They attracted idealists and desperados, but they never won the support of a whole class. In certain moments the radical Khawaridj were joined by other malcontents, but probably only for a short time. The achievements of the moderate Khawaridj were much greater, because they were more realistic and because at least one social group could identify itself with them.

The Ibadiyya opposed the principle of istirad, but on the other hand held, like all other Khawaridj, that belief in the true religion does not justify the sinner. According to their doctrine it is deeds that count, not the belief. In consequence these Kharidjites (as others) must have been much more scrupulous in their dealings and must have believed that honest economic activities are meritorious. Just as the pious English Puritans could demonstrate their religious merits by their economic activities, and did not resort to lax interpretations of religious precepts, so the Ibadi was a very honest merchant. Surely it is not by chance that the Ibadi merchants had great success everywhere and became the protagonists of the worldwide Moslem trade. Probably they introduced new methods in the international trade of their time, just as the Puritans did many centuries later in other parts of the world – a curious parallel. In any case the merchants became the mainstay of the Ibadite community everywhere, in Basra, in Oman, in East Africa and in Algeria. They helped the Ibadi missionaries and were themselves engaged in missionary work. The success of the moderate Khawaridj was, however, that of a religious sect, of a group of democratic dissenters. Even the democratic principles were enfeebled to a certain extent. However that may have been, the movement lost much of the social revolutionary character it had at the outset.

In estimating the successes and failures of this movement one should however distinguish between the Near East and other parts of the Moslem world. In the lands of the Fertile Crescent and in the adjacent countries of the Near East, the problem of the mawali was the crucial question. But the Khawaridj were, though egalitarians, still Arabs. They did not become the champions of the non-Arab Moslems.

However, the mawali found other champions. The most capable of them was a certain al-Mukhtar ('the Chosen one'). Though an ambitious and unscrupulous man, he was a true leader and he probably fought sincerely for the equality of rights of all Moslems. He appeared as the prophet of the Saviour, the offspring of Ali, who would establish justice on earth. His revolt began in Kufa, the metropolis of Western Irak where Ali had resided and which was the bulwark of the Shia, the party upholding the rights of his descendants to the caliphate. On the other hand, the number of the mawali in Kufa was considerable and they readily lent al-Mukhtar their arms.

The preaching of al-Mukhtar, who was an excellent speaker, had great success among the Shiites of Kufa, and at the end of the year 685 he seized the strategic points, first of all the citadel. As a gifted leader he succeeded in winning the support of other capable men, and especially that of Ibrahim b. Malik al-Ashtar, a son of Ali's famous general and himself a very capable commander. Most of the partisans of al-Mukhtar were mawali. Either he openly proclaimed their right to be considered equal to the Arab Moslems, or they felt instinctively that he fought for them. When they began to join him in large numbers, he bestowed upon them many rights which they had ardently desired. Even if he had been, at the outset, a Shiite leader like so many others, by force of circumstances he became in course of time the champion of the mawali, who alone sided with him. Indeed, it does not matter what his aims were at the beginning of his career. Whatever they were, he became the leader of a social revolt. According to the accounts of the old Arabic chronicler at-Tabari he was surrounded by mawali and most of his warriors were mawali.[20] Characteristically enough they were called Kafir kubad – the cudgel bearers – in contrast to the caliphal army, which was well armed with swords and lances. The relations of al-Mukhtar with the ashraf, the noble Arabs of Kufa, were strained from the beginning. Although he claimed to be the envoy of Muhammad Ibn al-Hanafiya, a son of Ali, who led a retired life, the 'nobles', who were aware of his egalitarian ideas, mistrusted him. So they defended the governor of Kufa against al-Mukhtar. All his endeavours to win them over were in vain, all the more as they were less inclined to fight against the government, as rich people mostly are. They could not forgive his having given the mawali a share in the booty, a measure which they considered a terrible insult to the Arab nation. They accused al-Mukhtar of having given the mawali horses and even of having liberated their slaves.[21] To them his revolt seemed to be a real social revolt, which to a great extent it really was.

The aims of al-Mukhtar were far-reaching. He aimed indeed at the overthrow of the caliphate and the establishment of a new social order in the whole of the Moslem empire. When his army had defeated the caliphal troops on the banks of the river Khazir in the year 686, almost the whole of Irak and a great part of Upper Mesopotamia and even Adherbeidjan fell to him and he appointed governors for all those provinces. But it was only for a short time that fortune smiled upon him. The nobles of Kufa left the town and joined the troops of the counter-caliph Ibn az-Zubair, who held Basra and the surrounding districts. The forces of his enemies put al-Mukhtar's troops to rout in two battles, one on the banks of the Tigris and the other near Kufa. Then he was beleaguered in the citadel of Kufa. Four months he resisted, and then was abandoned by most of his men and fell in battle in the year 687.

al-Mukhtar's rising had failed, but the mawali rose again. When Yazid b. al-Muhallab revolted in 720 against the caliph Yazid II, the mawali joined him, and at the end of the fifth decade of the eighth century they supported another rebel, Abdallah b. Muawiya. This latter revolt spread to many provinces of the Moslem empire and paved the way for another revolutionary movement which finally overthrew the Umayyad caliphate.

CHAPTER II

Agricultural Conditions in the Moslem Empire

Since the overwhelming majority of Near Eastern populations lived on the land, the impact of the Arab conquests will be gauged most clearly from an estimate of its consequences for the various branches of husbandry and the condition of the peasantry. Although a great part of the population produced itself the victuals it needed, the growth of towns gave rise to a lively trade in agricultural products. Agrarian life in the Near East was in the early middle ages very different from the closed economy which was so characteristic of Western Europe in that period. There certainly was some bartering, but urbanisation brought about the spread of a money economy in the countryside. These are facts which emerge from the historical sources at first sight. But the integration of so many countries in a new empire must have had an impact on the growth or decline of various crops and resulted in an upheaval in land tenure. The economic historian will, however, not be satisfied with the elucidation of these questions. He will want to find out whether these changes were connected with the introduction of new techniques.

a) *Land tenure*

Documentary and literary sources of the caliphal period show clearly that the changes brought about by the Moslem conquests were rather slow. The Arabs did not confiscate the lands whose owners had remained, and that was what the great majority had indeed done. So it was a long time before a new uniform Moslem system of land tenure was established in countries which had formerly belonged to different states.

According to the Arabic sources, the caliph Omar had thought of superimposing the Arabs as an army of occupation on the indigenous population, which should maintain them. But this idea, if he really conceived it, proved to be an illusion. The Arab conquerors were eager to get large areas of land in the Fertile Crescent and in Egypt, as in other countries. The caliph and his successors had to give in and distribute lands. The tribe of the Banu Badjila, which took a prominent part in the conquest of Irak, is said to have got no less than a quarter of the occupied lands. The lots which were granted to the Arabs were however mostly crown lands of the Sassanids or estates whose proprietors had abandoned them, such as the high Persian aristocrats. These estates were given to the land-hungry Arabs as allotments called katia, on very advantageous conditions: they were liable only to the tithe, whereas other landowners had to pay much higher taxes. The Umayyad caliphs too granted their favourite katias in all the provinces of Irak and Syria, where they settled Arabs near Antioch and on the Mediterranean coast. Umayyad princes too had katias in Northern Syria. So a new class of rich Arab landowners came into being. A great part of these katias were big estates, whose owners leased the land or much of it to poor peasants at a high rent. The difference between the tithe and these rents was their profit. It must have been sizable to account for the great interest which the Arabs had in seizing the lands of the Christian peasants. That they were eager to take possession of their lands in Upper Mesopotamia is borne out by the eloquent accounts of Dionysius of Tell Mahre, head of the Jacobite Church in that country, who lived at the beginning of the ninth century. The katias were in fact considered as private property: the proprietor usually did not live there; the tenants were *glebae adscripti*.

The growth of big estates meant a loss for the Treasury, and consequently some caliphs took measures to check it. The Umayyad caliph Yazid II (720–4) made an attempt to confiscate katias, but he aroused sharp protests and had to give up his projects. Moreover, he granted at least a part of the confiscated estates as new katias to high dignitaries. The Abbasids, who succeeded the Umayyads, gave their followers katias in various provinces. At the same time rich landowners began to bequeath their estates as endowments for religious purposes or for the benefit of their descendants. That was a way of avoiding confiscation and of safeguarding the future of the family. It meant also immobilisation of the property, and to a certain extent turned people from economic activity. But it guaranteed the preservation of the big estates and also made their parcelling out impossible. In Egypt a government office was established in 736 to manage the aukaf.[1]

Beside the Arab katia grantees there was everywhere a class of landowners who had middle-sized estates. In Irak there had survived a great part of the old Persian gentry, the so-called dihkans, who lived on the income from their landed property. Arabic authors of the caliphal period mention the dihkans living in small towns on the Tigris, such as Dair al-Akul, Djardjaraya, an-Numaniya and Madharaya. They had estates in the rural districts neighbouring these towns. The Arabic papyri show that even in Egypt there was a class of Moslem and Coptic landowners who leased and rented lands. Some of them made those agreements which are called by the Moslem jurisconsults muzaraa, i.e. a contract of lease obliging the tenant to deliver to the landowner a fixed share of the crop. Learning from these documents that Moslems living in the capital of Egypt rented crown land, one must conclude that they did so in order to let it themselves to tenants paying a high rent.[2]

All these landowners were, however, a rather small class of wealthy people, whereas the bulk of the peasantry consisted of small free-holders. That is at least the image of the peasantry of Upper Meso-potamia which emerges from the Syriac history written by Dionysius of Tell Mahre. It seems that in his days there were no latifundia in Upper Mesopotamia. But, as goes without saying, there were rich and poor peasants, and the Syriac author complains bitterly that the rich peasants exploited their poor brethren, e.g. when lump-sum taxes were imposed on the rural districts. Abu Yusuf, who wrote his treatise on the kharadj (land tax) at the end of the eighth century, alluded also to the existence of different classes within the peasantry. This Moslem author presumably had Lower Irak in mind. At the bottom of this social pyramid there was apparently everywhere a stratum of landless peasants, who hired themselves to those who needed their labour. Dionysius of Tell Mahre narrates how these agricultural labourers migrated to the places where there was employment. In Irak the land-less peasants, who had neither seed nor working animals, often leased lots of land at a rent of $\frac{5}{6}$ or $\frac{6}{7}$ of the crop.[3]

However, the basic fact of agrarian life, as reflected in the sources of the caliphal period, is the existence of a free peasantry, whose con-dition contrasted very much with that of the coloni of the Late Roman Empire and of the villains of feudal Europe in the middle ages.

Another striking feature of agrarian life in the Moslem empire was the ever-growing burden of taxation. The rules laid down by the Moslem jurisconsults distinguish, broadly speaking, between two categories of land liable to different taxes.

The lands given by the government to the Arabs and the estates of those native landowners who had embraced Islam at the time of the conquest were considered as tithe land. The caliphal government tried from time to time to impose the kharadj, the heavy land tax, on the tithe lands, but encountered strong opposition and had to renounce its plans. Moreover, from the middle of the eighth century it was very often compelled, because of lack of funds, to turn kharadj land, against a sizable payment, into tithe land. Nevertheless, the size of the tithe land remained somewhat limited as compared with the kharadj land. Tithe-paying was the privilege of people belonging to the higher strata of society.

The estates of all other landowners (beside the endowments) were liable to the kharadj. But analysis of the Arabic sources has shown that at the beginning of Moslem rule there was no uniform tax system in the countries conquered by the Arabs. In Irak, in Upper Mesopotamia, in Syria and in Egypt taxes were collected in conformity with the agreements made with the population at the time of the conquest, or in virtue of the rates established by the Moslem authorities after the conquest. In course of time the tax systems of the Moslem countries were more and more assimilated, but they remained nevertheless different throughout the reign of the caliphs.

As in the early Moslem period the officials who collected the taxes were everywhere those who had done so before the conquest. So there is a priori good reason to suppose that they did not change the old tax systems. In Irak the land tax was levied according to the rates fixed by the Persians, in Syria and in Egypt according to the Byzantine system. As the last Sassanid kings and the Byzantines had done, so the new Arab rulers levied in Irak, Syria and Egypt fixed sums proportional to the size of the estates. The old Arabic sources contain, however, two contradictory accounts of the land tax levied by the first caliphs in Irak. According to one tradition they, like the Persians, imposed on the djarib (1,592 square metres) a dirham, but they added a kafiz of grain (probably 48.75 kg of wheat). But according to other authorities the conquerors levied from a djarib of wheat land 4 dirhams, from barley 2 dirhams, etc. The tradition quoted in the first place would point to a rate of 0.5–0.6 dinar for the area corresponding to an Egyptian feddan, the other to 1.5 dinar. These are very different rates, but the Arabic authors say the lower rate was levied from the whole area of an estate, cultivated and waste, whereas the higher rate was levied from the cultivated area only. In Egypt the peasants had to pay a dinar and 3 irdabbs of grain in kind, altogether probably about 1.25 dinars.

In the eighth decade of the eighth century the peasants of Irak petitioned the caliph to change the tax system by levying a certain share of the crops, instead of a fixed amount. The advisers of the caliph agreed that this change would be profitable for both the government and the peasants. When there was a good harvest the income of the government would increase, at times of dearth it would safeguard the husbandmen. So the caliph al-Mahdi (775–85) established the system called mukasama, i.e. payment of a certain share of the crops. It seems, however, that the tax burden had increased considerably in the time preceding this reform, which was undertaken in order to relieve the peasants, for the rates of the kharadj as quoted by authors writing in the ninth and tenth centuries are very high. Lands which had not to be artificially irrigated were, according to them, liable to $\frac{2}{3}$ of the crops or even the half, lands irrigated by hydraulic engines to a quarter or $\frac{3}{10}$ of the crops. Moreover, the new tax system was not introduced everywhere, and even in Irak and in Upper Mesopotamia there were provinces where the kharadj was levied before according to the old system, the so-called misaha.

Altogether the gap between the status of the tithe land and the kharadj land widened more and more. Some Arabs who got crown lands had an even more privileged status: they paid a sum fixed once for ever, in virtue of an agreement made with the government (the so-called mukataa). There were, on the other hand, landless peasants who had to rent lots of land from the State according to the muzaraa system. The kharadj-paying peasants, the bulk of peasantry, were also liable to other taxes. They had to pay the wazifa, a tax destined to cover certain government expenses. This was not a regular tax, due at fixed dates, but payable when the authorities needed it. The non-Moslems had also to pay the poll tax, which was apparently a heavy burden. Both the Persians and the Byzantines had levied a poll tax from the peasants and from other low classes of society, but apparently it had been collected together with other taxes. The Moslems kept this system for some time, but later they began to levy the poll tax separately. One Syriac author says that it was Muawiya who established the new system, but another relates that it was Abdalmalik. Since the Moslem poll tax is often called 'the fugitive tax', it is highly probable that the Moslem authorities began to collect it separately when the number of the peasants leaving the villages increased. However that may be, it was very heavy. In Egypt every male Copt had to pay 2 dinars a year, in Irak and in other countries there was a sliding tariff for the poll tax, the rich paying 4 dinars, the middle class 2, and the poor 1.

Moslem authors, such as Abu Yusuf and Yahya b. Adam, who wrote treatises on the tax system, establish the rules and collect the evidence of their lawfulness, quoting the principles fixed by the first caliphs. But non-Moslem writers, who wrote the history of their communities at the same time, depict the practice of tax collection rather differently. Dionysius of Tell Mahre relates how taxes were levied several times, how the Moslem authorities imposed new additional taxes and charged even dead persons, obliging their descendants and relatives to pay for them. He recounts how the peasants of Upper Mesopotamia had to sell their crops to merchants in order to pay the amount required. These merchants were in collusion with the tax-collectors and paid them the half of the market price.[4] Even allowing for a great deal of exaggeration, one has the impression when reading this Syriac history that the tax system of the caliphs brought disaster on the peasantry of Upper Mesopotamia, and there is no reason to believe that the plight of peasants in other Near Eastern countries was better.

b) *The main crops*

The striking feature of Near Eastern agriculture in the days of the caliphs was the predominance of wheat. The Europeans, even those belonging to the upper strata of society, throughout the middle ages ate mainly rye bread. That is a fact attested by household books from various Western countries and by the accounts of noble and bourgeois families. It was only at the end of the middle ages that the upper classes began to eat wheaten bread. The Orientals, at least the town-dwellers, had white wheat bread from time immemorial. So wheat was the staple grain in the Near East under the reign of the caliphs, as it had been for many centuries before and would be for a long time to come. Bread made from barley and other cheaper grains was the food of ascetics. The predominance of wheat was a phenomenon common to all Near Eastern countries.

The accounts of the Irakian Treasury which have been included in the works of Arabic writers of the ninth and tenth centuries contain valuable data as to the extent of wheat growing and the cultivation of other grains. According to Kudama b. Djafar, the caliphal government in 820 levied as tax in kind from the provinces of Irak 177,200 kurrs (2,925 kg) of wheat and 99,721 kurrs of barley. There is, however, a discrepancy between these figures and the total of the taxes collected from the various provinces, as quoted by the same author. Summing up these other figures one finds that the quantity of wheat amounted to 88,600 (or perhaps 115,600) kurrs and that of barley to 105,921 (or perhaps 123,921) kurrs. These latter figures are probably more correct. Ibn Khurdadhbih provides us with data of the taxes paid in kind in 870 (approximately). They would have amounted to 73,650 kurrs of wheat, 78,750 kurrs of barley, and 8,900 (or perhaps 26,900) kurrs of barley and rice (mixed). These figures would indicate that the size of the wheat and barley crops was almost equal. Since the rate of the tax to be levied from wheat crops was higher, apparently corresponding to 19.5 kg per djarib against 16.2 kg barley, barley would even have been predominant. But the data provided by the Arabic authors show that barley was mainly grown in some districts whose soil was probably less adapted to wheat growing. Such districts were az-Zawabi, Babil-Khutarniya, Lower Falludja, al-Djubba-al-Budat, as-Sibani, as-Saila-hani on the Euphrates, and Baraz ar-Ruz, Upper Nahrawan, Lower Nahrawan and Badaraya-Bakusaya on the Tigris. The district of Kaskar alone produced perhaps 20,000 or 30,000 kurrs of barley and rice. Moreover, it should be taken into consideration that barley was mainly used for feeding animals. It is a point of interest, in this context, that the equilibrium between wheat and barley in Irak's agriculture can be traced from Sumerian times to the present day, when the proportion of wheat to barley is 41% to 47%.

Upper Mesopotamia was in the days of the caliphs a granary for the surrounding countries. It was a region which supplied Southern Irak with great quantities of wheat, probably shipped on the Euphrates and the Tigris. It was a wheat-growing country from ancient times and remained so until the first half of the tenth century. In Syria too wheat was grown almost everywhere, but there were some provinces which could export especially large quantities. Such wheat-growing regions were the provinces of Hamath, Hims and the Mediterranean coast in Northern Syria, Baalbek in Central Syria, and the Hauran, the Golan and Transjordan in the South. Even the Negev down to Eilat was in those days not a barren country as in later times, but still exported grain to other provinces.

Egypt, the granary of Rome and Byzantium in bygone days, pro-duced crops which so far exceeded its wants that considerable quantities could be exported to the Hidjaz and other countries. Egypt's wheat excelled also in its quality. Arabic authors of the caliphal period relate that some kinds of Egyptian wheat, e.g. the so-called Yusufi, were unequalled. The Said, Egypt's southern provinces, was the main wheat-growing region, but also the Fayyum and some districts in the Delta exported great quantities of wheat. Barley growing had begun to decline a long time before the Moslems conquered Egypt, and probably its crops decreased continuously in the caliphal period.[5]

The growth of the rice plantations, on the other hand, was a new phenomenon which in course of time changed the structure of agriculture in some regions of the Near East. In fact, rice had been planted in Irak in very remote times, but after the Moslem conquests it was grown much more than before. That was undoubtedly the consequence of the immigration of Persians into Irak. The mawali from Khuzistan and from the Caspian provinces were accustomed to rice, so that there was a growing demand for it in the big towns of Irak. It seems however that rice did not become a crop destined for mass consumption until the second half of the ninth century. For a long time rice was the food of the poor, and apparently great quantities of it were imported into Irak from neighbouring provinces of Persia. But later other people too began to eat rice and rice bread, when wheat bread became too expensive for them. However that may be, in the second half of the ninth century there were big rice plantations in some districts on the Euphrates such as Kussin, Sura, Sib al-asfal, Barbisama and Furat Badakla, in the district of Nistar near Baghdad, and in the districts of Kaskar and Djabbul on the Tigris. In sources referring to the second half of the ninth century there appear also Moslem scholars who are called ar-Razzaz – the rice merchant. That the advance of rice was rather slow is also borne out by the fact that rice plantations are not mentioned in the history of Upper Mesopotamia written by Dionysius of Tell Mahre at the beginning of the ninth century. Even in Egyptian sources from the early Moslem period rice is very seldom mentioned, although it was known there before the Moslem conquests.[6]

Studying the copious materials in the writings of the Arabic authors who deal with the various branches of horticulture and fruit growing, one is forced to the same conclusion: subsequent to Moslem conquests there were no great changes and those which took place were rather slow.

Dates were the staple fruit of the lands of the Fertile Crescent. They were grown in almost all districts of Southern Irak; mainly in those of

Basra, Wasit and Sarsar. But there were also large palm groves in the provinces north of Baghdad, in that of Daskara north-east of it, and in those of al-Anbar and Ana on the Euphrates, and even farther north. Date growing was undoubtedly an important branch of Irak's agriculture, and how voluminous the trade in dates was in many towns of Irak is borne out by the mention of religious scholars from Kufa and from Wasit whose family name was at-Tammar – the date merchant. The towns of Wasit and Basra were apparently the great centres of this lively trade.[7]

Horticulture was flourishing in Upper Mesopotamia and Syria. These two countries exported various fruits to the adjacent provinces of the caliphal empire. Several provinces of Syria, Lebanon and Palestine produced great quantities of apples; both Cis- and Transjordan had also figs, grapes and plums of many kinds.

All these branches of fruit growing had been cultivated in the Near East many centuries earlier, but after the Moslem conquests (although not immediately) other kinds were planted and fruits previously unknown were introduced. That this happened is probable, a priori, and there is also some evidence for this phenomenon in old Arabic sources. An author of the tenth century relates that the so-called raziki grape spread in Irak. This was a grape cultivated in the province of Taif in the Hidjaz. Much more important was the spread of certain citrus fruits. According to al-Masudi the orange and the lemon were introduced after the year 912 in Oman, whence they spread to Irak, Syria and Egypt. But since these fruits were to be found in the lands of the Fertile Crescent and in Egypt already in the ninth century, it seems that the Arabic writer had some other kinds of citrus fruits in mind, such as the cedrat.

On the other hand, there was a certain retrogression of the olive plantations, at least in some regions of the Near East. It is true that Palestine still produced great quantities of olives and olive oil, and if we can believe an Arabic geographer of the tenth century all the mountainous and hilly regions of Galilee and Central Palestine were covered with olive trees. Even some districts of Irak, e.g. that of Kufa, had many olive groves and could export their products to other countries. But in some provinces of Syria oil-growing villages which were based on monoculture declined. That happened on the Belus heights, a district between Aleppo-Antioch and Azaz-Afamiya. The decline of the olive plantations in this part of Syria certainly resulted from the loss of markets, for Syria had during many centuries exported olive oil to Southern Europe.[8]

The growing of industrial plants was undoubtedly in this period an important sector of Near Eastern agriculture. In Egypt, mainly in the Fayyum and the Delta, much flax was grown. Syria and Palestine produced considerable quantities of cotton. It seems that the province of Aleppo and the districts of Hula and Banyas were in that period the main centres of these plantations.[9] The growing volume of industry was a strong incentive to expand the cultivation of industrial plants. An early historian narrates that a cousin of the first Abbasid caliph founded in Eastern Syria the town of Salamiyya, dug there an irrigation canal and planted saffron. But there is no evidence of a sizable increase of all these plantations in the early Moslem period. As long as the growth of latifundia did not greatly change the structures of Near Eastern agriculture, the cultivation of industrial plants did not increase at the expense of the growing of cereals. So one arrives at the conclusion that in this period there were no major changes in Near Eastern agriculture as far as the various crops and the relative size of the different branches are concerned.

c) *Agricultural techniques and methods of work*

The yield of cereal cultures was in many parts of the Near East very much dependent on the efficiency of artificial irrigation, growing when the irrigation system was well maintained or improved and declining when the engines were spoilt. Whereas most lands in Upper Mesopotamia, Syria and Palestine were cultivated without irrigation by mechanical devices, the agriculture of Lower Irak and Egypt was conditioned by a rather complicated system of irrigation. In these countries there were systems of canals, dykes and coffer dams, the construction of which was very costly.[10] The expenses for the drainage of swamp land and the putting into operation of hydraulic engines were so great that small landowners were not in a position to carry out such schemes. So very much depended on the attitude of the government, that is, the rules which governed irrigation under the reign of the caliphs and the active interest which they took in its upkeep and improvement.

The Moslem jurisconsults who left us treatises on the State and the administration of the caliphs ruled that the digging of big canals ought to be paid for by the government. The construction of dams, outlets and other waterworks too was incumbent upon the authorities. Arabic historians, on the other hand, relate that the governors appointed by the first caliphs applied themselves immediately to this task. In the days of Omar they dug the canals which provided Basra and its surroundings with water. When these canals had been filled up they were dug out once more in the reign of the caliph Uthman. Ziyad, viceroy of Irak under the reign of Muawiya, dug the Nahr Makil near Basra. Yazid I (680–3), son and successor of Muawiya, was very much interested in irrigation and was therefore called 'al-muhandis' – the water-engineer; he repaired the irrigation of the Ghuta, the district surrounding Damascus. The governors of Irak in the days of the later Umayyads engaged in similar activities. Salm, a son of Ziyad, dug near Basra the canal called Harb, al-Hadjdjadj dug canals in the district of al-Anbar on the Euphrates and of Kaskar on the Tigris, Khalid al-Kasri – the canals Badjawwa, Barummana, al-Mubarak, al-Djami and others. The Umayyad prince Maslama, a son of Abdalmalik, was particularly interested in agricultural enterprises. He dug a canal from the Euphrates in Northern Syria, near the town of Balis. These activities were carried on by the Umayyads until the end of their reign. The caliph Hisham (724–43) dug the canals al-Hani and al-Mari, in the province of ar-Rakka. The Abbasids too dug and re-dug irrigation canals. At the beginning of their reign great constructions were still undertaken in the Diyala region. The foundation of Baghdad alone must have made that necessary. A complex system of branch canals had to draw irrigation water to fields lying far from the main canals. That was a gigantic project, judging by the thousands of brick sluice gates which have been found along the branch canals. Harun ar-Rashid dug near Baghdad the Katul, a canal east of the Tigris. The lands which could be cultivated by the water supplied by these canals were mostly katias, granted to those rich people who undertook the digging. One reads in an Arabic source that Khalid al-Kasri had from the estates lying by the canals he had dug a yearly income of 5 m dirhams. So rich and enterprising people used all possible means to reclaim waste land, whereas the peasants looked askance at the digging of canals, which aggrandised the big estates.[11]

The numerous accounts of these activities do not point to technological innovations within the irrigation system, which the Moslem rulers had simply taken over from their predecessors. The records in the writings of the Arabic historians show that those who drained the swamps and dug the canals were 'Nabataeans', i.e. natives of Irak and not Arabs. A famous native engineer was Hassan the Nabataean, who drained marshes in Southern Irak for al-Hadjdjadj and later for Hisham. The names of the hydraulic engines used by the Arabs testify to the same fact: most of them are Aramaic or Persian. In any case, the old sources contradict the supposition of some modern scholars who maintain that the Arabs transplanted devices used in Central Asia to the Near East. That is at least not true as far as the flourishing period of Moslem civilisation is concerned.

The Moslems used water-wheels and similar devices everywhere in order to raise water from the rivers and canals. There were two main types of water-wheels: the so-called sakiya, a wheel operated by an animal, and the noria (in Arabic *naura*), a big water-wheel with a chaplet of pots, operated by flowing water, usually a river. Such nauras were to be found in the great swamps of Southern Irak, on the Tigris and in Northern Syria, where some villages were called Naura or an-Nawair. These engines had been in use from time immemorial, as described by Vitruvius. Those mounted on the Orontes were famous already in the ninth century. They are described in a report of a certain Ahmad b. at-Tayyib who travelled in Northern Syria in 884. In Egypt there were sakiyas in the rural districts surrounding Bilbais and Damietta, on the Nile and elsewhere. They had pots of wood or clay and were thrown into gear by means of a horizontal wheel turned by camels or other animals. It goes without saying that in some places the peasants used more primitive devices, such as the daliya, a big beam with a jug for drawing water at its end. A small townlet in Upper Mesopotamia, near Kirkisiya, bore the name of this engine – ad-Daliya. Some provinces, on the other hand, had sophisticated irrigation systems. In certain districts of Eastern Irak water to irrigate the fields was led there from the canals and rivers by conduits of mortar and tubs which were placed one above the other.[12]

The big water-wheels were very expensive engines and at the same time they were easily spoilt. They were made of wood, which in course of time became rotten, and when the rivers were frozen in winter, they did not work at all. There is no evidence of improvements made by the Arabs, and that the technological level of agricultural work in general was in the early Moslem period rather static is also borne out by the description of water-mills in Transjordan which we find in the work of the tenth-century geographer al-Mukaddasi, which tends to show that such mills were very rare in that period in the Near East. The writings of the Arabic authors of the caliphal period contain also some reports on failures and setbacks sustained by the Moslem rulers when they tried to foster agriculture by improving irrigation. In the period of the first Abbasids many dykes on the Tigris and on the Euphrates were broken, and the endeavours of the caliphal government to repair them had only a partial success. Arabic authors say that as a consequence of these failures the area of Southern Irak which was covered by swamps from the end of the Sassanian period became larger.[13]

Reading attentively the accounts of the Arabic writers one becomes aware of the fact that the activities of the earlier caliphs and of their governors on behalf of Near Eastern agriculture were much more intense than those of the Abbasids. Apparently the age-long tradition of ancient agriculture, irrigation and soil conservation was still alive at the beginning of Moslem rule, whereas it vanished in the days of the Abbasids. A second observation must be made before estimating the attitude of the caliphal government towards agriculture: the Arabic authors recount the spectacular activities, such as the digging of big canals, but they keep silent on other duties incumbent on a far-sighted and prudent government which takes care of the interests of agriculture. Not the least among those tasks was in the Near East the maintenance of the terraces which preserved the fertile soil. Archaeological research has shown convincingly that at least in later times of Moslem rule this task was neglected.

Slowly but progressively another attitude towards the problems of agriculture prevailed. Surely the ever-increasing tax burden discouraged even well-to-do peasants from enterprises aiming at amelioration of soils as long as they were not considered absolutely necessary. But far more portentous was the change in the attitude of the government. Instead of the great care of the Byzantines and other preceding governments, the Arabs had a different approach to agrarian life.

Artificial irrigation as practised by the Arabs itself sometimes proved detrimental. Owing to perennial irrigation and unsuccessful drainage the soil deteriorated. It became alkaline, salt accumulating in the uppermost layers and forming a white crust. On the other hand, the irrigation canals were often neglected because of the peculiarities of Moslem law. According to the principles of the Moslem lawyers a landowner whose estate is not directly menaced is indeed not obliged to contribute to the repair of a burst dyke or canal. Further, if a crack or seepage of water from a private canal endangers the fields of a neighbour, the owner of the estate is not obliged to repair it.[14]

The information which the Arabic authors provide us on the methods of agricultural work, beside the irrigation canals and engines, is rather scanty. But collecting these records from various sources one is inclined to conclude that the Arabs did not improve the methods of agricultural work. There is only slight evidence of technological innovations in Near Eastern agriculture throughout the middle ages, whereas the history of European agriculture is the story of great changes and technological achievements.

The introduction of the wheeled plough brought great progress in European agriculture. The use of the mouldboard plough was another important innovation. In the Near East the peasants used the old wooden Mediterranean plough, a fact which astonished the French noble Jean de Joinville, who accompanied St Louis on his Crusade in Egypt. It is worthwhile to quote, in this context, the opinion of archaeologists who explain the great flourishing of Byzantine agriculture in dry areas of the Near East by the use of iron ploughshares. So the ploughing of the Moslems would have been less efficient than that of their predecessors. The adoption of the wheeled plough in Europe was connected with another great change – the use of horses instead of oxen for ploughing. In Western Europe peasants began in the tenth century to replace oxen by horses. This change again was possible because of a great improvement in harnessing, i.e. the introduction of the new stiff collar which rests on the shoulders of the animal. For as long as the peasants used collars of leather put on the neck of the horse, the animal's breathing was impeded and it could not do full work. But in the Moslem countries of the Near East the oxen or buffaloes were put to the plough as before.

There could be added other innovations made in European agriculture which apparently remained unknown or at least did not come into use in the Near East. Such innovations were the introduction of the iron-pronged spade, the scythe and the flail for threshing. The modern harrow, which is drawn by horses, was obviously unknown even in Moslem Spain. For the Hispano-Moslem agriculturist Ibn al-Awwam, who wrote in the twelfth century, gives a comprehensive account of it. Clearly he took it for granted that the readers of his book did not know it. The Moslem harrow was drawn by oxen.[15]

In compensation for all the shortcomings of Oriental agriculture, the odds of nature were in the favour of the Moslem peasants. The fertility of the soil was in many regions of the Near East so great that the harvests were rich even without improvements in agricultural methods. The yields of Western agriculture increased considerably when the two-course was changed to the three-course rotation. The Near Eastern peasants did not change the methods of fallowing. In Irak there prevailed the traditional system of winter-grown wheat or barley alternated with a fallow season. In Egypt fallowing was not absolutely necessary. Wheat was grown either after lucerne, broad beans or cucumbers, or after fallowing. The natural fertility of the soil in some regions, especially in Upper Egypt, made it possible to grow wheat on fields in successive years. Barley alternated with wheat or other crops, broad beans with barley. The Moslem peasants could also afford to work fields less frequently than the Europeans and they did less hoeing. There was no need of marling. There is however evidence of the use of salt earth as manure, an innovation made by Egyptian husbandmen in that period.

The yield ratio must have been very high in the early period of Moslem rule. According to Arabic authors of the later middle ages, who certainly quote earlier sources, the Egyptians sowed from $\frac{2}{3}$ to 1 irdabb of wheat on a feddan and harvested from 2 to 20 irdabb. In some provinces of Upper Egypt the quantity of seed which was sown was even smaller. These figures would point to an average yield ratio of 1:10. For an appropriate estimate of these indications one should compare them with the accounts of the yield ratio in medieval Europe. It seems that the yield ratio of grains in Western Europe in Carolingian times was 1:2–2:5. In the thirteenth century English agriculturists considered as reasonable yield ratio of wheat 1:5, of barley 1:8, of rye 1:7, and of oats 1:4. In fact the ratio was lower. On the average it was in England in that period perhaps 1:4 for wheat, 1:3.5 for barley, 1:5.5 for rye, and 1:3 for oats. But, characteristically enough, the yield ratio in Western Europe tended to increase, whereas it was on the decline in the Near East. On certain estates in Artois wheat yielded at the beginning of the fourteenth century 9 times or 13 times as much as had been sown. The Egyptian historian al-Makrizi, on the other hand, says that the harvests had diminished so much under Moslem rule that it was necessary to put aside a quarter or even a third of the crop in order to render cultivation profitable.[16] Undoubtedly the Arabic author had the later middle ages in mind. But the decrease of the crops had probably begun a long time before he wrote. It was the consequence of neglect, of old and tired methods of cultivation, of heavy taxation and of the attitude of a short-sighted government.

d) *Soil erosion and Near Eastern agriculture*

Some modern scholars have explained the contrast between the flourishing state of Near Eastern agriculture in ancient times and its desolation in later periods by the supposition of a progressive desiccation. The quantity of precipitations, they suggest, was much greater in antiquity than in the middle ages and the modern epoch, so that once fertile soil became arid. But the great majority of agriculturists have rejected this theory. The geologist Cl. Vita-Finzi surmises that more or less at the time when the Arabs conquered the lands of the Fertile Crescent there began a period of aggradation. The geological activity of the rivers underwent a change. Increasing erosion in the upper valleys led to more aggradation downstream. In the upper parts of the river basins soils were washed away and mountain villages had to be abandoned. Crests on which dams had been built were breached. The valley floor downstream was built up by silt-laden floods.[17] This geologist believes that increased erosion and deposition resulted from greater humidity. However that may be, there can be no doubt that soil erosion was one of the major calamities to befall Near Eastern agriculture in the middle ages.

In the Near Eastern countries, especially in the mountainous regions, rainfall is very heavy in the winter months, and the loose earth is easily washed away from slopes. A great quantity of silt is carried away through the gullies into the plains. Deposited there, it is sometimes most detrimental to agriculture. Outlets of wadis are choked and swamps are formed. When the porous earth has been removed springs disappear, and where there had been fertile land only barren rocks remain.

In antiquity Oriental agriculturists found a remedy for this great calamity – the construction of terraces to hold up the run-off. The soil of hill slopes was laid out in staircases of terraces, each about 90 cm high and protected by walls. In the hedges there were often tamarisks, which broke the wind, attracted moisture and bound the soil. Another way of conserving the fertile soil was to construct dams along the beds of brooks and rivers which prevented the floods from inundating the fields. Dams on the upper valleys of rivers impounded stormfloods in reservoirs and trapped the silt. After the Arab conquests these ingenious devices of the ancient agriculturists were often neglected and cultivation allowed to fall into decay. This is the conclusion reached by archaeologists and soil-conservationists studying the history of agriculture in various provinces of Syria and Palestine, where it depended to a great extent on careful and far-sighted management of the water resources.

The most characteristic example of what the change from ancient to medieval agriculture has brought about is the fate of the so-called Dead Cities in Northern Syria. This region, the old Belus heights, is called after the ruins of the ancient settlements which still stand as if enchanted on the barren rocky hills. It is an area of 1,150,000 acres where in antiquity and up to the Arab conquests agriculture had been the mainstay of a hundred flourishing settlements – a thriving economy. The fact that these settlements were close together leaves no doubt that agriculture was intensive and that water resources were sufficient. Spring-houses at places where nowadays there are no springs testify to that. The depletion of the soil and the decline of agriculture were the sequel of political and economic changes after the Arab conquests. When the monoculture of olives had to be abandoned the former inhabitants apparently left their villages, and semi-nomadic Arabs began to grow cereals. But as Bedouin usually do, they worked only patches of land in a very extensive way. So the soil was washed away and what remained are denuded hills. The American soil-conservationist W. C. Lowdermilk concluded that from 3 to 6 feet of good terra rossa have been removed. A clear proof of this phenomenon is the churches whose entrances have their lowest steps at 4½ feet above the present ground level. Ancient Roman roads standing on blocks much higher than the surrounding area are another proof.

Traces of ancient agriculture which have been found east and west of Hims point to the same phenomenon. Both on the deserted plateau of Kalat al-hisn, between Hims and the Mediterranean coast, and on the desert road from Hims to Palmyra ruins of oil presses and terraces show that what is at present arid and barren land had been in the antiquity fertile soil. The abandonment of terrace culture resulted in the decline of agriculture and subsequently also of other sectors of economy. Even in the Hauran, which remained until the end of the middle ages a granary of Syria, there must have been a good deal of erosion and loss of good soil. As a consequence of overgrazing the rich soil became much more exposed to the erosive forces of water and wind.

The havoc wrought by soil erosion in Palestine and Transjordan is visible to the layman. But soil-conservationists and archaeologists have collected valuable data concerning this phenomenon. In Galilee many patches of good soil have been washed away. At Sepphoris, for example, nearly twenty feet of débris were washed down from the hills on to the Roman theatre. The Roman theatre of Beth Shean is now covered by silt up to the top seats. Abandonment of the mountain villages was the consequence of soil erosion here as elsewhere. When the fertile soil was washed off the hills, the peasants could no longer make a living from agriculture and left their villages. Altogether there have been found in Galilee, on an area of 4,000 square kilometres, 460 abandoned settlements, which means 1.4 abandoned sites per 12 square kilometres. The connection between the abandonment of the terrace culture and the decline of agriculture is particularly obvious in Central Palestine, in the hilly land of Nabulus-Tulkarm, where the slopes are mostly steep or even precipitous. The soil-conservationists of the British Mandatory Government of Palestine found that only 8% of the precipitous slopes and 14% of the steep ones had any terracing which was effective in preventing soil from being washed away. On about half the slopes there are vestiges of ancient terraces. Nevertheless, at the time when the British soil-conservationists made their survey, 76% of the steep and 44% of the precipitous slopes were intensively cultivated. It goes without saying that this meant ever-increasing erosion.

The case of a bridge near Lydda is very instructive. It has been established that under this bridge, built in the year 1272, there had been another, Roman, bridge. The keystone of this ancient bridge had been more than 13 feet below the interior curve of the arch of the thirteenth-century bridge. The great difference in level is clearly the result of the filling up of the river-bed by alluvial deposits. This is shown by the investigation in 1938 by another officer of the British Mandatory Government, Colonel P. L. O. Guy, of the abandoned villages in the catchment area of the Wadi Musrara, over which the bridge was built. This area comprises the hill land between Lydda-Ramla and the mountains of Judaea and Ramallah in the east. The following table summarises the results of Guy's survey of an area of 805.7 square kilometres, of which 240 lie in the plain (up to 100 m above sea-level), 260 on the foothills (100 to 300 m above sea-level) and 300 in the mountains. This survey shows that abandonment and decline of agriculture was a serious phenomenon in the mountainous regions. It was the sequel to soil erosion which denuded the hills, washing off the fertile soil. This is clearly visible on the map of the abandoned villages in the Musrara area (see p. 54).

Another aspect of the same phenomenon has been dealt with by Y. Karmon, a geographer who has shown that in the coastal plain of

Abandoned villages in the Musrara catchment area

	elevation above sea-level	occupied	abandoned	percentage of abandonment
plain	below 100 m	32	4	11%
foothills	100–300 m	31	65	67%
mountains	over 300 m	37	124	77%

Palestine the decline of agriculture and the abandonment of villages was widespread on the Mediterranean coast, where silting up of the brooks and wind erosion resulted in the growth of swamps and spread of dunes, while, on the other hand, from the Arab conquest to the Crusaders' period the number of settlements did not diminish in the Eastern belt of this region, where kurkur slopes, fertile silt and an adequate water supply made it possible to harvest twice a year. Karmon's results are summarised in the following table:

Abandoned villages in the Sharon plain

	Western belt	Central belt		Eastern belt	Total
		Sandhills	Swamps		
Roman-Byz. period	28 + 2 port towns	7	21	33	91
Crusaders' period	8	5	4	35	52
1800	4	4	—	17	25

So 42.8% of the settlements in this area were abandoned from the Arab conquest to the Crusaders' period. The difference between the rate of abandonment on the coast line and in the Eastern belt is conspicuous.

The British soil-conservationist F. H. Taylor has arrived at the conclusion that from 2,000 to 4,000 million cubic metres of soil have been washed off the western side of the Judaean hills since Roman times. That is a quantity sufficient to make 4,000–8,000 square kilometres of good farm land. A. Reifenberg concluded that the quantity of silt carried down the wadis by the floods in Palestine, north of a line from Jericho to Gaza, is 7–9 million cubic metres a year. That would mean that from this area of about 8,000 square kilometres 2 m of good soil have been washed away since Roman times.

Archaeologists researching in the Negev, the desert of Southern Palestine, have become aware of the astonishing achievements of ancient agriculturists in that area. The results of their research bear out the suppositions of soil-conservationists who maintain that the careless methods of cultivation have brought about the great decline of agriculture in the course of the last 1,300 years.

At the present stage of research there remains no doubt that this region, which has been considered arid and absolutely unfit for agriculture, was cultivated up to the Arab conquest and even later. Archaeologists conclude that the Negev reached its highest point of development in the Byzantine period, and that the age of Justinian marked the culminating point. Areas never cultivated before were then developed. The methods by which ancient agriculturists succeeded in making this region fertile were terracing and very skilful use of the water resources. The extent of soil erosion and deposition of débris in this region is clearly shown by the great amount of soil deposited at archaeological sites. At Tell Duwair, the ancient Lakhish, 5 feet of earth have been deposited on the Roman road since the third century. It would however be erroneous to believe that after the Moslem conquests there was a real cataclysm in the agricultural history of this region. In fact there was rather a progressive decline. Cultivation of cereals and other branches of agriculture were still carried on and settlements were still built, as is borne out by archaeological evidence.

The American archaeologist Nelson Glueck, who has thoroughly studied the vestiges of Nabataean culture in Transjordan, concluded also that the terraces on the hills had been neglected since the end of the Byzantine period. But even this scholar dwelt on the fact that agricultural life did not disappear suddenly. According to him it lingered on for about 500 years. The amount of terracing in this region must have been very great indeed. It has been found that almost all the slopes of big wadis were terraced, even those whose gradients are up to 80%. But when the terraces were neglected erosion annihilated the once flourishing agriculture. Lowdermilk found in the Sik, the gorge leading to the site of Petra, a fragment of a water conduit covered with erosional débris to a height of 3 feet. The conduit itself is at present 7 feet above the floor of the gorge. That means that at some time 10 feet of débris had been deposited there.

The research of Nelson Glueck, who has investigated 500 archaeo-

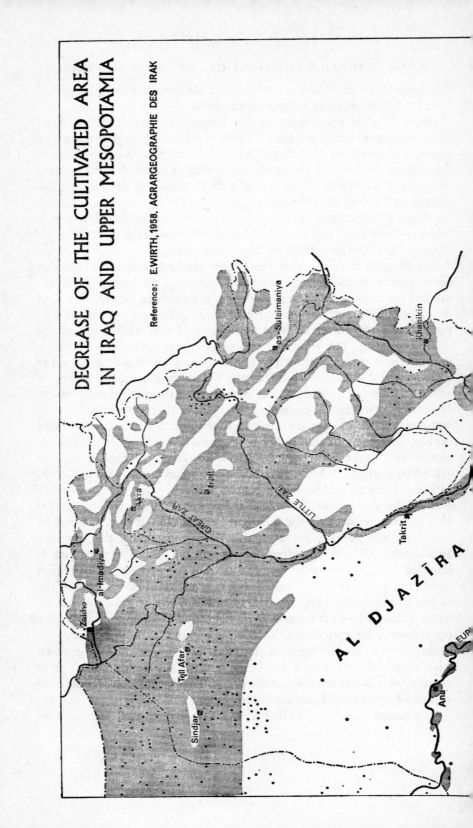

DECREASE OF THE CULTIVATED AREA
IN IRAQ AND UPPER MESOPOTAMIA

Reference: E.WIRTH, 1958, AGRARGEOGRAPHIE DES IRAK

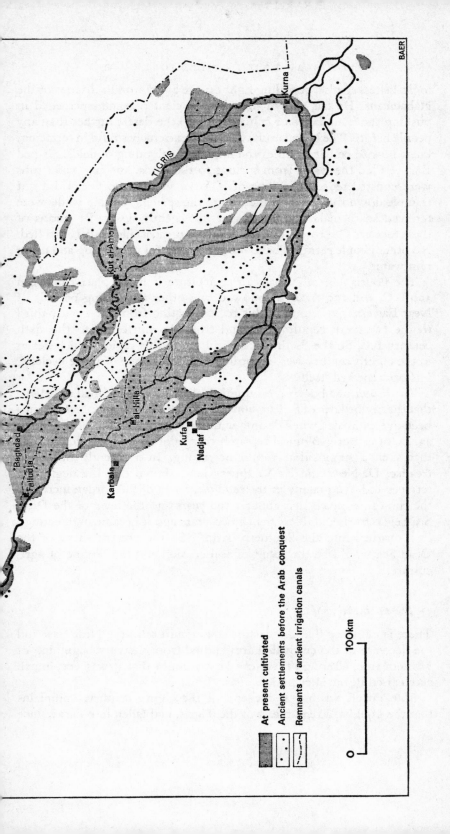

At present cultivated

Ancient settlements before the Arab conquest

Remnants of ancient irrigation canals

0   100km

BAER

logical sites, sheds a revealing light on the agricultural activities of the Nabataeans. He has shown that these ancient peasants succeeded in pushing the boundaries of cultivation into the desert further than any people before. The Nabataeans, who were extremely skilful in terracing, knew how to embank gullies and impede the flooding of fields. Shaped channels led the water from springs to the fields, and big water tubs were constructed on the tops of hillocks so that the flocks did not trample down the crops on the way to the springs. Certain wadis were terraced so to make the floodwater flow gently down. By means of these terraces the erosion and the floods were most efficiently controlled. No other people seems to have been so successful in catching and using rain water.

The flourishing of Nabataean agriculture is to be placed between 300 B.C. and 200 A.D. It followed two other flourishing periods of Near Eastern civilisation in this region, lasting from the twenty-third to the twentieth century B.C. and from the thirteenth to the sixth century B.C. So the decline of agriculture in this region which began in the eighth century was, according to Glueck, one of those cycles.[18] History repeated itself.

The reader of a book on economic history may be inclined to believe that the importance of soil erosion as a secular phenomenon has perhaps been overestimated when dealing with its consequence for Near Eastern agriculture. But geological research continuously adduces new proofs that such a supposition would be wrong. In a recently published treatise, D. Neev and K. V. Emery have shown that the neglect of terraces and overgrazing in the catchment area of the Jordan increased the run-off so much that about 1,500 years ago the level of the Dead Sea began to rise, and less than 1,000 years ago it became high enough to transgress into the Southern basin.[19] So the present shape of the Dead Sea would be the result of soil erosion and the decline of agriculture.

e) *The cultivated area*

There is evidence that the decline of agriculture in the Near East and the decrease of the cultivated area started from the very beginning of Moslem rule, although there can be no doubt that it was very much accelerated in the later middle ages.

Abu Yusuf, writing at the end of the eighth century, complains that the Djukha, a region east of the Tigris, had fallen into decay since the Arab conquest. He says that the water resources of this once fertile region have vanished and its agricultural produce has shrunk to nothing. Other Arabic writers confirm this statement and say that the Djukha had once been the most fertile region of Irak. In another passage Abu Yusuf speaks in general terms about the decline of Irak's agriculture since its conquest by the Moslems. He says that the cultivated area which had become waste since that time was so large that it would be impossible to bring it back under cultivation within a short time.

The decrease of the cultivated area was connected with the disappearance of many villages. The peasants left their villages and went to live in the towns. The American scholar Robert McC. Adams, who has made an archaeological survey of the province of Diyala in Eastern Irak, has shown the considerable decrease of villages in the early Moslem period. The results of his research, based on surface reconnaissance, can be summed up as follows:

Number of villages in the Diyala province

	Sassanian times	Early Moslem times
large villages	59 (356 ha)	57 (327 ha)
small villages	308 (440 ha)	234 (367 ha)

Average area of villages

	Sassanian times	Early Moslem times
large villages	6 ha	5.7 ha
small villages	1.4 ha	1.56 ha

So in this province covering an area of 12,493 square kilometres, already in early Moslem times 24% of the villages had been abandoned. The number of abandoned settlements in Upper Mesopotamia suggests also that the decrease of cultivation in this area was sizable, but so far no thorough research has established the date of the abandonment.

The findings of Colonel Guy, who made a survey of deserted villages in the hill country stretching from Lydda-Ramla to Ramallah and the mountains of Judaea are summed up in the following table:

	Occupied at present	Abandoned	Total
Wadi Musrara area	100	193	293
Wadi Djindas area	42	95	137

Although these figures refer to the whole of the Moslem period they are quite surprising. In the area investigated by Guy, 70% of the villages have been abandoned.

The decline of Southern Judaea under Moslem rule is obvious. In Joshua 15, 48–57, one reads that South of Hebron there were at the time of its conquest by the Israelites 30 cities, with villages surrounding them. At the beginning of the nineteenth century there were in this district 90 abandoned settlements, against 5 inhabited villages. As this district covers 960 square kilometres, there was one village for every 18 sites on 192 square kilometres.

The number of agricultural settlements which existed in the Negev in Nabataean and Byzantine times must have been considerable. They have disappeared almost altogether and been replaced by Bedouin camps. Population has dwindled. While the population at its height is estimated at 80–100,000, in 1931 it was 50,000.

Altogether, there were in 1931 in Cisjordan Palestine 934 villages, against 1,790 abandoned settlements, which means that the numbers of inhabited settlements amounted to a third of those existing in ancient times. But this number includes 124 colonies founded after the establishment of British mandatory rule.

Even in Egypt the cultivated area must have become smaller during the eighth and the first half of the ninth century. The Egyptian historian al-Makrizi, who quotes many ancient and reliable sources, says that in the middle of the ninth century the country was in a state of decay, with dire effects on the revenue of the government. A modern Egyptian scholar has concluded that the cultivated area amounted in the days of the caliph Hisham (724–43) to 3 m feddans, but under al-Mamun (813–33) to 2,128,500 feddans only.[20]

Against the evidence of abandonment of villages and other proofs of agricultural decline, there are in the old Arabic sources many records of colonisation of waste land. These accounts leave no doubt as to the efforts made by wealthy persons, princes and governors, to bring fallow land under the plough. Many of these texts refer to Southern Irak.

As a consequence of the bursting of dams a great part of Lower Irak had been inundated by the Euphrates and Tigris and a large area of cultivated land had become swamp. This disaster had happened long before the Arab conquest, and the Persian kings had vainly tried to repair the damage. When anarchy increased at the time of the invasion of Irak by the Arabs things went from bad to worse, and the Great Swamp was formed, covering an immense area between the two great rivers, from Kufa to the environs of Basra. The Tigris shifted from the eastern (present) bed to the western and flowed into the Swamp. This change turned all the country bordering on the old channel into a desert. The Umayyad governor Khalid al-Kasri tried to restore the river to its old channel, but in vain.[21]

On the other hand, various attempts were made to drain the marshy lands and apparently they were, at least partly, crowned by success. The Arabic writers recount that in the reign of Muawiya, the first Umayyad caliph, Abdallah b. Darradj, reclaimed from the swamp land which yielded 5 (or according to others even 15) million dirhams. He built dykes and drained the marshes, so that parts of them once more became cultivable. Ziyad b. Abihi, the governor of Irak in the days of Muawiya, was a great coloniser. He secured lands by all possible means and gave katias to his daughters where they dug canals and settled peasants. Also his lieutenants colonised waste lands. Some of the dykes built under the first Umayyad, however, burst as early as the end of the seventh century, and according to the Arabic historians the viceroy al-Hadjdjadj refused to repair them in order to take his revenge on the dihkans, his enemies. But the famous viceroy dug (or re-dug) several canals which irrigated large areas and made cultivation possible. Such were the Sarat Djamasp, a loop canal branching off the Great Sarat, and the Zabi, connecting this big canal with the Tigris. The lands irrigated by these canals were thereupon brought under cultivation. al-Hadjdjadj's colonising activities were manifold. He colonised also lands which had been drained by Abdallah b. Darradj, bestowing waste land on Arabs who dug canals and cultivated the soil.

The most active in colonising among the Umayyad princes and dignitaries was Maslama, a son of the caliph Abdalmalik. He was a real entrepreneur, and colonised waste land in several provinces of the Fertile Crescent. The Arabic authors relate that he spent 3 m dirhams for repairing the dams which had burst in Southern Irak and reclaimed a vast area of fertile land by draining marshes. He dug also the two Sib canals, in the district of Sura near Kufa, and settled many peasants there. According to these accounts many peasants of neighbouring districts handed their estates over to Maslama and became his clients. In Upper Mesopotamia, east of the river Balikh, Maslama built a castle ever since known by his name – Hisn Maslama. A canal from the Balikh supplied water to the castle and the surrounding area, which previously had no artificial irrigation. In Northern Syria, between Aleppo and Balis, this Umayyad prince built a new village and another castle called Kasr Maslama. The old Arabic authors mention also the colonising activities of Said, a brother of Maslama, who brought waste land near ar-Rakka under cultivation, and from papyri one learns that Kurra b. Sharik, the Umayyad governor of Egypt (709–14), founded sugar plantations.[22]

Not only princes and governors colonised waste land in that period, but also other rich and enterprising people. It goes without saying that many of them were relatives or friends of high dignitaries. Moslem law, which began to develop at this time and embodied the rules fixed by the authorities, was favourable to such enterprises. Those who colonised fallow land enjoyed tax privileges.

In Northern Syria Muawiya settled Moslem soldiers, who served as true military colonists in frontier regions. The Umayyad caliph gave them katias in the districts around Antioch and on the Mediterranean coast of Syria. In Upper Mesopotamia too abandoned estates were given to Arabs. The lands abandoned by the Persian nobles and marshy land in Southern Irak were a favourite region for Arab colonisation. Abdallah b. Amir, who was until 664 governor of Basra, granted his uncle Umair an area of 8,000 djarib, and the grantee brought them under cultivation, digging a canal for the irrigation of the fields and gardens. Even Ibn Amir's mother had several canals dug. Abdallah b. Amir himself caused canals to be dug in the district of Basra and on the way from Basra to Mecca built a palace surrounded by artificially irrigated gardens in an-Nibadj, a place in Northern Arabia, and nearby a village, called al-Karyatani. A daughter of his also dug a canal which irrigated lands near Basra. Ziyad b. Abihi used to grant waste land as katias on the condition that they should be cultivated within two years. Otherwise he took them back. In those days there were in Southern Irak families which were especially interested in colonising work and invested great sums in it. Such a family was that of Abu Bakra. In Arabic sources one finds the names of several men belonging to this family who were active in these enterprises, such as Ubaidallah, his sons Bashir and Abu Bardhaa and Abdarrahman b. Abi Bakra. Later a great part of their estates near Basra was confiscated by the Abbasid caliph al-Mamun.

The Arabic authors whom we have quoted so far wrote in the time of the Abbasids, and were inclined to denigrate the Umayyad caliphs and extol the merits of their successors. But a mere glance at their writings is enough to show that the colonising activities of the Abbasids were much more limited. One reads in the Arabic sources that the caliph al-Mahdi (775-85) dug near Wasit the Nahr as-Sila canal and colonised the lands bordering on it and that Harun ar-Rashid (786-809) reclaimed land in Central Palestine which had become waste. Khaizuran, the mother of Harun ar-Rashid, was apparently also very prominent in colonising work. But altogether these activities of the 'Blessed dynasty' were far from being equal to the colonisation undertaken by the Umayyads.[23]

That this is not a mere guess is borne out by indirect evidence. The accounts of the revenues yielded by the taxes of the Near Eastern countries show clearly the decrease of the cultivated area, for the land tax, the kharadj, yielded more than all the others. The figures given in these accounts are summarised in the following tables:

Revenues from Irak

Name of reigning caliph (governor) or date	in dirhams	converted into dinars
after the Moslem conquest	128 m	12.8 m
Muawiya (661–680)	100 m	10 m
Ubaidallah b. Ziyad (680–686)	135 m	11.2 m
al-Hadjdjadj (694–714)	118 m	9.83 m
Omar II (717–720)	120 m	10 m
Yusuf b. Omar (738–744)	100 m	8.3 m
Harun ar-Rashid (786–809)	134,980,000	6.75 m
819	108,457,650	5 m
870	78,309,340	3.12 m

With all the reservations due to figures transmitted by medieval authors and to the errors in the conversion of dirhams into dinars, these data leave no doubt as to the considerable decrease of the tax revenue from the middle of the eighth century.

The data which the Arabic authors quote from the documents concerning the tax revenue from Upper Mesopotamia are scanty:

Revenue from Upper Mesopotamia

Name of caliph or date	Provinces	dirhams	converted into dinars
Harun ar-Rashid (786–809)	Mosul, Tarik Furat 24 m Diyar Mudar, Diyar Rabia 34 m	58 m	2.9 m (without payment in kind)
819	Tarik Furat, Mosul, Diyar Mudar, Diyar Rabia	20,835,000	1 m
870	Tarik Furat, Mosul, Diyar Mudar, Diyar Rabia	17.3 m	692,000

In this table the decline is not less conspicuous.

For the tax revenue from Egypt the data found in the Arabic sources are more copious. In the following table they are arranged in two columns, one comprising the gross revenue and the other the amounts sent to the Exchequer in the capital:

Revenue from Egypt

Name of caliph (governor) or date	gross revenue	amount sent to the caliph
Omar I (634–644)	12 m dinars	
647	14 m dinars	
662	5 m dinars	
Sulaiman (715–717)	12 m dinars	
725		2,723,837 dinars
al-Mahdi (775–785)		1,825,500 dinars
Musa b. Isa (786–796)	4 m dinars	2,180,000 dinars
Harun ar-Rashid, cca 800		2,920,000 dinars
819		2,500,000 dinars
al-Mamun (813–833)	4,257,000 dinars	
827		3 m dinars

Since the data from the beginning of the Moslem period may be considered suspicious, one might infer from this table that the tax revenue from Egypt was fairly stable. That would, however, be a mistake. In fact there was no catastrophic decrease of the total of Egypt's tax revenue, because the authorities had the rates raised. Apparently they did so from the beginning of the eighth century. The fact that in its third decade the peasant revolts began seems to bear out this supposition. In the first half of the ninth century the land tax paid in money was raised from 1 dinar to $1\frac{1}{2}$ dinar, and later it rose to 2.5 dinar and even more. The tax paid in kind rose at the end of the Umayyad period from 3 irdabbs to 5 irdabbs of grain and even more.[24]

All these data point to the decrease of the cultivated area. The rise of grain prices is further evidence of this phenomenon. It was certainly not a consequence of climatic changes, i.e. a desiccation causing a decrease of crops. The measurements of the nilometer, as related by Arabic authors, show indeed a decrease of the average level of the Nile inundations, but, on the other hand, there is good reason to believe that the quantity of precipitation in the lands of the Fertile Crescent increased up to the middle of the tenth century. So one must necessarily conclude that the rise of grain prices was due to the decrease of the cultivated area and to other factors. The decrease of the cultivated area cannot have been anything like a sudden change, nor a sizable one. For the demand for grain being fairly constant, prices reacted vigorously as soon as the equilibrium was even slightly changed, e.g. by decreasing cultivation.

There arises the question why the rise of grain prices did not stimulate new colonisation. Why did the Umayyads, the true Arab tribal kings, engage in colonisation, whereas the Abbasids were much less active in this field? To this question several answers could be given.

It may be that any large areas of waste land which could with the means available be brought under the plough had already been colonised in the period of the Umayyads. Further, the social stratification of the Near Eastern peasantry should be taken into consideration. In the period in question the bulk of peasantry consisted of small freeholders who had not sufficient capital for colonising enterprises. Even in medieval Europe colonisation was mainly carried on by feudal lords. The rich landowners of the Near East apparently invested their capital in agricultural and commercial enterprises which yielded great profits within a short time. Such enterprises were rice plantations or the import of wheat from Upper Mesopotamia to Irak.[25]

Overpopulation, whether in the countryside or in the towns, or a rise in grain prices need not necessarily result in colonisation on a great scale, as economic historians studying various periods have realised. G. Duby concluded that notwithstanding the overpopulation of the villages of Western Europe in the Carolingian period, technological incapacity impeded colonisation on a great scale. M. Postan, referring to the rise of grain prices in Western Europe in the thirteenth century and the slackening of colonisation, developed a thesis rightly called after him the 'Postan thesis', namely that these two phenomena are not at all contradictory. Rising grain prices in England caused marginal land to come under the plough. Pastures and meadows grew scarcer, so that the peasants could keep fewer animals. Manures and consequently harvests diminished. On the poorer soils poorer grains had to be grown. So the rise of grain prices resulted in undernourishment and finally in epidemics which brought about a new equilibrium.

So there is sufficient evidence of the supposition that the cultivated area in the Near East decreased under the caliphs, and this supposition is not contrary to other phenomena of its economic development.

f) Condition of the peasantry

Did the establishment of Moslem rule improve the state of the peasants or make it worse?

The decrease of the cultivated area and the abandonment of the villages does not necessarily show that their condition worsened. For it may be that many peasants were absorbed in other branches of production. But in fact there is first-hand and reliable evidence of a deterioration in the conditions of peasant life.

The tax burden apparently increased to a great extent in the two hundred years which elapsed from the Arab conquests to the middle of the ninth century, and despite the rising prices of agricultural products it became very difficult for the peasants to pay the imposts. The accounts of the Christian writer Dionysius of Tell Mahre are very eloquent on this point and he is surely a trustworthy witness, for he voices the bitterness of the peasantry. In his *History* one reads that the peasants borrowed money from the townspeople at high rates of interest in order to pay the taxes and defray their expenses. The antagonism between the peasants and the townspeople must have been very great, as one finds in Dionysius's work stories about the pillaging of the barns of the town-dwellers by the peasants.[26] Needless to say, these poor peasants could not afford technological innovations. Dionysius of Tell Mahre describes conditions in Upper Mesopotamia in the second half of the eighth century. But there is little doubt that the situation of the peasants was more or less the same everywhere and throughout this period.

A consequence of the heavy tax burden and the hopelessness of broad strata of the peasantry was the flight from the land, a major phenomenon of social life in the caliphal empire. Of this there is plenty of evidence, both in literary sources and in documents, such as Greek and Arabic papyri from Egypt. All of them depict in colourful terms the pitiful condition of the fugitive peasants, who were chased by the authorities like wild beasts. In order to prevent the abandonment of villages and the consequent decrease of the land tax, the main source of the government's revenue, the government set up special services to catch the runaway peasants and to bring them back to their villages. It issued orders that for this purpose the most drastic methods should be employed.

Moslem authors recount how al-Hadjdjadj, when he became aware of the decrease of the land tax owing to the flight from the land, took measures to have fugitive peasants sent back to the villages. According to Dionysius of Tell Mahre the flight from the land was a major phenomenon of agrarian life in Upper Mesopotamia in the second half of the eighth century. Everywhere in the districts of Nisibin, Amid, Harran and Edessa the peasants left their villages. People fled from village to village, seeking a secure refuge. But the chiefs of the villages denounced them to the authorities or exploited their precarious condition. Searches were made in the countryside and it was incumbent on the chiefs of the villages to help the authorities. There were officials who had to mark the peasants with signs indicating their village.

The accounts of the phenomenon in Egypt are particularly numerous. Christian-Arabic writers relate the abandonment of villages by peasants in Lower Egypt, and the papyri of Aphrodito deal with it in Upper Egypt in the days of the governor Kurra b. Sharik. From all these sources one learns that the Egyptian peasants were in the period of the caliphs *glebae adscripti* as they had been under the rule of the Byzantines. The number of those who tried to emancipate themselves and their families from this bondage must have been considerable. Time and again the government issued orders to discover where the fugitives had gone and to send them back to their villages. The runaway peasants who were caught were fined 5 dinars, a very great sum for these poor men, and even the officers in charge of the administration of the villages where the fugitives had been found were punished. The fugitives were not only fined, but also scourged 40 lashes and nailed to a wooden yoke. Anyone providing information on fugitives got a payment of 2 dinars, whereas those who gave them shelter were fined 10 dinars. The papyri show clearly that the local authorities were often reluctant to deliver the fugitives who had found refuge in their districts, because they contributed to the taxes (although they paid less there than in the villages whence they had fled). Sometimes the authorities of the rural districts to which the fugitives had been repatriated had to guarantee that they would not flee again. In order to maintain strict control a system of passports was established. Those who were caught without a passport were fined, and ships on which they had travelled were to be burnt. Such were the orders given by Usama, the successor of Kurra b. Sharik. But despite all the measures taken by the caliphal government the flight from the land continued through the ages. It was a grave problem even in the second half of the eighth and in the first half of the ninth century.[27]

The pitiful state of the peasants produced many revolts, which, however, were no more than outbursts of discontent, lacking any long-term objective.

In the year 751 there was a peasant revolt in Upper Mesopotamia, in the province of Mayyafarikin, but apparently it was quelled without difficulty. Then in 774 a capable leader, whose name was Razin, succeeded in stirring up the peasants in several provinces of Upper Mesopotamia. The revolt began in the district of Tutis in Armenia and spread to those of Arzan and Mayyafarikin. Many rich landowners' houses were burnt, and although the rebels were mostly Christians they attacked churches. The officers of the caliphal government who were caught by the rebels were killed without mercy. But, as in almost all similar cases, the rising was suppressed by the caliph's troops without much trouble.

The peasant revolts in Egypt were much more numerous, probably because the garrisons of the caliphal troops were weaker there and because the bitterness of the peasants was intensified by the religious antagonism between the Copts and the Moslem government. However that may have been, the revolts of the Copts resulted in much bloodshed. Almost all the revolts were occasioned by the vexatious burden of the taxes. The first revolt broke out in the Delta or more precisely in the Eastern Hauf, in the year 725. In the middle of the eighth century there followed several other revolts, in 739 in Upper Egypt, in 750 in the district of Samannud, and then in that of Rashid. During this last revolt the Bashrudites, a group of very primitive Copts, conquered Rashid and killed all the Moslems. In the second half of the eighth century the peasant revolts in Egypt became more frequent. All of them were provoked by fiscal causes. In the year 753 the peasants revolted once more in the district of Samannud, in 767 in that of Sakha, and in 773 in the villages surrounding Balhit. A new revolt broke out in 794 when the Arabs began to join the rebels. Other revolts followed in 802 and 807. But it seems that all of them were local movements, outbursts of despair and hatred of the Moslem government.

In the year 831 there was a general revolt of the Egyptian peasants, and this time too the Arabs joined the Copts. The peasants rose in both Upper and Lower Egypt, in the provinces of Alexandria and Damira. In Upper Egypt an Arab tribe, the Banu Mudlidj, a clan of the Banu Lakhm, was the most active group. The revolt was put down by the valiant Turkish general Afshin, although not without encountering stubborn resistance; for the Arabic authors relate that he had to fight several battles. In the Eastern Delta the resistance of the peasants must have been especially strong, and a very great number were killed by Afshin's troops. This revolt aroused great emotion, and before it was crushed the caliph came to Egypt. But all his endeavours and the intervention of the Coptic clergy were fruitless. The fierce Bashrudites, who fortified themselves in the marshes of the Delta, continued their desperate fight until the end. When the troops of the caliph had finally gained the upper hand, many of the women and children were sold as slaves, the men exiled to Irak.

The greatest peasant revolt in the first two hundred years of Moslem rule in the Near East was, however, the rising of the Palestinian and South Syrian countryfolk in the year 841. This rebellion began in Transjordan under the leadership of a certain Abu Harb. He posed as a religious leader or perhaps as a prophet, as many other revolutionaries did in those times. He veiled his face and urged his followers to 'do good and to abstain from wrong'. At first the poorer peasants joined him, later also the rich landowners. Then the Yemenites in Southern Syria made common cause with him, so that finally the number of the rebels grew formidable. The caliphal army sent against Abu Harb had to turn aside to quell the revolt in the province of Damascus, which looked much more dangerous. When this rising had been put down, the army of the caliph defeated Abu Harb also. According to Arabic historians the last battle was fought near Ramla, in 842, showing the revolt had spread to Southern Palestine too.[28]

It failed because, unlike European peasant revolts, it was not supported by other classes. The peasants alone were too weak.

CHAPTER III

The Heyday of the Moslem Empire

The downfall of the Umayyads in the year 750 and the accession of the Abbasids to the throne of the caliphs meant much more than a change of dynasties. The whole régime underwent a complete transformation. The rule of the Umayyads was a kind of military occupation by Arab tribal kings, who had superimposed themselves upon the Byzantine and Persian administration. The Abbasids, on the other hand, made a great effort to accomplish the aspirations of the orthodox Moslems, who had supported their revolt, and to build up a true theocracy. Whereas under the Umayyads the various countries conquered by the Arabs had continued to be diverse cultural and economic regions, the Abbasids welded them into a great Moslem empire.

The military and political power of the Abbasids began to decline a short time after their accession to the throne, the scope of their rule progressively shrinking. But at the same time the economic cohesion of the Moslem countries became stronger. Those countries which no longer recognised the suzerainty of the caliphs did not sever their economic links with the other parts of the empire. So, in the course of the ninth century, a gigantic economic unit, based on commercial exchanges, came into being, a unit never before equalled in the history of the old world. The economic ascendancy of the Abbasid empire over other regions of Asia and Africa, and even more over Western Europe, was overwhelming, and it lasted a relatively long period – about two hundred years.

a) *The empire of the Abbasids*

The collapse of the Umayyad régime was the result of a long and intense propaganda carried on by the emissaries of the Abbasids, a branch of Mohammed's family, who claimed to be the champions of true Islam. Their subversive activities had begun in 718, a revolt breaking out in Eastern Persia in 747 and being crowned by a decisive

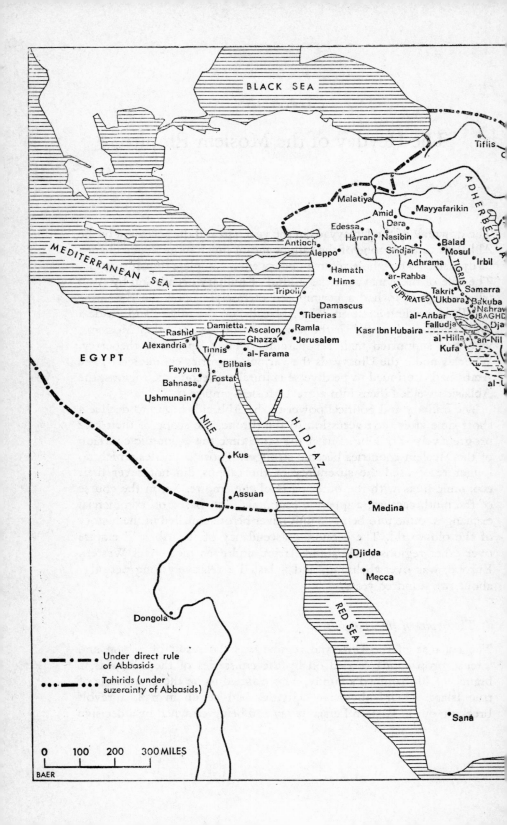

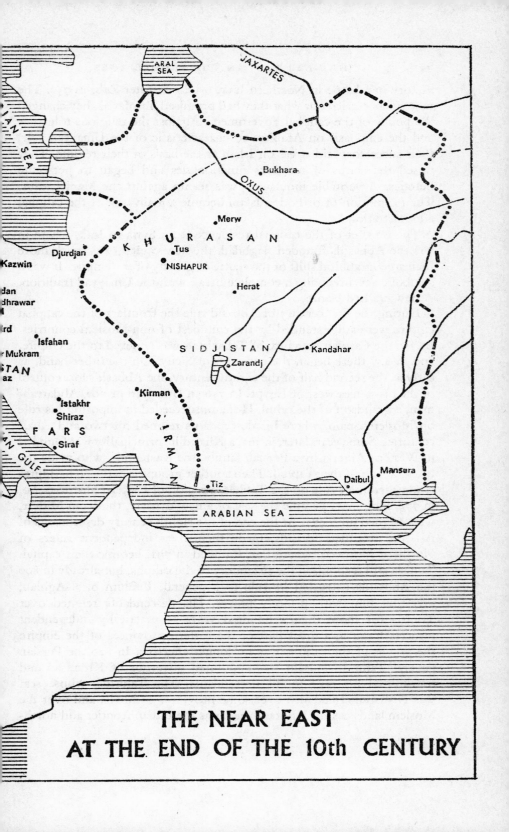

THE NEAR EAST
AT THE END OF THE 10th CENTURY

victory in a battle in Northern Irak, on the Greater Zab, in 750. The new rulers carried out what they had promised, insofar as they changed the policy of the caliphal government. Against the religious tolerance and the emphasis on Arabism so characteristic of the Umayyad rule, their successors laid stress on Islam as the basis of their régime. They raised the status of religious functionaries and began to persecute heretics. A veritable inquisition was set up against the Manichaeans. The promotion of orthodox Islam became a main task of the caliphal administration.

The transfer of the caliphal residence from Syria to Irak, where in 762 the Abbasids founded Baghdad, the new capital, was much more than a geographical shift of the centre of gravity of the empire. It was a symbolic act, involving a complete break with the Umayyad tradition. A new era had begun.

During the first century of Abbasid rule the frontiers of the caliphal empire were still extended by the conquest of non-Moslem countries. In 759 the Caspian province of Tabaristan was annexed to the empire, and in 827 there began the conquest of Sicily. On the other hand, as early as the second half of the eighth century, the Abbasids lost control of the provinces west of Egypt. In 756 an Umayyad prince, Abdarrahman, a grandson of the caliph Hisham, succeeded in imposing his rule on Moslem Spain, where his descendants reigned for two and a half centuries. Some years later, in 761, a Kharidjite principality was founded in Western Algeria by a Persian family, the Rustemids, who made the town of Tahert their capital. Then another group of Berber Kharidjites established their rule on the Tafilelt, a region of Eastern Morocco. So, in 772, Sidjilmasa became the seat of a new dynasty, the Banu Midrar, who reigned until 977. At the end of the eighth century descendants of Ali, the so-called Idrisids, made themselves independent rulers of Northern Morocco, where Fez, founded in 791, became their capital. Tunisia still recognised the suzerainty of the caliphs, but already in 800 the Abbasids entrusted its rule to a general, Ibrahim b. al-Aghlab, investing him with princely power. His descendants reigned over Tunisia for more than a hundred years as practically independent princes. Even in a great part of the eastern provinces of the empire the power of the caliphs was no longer effective. In 820 the Persian general Tahir b. Husain was appointed governor of Khurasan and transmitted his post to his descendants. The Tahirids, whose seat was Nishapur, ruled also over some provinces of Media and over the Moslem lands east of Khurasan as far as the Indian frontier and northwards to the boundaries of the caliphal empire. Formally they were only governors, but their authority was so firmly established that the caliph could not have transferred their dominions to anyone else.

It was not only because of the hereditary reign of semi-independent governors that the power of the Abbasids declined. The ever-increasing influence of Turkish officers became an even greater danger to the dynasty. Already in the second half of the eighth century Turks began to play a great role in the army of the Abbasids. Some of them had been brought to the Near East as prisoners of war or slaves, others had hired themselves as mercenaries. As their numbers increased their officers won great influence on the government, and in the middle of the ninth century they had become true praetorians, appointing and deposing caliphs at their will. They also became proprietors of big estates, both in Irak and in other Near Eastern countries.[1]

The character of the Abbasid revolt has been much discussed by Orientalists. In the nineteenth century most of them held it to be an Iranian reaction to the rule of the Arabs, and even expressed the opinion that the civil war between the brothers al-Amin and al-Mamun (811–13) was a conflict between Persians and Arabs. But according to recent research the contest was rather inter-Arab, although there was a substratum of national antagonism.[2] But for the social historian it is much more relevant to consider the consequences of the Abbasid take-over. The traditional Orientalists have stressed time and again the strong Iranian impregnation of the Abbasid régime. In fact, the accession of the Abbasids to the throne meant the seizure of power by another class. Instead of the Syrian Arab clans and other groups of pure Arab descent, a new Persian-Arab aristocracy took control. The revolt of the Abbasids in Khurasan, led by the great leader and general Abu Muslim, was accompanied by or had as a consequence a mass conversion to Islam of the Persian gentry.[3] The role of the Barmekid viziers in the reign of Harun ar-Rashid is symbolic of the great change in the social hierarchy of the caliphate under the first Abbasids. The lower classes of the inhabitants of Baghdad, who fought desperately against the Persian army of al-Mamun, had perhaps an unconscious sense of this class antagonism.[4] The reign of the Tahirids in Persia was a restoration of the rule of the old Persian aristocracy.

The hegemony of this Persian-Arab aristocracy, the Neo-Sassanian empire, lasted however no more than three generations. It came to an end in the reign of the caliph al-Mutasim (833–42), when the Turkish guards attained overwhelming power. The Arabs were struck off the pay-roll of the army, and the Turkish generals became the almighty dictators of the caliphate.

It goes without saying that the re-establishment of the rule of the Persian aristocracy provoked revolutionary movements, whose social substratum is clearly visible beneath the biased reports of the orthodox Arabic chroniclers. There is no doubt that some of the revolts which convulsed the Abbasid reign in the eastern parts of the empire had a predominantly religious background. Among the rebels were supporters of the house of Ali, feeling themselves betrayed by the Abbasids, who had posed as the champions of the 'family of the prophet' and finally established their own rule instead of that of the descendant of Ali and his wife Fatima, who was the prophet's daughter. There were also groups of religious extremists who, dreaming of the foundation of a perfect Moslem theocracy, were disappointed by the new régime.

The Kharidjites continued their perennial struggle for a democratic society. There were several revolts in the lands of the Fertile Crescent and in the Iranian provinces. They revolted in Upper Mesopotamia in 736 and in 747. In 779 they rose in Upper Mesopotamia and Northern Syria and in 784 again in Upper Mesopotamia. In the reign of Harun ar-Rashid the Kharidjite risings were quite frequent. They revolted in 791 in Khurasan, in 795 in Upper Mesopotamia, and then in 796 there began in Eastern Persia the revolt of Hamza b. Atrak, who continued his fight for some years. Then, in the year 807, there was another rising of the Kharidjites in Irak.

The accounts of other great revolts in Persia point clearly to their social-revolutionary character. The old Arabic historians dwell on the confused, syncretic religious ideas of the rebels and they were accused, like so many social-revolutionary movements in the middle ages, of libertinism. In fact, there still existed in Persia remnants of the Mazdakite movement, the curious communism of the Sassanian period.

Speaking of the revolt of Sinbadh in 754, the Arabic chroniclers do not omit to connect him with Mazdakism. The leader of another revolt which broke out in Khurasan in 767 was Ustadhsis, a fuller, i.e. a proletarian. The revolutionary movement led by the so-called 'Veiled Prophet', al-Mukanna, was apparently a much more dangerous outbreak of popular discontent. His followers were mostly peasants and included Mazdakites. The centre of the movement was in the Transoxanian province of Sughd, but it spread also to Bukhara and other adjacent regions. When it was suppressed after hard fighting in 780, another revolt in the Caspian province of Djurdjan had already begun.

Characteristically enough, these rebels, called the 'Red ones', were also accused of sexual promiscuity. In 796 and in 808 there were new risings of the 'Red ones'. The greatest revolt against the Abbasids in the first half of the ninth century was, however, that of Babek, who defied the caliphal armies in Adherbeidjan and in the Caucasian provinces for more than twenty years (816–38). Babek was a true proletarian who had made a living in a variety of jobs. As usual, when speaking of revolutionary movements, the pious chroniclers accuse the followers of Babek of libertinism and other crimes, but their accounts leave no doubt as to the social-revolutionary character of this revolt. One Arabic author clearly points to the fact that Babek was supported mainly by people from the lower strata of society.

The revolt of Mazyar b. Karin, prince of Tabaristan, in 939 was accompanied by a social revolution 'from above'. Trying to restore the old Persian state and the Zoroastrian religion, he made use of the social antagonism between the Persian peasants and the rich landowners. He incited the rebels to plunder the houses of the wealthy and undertook to expel the Moslems from the towns.

In Baghdad, where strong military forces were stationed, the discontented lower classes had mostly to keep quiet. But there were groups of desperados and bandits who lived outside the society and took their revenge by acts of robbery. From the days of al-Mamun (813–33) the chroniclers mention from time to time the 'ayyarun' or 'shutter'. But they speak also of the 'White ones', i.e. dissenters who had syncretic ideas. These texts show that even in Baghdad there were groups dreaming of social revolution, though adding to their true aims a religious superstructure. In time of civil war the mob sided with one party, opened the prisons and liberated the prisoners. The people of Baghdad as a whole were very much opposed to the Turkish army and rose against it when conditions were propitious.[5]

But thanks to the military strength of their Persian and Turkish regiments the Abbasids succeeded in quelling all the revolts and in realising their great scheme of knitting together the lands conquered by their predecessors into a uniform empire. Their efforts were crowned by full success. Islamisation and Arabisation made great progress, and at the same time the countries of the Near and Middle East became an economic unit, which distinguished itself by intense industrial and commercial activities. It is not an exaggeration to speak of a true economic miracle, performed under the guidance of the Abbasid government.

The formerly Byzantine and Persian countries became engaged in a manifold exchange of their agricultural and industrial products. Certainly there had been commercial relations between Syria and Persia before the lands of the Fertile Crescent were conquered by the Arabs, and it is true that the custom houses posted on the old frontiers and elsewhere did not disappear under the rule of the caliphs.[6] But there can be no doubt that trade between Egypt and Syria, on the one hand, and Irak and Persia, on the other hand, increased to a great extent when all these countries were united under the sceptre of the caliphs. The growth of trade between countries which had belonged during many centuries to different economic regions was slow but continuous, and had tremendous consequences for the economic life of the Moslem lands.

In the period before the Moslem conquests trade between the Byzantine and Persian empires was mainly an exchange of luxury articles, but under the Abbasids considerable quantities of articles destined for mass consumption, textiles and victuals were exchanged between distant provinces of their vast empire.

Grain was shipped from Northern Mesopotamia to Southern Irak, olive oil from Syria, Palestine and Tunisia to Egypt. Dates from Irak were exported to many provinces of the Moslem world. Khuzistan, Makran and Yemen produced sugar, Syria was famous for its fruit-culture, the products of which were highly appreciated in Irak and in Egypt. Barca supplied Egypt with cattle for slaughter. The textile industries of Khurasan, Bukhara and Samarkand exported their cotton goods to all the provinces of the Near East. The cotton cloth of Herat, Merw and Nishapur was sold everywhere. The Caspian provinces produced silk and woollen stuffs renowned in all parts of the Abbasid empire. Khuzistan and Fars, the two provinces of South-western Persia bordering on the Persian Gulf, exported precious silk and cotton fabrics, Armenia its famous carpets. Egypt had from time immemorial a highly developed linen industry, and when it was united, under the sceptre of the caliphs, with Irak and Persia, these latter countries became a big market for its products. The North African provinces, lastly, exported coarse woollen fabrics, destined for the lower classes of Oriental society.[7] There can be no doubt that the increase in the volume of trade ushered in a flourishing period for many towns. Industrial production was growing steadily, prices and salaries were rising, the demand for skilled labour was considerable, the population of the urban agglomerations increased more and more. In other words, the

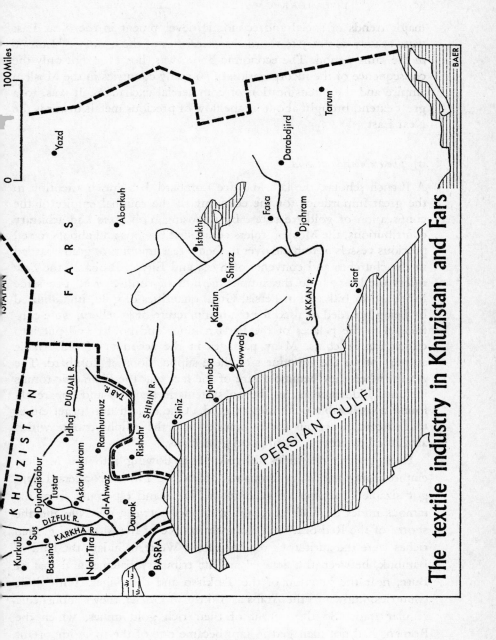

The textile industry in Khuzistan and Fars

Map labels:

100 Miles
0

BAER

FARS

Yazd
Abarkuh
Istakhr
Fasa
Shiraz
Djahram
Darabdjird
Tarum
Kazirun
Siraf
SAKKAN R.
Tawwadj
Djannaba
Siniz
SHIRIN R.
Rishahr
TAB R.
Ramhurmuz
Idhaj
DUDJAIL R.
Askar Mukram
al-Ahwaz
Daurak
Tustar
Djundaisabur
Sus
Kurkub
Bassina
DIZFUL R.
KARKHA R.
Nahr Tira
BASRA

KHUZISTAN

ISFAHAN

PERSIAN GULF

major trends of social and economic development in the Near East were exactly contrary to those characteristics of the history of Europe in the same period. The economic boom was, however, not only the consequence of the incorporation of so many countries in the Moslem empire and the intensification of commercial exchanges. It was, to a great extent, brought about by the flow of precious metals towards the Near East.

b) *The expansion of gold*

A French scholar, the late Maurice Lombard, has drawn attention to the great importance for the economy of the caliphal empire of the confiscation of gold treasures. By imposing high taxes and arbitrary contributions, the Moslem rulers compelled bishops and abbots to sell precious vessels or to hand over to them great amounts of gold hoarded in the churches and convents of Syria and Egypt. Probably the new rulers used as a rule the simple method of confiscation. The same happened in Irak and in Persia. Great quantities of gold, immobilised by being hoarded or used for the manufacture of jewellery, were confiscated in the palaces of the Persian kings and nobles and put into circulation as coins. Many passages in the accounts of old Arabic authors prove the soundness of these suppositions of Lombard. The Arabs, when they became aware of the fact that the Pharaonic tombs included hidden treasures, began systematic searches and apparently found considerable quantities of gold.[8] One should not forget either that in certain periods the Byzantines paid the caliphs tribute which amounted to great sums of good gold coins.

Even greater quantities of gold were flowing into the Moslem empire from various auriferous regions adjacent to its frontiers. Egypt got sizable quantities of gold from Nubia and especially from the famous mines of Wadi al-Allaki, a district between the Nile and the shores of the Red Sea.[9] But the main source of the Moslems' golden riches were the auriferous regions of the Western Sudan, the land of Bambuk, between the Senegal and its tributary Faleme, and that of Bure, near the junction of the Tinkisso and the Niger. With these countries, known to the Arabs as Takrur or Ghana, they established a regular trade. So the output of their rich gold mines, which the Romans had not managed to tap, became one of the most important factors in the Moslem empire's economy. The stream of gold which thenceforth flowed from the Western Sudan to the Near East stimulated its economic life to an extent previously unequalled.

The gold of 'Ghana' was transported to the Near East by several routes. The most westerly route was that which reached Sidjilmasa and led therefrom to Tlemcen and through the littoral of North Africa to Egypt. This route always remained a very important one and, characteristically enough, Ibn Haukal, a tenth-century geographer, says that the ruler of Sidjilmasa levied 400,000 dinars every year as duties from the trade of his capital. A second route led from Walata to Taghazza and beyond to Touat and the Mediterranean coast. Two other routes connected Gao, an important commercial centre on the Niger, with Egypt: one led from this town to Tadmekka and Ouargla and on to the Mediterranean coast; the other led to Takedda, the Air Massif and Tibesti and by way of the oases of Kufra, Dakhla and Kharga to Upper Egypt. But there was also a trade route which connected the Western Sudan with Egypt by caravan routes south of the Sahara, through the land of Kanem and north of Lake Tchad. There is evidence of the intense commercial relations between the Western Sudan and Egypt, which began to flourish in the eighth century, not only in many passages in the works of the old Arabic geographers, but also in the accounts of people from 'Takrur' who settled in Egypt even in that early period.[10]

Since the trade with the Western Sudan was closely connected with the progress of the Moslem conquests, and the occupation of North Africa was not accomplished before the beginning of the eighth century, the increase of the gold circulation in the Near East, although continuous, was slow. The first caliphs and the Umayyads did not change the monetary system of the lands which had come under their control. The mints in Egypt and in Syria struck Byzantine nomismata bearing in addition to the Greek inscriptions Arabic legends or images of the caliphs. In the formerly Sassanian countries they coined old Persian silver direms, displacing the name of the Persian king by that of the caliph or of the Umayyad governor. In Egypt and in Syria there were under the Umayyads many mints emitting bronze coins, modelled after the Byzantine follis, often with bilingual inscriptions and suppressing the name of the Byzantine emperor. It was only at the end of the eighth century that the caliph Abdalmalik could undertake a reform of the monetary system and strike true Moslem coins. The new gold coin, the Moslem dinar, which was minted in 696 (77 of the hidjra), was of a new type, different from the Byzantine nomisma.

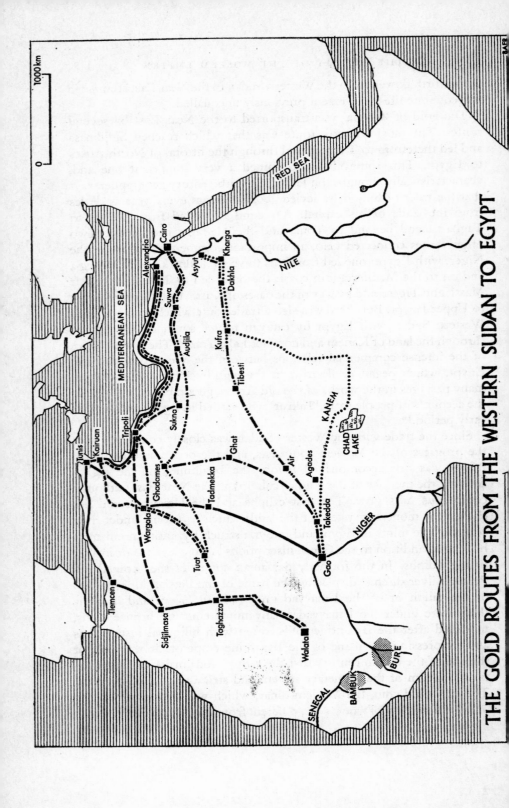

THE GOLD ROUTES FROM THE WESTERN SUDAN TO EGYPT

It was a purely epigraphic coin and its weight was 4.25 g, against 4.55 of the Byzantine gold coin. Two years later new Moslem silver coins were emitted – the dirhams, whose weight was 2.97 g, compared with the heavy Arabic-Sassanian direm weighing 3.98 g. These two coins were from that time accepted as the legal (canonical) Moslem currency, and they remained unchanged by the rulers of the Moslem world for many centuries.[11]

Under the later Umayyads gold coins were struck only in Damascus and circulated mainly in the former Byzantine provinces, whereas Irak, Persia and the adjacent countries remained the 'silver area', as from time immemorial. Even in the first half of the ninth century the payment and reckoning of great sums were made in Irak in silver dirhams.[12] But as the flow of gold from the Western Sudan increased more and more, a great change in the monetary system of the Moslem empire began. Lands whose currency had for many centuries been based on silver only went over to bi-metallism. There is no need to stress the tremendous consequences of this for all sectors of economy. The purchasing power of gold diminished and prices rose, but people were induced to invest money in industrial and commercial enterprises.

The numismatic collections provide us with many indications as to the expansion of gold. In 842 the striking of gold coins began in Merw, in 849 in Rayy, in 861 in Samarkand, in 862 in Shash, in 882 in Kazwin, in 884 in al-Ahwaz and in Hamadhan, in 885 in Adherbeidjan. So a bi-metallist currency system was established in the eastern part of the Moslem empire. The Arabic geographers of the tenth century relate that in their days the provinces of Fars, Kirman and Bukhara were still silver countries, whereas Armenia, Adherbeidjan, Arran, Media, the Caspian provinces and Samarkand had gone over to bi-metallism. The great change in the monetary life of the Moslem empire is borne out by the entries in the budgets of the caliphate. Whereas the revenues from Irak are calculated in the budget of 874 in dirhams, they are specified in 915 in dinars.[13]

The mints of the caliphal empire were also well supplied with silver ingots, for the Moslem armies had conquered most of the argentiferous regions of Central Asia. So the rich output of the silver mines of Afghanistan, Eastern Persia and Transoxiana supplied the mints of the Near East with sufficient stocks. Arabic geographers speak of the great quantities of silver extracted from the mines of Pendjhir in Afghanistan, but the output of the mines of the neighbouring town of Djarbaya and of those of Transoxiana must also have been considerable. Consequently the Moslem mints could almost always emit sizable quantities of dirhams.

If the exchange rate of the dinar in Irak and in Syria in the Umayyad period was really at least 10 dirhams, as we infer from the writings of the old Moslem jurisconsults, the gold-silver ratio would have been 1:8.5. After the accession of the Abbasids to the throne the exchange rate rose to 12 dirhams, so that the gold-silver ratio became 1:8.4. This low ratio, which shows the relative decrease of the purchasing power of gold, is a clear proof of the great change which the flow of Sudani gold had brought about in Near Eastern economy. In the ninth century the supply of silver from Central Asia must have increased, for the exchange rate of the dinar rose continually. Even assuming that the dirhams were debased, the value of gold must have risen again.[14]

Against the oscillations of the gold-silver ratio, due to changes in the supply of those metals and to other reasons, the remarkable stability of the intrinsic value of the dinar is the most striking feature of the monetary system of the caliphate. The expansion of gold output and the foundation of new mints did not result in the debasement of the dinar. The dinars coined by the caliphal mints were distinguished by their excellent quality throughout the ninth century.

From the beginning of the emission of Moslem gold coins the gold content of their alloy was very high. Measuring some hundred dinars in the collection of the American Numismatic Society, A. S. Ehrenkreutz arrived at the following results, so far as Umayyad dinars of the Near East (Arabia excluded) are concerned:

Umayyad dinars

89%	90%	91%	92%	93%	94%	95%	96%	97%	98%	99%	100%
No. of speci- mens 1	1	1	1	1	1	3	40	22	22	3	—

So the dinars consisting of 96% gold represent 42% of the Umayyad gold coins, the next group being those of 97% and 98%. Altogether these three groups represent 88%. The standard was probably 96% at the beginning and later, in the days of the caliph Hisham (724-43), 98%. The average weight of 177 Umayyad and early Abbasid dinars has been established as 4.19 g. The high-percentage alloy of Hisham's dinars may have been connected with the centralisation of gold minting. For prior to Hisham's reign dinars were struck in Damascus, Hidjaz, Egypt, Tunisia and Spain, whereas this caliph centralised their emission in Damascus.

The Abbasids, who transferred the seat of the caliphal government to Irak, suppressed the Damascus mint. The dinars emitted by the first caliphs of this dynasty bear no indication of the mint and are therefore called by numismatists 'mintless dinars'. The results of Ehrenkreutz's research into the alloy of these early Abbasid dinars are summarised in the following diagram:

Abbasid mintless dinars

	below 89%	89%	90%	91%	92%	93%
No. of specimens	4	3	3	5	4	3

	94%	95%	96%	97%	98%	99%	100%
No. of specimens	16	15	36	17	13	1	1

Once more we may conclude that 96% was the standard, for this group comprises 29.7% of the early Abbasid dinars examined by Ehrenkreutz, against 17% where the alloy is 97%. It seems, however, that through the period of the Umayyads and the early Abbasids the standard of fineness of the Egyptian dinars was always higher than that of the gold coins struck in Syria and Irak and amounted to 98%. After the death of Harun ar-Rashid in 809 and during the civil war which ensued, the caliphal mints had to debase the dinar, but that was a temporary phenomenon due to a political crisis. When the rule of al-Mamun (813–33) was firmly established, the old standard of the dinar was restored. The dinars coined by the Abbasid caliphs from al-Mutasim (833–42) to al-Mutamid (870–92) have mostly an alloy of 96–98%. Also the weight of the Abbasid dinars was almost that considered as canonical. The great majority of the gold coins emitted by the caliphs in this period weigh from 4.06 to 4.3 g.

The excellent quality of the dinar was certainly not only the result of sufficient supply of gold, but also the consequence of technological ability, or perhaps even progress. The Moslem minters had a thorough knowlege of cupellation, of the separation of gold and silver by means of nitric acid and of the extraction of gold and silver by amalgamation with mercury. The earthy compound, containing residue, was pounded, mixed with mercury and washed away by water. The gold ore was purified by a repeated operation of submitting it to fire. Silver was separated from copper and chrysocolla by fusing it with lead, being dissolved in crucibles which were kept under intense heat sustained by blowing with bellows. Lastly, the Moslem minters knew how to use effective check-measures so as to secure a great accuracy in the adjusting of the alloy.[15]

The emission of great quantities of excellent gold and silver coins had far-reaching consequences for the economic life of the Near East. When so many gold coins were put into circulation, people were less inclined to hoarding. On the contrary, the intense circulation of dinars resulted in an increase in the consumption of various goods. This phenomenon, again, brought about a steep rise of prices. An Arabic author quotes the caliph Harun ar-Rashid as saying that in his days a dinar had less value than a dirham in the days of al-Mansur (754–75). As the value of gold and silver was not the same in various provinces, and as the gold-silver ratio often changed, banking began to flourish and new techniques were developed. But the phenomenon which is perhaps the most characteristic feature of the economic life in the caliphal empire (and later in its successor states) is the low rate of interest. Whereas an interest of 20% was customary in wealthy European towns, people lent money in the Near East till the time of the Crusades for 4–10% on the average,[16] showing how great were the quantities of money in circulation.

c) *Demographic growth*

The Moslem conquests and the creation of an economic unit stretching from the frontiers of China to the shores of the Atlantic Ocean ushered in a long period of demographic growth, as a consequence of the economic upsurge, of the religious attitude of all classes of society and, last but not least, of the hopefulness with which people looked forward to the future, both their own and that of their community. The increase of population was certainly not a result of the spread of polygamy. It was noticed by the ninth-century Arabic author al-Djahiz that polygamous Moslem families had fewer children than the Christians.[17]

The increase of the population of Irak was the most conspicuous. The number of the Arabs who settled in Irak after the conquest was very considerable. The biographical dictionaries, an important branch of Arabic historical literature, contain numerous biographies of scholars who immigrated in this period from Iranian countries to Irak. But surely we may suppose also that many merchants and people of other classes came to live in Irak, when this country became the centre of a great empire under the Abbasids. The numerous slaves brought from Africa and elsewhere, and the Turkish military from Central Asia, certainly represented also sizable additions to the autochthonous population. According to some medieval Oriental sources, the caliph al-Mutasim alone bought 70,000 Turkish slaves for his guards in the nine years of his reign.[18]

In the Abbasid period public health must have improved remarkably, as there were apparently few outbreaks of pestilence or other epidemics. Under the Umayyad caliphs Irak had been infested by numerous epidemics, some of which are expressly specified as bubonic plague. Although most of these epidemics were local ones, they must have taken a heavy toll from the inhabitants of Irak, especially in the big towns of Basra, Baghdad and Wasit. In 639 there was an outbreak of bubonic plague in Basra, in 669 and in 673 there were epidemics in Kufa, and in 688-9 there was again a heavy epidemic of bubonic plague in Basra. In 706 Basra was once more visited by the plague and at the same time there was an epidemic in Wasit. Other outbreaks occurred in this latter town in 732 or 734 and in Basra in 745 and 749, in Upper Mesopotamia in 705 and in 745. On the other hand, the Arabic authors very seldom mention epidemics in Irak after the accession of the Abbasids to the throne. One reads of outbreaks of plague in Irak in 763 and in Upper Mesopotamia in 774. In the last mentioned year Upper Mesopotamia was also haunted by smallpox, measles, dysentery, dropsy and other illnesses. There were other epidemics in 775, 836, 863 and 872. This last epidemic raged in all the provinces of Irak, but is not identified.[19] So there is good reason to believe that the population of Irak increased considerably from the middle of the eighth century, as is further shown by the foundation of many urban settlements which became populous towns.

Basra and Kufa, which had been founded after the conquest of Irak as military camps and had become large towns, grew steadily throughout a long period. Basra reached its zenith after the accession of the Abbasids at the end of the eighth century and the beginning of the ninth. Kufa began to decline but was still an important town. Wasit remained a big town through the successive reigns of Umayyads, Abbasids and later dynasties.

New towns were founded in all the provinces of Irak. an-Nil, built by al-Hadjdjadj, on the southernmost canal connecting the Euphrates and the Tigris, became the chief town of a district. Kasr Ibn Hubaira, which had been founded by Umar b. Hubaira at the end of the Umayyad period, was an important centre of Irak's textile industry and according to a tenth-century geographer a large town. Among the towns founded in the first century of Abbasid rule, Baghdad, the new capital built in 762, was the foremost. Two years later, the caliph al-Mansur founded near ar-Rakka a new town which replaced it in course of time and became an important commercial and industrial centre. Harun ar-Rashid, who resided there some time, built a new palace, and the town finally became the capital of the province of Diyar Mudar. ar-Rahba, on the Euphrates, was founded in the days of al-Mamun and was a large town in the tenth century. In 836 al-Mutasim founded Samarra, on the Tigris, which replaced Baghdad as the residence of the caliphs for more than half a century. The town of Djazirat Ibn Umar, in Upper Mesopotamia, was founded in the middle of the ninth century and became soon an emporium for the trade of Irak with Armenia and Byzantium. Smaller towns in Irak which were built or rebuilt by the Moslems were the two al-Haditha. One of them, lying near the junction of the Greater Zab and the Tigris, was rebuilt by Marwan II, the last Umayyad caliph. The other al-Haditha, called Hadithat an-nura ('of the chalk pit') and lying on the Euphrates, had been founded in the days of the caliph Omar I. In connection with the foundation and development of towns in Irak under the first Abbasids, the frontier fortresses should not be overlooked, for these towns not only attracted pious Moslems who came to fight the Byzantines, but sometimes also became centres of a lively trade with the surrounding regions. Such frontier towns founded or rebuilt by the first Abbasids were al-Haruniyya, Ain Zarba, Malatiya, al-Hadath and Hisn Mansur.[20]

As against the numerous new towns founded by the Arabs, there were few ancient towns which decayed in this period. One of them was al-Hira, the former capital of the Lakhmid kings, which declined progressively. Another, much more important, urban centre, which fell into ruins after the Arabs had conquered Irak, was Ctesiphon, the capital of the Sassanian kings.

But we cannot of course be satisfied by collecting accounts of the foundation of new towns which were considered large by the old Arabic geographers. We would like to know what were the numbers of their inhabitants or even guess the total of Irak's population. Archaeologists who have measured the area covered by some of these towns provide us with data which render some guesses feasible, but cannot save us from embarking on rather venturesome conjectures.

It has been established that Baghdad at the heyday of the Abbasid period covered about 7,000 ha, about 5 times as much as tenth-century Constantinople and 13 times as much as Ctesiphon. The American scholar J. Lassner, who has specialised in this field of research, is inclined to suppose that the town numbered 560,000 inhabitants. But another very competent scholar concluded that the Abbasid capital had fewer than 200,000 inhabitants. The area of Samarra too was very extensive, the town covering 6,800 ha, but a great part of it apparently comprised palaces and gardens. The area of most other towns was rather small: ar-Rakka covered 192 ha and Mosul 292 ha. Basra, on the other hand, was a large town, covering 3,000 ha. A scholar who has carried out thorough research into its history concluded that it had 200,000 inhabitants in the ninth century. Kufa had perhaps three-quarters of the population of Basra.

Estimates of the population of whole regions are of course even more risky. But they convey some notion of the trend of demographic development under Moslem rule. An American archaeologist who has made a survey of the sites of abandoned settlements in the Diyala province, east of the Tigris, has concluded that in the heyday of Abbasid rule it had together with Baghdad 840,000 inhabitants.[21] In 1965 the modern republic of Irak had 8,261,527 inhabitants. But adding the provinces of Upper Mesopotamia now belonging to Turkey, i.e. Sairt, Mardin, Mush, Marash, Diyarbekr, Malatiya and Bitlis, one arrives at a total of about 10 millions. Baghdad and the Diyala province represent a fifth of this number. Perhaps we can safely assume the same proportion for the Abbasid period and conclude that Irak and Upper Mesopotamia then had 4 million inhabitants.

The most characteristic phenomenon of the demographic development of Irak in the Abbasid period was undoubtedly the growth of the towns. Comparing the sites of the Sassanian and Abbasid periods, the same American archaeologist has elaborated the following table:

	Sassanian period	Abbasid period
imperial cities	1 (540 ha)	2 (13,800 ha)
towns	8 (1,244 ha)	4 (730 ha)
small towns	4 (188 ha)	6 (265 ha)
small market towns	35 (599 ha)	20 (344 ha)

That in the Abbasid period many more people lived in big urban settlements will emerge from the calculation of the average area of the same sites:

	Sassanian period	Abbasid period
imperial cities	1 (540 ha)	2 (6,900 ha)
towns	8 (155 ha)	4 (182 ha)
small towns	4 (47 ha)	6 (44 ha)
small market towns	35 (17 ha)	20 (17 ha)

So there can be no doubt that there was a tremendous phenomenon of urbanisation. It would, however, be wrong to suppose that the big towns grew mainly at the expense of the small market towns and the villages. Many texts in the old Arabic sources show convincingly that towns like Baghdad and Basra attracted people even from distant countries.[22] In any case the main trend of demographic development was urbanisation, contrary to the major trend of the social history of Europe in the early middle ages, when the towns mostly disappeared. Urbanisation was accompanied by other phenomena which contrasted very much with the economic development of Europe in the same period. When the towns grew the money economy spread into the countryside. This phenomenon alone made life in the Moslem world very different from that of medieval Europe.

The population of Syria must have increased, though slowly, under the caliphs. Beside the immigration of Arab tribes during the occupation by the Moslems and subsequent to it, which was probably not altogether balanced by the exodus of Christian Arabs and Greek town-dwellers to Byzantium, there was through this period a continuous immigration of people from many countries, Persia and elsewhere, who came to live in the frontier fortresses. This immigration fostered a conspicuous growth of these towns, the so-called 'thughur'. Tarsus and al-Massisa became large and flourishing towns to the fortification of which all the caliphs paid great attention. Near al-Massisa, on the other bank of the river Djaihan, a new town, Kafarbayya, sprang up. Farther to the south, on the sea-shore east of Antioch, the town of Iskandaruna (later known as Alexandrette) was founded in the days of the caliph al-Wathik (842–7). The biographies included in the old Arabic 'Who's Who' show the great attractive power of these towns even for merchants and other people.[23] Ramla, in Southern Palestine, which had been founded by the Umayyad caliph Sulaiman (715–17) as his residence, became a flourishing emporium and remained an important town through three centuries.

The record of the epidemics which infested Syria in the first two centuries of Moslem rule is similar to that emerging from the chronicles of Irak: there were quite frequent outbreaks of plague under the Umayyads. After the conquest of Syria there was a terrible outbreak of plague in 638–9, followed by similar epidemics in 676 and in 698. This last epidemic, expressly identified as bubonic plague, took a heavy toll of Syria's population. In the first half of the eighth century there were at least five outbreaks of plague in Syria, in 717, 719, 725, 733–4 and 745. In the same period there were several earthquakes which wrought havoc in some of the biggest towns of Syria. In 713 there was an earthquake in Antioch and the surrounding region, and others followed in 717, 748 and 749, of which the last two caused great damage in Damascus. From the beginning of the Abbasid period an old Arabic author reports an epidemic of bubonic plague, which in the reign of Harun ar-Rashid carried off many people in Palestine. It may be that it was a local epidemic, but whereas the plague seems to have disappeared in Syria under the Abbasids, the country was, in the middle of the ninth century, afflicted by several heavy earthquakes. In 835 Antioch was almost destroyed, in 847 the range of the seismic movement stretched from Damascus to Antioch, in 848 there was another earthquake in Damascus. In 853 Tiberias suffered an earthquake, in 856 and in 859 the whole of Syria.[24] It is reasonable to suppose that the epidemics in the period of the Umayyads and the earthquakes in the Abbasid period slowed down the natural increase of Syria's population.

Judging according to the built-up area of Syrian towns in this period one must conclude that the country had no really big towns. Aleppo covered 56 ha (to which could be added 5½ ha of the citadel), Damascus 125 ha, or together with the suburbs 133 ha. So these towns could not have had more than 10–20,000 inhabitants each.

The total of Syria's population at the time of the Moslem conquest may have been 3–3.5 millions. There is good reason to believe that owing to the epidemics and the wars it did not increase very much in the period of the Umayyads. Under the Abbasids there was surely a slow but steady growth of population.[25]

Studying the rather uncertain data concerning Egypt's population in the periods of the Umayyad and first Abbasid caliphs, one arrives at similar conclusions: there was apparently a continuous growth of population. At the time of the conquest Egypt probably had 4 or 4½ millions of inhabitants. But soon after the conquest there began a continuous immigration of Arab tribesmen, in clans large and small and, on the other hand, through the reign of the Umayyad caliphs Egypt was free from civil wars or revolts which would have resulted in loss of many lives. Even the epidemics mentioned in the Arabic sources are insignificant in number; according to the Arabic historians there were in this period outbreaks of plague in 686, 680–90, 704, 751 and 832. On the other hand, urbanisation was much less conspicuous in Egypt than in Irak. Fostat, the new capital, did not reach 100,000 inhabitants.[26] But smaller towns probably increased more or less continuously, absorbing runaway peasants and slaves. So both the total of Egypt's population and the number of consumers of victuals grew.

Demographic growth, which was a major phenomenon of social life in the empire of the caliphs, led to a rise in prices and salaries. Many passages in the writings of the old Arabic authors, data collected from the papyri and other sources point to this fact. But although this was a general phenomenon of the economic life of the Near East in this period it did not occur at the same rate in all the various countries. Since it was a long time before they became one economic unit, the rise of prices began in some regions earlier, in others later. There can also be no doubt that this phenomenon was the effect of several causes, whose importance varied from place to place and in successive periods. Surely, the rise in the prices of grain was brought about by the circulation of much greater numbers of gold coins. The demographic growth and first of all the progressive urbanisation, that means the increase of the numbers of consumers, were other reasons of this phenomenon.

In Syria the prices of victuals must have risen considerably as early as the second decade of the eighth century, for an old and reliable

Arabic author relates how people came to the caliph Omar II (717–20) to complain about the dearth. Similar complaints are to be found in papyri dating from the same time.

In Irak grain prices apparently rose almost continuously from the beginning of Abbasid rule. According to Dionysius of Tell Mahre, the commercial price of 30–40 djarib of wheat in Upper Mesopotamia in the 70s of the eighth century was 1 dinar. That means that 100 kg cost 0.125 dinars. In Southern Irak prices may have been higher, but we have no records from that period. Two accounts from the tenth century clearly illustrate the continuous rise of prices. According to Kudama b. Djafar, who wrote in the first quarter of that century, the average price of 100 kg of wheat in Southern Mesopotamia was 1.36 dinar. The geographer Ibn Haukal, on the other hand, relates that when he visited Upper Mesopotamia in 969 the same quantity there cost 1.51 dinar. Those were, to be sure, the wholesale prices; how much the retailers' profits increased them we do not know.

As far as wheat prices in Egypt are concerned, the papyri and other sources provide us with many details. They are contained in the following table:

Wheat prices in Egypt under the reign of the caliphs

date	price of an irdabb (= 6 waibas)
699	$\frac{1}{8}$ dinar
706–707	1/12 dinar
709	1/13 dinar
714	very low prices, 1/25 dinar
715	1/10 dinar
743	1/14 dinar, then dearth: 1 mudd $\frac{1}{2}$ dinar
8th cent.	1/10 dinar
beginning of 9th cent.	1 irdabb + 2$\frac{1}{2}$ waibas = 1 dinar
9th cent.	1$\frac{2}{3}$ irdabb = 1 dinar
,,	3 irdabbs + 1 to 2 waibas = 1 dinar
,,	2$\frac{1}{2}$ to 3$\frac{1}{3}$ irdabbs of best quality = 1 dinar
,,	2 irdabbs + $\frac{1}{4}$ waiba = 1 dinar
,,	2 irdabbs = 1 dinar

This table shows clearly that the price of an irdabb, apparently of 109.6875 kg, in the eighth century was $\frac{1}{13}-\frac{1}{10}$ dinar, whereas it rose in the first half of the ninth century to $\frac{1}{4}-\frac{1}{2}$ dinar. So the average price of 100 kg wheat would have been 0.075 dinar in the eighth century and in the first half of the ninth century more than 0.3 dinar. This steep rise in prices in the first half of the ninth century was probably connected with revolts and civil war, and was therefore to some extent a temporary phenomenon. For the data which have been found so far show the difference between the rise of grain prices in Irak and in Egypt. The rise (as far as the secular trend is concerned) was considerably smaller in Egypt, probably because in that monetary system gold coinage was no innovation and the increase of the population was more limited.

As so often happens, wages were lagging behind, rising much more slowly than the prices of victuals and of other articles. In Irak a highly qualified craftsman, such as a tailor or mason, in the second half of the eighth century earned 5-6 dinars a month, which would be comparatively high pay. As to the wages of simple journeymen, we find some data from the end of the eighth and from the ninth centuries. According to different sources a mason in the days of Harun ar-Rashid earned $1\frac{1}{2}$ dinars a month, whereas a rich man's chief cook in the first half of the ninth century got 1 dinar with portions of food. But notwithstanding the continuous rise of the cost of living, a glass-cutter earned no more in the second half of the ninth century than 1.3-1.5 dinars a month.

In Egypt, in the first half of the eighth century the monthly salary of a journeyman was $\frac{1}{2}-\frac{3}{4}$ dinar. According to papyri of Aphrodito, dating from this period, a worker employed in the vineyards of the caliph in Fostat had $\frac{5}{8}$ dinar a month, workers who had to repair ships $\frac{3}{4}$ dinar, and Egyptian workers employed in the construction of the Great Mosque of Jerusalem $\frac{7}{12}-\frac{2}{3}$ dinar. Skilled craftsmen, however, in the same period earned $1\frac{1}{4}-2$ dinars. The monthly wages of carpenters were $1\frac{1}{4}$, $1\frac{1}{3}$ or $2\frac{1}{4}$ dinars, and those of an expert craftsman in ship-building amounted to 2 dinars. A caulker got $1\frac{1}{2}$ dinars a month, a smith $1\frac{2}{3}$ or $1\frac{3}{4}$ dinars. But in the fourth decade of the ninth century, when prices had risen very much, many weavers in Lower Egypt earned no more than $\frac{3}{4}$ dinar, and at the beginning of the tenth century the sum of 1 dinar was apparently the usual pay of a journeyman.[27]

So inflation and demographic growth had resulted in the deterioration of the workers' situation. However, most of the data which one finds in the sources refer to the minimum wages, and there is good reason to believe that they fell more steeply, as always, than the wages of the skilled workers.

The question arises why public health improved in the Abbasid period, with a consequent decrease of epidemics, despite the rise in prices and the fall of real wages. One may conjecture that mortality in the Umayyad period was so high that a certain recovery took place under the reign of the Abbasids. It is also probable that the growth of towns was much slower in this period. Basra and Kufa had become large towns in a short time, while Baghdad grew apparently at the expense of other towns. Further, one should not forget that the wars of conquest helped to spread epidemics.

d) *Technological progress*

The flourishing state of the Near Eastern economy in the period of the first Abbasids and the growth of many towns was to a great extent associated with industrial efficiency. The Moslems improved methods of production in the industrial enterprises which they had inherited from the former rulers, the Persians and the Byzantines. They developed new branches of old industries and created new ones. It is worth emphasising that technological progress was made, in contrast with the ideas of a certain school of economists, at a time when labour was cheap and slaves abundant.

As everywhere in the middle ages, the textile industries in the Near East were the most important. The old linen industry in Egypt kept its old reputation under Moslem rule and won new markets. In the industrial centres of Lower Egypt, in the towns of Tinnis, Damietta, Dabik, Shata, Bura, Damira, Tuna, Abwan and Difu, various kinds of linen were produced. Some manufacturers specialised in the production of white linen, others in coloured fabrics or brocaded linen (dikk). The fine linen fabrics called sharb and kasab were world famous, and the gold-embroidered and figured stuffs (*muwashsha*) produced in Alexandria were also highly esteemed. The province of Fayyum and the towns of Bahnasa and Akhmim in Upper Egypt were other centres of the linen industry. But Egypt also produced woollen fabrics renowned for their quality. An Arabic writer of the ninth century says that the best woollen garments came from Egypt. The products of the Egyptian textile industries were exported to many other countries. Several texts in the writings of the old Arabic authors show how highly they were esteemed in Irak and elsewhere.[28]

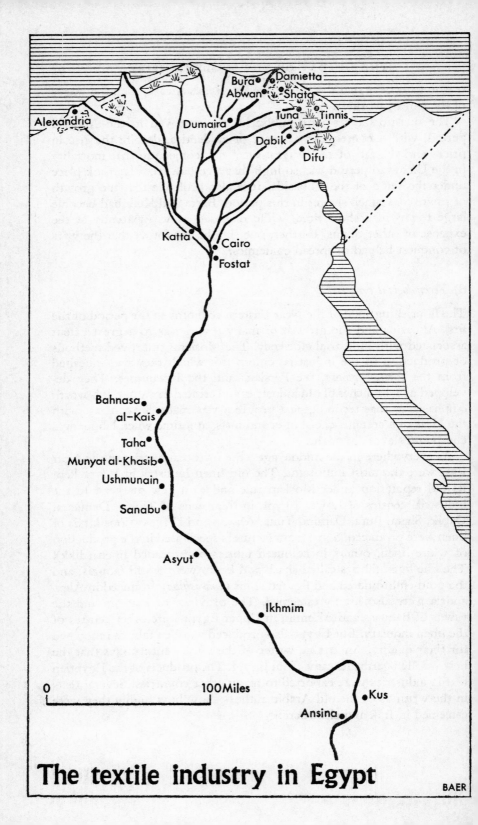

The textile industry in Egypt

BAER

Both Syria and Irak had renowned silk manufactures. In Syria and Palestine the most important centres were Damascus, Ascalon and Ghazza. Aleppo produced cotton garments, Tiberias carpets, while in some villages of Galilee there was a domestic industry producing various textile fabrics. The different silk fabrics of Irak, such as the siklatun, silk interwoven with gold, and other brocades, filoselle (called *khazz*) and satin were renowned for their quality. The most important silk manufactures of Irak were located in Baghdad, Basra and Kufa. In Baghdad there were also manufactures of cotton, and its *attabi* fabrics were famous everywhere. Wasit produced curtains, the province of Maisan, in South-eastern Irak, carpets, and Takrit had an excellent woollen industry. In Northern Mesopotamia, Mosul and Nisibin there were great weaving centres which produced various kinds of garments, curtains and carpets. The products of the textile industries of Irak and Northern Mesopotamia were exported to all parts of the Moslem world.[29]

As many of these industries (or more precisely most of those which were not located in the towns founded by the Arabs) had existed long before the Moslem conquests, their structures probably remained unchanged. In the great industrial centres there were royal factories, called by the Arabs tiraz, which had to supply the government. There were also flourishing private industries in several regions, both in the towns and in the villages. It was a striking feature of the industrial structures in the Moslem empire that most workers were free men. The labour force did not consist of slaves.[30]

The great advance of the textile industries in the time of the caliphs was an indubitable result of the unification of many countries into a great empire, which was gradually becoming an enormous economic unit.

In the days of the caliphs the supply of the raw materials became much easier than before, as access was obtained to materials from quite distant regions. The wool of the Maghreb could be used in Egypt's manufactures, and the renowned Armenian wool was exported for use elsewhere. The possibility of obtaining colouring matter from various and even remote provinces of the caliphal empire was equally important in a period when people were so keen to wear variegated garments. Saffron, a dye very much in demand, could be obtained from several districts of Media where it was produced in a number of excellent varieties. The saffron of Isfahan, Hamadhan, Rudhrawar, Nihawend and Barudjird was exported to many other provinces of the

Moslem empire. Not less esteemed was the saffron of Tabaristan. The crimson for which the Armenian carpets were so famous was imported from Western Persia and Irak, and it was also employed in Egypt's textile industry. The Near Eastern textile industries could use Brazil-wood imported from India, indigo from the South Persian province of Kirman and from certain provinces of the Maghreb. Alum, used to strengthen the colours, was an Egyptian product, and was exported to many other countries.[31]

The intense trading activity between the Moslem dominions resulted in an exchange of knowledge or, more exactly, in the imitation of industrial techniques. The flourishing textile industry of Khuzistan began to imitate Egyptian fabrics, such as those manufactured in Dabik. On the other hand, Armenian upholstery was imitated in al-Ushmunain, in Upper Egypt. The silk industry of Irakian towns founded by the Arabs, such as Basra, Kufa and Baghdad, was undoubtedly strongly influenced by the methods of the industries in South-western Persia, whence so many of their inhabitants had come. On the other hand, the textile industry of Upper Mesopotamia certainly employed Armenian methods.[32]

Similar conclusions can be drawn from the data concerning the glass industry of the Near East in the Abbasid period. Irak and Upper Mesopotamia already had flourishing glass manufactures in the fourth and third millenia B.C. Instructions for glass-making have been found in cuneiform texts. From these we learn that the ancient Mesopotamian glassmakers constructed different types of kilns and used bellows to obtain high temperatures. They also developed methods for cooling off the glass outside the kiln, so that they could produce both transparent and opaque glass. Syria and Palestine too had a renowned glass industry from time immemorial, using the silicate extracted from the white pebbly sand of the seashore. In Egypt, Alexandria and some towns south of the present Cairo, such as Madinat al-Fayyum and al-Ushmunain, were the main centres of the glass industry. The excellent quality of the Egyptian glass was certainly attributable to the alkali found in the Salt Sea of Wadi Natrun. After the Moslem conquest a glass industry developed in Fostat and in other towns. In Irak, Basra became a famous centre of the glass industry. The old Arabic authors provide us with many details on the kinds of glass and glass vessels produced in the Near East, and archaeological finds corroborate their accounts. The glassmakers of the caliphal empire produced transparent and opaque glass, enamelled glass and vitreous paste, consisting of variegated glass, and vessels of glass covered with gold and coloured ornaments. A Chinese author praises the quality of the Near Eastern opaque glass, saying that it is made by burning oxide of lead, nitrate of potash and gypsum. To these materials the Near Eastern glassmakers added borax, which made the glass elastic and indifferent to temperature.

Specialists who have studied the style of Egyptian glass products dating from the ninth and tenth centuries have concluded that the glass industry of this country was in that period very much influenced by the methods employed in the factories of Irak. The ornamented crystals manufactured in Egypt in the Abbasid period show this influence clearly. But as far as some other kinds of glass are concerned, Egypt's factories decisively influenced the manufactures of Irak. Glass vessels found in Samarra show Egyptian influence, or may even indicate that Egyptian glassmakers were called to the new residence of the caliphs.

There can be no doubt that in that period glass manufacture was an important sector of Near Eastern industry, a fact to which many accounts of the export of glass products to remote countries bear witness. The flourishing condition of this industry is therefore another example of the effect of the Moslem conquests on the economy of the lands henceforth united under the sceptre of the caliphs.[33]

But whereas this and other industries had existed a long time before the Arab conquests, the introduction of the paper industry into the Near East was a great achievement of the Moslems. The replacement of the fragile and expensive papyrus by Chinese paper ushered in a new epoch in the civilisation of the Old World.

It is now a well-established fact that the production of rag paper was introduced into the Moslem empire by Chinese prisoners of war who were brought to Samarkand in 751. These Chinese papermakers taught the Moslems the pounding of textile fibres in stone mortars and methods of chemical maceration. Further, they transmitted to them the technique of sizing the paper with starch glue or loading it with starch flour. From that time Samarkand had a famous paper industry, whose products were sold to all parts of the Moslem world. At the end of the eighth century paper mills were founded in Baghdad, and the Baghdadi paper became known for its good quality. The paper industry spread also to Arabia, where manufactures were founded in the provinces of Tihama and Yemen, and farther west to Syria and Egypt. In Syria paper was manufactured in Damascus, Hamath and

Manbidj, whereas in Egypt Fostat and the small town of Bura became centres of the new industry. The relatively great number of papermakers, called 'warrak', 'kaghidi' and also 'karatisi' (which originally meant papyrus-maker and in course of time came to mean papermaker), who are mentioned or whose biographies are included in the biographical collections of this period, is clear evidence of the great development of the new industry. Large towns had also their paper markets where people came to buy paper and to have books copied. When paper mills sprang up in so many countries and paper became an ordinary product, many different kinds were produced and the methods of production were continuously improved. Whereas at the beginning only small sheets were manufactured, later on large ones of various sizes were produced.[34] The introduction of paper, of course, provided employment to many people and contributed to the development of towns. It promoted also all branches of trade and banking, since it rendered bookkeeping much easier.

e) Foreign trade

For the sake of an appropriate estimate of the importance of foreign trade for the economy of the Moslem empire, one should never forget that the overwhelming majority of its inhabitants lived in the country and made a living from agriculture. But the great difference between the structures of the Near Eastern society and the Christian Occident in the early middle ages was the existence of many populous towns in the Moslem empire. These towns had a considerable importance for the economy of the empire as a whole and especially for its commercial relations with other parts of the Old World.

These commercial exchanges were manifold and of a very different character. Although Byzantium was during four centuries the traditional enemy of the Moslem empire and intermittent warfare went on through the ages, the Moslems engaged also in a continuous trade with the Byzantines. It seems that Trebizond was the Byzantine emporium where the Moslem merchants got the greatest part of the Greek products, brocades and others, which they wanted to acquire.[35]

The trade with pagan countries of Africa was much more important for the economy of the Moslem Near East. It was probably through many centuries the most profitable branch of foreign trade, for the Moslems exchanged very cheap products against gold. The inhabitants of the Western Sudan had a great need of salt. An Arabic author of the eleventh century speaks of tribes who simply exchanged for salt an equal weight of gold. The geographer Ibn Haukal who wrote in the second half of the tenth century, says that the people of Kugha, which was apparently Gungia, east of Ghana, depend completely on the rulers of Audaghost, whence salt is imported to them, coming from the Moslem countries. According to this author a load of salt fetched 200–300 dinars. al-Bakri, on the other hand, lists the imports of Kugha, a town west of Ghana. It imported salt, cowries, copper and spurge, the last two articles being most in demand. Describing Audaghost, a great emporium of the Western Sudan, al-Bakri says that it imports grain, fruit and raisins. Wheat, he says, costs 6 mithkals a kintar. Further, he relates that garments and vessels of copper are also imported there. In other passages al-Bakri mentions also the import of salt into the Western Sudan. A part of it came from the Maghreb, and some was brought from the Near East. According to al-Bakri, salt was used in some places as money. As the gold trade in this region probably did not change through many centuries, one may even quote later authors who relate that beads were one of the articles much in demand in the Western Sudan and therefore imported by Moslem merchants. So salt, beads, copper vessels and other cheap merchandise were exchanged by the Moslem traders for gold and no doubt for slaves. In later periods Egyptian textiles may have played a greater role in imports to the Western Sudan.[36]

The commercial activities of the Moslems in the Western Sudan must have been intense. For the Arabic authors of the tenth and eleventh centuries relate that there were in all major towns Moslem quarters whose inhabitants were probably to a large extent North African and Egyptian merchants. Such merchant colonies existed in Ghana, Kugha and Kawkaw (Gao on the Niger). In his description of Audaghost al-Bakri says explicitly that one finds there the same people as in every big Moslem town.[37]

Although Maghrebin merchants played a great role in the Sudan trade, one should take into consideration that many of them were agents of Egyptian traders. The trans-Saharan route was probably to a great measure under the control of Egyptian traders.

As far as the commercial exchanges between the caliphal empire and the Western Sudan are concerned, there is good reason to rely on the witness of late authors, for scholars are almost unanimous that there were during long periods few changes in this long-distance trade. But the history of the commercial relations of the Moslem Near East with

Western Europe have been the subject of animated debate ever since the great Belgian historian H. Pirenne put forward his thesis.

According to Pirenne the conquest of the African and Spanish coasts of the Mediterranean, the naval activities of the Moslems and later the occupation of the large islands at the centre of the inland sea had tremendous consequences for the economic life of all adjacent regions. The Mediterranean had been for many centuries a kind of channel through which merchandise and ideas were transmitted from the Near East to Europe and *vice versa*. The migrations of the German peoples and the occupation of a great part of the Roman empire by these tribes had not changed their social structure. The Germans had superimposed themselves upon the old social hierarchy and had fairly soon been amalgamated with the autochthonous populations. Therefore the so-called Völkerwanderung did not bring about a break in the economic and cultural development of Europe, and did not mean the beginning of a new era. But when the Arabs had established their rule over the eastern, southern and western coasts of the Mediterranean, it became the frontier between two civilisations, strange, unknown and hostile to each other. What had been a great lake on whose shores rulers, laws, religion and language were the same or similar became the scene of naval warfare and piracy. Trade disappeared almost altogether in the Mediterranean in the course of the eighth century. Spices, precious silk fabrics and other Oriental articles were hardly to be found in Western Europe. Moreover, with the extinction of foreign trade, there perished the towns where it was carried on. The rulers of Western Europe no longer minted gold coins, because there was no need of them. The time of the self-sufficient manor had come, and the coronation of Charlemagne, in 800, formally initiated the middle ages, the feudal period.

Pirenne's thesis has aroused sharp criticism, and many students of European history have collected texts showing that the Moslem conquests did not result in a complete interruption of commercial exchanges between the Near East and the Christian Occident.[38] But Orientalists have seldom dealt with the questions raised by Pirenne, though the Oriental sources contain materials by recourse to which the ideas of the Belgian historian may be proved or disproved.

Arabic, Greek and Latin sources yield data showing that notwithstanding the frequent wars between the Moslems and the Byzantines maritime trade was sometimes carried on between the two empires. According to Latin sources, Moslem ships anchored in South Italian ports in the first half of the eighth century, and a Frankish monk relates how he and two companions embarked in 870 in Bari on two ships which transported a great number of Christian prisoners to Egypt (to be sold as slaves). He says that other ships, with even more captives, sailed to Tripoli. Indeed, there can be no doubt that through this period trade was going on between the Christian towns of Southern Italy and the Moslem ports of North Africa.

But the picture of conditions in the Mediterranean which emerges from the accounts of the Arabic writers is of a situation which rendered impossible the continuation of regular and wholesale trade between the Moslem ports of the Near East and the Byzantine and Occidental countries. Time and again the Byzantines launched naval expeditions against the Moslem ports. They attacked Damietta in 709, in 739 and again during the civil war between al-Amin and al-Mamun. Conditions in the Mediterranean worsened very much in the first half of the ninth century. In 814 a group of Spanish Moslems occupied Alexandria and made it the base for their intensive piratical activities. Later, in 827, they left Alexandria for Crete, from which they threatened the Christian ships and ports even more. Meanwhile, the Moslem rulers of Tunisia had launched the great offensive against Sicily, the bulwark of Byzantine seapower in the Central Mediterranean, and in 831 they took Palermo. During the following twenty years the Moslems had great successes. In 838 Brindisi was conquered; in 841 Bari, the occupation of which lasted thirty years, and in 843 Messina were taken. Then there began a counter-offensive by the Byzantines, who landed on the coast of Northern Syria. In 853 and again in 859 they occupied Damietta, and these expeditions seem to have wrought havoc in these and other Egyptian coast towns. But in the last third of the ninth century the Moslem war fleets had the upper hand in this long naval war. Under the efficient leadership of two great admirals, Leon of Tripoli and Yazaman of Tarsus, they defeated the Byzantines several times and in 904 they sacked the port of Salonica. The Byzantines took their revenge by the conquest of Cyprus and a new invasion of Northern Syria. However, in 911 and 915 the Moslem admiral Damian defeated them again.

Collecting the accounts of these numerous naval expeditions, one is inclined to believe the statement of a contemporary Arabic geographer that Moslem and Byzantine ships attack each other's littoral, sacking the towns and taking much booty. Often, he says, they gather a hundred or even more warships and make naval war. So there was almost permanent state of war in the Eastern and Central Mediterranean, and regular trade between the Near East and Southern Europe became for 250 years impossible. Another Arabic geographer of the same period speaks of the Byzantine ships which lie in wait for the Moslem merchant vessels along the coasts of Syria and Egypt.

The abandonment of the Syrian and Egyptian coastal towns was partly the consequence of the exodus of many Greek inhabitants, most of them belonging of course to the upper strata of society, who left after the Moslem conquest for the provinces remaining under Byzantine rule. Certainly there were many merchants among these emigrants. When insecurity became endemic on all the shores of the Eastern Mediterranean and trade became impossible, the decline of these towns became even more conspicuous. If trade had been possible, new inhabitants, brought by the Umayyad caliphs to the Syrian ports, would have resumed it. But since it was too dangerous, people left these towns. The caliphs Muawiya, Abdalmalik and Hisham tried to keep them alive, probably for strategic reasons. They rebuilt the decayed quarters of Tyre, Caesarea and Acre, but their efforts were in vain. When Lattakia, an important port in Northern Syria, was left in flames by the Byzantines in 715, it remained for at least 60 years in ruins. The copious materials in the collections of Arabic biographies of this period shed light on the conditions of these towns. Whereas they contain many biographies of people who left Irak and Persia from the middle of the ninth century for the flourishing towns on the Byzantine frontier, for the towns of Central Syria and for the great urban settlements in Egypt, the number of those who came to live in the coastal towns of Syria and Palestine was, according to these sources, very small.[39]

So the Orientalist finds in his sources many texts which seem to support Pirenne's supposition of an interruption of regular and wholesale trade in the Mediterranean. The texts which he can adduce refer, however, mostly to military activities, and being typical accounts of medieval authors they do not explain the somewhat astonishing superiority of the Moslems over the warlike, well-equipped and well-trained Byzantine fleet.

In order to be a match for the Byzantine navy, which had relatively sophisticated equipment and weapons, the Moslems must have reached a considerable degree of technical parity. Therefore one finds very persuasive the theory of a modern scholar that the Arab fleets were already using the so-called lateen sail in the Mediterranean in the ninth century. This triangular sail, the upper edge of which is held up by a long yard, called an antenna, and rigged aslant towards the stern, is much easier to control from the deck than the ancient square sail, especially when the wind is not too strong. It was apparently invented by the Byzantines and very soon taken over by the Arabs.[40]

However that may be, the military achievements of the Arabs and the state of war in the Mediterranean resulted in an interruption of international trade. This situation is also reflected in another branch of Arabic literature, i.e. in purely geographical works. The writings of the Arab geographers of the ninth century and of the beginning of the tenth century reveal an almost complete ignorance of the geography of Europe. Even the European shores of the Mediterranean were unknown to the Arabs. This is a clear proof that there were no trade relations. The book of Ibn Khurdadhbih, who wrote in 846 and made additions to his work until 886, is a good example of the Arabs' geographical knowledge. Whereas this scholar had a very good knowledge of the geography and administration of the Byzantine empire and included interesting chapters on India and China, he knew nothing of the Christian Occident. Narbonne, which had been captured by the Franks in 759, is for him still a Moslem town. The Tyrrhenian Sea is virtually a region still to be explored. The same ignorance is revealed by the *Geography* of al-Yakubi, written in 891, and that of Ibn al-Fakih, dating from the beginning of the tenth century. All Arab geographers of this period confuse Rome and Constantinople and repeat legendary stories which they had picked up from spurious sources. Suffice it to quote Ibn al-Fakih's statement that the distance of Rome from Constantinople is – one year (i.e. a journey of one year).[41]

The *Geography* of Ibn Khurdadhbih contains, however, an account of the activities of a group of merchants which carried on a worldwide trade, an account which has great importance for the study of the Pirenne thesis. According to Ibn Khurdadhbih, there was in his days a group of Jewish merchants, called Radhanites, who engaged in the exchange of goods of the Christian Occident and of the Far East. The Arabic author specifies the various routes by which they travelled from the kingdom of the Franks to the Far East and back. Some of them travelled by sea to Egypt and thence sailed on the Red Sea to India. Others went to Syria and beyond to Irak and embarked in the Persian Gulf. A third route led from Spain along the coast of North Africa to Egypt and through Palestine, Syria, Irak and Southern Persia to India, a land route from the starting-point to the destination. The traders who chose it continued, according to Ibn Khurdadhbih, their journeys by land from India to China. The fourth route was also a land route, leading from Central Europe through Russia to Northern Persia and beyond through the lands of the Turks to China. These itineraries have given rise to some questions, but for our subject it is much more relevant to dwell on the merchandise which the Radhanites, according to Ibn Khurdadhbih, carried from Western Europe to the Near East and from China and India to the Mediterranean world. He says that they exported from the Occident eunuchs, slaves, brocades, furs and swords. These commodities were typical luxuries. From the Far East they imported costly merchandise, such as musk, aloe wood, camphor and cinnamon. So the Radhanites were engaged in a trade in very expensive articles, not intended for mass consumption. Their trade was probably not a regular one and they could engage in it because they belonged to neither the Christian nor the Moslem world. Although there were other merchants who crossed the frontier – a kind of iron curtain – which had been set up between the Christian and the Moslem empires, the account of the Radhanites' trade tends to prove that there was no regular trade between the two hostile civilisations.[42]

Many historians have, however, maintained that trade between the Moslem empire and Europe was not discontinued, but had merely changed its routes. So the Pirenne thesis cannot be judged duly without collecting the accounts which one finds in Arabic literary sources of the origin of those articles which could have been imported from Europe.

Among these articles slaves (eunuchs) and furs hold the first place. As far as slaves are concerned, many accounts of the Arabic authors of this period show convincingly that the great majority of them were brought to the Near East from Africa, from Russia and the adjacent Slavic countries and from Central Asia. Most of them were indeed Negroes, Slavs and Turks. The Arabic story-tellers attribute to Harun ar-Rashid the observation that the number of black slaves in Baghdad is countless. Collections of sailors' stories even include accounts of slave raids made by cunning Arab slave-hunters in East Africa. Juridical texts of Jewish jurisconsults who lived at that time in Irak point also to the African origin of most slaves. These Negroes were the house slaves. Those destined for military service were mostly Turks. It seems, however, that a certain change occurred at the beginning of the tenth century. Whereas in the eighth and the ninth centuries most house slaves had been Negroes and the eunuchs Greeks, in the tenth century many Turkish and Slavic slaves were imported into the Near

East and the eunuchs were brought from Spain. As the quality of various kinds of furs has been discussed repeatedly by old Arabic authors, we have copious information about their origin. According to a trustworthy author of the ninth century, the most precious furs were those imported into the Near East from the Caspian provinces and from Khwarizm. The import of Russian furs had already begun a long time ago and was to develop very much in the tenth century.[43]

Summarising all the texts referring to the foreign trade of the Moslem empire under the reign of the first Abbasids, one is bound to conclude that Pirenne was right in supposing that there was an almost complete interruption of commercial exchanges between the Near East and the Christian Occident lasting more than 250 years. The accounts of the Arabic writers on the origin of slaves and furs show that there was no change of trade routes. Before the middle of the tenth century there was only sporadic trade between the Moslem Near East and the Christian Occident.

On the other hand, the commercial relations between the Near East and India and the lands beyond it had never been discontinued, although their volume and their character changed from time to time. Persian traders and merchants of Oman, whose towns had a mixed population of Arabs and Persians, engaged in trade with India throughout the reign of the Umayyad and Abbasid caliphs. In the period of the Umayyads Oman was apparently the main centre of this long-distance trade. Arabic texts referring to this period show that in the Near East were to be found Indian products, e.g. arms, mail and teak-wood. Indian and Chinese ships visited the Persian Gulf and Moslem traders went to India. In about 700 there was a colony of Moslem merchants in Ceylon. Moreover, a great change had occurred in the trade with the Far East after the Moslem conquests. Whereas before Ceylon had been the meeting-place where Near Eastern and Chinese traders exchanged their goods, the Moslem merchants carried on vigorous activity in China itself. The Chinese author I-Tsing speaks of Persian ships which came to Canton in 671. The Buddhist teacher Vajrabadhi saw in Ceylon in 717 not less than 35 Persian ships which sailed to Canton. Another Buddhist pilgrim, Hui-Chao, says in 727 that the Persians come to China to buy silk. In old Arabic sources even the names of some China traders of the late Umayyad period have been found. One of them was Abu Ubaida Abdallah b. al-Kasim, an Ibadi Kharidjite. The number of Moslems in the Chinese emporia must have increased continuously, for in 748 a Chinese priest noticed the existence of a village inhabited by Persians on the island of Hainan. In Khanfu there was a big colony of Moslem traders. In 758 the Arab traders in Canton became involved in civil war and two years later a thousand of them are said to have been slain.

Notwithstanding the numerous accounts of the commercial activities of the Moslems in the Far East in the time of the Umayyads, one should not forget that it was a period of conquest and civil war. The Arabs were not yet accustomed to luxury, and there was not yet a great demand for the precious articles of India and China. But the Umayyads apparently had a great interest in establishing good relations with the Chinese, for they sent their emperors many embassies.[44]

A new period in the history of Moslem trade with the Far East began after the accession of the Abbasids to the throne of the caliphs. The luxurious life of the new dynasty, which was imitated by their viziers and other high dignitaries, meant that the perfume and other precious merchandise of the Far East were much more in demand than before. So the trade with India and China grew in volume. It was carried on by land and, preferably, by sea. The caravan routes from Transoxiana to China were considered long and difficult. But the caravan trade between Sind, the north-western province of India occupied by the Arabs, and Eastern Persia was quite lively. Nevertheless, the seaborne trade with India and China was much more important. At the end of the eighth century the Moslems returned to Canton and the trade with China grew continuously. Arab colonies sprang up in towns where they had not existed before.

Irak had become not only the political but also the economic centre of the Moslem empire and therefore the Persian Gulf was the main route of the great Indian trade as it had been in Sassanid times (before the Byzantines had tried in the sixth century to divert it to the Red Sea). The port of Basra, al-Ubulla, was the starting-point of this main line of world trade in the early middle ages. Siraf, a coastal town of South-western Persia, Sohar and Muscat in Oman were others. Some of the merchant vessels sailed along the southern coast of Persia to the ports of North-western India, others put out to the open sea and sailed to Malabar, where Kulam was the destination of most of them. From there they continued their voyage sailing through the Park Strait or south of Ceylon and then to the Nicobar Islands and farther to Kalah, a port of Malaysia, and finally to Canton. Trade with Sumatra seems to have been fairly lively, whereas there is no indication as to trade with Borneo or the Moluccas. Korea was beyond the reach of

Arab trade until the middle of the ninth century, but in the second half of it the Moslem merchants began to visit this country too.

This long-distance trade had become possible when the Arabs had acquired considerable nautical knowledge and learnt to take advantage of the monsoons. The north-west monsoon enabled the ships to cross the Indian Ocean from Oman to Malabar in the months November-December, whereupon they continued their voyage with the southerly monsoon in the China Sea. After spending the summer in Chinese ports, the Arab traders returned with the north-east monsoon to the Malacca Strait and sailed back to the Persian Gulf driven by the southeast monsoon. So, altogether, a voyage to China would have taken a year and a half. There was also another maritime route from the Near East to India, namely that from Egypt through the Red Sea and via Aden. Studying the Arabic sources of this period one becomes aware, however, of the fact that it then had less importance for the great Indian trade.[45]

The Arabic authors of this period and others referring to it provide us with plenty of information on the articles which the Near Eastern traders imported from India and China. They brought camphor, musk, cinnamon, cloves, canella, cardamom, galanga, nutmeg, aloe wood, sandal wood, perfume, Brazil-wood and other spices and dyes. From China they imported silk, and from India also precious stones. From the coast of East Africa they brought ambergris and ivory. The great majority of these articles were very expensive; they were typical luxury articles. Timber, so much needed in the Near East and in this period not imported from Europe, was probably the most important exception. The character of the trade which the Moslems carried on with the Far East in this period is shown by the almost complete absence of the Indian article which held the first place in the great Levantine trade of the later middle ages, namely pepper. In one of the oldest Arabic sources one finds an explicit statement as to the nature of the merchandise imported from India. In the travel book of the merchant Sulaiman we read that the Moslems import from China, for several reasons, small quantities of precious articles.[46]

f) *The rise of Moslem bourgeoisie*

Under the reign of the first Abbasid caliphs a new class of Moslem bourgeois began to play a great role in the economic, political and cultural life of the Near East.

In part it was autochthonous. Persians who had settled in the lands of the Fertile Crescent, Aramaic-speaking Christians and Copts who had embraced Islam and had made money by trade. But this bourgeois class comprised also many Arabs whose fathers had been merchants in the towns of Arabia and who stuck to their profession. Others were Arabs who had become purveyors to the armies of the caliphs and had enriched themselves. Some had served in the Moslem armies on campaign and later become merchants specialising in the trade in luxury articles, such as precious stones, perfume and slaves, or, more often, in textiles. The trade in textiles was without doubt very profitable, since the prices of industrial products probably rose much more than those of agricultural ones. This was one of the consequences of the new style of life introduced by the Abbasid caliphs. Service in the caliphal administration was the origin of many other fortunes. From the beginning of Moslem rule the governors and their staffs used their position to acquire great riches.

Needless to say that in these days of boom all kinds of devices were used to become rich, and money was in certain classes considered the only thing of real value in this world. The Arabic writers of the ninth century depict this atmosphere in colourful terms.[47] The new rich invested part of their money in credit business. Old Arabic sources leave no doubt that already at the end of the eighth century credit arrangements of different types were quite common in both trade and industry. One of them was the so-called mudaraba (or kirad) – the Moslem form of the commenda. This was a loan given to a merchant traveller against a share of the profit to be realised and without imposing on the agent any liability for losses. Generally speaking, credit was considered by the Hanefite school of Moslem jurisconsults as a lawful kind of investment, even at the beginning of the Abbasid period. But the new rich usually invested a part of their money also in rural estates. It seems, moreover, that they were so much interested in acquiring such estates that they used all possible means to get possession of them. Some enterprising and wealthy businessmen became tax-farmers, a most lucrative business.[48]

The new Moslem bourgeoisie adapted itself very soon to the aristocratic way of life cultivated by the old Persian nobles who had become Moslems and by the Arab chiefs. Some of them justified themselves by playing the part of Maecenas, while at the same time pious theologians collected sayings of Mohammed, more or less authentic, which were favourable to the acquisition of riches. Other men of letters too praised

wealth and wealthy people and extolled the professions of the first
Moslems to be merchants or craftsmen. Many merchants became
themselves interested in the sciences of Islam, i.e. in the Koran, the
oral tradition and law, and, as it has always been, not a few of their
sons devoted themselves entirely to the scholarly life. So it can be seen
from the study of the Arabic collections of biographies that most
theologians of this period belonged to the bourgeois class, i.e. were
merchants or sons of merchants. H. J. Cohen, scrutinising these biographical dictionaries, has found 4,200 scholars whose occupations are
mentioned. Certainly his conclusions should be accepted, as he very
honestly avows, *cum grano salis*. Because of the intricacies of the Arabic
language one cannot be sure whether the epithet given to a man points
to his profession or to that of one of his forefathers and, secondly, there
is the ambiguity of so many Arabic professional names which denote
both the manufacturer and the seller of a certain product. At all events,
the major result of Cohen's research is very impressive. He has found
that 60.6% of Moslem theologians in the ninth century were merchants,
a third of them being traders in textiles. Furthermore, he arrived at the
conclusion that from this point of view no change followed from the
establishment of Abbasid rule.[49]

As the majority of the Moslem jurisconsults belonged to the merchant class, it is quite understandable that the juridical principles
developed in Irak, under the first Abbasids, by the very influential
school of Hanefite lawyers to a very great extent reflected commercial
practice. Their rules were modelled on the law merchant of Near
Eastern traders in this period. This is convincingly borne out by the
consistency between these rules and the merchants' customs illustrated
by the Judaeo-Arabic letters which date from the eleventh and twelfth
centuries and have been found in the Cairo geniza. The old Hanefites
distinguished themselves by a deep understanding of the necessities of
trade and the interests of merchants. That is the conclusion which
must be drawn from the study of the chapters in the law books which
deal with commercial transactions. The use of 'juristic preference'
(*istihsan*) instead of establishing by strict analogy a law which would
be opposed to the interests of the merchants, is a striking feature of the
Hanefites' juridic reasoning. Profit-making is the touchstone by which
many transactions are judged by this school of lawyers. Further, they
take commercial practice very much into consideration in establishing
their rules.[50]

Between the period in which the new Moslem bourgeoisie had

become an economic factor to reckon with and the time when it began to play a role in political life almost a century elapsed. The new bourgeois had to wait a long time before they obtained positions at the top of the hierarchy of the Moslem empire. The Persian gentry, the dihkans, had already under the reign of the Umayyads occupied a prominent position in the caliphal administration. The predominance of the Persian aristocracy under the first Abbasid caliphs was a striking feature of the change brought about by the new rulers. The role of the Barmekids was a sign of that. But in the days of the caliph al-Mamun (813–33) the upper bourgeoisie began to climb the ladders of the social hierarchy. Several texts in the great chronicle of at-Tabari point to the high position held by Djafar b. Dinar al-Khayyat, a native Iraki, in the caliphal army under al-Mamun and his successors. But, needless to say, the role which the bourgeois began to play in the civil administration was much more conspicuous. al-Mamun's successor, al-Mutasim, had at the beginning of his reign (833–42) appointed to the post of vizier al-Fadl b. Marwan, a landowner of rather humble origin. Then a merchant, Ahmad b. Ammar at-Tahhan ('the miller'), became his secretary and for a short time he fulfilled most of the vizier's tasks. But al-Mutasim became dissatisfied with his services and appointed as his vizier Muhammad b. Abdalmalik az-Zayyat ('the oil merchant'), a man belonging to a family of rich merchants in the town of Daskara and later in Baghdad.[51] From that time the bourgeoisie of Irak shared the government with the commanders of the Turkish guards of the caliph. A class of rich landowners who held high posts in the caliphal administration emerged from the new Moslem bourgeoisie and were in control of the caliph's diwans. This class of kuttab (high officials) became a very influential group, to be distinguished from the theologians, who represented another wing of the new bourgeoisie.

In view of the expansion of gold, the prosperity of industry and foreign trade and the rise of a new and rich Moslem bourgeoisie there arises the question why a true capitalism did not develop in the empire of the Abbasids. For there can be no doubt that in the time of the Abbasids the Near Eastern economy reached the state of pre-capitalism.

That a class of merchants and rich landowners in the Moslem empire carried on activities by methods of rational capital accounting and that there was a relatively free market does not characterise this economy as truly capitalistic as Max Weber, for example, has defined it. To quote Weber: 'A whole epoch can be designated as typically capitalistic only as the provision for wants is capitalistically organised to such a predominant degree that if we imagine this form of organisation taken away the whole economic system must collapse.' Some sectors of the Near Eastern economy in the Abbasid period may have had a capitalistic character, its economy as a whole did not. The accumulation of capital was not so great that it could control the production of the Near Eastern industries. There were, it is true, relatively big industries producng for export, but they were not managed by traders who sold their products in other countries, as did the great capitalists of Florence in the fourteenth century. The structures of the industries were not uniform. There were royal industries and private industries; in some slave labour was used and in others not. In some manufactures, as in the domestic industries located in villages, the tools probably belonged to the worker, in others they were the employer's. It goes without saying that we cannot estimate the volume of the different sectors of industry. In any case there is no reason to suppose a crushing predominance of the big industry which would have given the Moslem empire's economy a true capitalistic character.[52]

The Moslem prohibition of lending money at interest was certainly neither an obstacle to the development of a true capitalistic economy, nor did it confer a monopoly of banking on non-Moslems, as Massignon has maintained. Moslems did, in fact, evade the law of usury.[53] But the Moslem law of inheritance probably impeded the accumulation of capital in rich merchant families. According to this law the testator can make disposition of no more than a third of his property, while at the same time a bequest to one of the legal heirs is invalid without the consent of the others. In cases where no will has been made the property must be divided among those heirs whose shares are specified in the Koran and in the oral tradition of Mohammed's sayings. They are twelve in number and their shares are liable to variations according to circumstances. Further, there are agnatic heirs who take a residuary share. As the agnatic heirs include ascendants (father, grandfather, brother, the offspring of the grandfather, etc.) the Moslem law of inheritance resulted in frittering away the big properties. For it can rightly be asserted that the bulk of the property, according to this law, went to the residuary heirs, whose number was in most cases considerable.

The commercial activities of the Moslem governments also hampered the development of a capitalistic economy. In almost all Moslem countries and in all periods the princes engaged in trade. They sold great quantities of grain which they had collected as taxes and they took a share in foreign trade. The princes had ships to export the precious products of India and of their own countries to the Maghreb and elsewhere. On the one hand there was freedom of enterprise, on the other hand private industry and private trade had to sustain the competition of the princes. The commercial activities of the governments partly corresponded to the needs of supply, e.g. of war materials such as timber and iron, lacking in the Near East, or with grain necessary for the provision of the large towns. In any case, the participation of the princes in trade was a great obstacle to the development of capitalism. The great Moslem sociologist Ibn Khaldun was fully aware of that and severely condemned it.[54]

Another reason for the peculiar development of the Near Eastern economy was the lack of security. In the middle ages a successful merchant living in a European town had not to fear that his property would be arbitrarily confiscated by the prince. In the Oriental world this squeezing of the rich was usual. Where burghers had no municipal autonomy and the State had to defray by means of land-tax the enormous expenses of an uncomfortably powerful army, the imposition of arbitrary 'contributions' (musadara) on rich bourgeois, high officials or merchants often seemed to the government to be the only way to get money urgently needed. These confiscations of private property, which became a striking feature of social life in the Moslem world, began in a very early period. Even the collection of the taxes imposed on the merchants often meant a confiscation of part of their goods and money. Dionysius of Tell Mahre describes in eloquent terms the predatory methods used by tax-collectors in Upper Mesopotamia in the second half of the eighth century.[55]

The shortcomings of the Moslem régime were, however, to become more obvious in later periods. Under the first Abbasids the Moslem bourgeoisie was still a new class, rising in the social hierarchy of the caliphal empire. It became even a powerful class and a factor to reckon with. It seems that many Orientalists have overlooked the fact that for three hundred years the Near Eastern bourgeoisie tried to resist the feudal lords and that the struggle between these two classes was one of the leitmotifs of Oriental history.

CHAPTER IV

Disintegration of the Caliphate

The boom in the Near Eastern economies came suddenly to an end and the unity of the Moslem empire was shattered when some thousands of slaves revolted in the swamps of Southern Irak. The caliphs had overcome dangerous outbreaks of religious dissent and of social discontent disguised as sectarian movements, and their armies had subdued revolts of Arabs and Persians whose leaders belonged to the highest strata of Moslem society. But this new revolt, which proved so fateful, was the rising of the most despised class – the Negro slaves. Not all the rebels, indeed, were Negroes, but most of them were. It was their desperation and fury which gave them strength to hold their own against the caliphal armies. For fourteen years they frightened half of Irak and the adjacent regions. All the forces of the caliphal government had to be mobilised to suppress these daring rebels. So the revolt had far-reaching consequences. Great countries broke away from the caliphate and became independent kingdoms. The strain upon the provinces which remained faithful to the caliphs aggravated the social tensions within Near Eastern society and paved the way for the downfall of the old régime.

a) *The slave revolt of the Zindj*

Arabic historians, imbued with the spirit of rigid orthodoxy and faithful to the cause of the caliphs, are bitterly hostile to these rebels. The medieval chroniclers speak with abhorrence of 'the abominable' – the leader of the revolted slaves. They depict him as a bloodthirsty tyrant who killed women and children; they even accuse him and his followers of cannibalism. Modern Orientalists have seen him as an ambitious man who roused the slaves in order to carve out for himself a princely dominion. But he was not an impostor, nor were his followers simple robbers. The revolt of the Zindj was an authentic social rising, and its leader had well-defined ideas.

The scene of the revolt was the southernmost part of Irak, the geography of which was at that period very different from present conditions. Both the Euphrates and the Tigris spread out and became lost in the Swamp which covered the greater part of Lower Irak. It stretched from Kufa, where it received the waters of the Euphrates, to Basra and covered an area 50 miles across and about 200 miles in length. North of Basra the Swamp drained out by the Abul-Asad canal into the estuary of the Shatt al-arab. The region of the estuary was marsh land, intersected by numerous canals which were exposed to tidal fluctuations. In course of time most of it had been covered with nitrous layers which made cultivation impossible.

But these nitrates could be used for certain purposes and the earth below it could, when cleared, be fertile. So enterprising Basra business-men used slave labour to remove the upper layers. Most of them were Negroes brought from East Africa, called in Arabic Zindj. Although some free workers joined them, the enterprise was organised as slave work. Groups numbering from 50 to 500 workers, called 'sweepers', removed the nitrous layers, piling them up in mounds, so that the land became arable. Task-masters, probably freedmen of the employers, kept strict discipline and provided the slaves with poor food. The life of these 'sweepers' was a hopeless one, but it developed a group spirit, and their great numbers, amounting to many thousands, gave them the consciousness of strength. Moslem ascetics who happened to live in this region had conveyed to them some of the ideas of Islam, such as the natural rights of men and notions of social justice. So there were all the conditions for a social revolt: the concentration of capital in Southern Irak had brought about a concentration of labour, masses of desperate workers were longing for rescue. They only needed a leader, and eventually he appeared.

This was a certain Ali b. Muhammad, who hailed from Verzenin (near the modern Teheran) and pretended to be an offspring of the caliph Ali. His Alid origin is doubtful. According to Arabic historians, people believed that he belonged to the tribe of Abdalkais. He was certainly very ambitious, but also very gifted. He was by no means an ascetic, for he was happy to join in looting. His career seems to have been quite unusual. First he tried his luck as a poet at the court of the caliph at Samarra. Then he attempted to stir up a revolt in the province of Bahrain, but failed. Thereupon he embarked on the career of a religious leader and appeared as a soothsayer and even prophet. When the number of his followers increased, he was, however, compelled to leave the town of al-Ahsa, whereupon he went to the Bedouin and finally to Basra. There he continued his activities and failed once more. He had to flee, and his followers were imprisoned. But he had not yet lost his courage. Once more he pretended to possess supernatural knowledge, and preaching his heretical doctrine in Baghdad he had some success. Upon the dismissal of the governor of Basra he returned to the great emporium, which had always been a hotbed of sectarians and revolutionaries.

But this time he found a stage for his activities outside the town. The slave masses employed by the capitalists of Basra as sweepers in the surrounding marshes seemed to be a more propitious field. At the beginning of September 869 he began to rouse the sweepers, promising them that he would lead them to freedom, give them property and remain faithful to them to the end. Since the slaves were probably sceptical as to his real intentions, he took solemn oaths that he would not betray them. Ali b. Muhammad was an excellent speaker, and had his speeches translated for those who did not understand Arabic. Addressing the poor slaves he spoke of the misery and hopelessness of their present lot and held out the prospect of a splendid future, houses of their own, money and – slaves. As other prophets used to do, he wore a veil over his face, so his outward appearance was in keeping with his preaching. Needless to say he had great success.

Devout Arabic court historians, who tell us this story, describe Ali b. Muhammad as an unscrupulous impostor. But in fact he aimed at the overthrow of the existing régime and the establishment of a new social order. The trappings of a heresiarch were necessary to rouse the lower strata of society. When he claimed to be a descendant of Ali he appealed to the belief of the Moslems that his offspring, the lawful heirs of the caliphate, would restore the pure Islam, with the social justice it implied. He dwelt very much on his noble ancestry and had it engraved on his coins. The legends of the coins he struck are outspoken: he calls himself 'al-Mahdi Ali b. Muhammad' – the Redeemer.[1] So he pretended to be the Redeemer whom all Moslems believe will come at the last day. He maintained that he was fighting not for worldly aims, but for the restoration of the true religion. That is a feature characteristic of many medieval social revolts. Ali b. Muhammad had banners bearing the verse of the Koran (9[112]) which was a watchword of the Khawaridj. He had it also engraved on coins. So he fought for the ideas of the Khawaridj, for equality and social justice as conceived by the Moslems. The idea of evangelical poverty would have sounded strange to them. Ali b. Muhammad preached that all should have property, houses and slaves, not only the rich Arabs in Basra and Baghdad. In fact, Islam had not abolished slavery. The doctrine of Ali b. Muhammad, as far as we may glean from the fragmentary indications in hostile sources, combined two main streams of social revolt in the empire of the caliphs. According to at-Tabari he had his slogans written on the banners in green and red – the colours of the Alids and the Khawaridj. at-Tabari and other Arabic authors are concerned with the question whether he was really a descendant of Ali. For the modern historian this is irrelevant. We must conclude that the rising of the Zindj was a social revolt disguised as a religious movement. His followers were almost exclusively slaves or true proletarians. Among his officers there were Yahya b. Muhammad, a weigher of grain, Sulaiman b. Djami, a black freedman, Muhammad b. Salim, a butcher, Fath al-hadjdjam, a phlebotomist (a despised profession).

The accounts given by the Arabic historians of the progress of Ali b. Muhammad's revolt are more detailed than those dealing with his teaching. He tried to win over the peasants, but had only partial success. Some villages, most of them no doubt settlements of poor tenants, joined the rebels, whereas others applied to the caliphal army, promising it reward for action against the Zindj. The slaves, however, did not hesitate. Everywhere they flocked together to swell the forces of Ali b. Muhammad. Soon he commanded troops of various origins. Although most of them were Negroes, there were some regiments of whites, such as the Furatiyya and Nuba. The problem of manpower did not worry the rebels, but that of weapons did. When the revolt started Ali's followers had no weapons. But when they won their first successes and took booty, they also seized weapons. Ali b. Muhammad proved to be a very able general. His campaign was distinguished by the great efficiency of his scouting. He always knew of the movements of the government troops and could take the necessary measures. The method of fighting which the Zindj developed gave them a clear superiority over the caliphal troops. Whereas the army of the caliph was composed of cavalry which could not move easily in the marshes of the Shatt al-arab, the Zindj, armed with slings and arrows, attacked them from side-canals overgrown with reed. The caliph's troops were suddenly charged by an invisible enemy and suffered heavy losses. Many were drowned, and those taken prisoners by the rebels were executed, a frequent practice of rebels to terrify their enemies. Success brought success. Some clans of the Banu Tamim began to help the Zindj by supplying them with victuals. The rebels could not, however, rely on the Bedouin alone. They imposed on the villages which submitted to them the supply of certain quantities of victuals and sacked those which opposed them. The number of the latter was the greater, for the bulk of the peasantry adopted a decidedly hostile attitude towards the Zindj, and the antagonism between the two classes was sharp.

At the end of October 869 the Zindj were in a position to attempt an attack on Basra, but they were repelled. Some time after this first abortive attempt on the capital of Southern Irak, they built themselves a new town, 'al-Mukhtara' (the Elect City). This new town, situated on the canal Nahr Abi l-Khasib, south-east of Basra, became the head-quarters and seat of the government which they set up for the region under their control. In June 870 they took al-Ubulla, a large town at the place where the Ubulla canal flowed into the estuary. It was then a rich town and the booty was considerable. The repercussion of this blow was felt in all the districts of Southern Irak. The town of Abbadan submitted to the Zindj and promised to deliver them weapons and slaves. Two months later they were already so strong that they could venture to invade Khuzistan, one of the richest provinces of the caliphs and famous for its industries. They took al-Ahwaz, its capital, and came back covered with glory and laden with booty. This exploit gave them courage for a new and daring undertaking, and once more they had success: they cut Baghdad's supplies from the south, inter-cepting the ships on the Tigris. In September 871 they took Basra. This was their greatest success. The booty was enormous, and they freed many Negro slaves. Arabic chroniclers say that after the conquest of Basra many of the Zindj had ten slaves. The rebels left the town, but tightened their grip on Khuzistan. In 873 they conquered al-Ahwaz once more. When in 876 the caliphal army was engaged in a war with a Persian rebel, the Zindj advanced to Central Irak and in-vaded the province of Wasit. In 878 they took this large town, and in the following year Djabbul, an-Numaniya and Djardjaraya, three towns on the Tigris. They could not hold these places, but remained in the province and built a new town of their own, al-Mania. In Khuzistan a Kurdish rebel recognised their suzerainty and gave over to them the town of Ramhurmuz.

So in 879, ten years after their rising, the power of the Zindj was at its height. al-Mukhtara had become the capital of a state comprising large parts of Southern Irak and Khuzistan. The provinces conquered by the rebels were governed by officers, as usual in the Moslem world.

In al-Mukhtara they established a real government, with a Treasury, a Chancery and judicial authorities. But this was the year when the tide turned.

al-Muwaffak, the brother of the caliph al-Mutamid and the real master of the Abbasid capital, prosecuted the war against the Zindj with caution but also with persistence. For a long time he was occupied by the contest with other rebels, but he had not neglected the campaign against the Zindj. He had entrusted his lieutenants with the continuation of the war, and in fact his son Abu l-Abbas took al-Mania in 880. At the beginning of 881 al-Muwaffak left for Khuzistan, and when he came back a year later he launched the great attack. His army laid siege to al-Mukhtara. The besieged Negroes closed the waterways by erecting dams, or even with chains, so that the big ships of the imperial army could not move on. But the regiments of al-Muwaffak were continuously reinforced, and in course of time he succeeded in cutting off the supplies of the besieged town, and as the siege dragged on food became scarce in al-Mukhtara. In July 881 his troops penetrated into the town for the first time. When al-Muwaffak was wounded at the end of 882 fighting ceased for some months, but at the end of April 883 military activities were resumed, and the final attack was launched. After four months of bitter fighting al-Mukhtara was taken and Ali b. Muhammad killed. The slave revolt which had lasted fourteen years was subdued.[2]

Just as there can be no doubt as to the circumstances which rendered the successes of the Zindj possible, so it is not difficult to understand their final failure. The leader of the slaves did not succeed in winning over sizable sectors of other classes. Neither the peasants nor the town proletariat allied themselves with the Zindj. The slaves alone were too weak, notwithstanding their great number. But how to explain the attitude adopted by the lower strata of Oriental society? Why did the petty merchants and craftsmen of Baghdad volunteer for the war against the Zindj? Why did the poor tenants in the small hamlets of Southern Irak not join them to the last man? It is easy to understand the antagonism between the Zindj and the wealthy peasants in whose villages they looted precious vessels, jewels, gold and silver; in many villages, however, there lived tenants who were themselves considered serfs.

Probably the industrial proletariat in the towns of Southern Irak was numerically too weak, for the towns of the Near East were predominantly commercial centres. So the religious antagonism between the heretical Zindj and the other classes faithful to orthodox Islam became paramount. Secondly, there was the natural antipathy between black and white people. For racial feeling ran high in those times; the Negroes were held in contempt, in spite of the teachings of Islam. At the beginning of the revolt many black soldiers deserted from the imperial army and joined the Zindj. But only an insignificant number of proletarians in the towns went over to the rebels. Thirdly, we must take into consideration the antagonism between sedentary populations and Bedouin. The support they received from some Bedouin clans made them suspect to the peasantry, which abhorred the nomadic robbers. The Bedouin themselves were not reliable allies. They were interested in looting and the profitable exchange of goods and for the sake of these were always ready to go over to the other side.

So the slave revolt failed through lack of support from other classes. But the Moslem empire had been considerably weakened during the long years of fighting, when the flower of the imperial regiments had to be sent into the swamps of Southern Irak. The interruption of commercial relations put a heavy strain on the middle classes in the large towns of Irak. The great merchants who supplied the army carried on a lucrative business, but others suffered severe losses when the Zindj captured merchant ships with their cargoes and trade with the lands on the Persian Gulf became impossible. The rise in prices, when the supply was cut off, impoverished petty merchants. Craftsmen lost customers who could no more afford to pay for their products. The increase of social tension in Irak and the neighbouring countries was the outcome of the slave revolt. But it had even more fateful consequences.

b) *Dismemberment of the caliphate*

The revolt of the Zindj was a decisive phase in the history of the caliphal empire. The disruptive forces became so strong that they brought about its decomposition. North Africa had broken away a long time ago. During the long war against the revolted slaves, and shortly afterwards, many other countries separated themselves from the Abbasid caliphate. The difficult situation in which the rulers of Baghdad found themselves was the opportunity for high-spirited leaders to establish their rule in various parts of the empire. It seems, however, that their success corresponded to the wishes of the upper classes in these countries. As industrial development was too slow to absorb the plentiful supply of men, and the war with the Byzantines and the pagan Turks had slowed down and no more provided an outlet for the unemployed, there were everywhere many young people who readily joined revolutionary movements or hired themselves to those who would employ them. In many provinces social-revolutionary tendencies were perceptible. New social forces were at work, directed against the old Arabic-Persian aristocracy. The Dulafid prince Abdal aziz who ruled over Karadj, between Hamadhan and Isfahan, had in 867 an army of 20,000 *saalik*. This word means in Arabic: poor, beggar and also robber. It meant in this case probably 'landless proletarians'. The recrudescence of Bedouin brigandage became a general phenomenon, and sectarian movements aiming at social upheaval sprang up in various sectors of the sedentary population. A certain Muhammad b. Harun, who had been a tailor and then a highway robber, rose at the beginning of the tenth century in Rayy. The Arabic chroniclers report that he assembled herdsmen and criminals and embarked on revolutionary activities. At times he hired his forces to those who needed them, and when in 902 a party of the inhabitants of Rayy called him in he entered the town, killed the governor, and himself became ruler of the district. He was, however, expelled a year later by the king of Bukhara. The Arabic authors say that his following numbered 8,000 men.[3] This was a true social revolt.

It can easily be understood that the upper strata of society, the wealthy and middle bourgeoisie were frightened by social unrest, and that these classes readily supported rulers who could guarantee them the security necessary for their economic activities and the maintenance of the social order. A situation had been created in which firm rule was needed. All those who had property were convinced that only the army could restore order and warrant a minimum of security. It did not matter that the new rulers hailed from the lower classes or had seized power with their help. Often the antagonism between the sedentary population and the Bedouin was much stronger than the tension within the townspeople and the peasantry. Anyone who could restore security was welcomed. As the power of the caliph was at a discount, it came about that every energetic general who commanded a well-equipped, trained and faithful corps could carve out for himself a principality.

For a long time the army had been satisfied with ruling behind the scenes. Now the generals strove to become independent princes, and their ambitions, like those of other leaders, became the decisive factor in the course of events. The rank and file was bound to these generals by ties of personal attachment. Many of these military chiefs were Turks, others were Persians or Arabs or belonged to other nations. Some of them, although setting out to establish their personal rule, represented national aspirations. Indeed, everywhere particularism and the desire for national independence became uppermost. But in this interplay of opposed tendencies personal ambition was the strongest force. The generals go over from one party to the other and later use their forces to fight on their own account. When appointed by the caliph governor of a province, a general would revolt against him and declare himself independent. Even when such a governor recognised the suzerainty of the caliph, he became in fact an independent prince. The empire of the caliphs was torn in pieces and was never to revive. But the new princes brought their subjects security, gave them a stable government, improved the economic situation and earned their gratitude.

When the Zindj revolt broke out, the central provinces of the empire and the Iranian countries were still under the direct administration of the caliphs, or governed by vassals who were more or less faithful to them. During the slave revolt all that changed. In this period the Tahirids ruled not only over Khurasan as before, but also the provinces east and north of it, to the Indian border and to the boundary of the pagan Turks. They had always remained faithful to the Abbasids. But Muhammad b. Tahir II, who became ruler of Persia in 862, had not the talents of his predecessors. Meanwhile a rebel had succeeded in establishing an independent state in Sidjistan, the easternmost province of Southern Persia. His career was characteristic of the conditions prevailing. Sidjistan was torn up by the Khawaridj and the peaceful population suffered much. The Khawaridj had villages of their own, i.e. had won over a part of the peasantry. Yakub b. Laith, the new ruler of Sidjistan, was of humble origins. He was the son of a peasant and had become a coppersmith, his brother Amr a mule driver or mason. Then he was a 'brigand', probably a Kharidjite. But in those days the Arab-Persian aristocracy gave way to other groups, these Persian proletarians being one of them. The Tahirid governor left the country, having been supplanted by the 'volunteers' fighting against the Khawaridj. Yakub as-Saffar (the coppersmith) switched over to them, was appointed by their leader governor of the town of Bust, and in 867 was in control of the whole of Sidjistan and some adjacent regions. He began to fight the Tahirids and occupied Herat, Kirman, and for some time Fars. He was supported by the lower strata of society, and his close collaborators were proletarians. One was called 'the Turkish slave', another 'the naked one', a third 'the weaver'. In order to avert his advance to the centre of the empire, al-Muwaffak entrusted him with the government of Balkh and Tokharistan. In 870 he conquered other provinces of Khurasan and in 873 Nishapur, the capital of the Tahirids. When the caliph refused to recognise him as king of Khurasan, he marched against Baghdad and although he was defeated in 876, he retained Fars and Khuzistan, the two provinces of Persia which were nearest to Irak.

The Arabic historians narrate the military exploits of Yakub b. Laith and do not dwell on other aspects of his reign. But from some passages in their writings we learn that everywhere he restored peace and security and that his army was very much attached to him. So it was not only his prowess and ability that explain his success, but also the desire of his subjects to have a stable and efficient government. We are told that he destroyed the bulwarks of the Khawaridj and that the inhabitants of Sidjistan regarded him as their saviour. The upper bourgeoisie enjoyed the security and the stability of the new régime, while the lower classes rejoiced at the downfall of the aristocrats. The establishment of Saffarid rule was indeed a social upheaval. For in the Oriental world a social revolution had not the same meaning as in the medieval Christian world, or in modern times. When we speak of social revolution, we think of equality, of the abolition of privileges. This is because we are imbued with Christian ideas and often consider opulence a vice. But the Moslems regarded the overthrow of the ruling class as a social revolt. Yakub b. Laith set up battalions which were famous for their riches. They bore maces of gold and silver, the intention of Yakub being to impress people by their appearance.

Amr b. Laith, his brother, who succeeded him after his death in 879, was not as able a ruler, but continued for many years the struggle for the Iranian provinces. The later Saffarids were even less talented princes and were happy when they succeeded in holding Sidjistan.[4]

The coppersmith established his power in Sidjistan some years before the Zindj revolt, and made his conquests in the years when the caliphal army was occupied by the contest with the slaves. About the same time a family claiming descent from Ali founded a principality in Tabaristan, annexed to it the adjacent country of Djurdjan, and held these provinces for 64 years (864–928). The accession of this Alid family descended from Zaid b. Ali was the outcome of a conflict between the native peasantry and the Tahirids. When one of these princes tried to seize a no-man's-land used as pasture, the peasants revolted and chose the Alids as leaders. The new rulers apparently redistributed land.[5] If the Zindj had not checked the forces of the Abbasids, they would probably have found means to subdue them. But their army being engaged in the war with the slaves, they had to acquiesce, and the Alids could even expand and conquer the province of Rayy, which they held for twenty years.

At the end of the ninth century and at the beginning of the tenth, when the caliphs were threatened by new revolts in the central provinces, the Turkish general Muhammad Ibn Abi s-Sadj became an almost independent prince of Adherbeidjan and made great efforts to annex to his dominions some provinces of Media. The reign of this dynasty lasted from 889 to 930.

A much more powerful dynasty was that of the Samanids, a family of Persian nobles which from the beginning of the ninth century held high posts in the administration of the Iranian provinces. Ismail b. Ahmad (892–907) added to Ferghana, his dominion of old, Samarkand and also Khurasan; which he took in 900 from the Saffarids. Then he conquered the Caspian provinces and some parts of Media. The power of the Samanids was at its zenith under his grandson Nasr b. Ahmad (914–43), when their realm comprised almost the whole of Transoxiana and what is now Persia. It stretched from the Jaxartes to the shores of the Indian Ocean. Although the Samanids, whose residence was in Bukhara, recognised the suzerainty of the caliphs and paid them tribute, they severed the ties linking the eastern provinces to Baghdad. They represented the old Persian aristocracy and gave back the estates which in Tabaristan had been taken by the Alids from their legal owners and given to the peasants. On the other hand, they promoted the revival of the Persian culture. The exploits of the Samanids survived their rule, which, like that of so many Moslem dynasties, did not last more than three generations. They held Bukhara and Transoxiana until 999, but in the middle of the tenth century lost Western Persia. New dynasties, such as the Ziyarids, made themselves independent in the Caspian provinces and Media.

So more or less short-lived dynasties supplanted each other in the Iranian provinces of the Moslem empire, but Arab rule was ended and the caliphs had lost control. There were only two Persian provinces where they could maintain their government. They were Khuzistan and Fars, the provinces bordering on the Persian Gulf, although even there the caliphs had to fight time and again against insurgents. But at the same time their government crumbled in Syria and Egypt. The loss of these countries was a severe blow for the caliphs, for both political and economic reasons. Whereas Persia had been given up a long time ago and was ruled by a vassal dynasty, the Tahirids, Syria and Egypt were under the direct administration of the caliphs. These two countries broke away from the caliphate exactly at the time of the Zindj rising. This was surely no coincidence.

Ahmad b. Tulun, who became the first independent Moslem king of Egypt, was the son of a Turkish slave. He came to Egypt in 868 as the lieutenant of a high-ranking dignitary who had been appointed its governor. But he equipped a strong army, purchasing a considerable number of military slaves. When al-Muwaffak considered too small the sum paid by Ahmad as assistance for the Zindj war, an open clash ensued and an imperial army was sent in 877 against the governor of Egypt. But the attempt to turn out Ibn Tulun failed and instead he occupied Syria. When in 882 al-Muwaffak had him cursed from the pulpits of the mosques, Ahmad retorted by applying the same measure to al-Muwaffak. So the rupture was complete. Ahmad's son Khumarawaih (884–96) was formally recognised by the caliph as king of Egypt, Syria and the adjacent provinces of Northern Mesopotamia, and Barca in the west. The caliph appointed him, in 893, ruler of these countries for a period of 30 years in return for 300,000 dinars a year. Compared with the tax-revenue of Egypt this was little more than a symbolical payment. This agreement was indeed the apogee of the Tulunid power. After the violent death of Khumarawaih – he was murdered by his slaves – two sons and a brother succeeded him. They could not maintain their independence and in 905 Egypt renewed its obedience to the caliph. The Tulunid state had been the creation of one great general and gifted ruler, and after his death it disappeared.

The account we read in the Arabic historians of the reign of Ibn Tulun and of his son may be adduced as proof of the efficiency of the new régime and the relief the new rulers brought to their subjects, who had suffered from the vexations and extortions of the governors appointed by the caliphs. Whereas these governors, whose terms of service were not very long, were not at all interested in the welfare of their subjects or in the economic development of the provinces they administered, the new independent rulers made serious efforts to develop the national economy. Until the accession of Ibn Tulun, the Egyptian Treasury had every year delivered to the caliphal government a huge sum in net tax-revenue, but afterwards it remained in the country. It is true that the expense of the army increased very much and amounted under Khumarawaih to no less than 900,000 dinars a year. Even so, the surplus of the tax-revenue was a great sum.

The Tulunid régime brought, first of all, stability and with it a normal course of economic activity. Ahmad b. Tulun took various measures to increase agricultural production. He had the canals repaired by which the fields were irrigated and had others dug. The dams which had been damaged were restored. He forbade also certain practices of the tax-farmers which were a heavy burden on the peasants. The tax-farmers, on some pretext or other, used to cancel the agreements with the peasants and impose higher taxes on them. Ibn Tulun also forbade the officials and tax-collectors to levy the imposts called 'presents' and 'assistance money'.[6] As always, when the peasants hoped to have greater profits, they cultivated more land and production increased. The same happened in other sectors of Egypt's economy and a new prosperity began. Grain prices were lower than at any time since the beginning of the tenth century. Arabic historians report that in the days of Ibn Tulun one got for a dinar 10 irdabbs of wheat (then in the capital 73.125 kg), and in the days of his son Khumarawaih 5 irdabbs. Calculating the price of 100 kg of wheat in that period and comparing it with average prices in earlier periods of Moslem rule in Egypt the drop is even more obvious.[7]

Average wheat prices in Egypt
(eighth–ninth centuries)

beginning of eighth century	0.075 dinar
first half of ninth century	0.3 dinar
reign of Ibn Tulun (868–884)	0.173 dinar
reign of Khumarawaih (884–896)	0.274 dinar

According to the Arabic authors the prices of other products fell too. The equipment of the new army, supply for the campaigns in Syria, the maintenance of the splendid Tulunid court and the building of the new capital al-Katai, on the other hand, provided work for many craftsmen and new possibilities for enterprising businessmen. It goes without saying that the people rejoiced at the improvement of economic conditions.

Prices fell, although in the days of Ibn Tulun Egypt was probably richer in gold than in any preceding period of Moslem rule. The Arabic writers tell us the story of a hidden treasure of gold coins found by Ibn Tulun – a medieval way of explaining the riches of this ruler and the high standard of his dinars. The stability of the currency was indeed another aspect of the remarkable economic prosperity; the dinars struck by the Tulunids had a very high standard of fineness. A. S. Ehrenkreutz, weighing Tulunid dinars, arrived at the following results:[8]

Fineness of Tulunid dinars

							%						
per cent of gold	88	89	90	91	92	93	94	95	96	97	98	99	100
Ahmad b. Tulun (868–884)	1									1	2	1	
Khumarawaih (884–896)							4	1	2	4	2	1	
Djaish (896)										1	2		
Harun (896–904)							5	1	3	2	2		

This table is also interesting for another reason: it shows that conditions changed immediately after the death of the founder of the dynasty; his successors could not maintain the same standard of fineness. Nevertheless it remained very high. Further evidence of the economic recovery of Egypt under the rule of the Tulunids is the increase of the tax revenue. Whereas the total of the kharadj had considerably diminished since the Arabs conquered Egypt and probably came to its lowest ebb just before the accession of Ibn Tulun, it increased very much under his rule. Even allowing for greater efficiency of the tax-collectors, together with the other phenomena, it bears out the new prosperity. The particulars found in various Arabic sources are summed up in the table on p. 129.[9]

After the downfall of the Tulunids in 905 Egypt came again under Abbasid rule and was once more administered by governors appointed in Baghdad. Their government proved not only inefficient but disastrous. They were usually dismissed after a short term, but strove for a new appointment. One of them, Tekin, in fact held the post three times. The intrigues resulted in armed conflicts. The antagonism

Tax revenue from Egypt

	gross revenue	amount sent to the caliph
827		3 m dinars
868		800,000 dinars
Ahmad b. Tulun (868–884)	4.3 m dinars	
Khumarawaih (884–896)	4 m dinars	

between the heterogeneous regiments of the army increased, and Turkish and Berber battalions fought pitched battles. There was plundering by disbanded troops. Economic conditions deteriorated, prices rose and the gold currency was debased. The standard of fineness of the dinars struck in Egypt in that period is a clear indication of these conditions.[10]

Fineness of Egyptian dinars in the first third of the tenth century

	%												
per cent of gold	88	89	90	91	92	93	94	95	96	97	98	99	100
al-Muktafi (902–908)	1						1			1			
al-Muktadir (908–932)	1	1	1	2	1	5	6	2	4	1			
ar-Radi (932–934)	10	1											

The great number of dinars having less than 90% gold shows clearly how much the Treasury of Egypt was impoverished in that period.

But the caliphal administration, no longer equal to its task, soon came to its end, and a new dynasty, more or less independent, took over. Muhammad b. Tughdj, whom the caliph appointed ruler of Egypt in 935, was descended from the princes of Ferghana, and like those Turkish princes was called Ikhshid. He followed the example of Ibn Tulun. Once more a mighty army was equipped, composed of mercenaries and slaves from various countries. The figures given by the chroniclers must be very much exaggerated – they speak of 400,000

soldiers – but there can be no doubt that it was at that time (he reigned
from 935 to 946) the strongest in the Near East. As Ibn Tulun had
conquered Syria, so the Ikhshid succeeded in 942 in annexing this
country to his dominions. Two years later the caliph entrusted him
with the government of Hidjaz. As to economic conditions, his government achieved as much as his great predecessor. The new stability
brought about prosperity. Once more attention should be drawn to
the gold currency as unmistakable evidence: the dinars of the Ikhshid
and his successors were distinguished by their high standard.[11]

As Egypt had been lost to the caliphs, so was Syria, notwithstanding
temporary restoration. After the fall of the Tulunids, the country was
administered by governors appointed by the caliph until the Ikhshid
had occupied the greater part of it. But at the same time a new dynasty
established its rule over Northern Syria and contested Central Syria
with him. This dynasty, the Banu Hamdan, were tribal chiefs of the
Banu Taghlib. Their achievement was the checking of the Bedouin,
whose power and brigandage had considerably increased in both
Northern Mesopotamia and Syria. Being themselves Bedouin chiefs
they knew how to handle these daring tribes and the caliphs had to
acquiesce in their rule.

The ancestor of this princely family was Hamdan b. Hamdan, chief
of a clan living in Upper Mesopotamia. He fought many battles in the
last twenty years of the tenth century, sometimes supporting the
caliphal government, sometimes siding with rebels, until he was
caught in 895 by the imperial troops. His son Husain too was for some
time a general in the imperial army, and in 911 was appointed governor
of a province of Upper Mesopotamia. But later he rose against the
government of the caliph, was defeated and in 918 executed. In spite
of their treachery, the caliphs again had recourse to their services
because of their great interest in a stable government in Upper Mesopotamia, which supplied Irak with great quantities of grain. The
Hamdanids were a powerful clan, capable of guaranteeing a minimum
of security, so that the caliph could not help but appoint them once
more as governors. Abu l-Haidja Abdallah, who became governor of
Mosul in 905, was the real founder of their princedom. Neither he nor
his successors severed the links with the caliphate, but the recognition
of the caliphal suzerainty was only nominal, and in fact they were
independent rulers. At first his son Nasir ad-daula Hasan succeeded
him in Mosul, whereas his brothers Nasr and Said became governors

of the provinces of Diyar Rabia and Diyar Bakr, but later Hasan ruled over the whole of Upper Mesopotamia.

In 943 the Hamdanids began to build up their power in Syria. Saif ad-daula Ali, a brother of Nasir ad-daula, occupied Northern Syria as far as Hims and waged war against the Ikhshid. The war ended with the division of Syria, the northern part falling to Saif ad-daula, the southern to the Ikhshid. Arabic chroniclers extol the exploits of Saif ad-daula in the wars with the Byzantines, but his achievements on another front were not less important. Northern Syria was one of the regions where the raids of the Bedouin had become very frequent, with pernicious effects on the peasantry and the inhabitants of small townships. Saif ad-daula's strong arm was badly needed, and he undertook time and again the struggle with the tribesmen. In 949 he expelled some clans of the Banu Ukail and Kushair b. Kab from Northern Syria, in 954 he undertook a great campaign against the Banu Kilab, and in 955 he had to face a general revolt of the Bedouin. Participating in this revolt were clans and sections of heterogeneous tribes which usually opposed each other, Kalbites and Tayy, who were Yemenites, Numair b. Amr, Kab and Kilab b. Rabia who were Kaisites. In June 955 a great battle fought near the town of Salamiyya ended in a splendid victory for Saif ad-daula. It had far-reaching consequences. One was the new ascendancy of the Banu Kilab, who had betrayed the other rebels and ever since enjoyed a privileged position in Northern Syria. In course of time they were to become its masters. The Hamdanid state in Northern Syria was, however, the achievement of one great warrior, Saif ad-daula. When he passed away, it was doomed to disappear.

For in the history of the Near East the end of the ninth century and the first half of the tenth were the time of great generals. But their exploits were no more than an interlude. The social and economic development of the central provinces of the caliphate had created conditions which necessarily brought about a complete change in the structure of the Moslem states. The great political crisis ushered in by the Zindj revolt had deepened the cleavage between the social classes. The régime of the caesaro-papist theocracy was no more in keeping with necessities and had to disappear. It had to be replaced by a new socio-economic order. But before this inevitable change was made, the rulers in Baghdad had recourse to other expedients. A period of transition began, characterised by social tension, upheavals and intense agitation.

c) *Apogee of Moslem pre-capitalism*

At the beginning of the tenth century the civilians were still in control in Irak and the other provinces which had remained under the sway of the Abbasids. A costly court lavishing enormous sums of money was the focus of political intrigues. The expenditure on the wars necessary to preserve the remaining provinces from rebels and invaders amounted to millions of dinars. In peacetime the pay of the Iraki army amounted, in the days of the caliph al-Muktadir (908–32), to a million dinars a year.[12] A highly technocratic bureaucracy had to satisfy the demands of the pay office, but it encountered increasing difficulties. Behind the civilian government there was a most influential politicised army whose power was ever-growing and which began to be the arbiter of the various pressure groups. The day was approaching when it would openly take over.

The army was composed of heterogeneous elements, among which an often passionate rivalry prevailed. There were the masaffiyya and hudjariyya, infantry regiments which composed the caliphal bodyguard. There were cavalry regiments called after the generals who had re-cruited them. These different regiments comprised mercenaries, and slaves bought for the military service called mamluks. They hailed from many parts of the Moslem world and various non-Moslem regions. The Turks, both as mercenaries and slaves, were always a very strong element in the army, but there were also many battalions of Dailamites, originating from the mountainous borderland on the southern shores of the Caspian Sea, Berbers from Morocco and Negroes from the Sudan. The Dailamites were very numerous in the army of Saif ad-daula, the Bedouin king, who revived the tradition of the tribal chiefs of his race. Generally speaking, the composition of the army of the central government and of the provincial armies was more or less the same. Even the governors of the provinces enlisted mercenaries and bought slaves.[13] But the number of the Maghrebins in the Egyptian army was of course much more considerable. In the armies of Ibn Tulun and the Ikhshid there were also mercenaries and slaves hailing from Christian countries, called 'Rumis' and 'Slavs', and many Negroes. But the Turkish mamluks were probably the strongest element in their armies. Ibn Tulun had also many Dailamites in his army. The Egyptian rulers also recruited Bedouin. In the Tulunid army the Turkish element was predominant in the ranks of the officers, in that of the Ikhshid there were also many officers who belonged to other races.[14] As long as these heterogeneous elements served under a great military chief, the feelings of mutual animosity and jealousy were subdued by the affection and awe inspired by his personality. But when there was no such chief at their head, their rivalry resulted in fighting.

Both the Iraki army and the provincial armies were in that period paid in cash. This is a striking feature of the socio-economic régime of the caliphal period, characterised by its money economy. But what were the soldiers paid? Any assertion on this subject must remain somewhat conjectural, as the indications to be found in the Arabic sources can be misleading. For the Arabic authors speak about the 'month' or the pay-period (*nauba*) of the soldiers (or other salaried personnel). These 'months' were, however, very different. For some regiments or categories of soldiers the month numbered 50 days, for others 60 or even 120. So we must beware of traps. Fortunately the writings of some Arabic historians contain more precise data.

Hilal as-Sabi reports that under al-Mutadid (892–902) and al-Muktafi (902–8) the mamluks got 7 to 12 dinars for 50 days and later 12 or 16 dinars. So their monthly pay would have been first 4.2 or 7.2 and later 7.2 or 9.6 dinars. There can be no doubt that among these mamluks were horsemen, recruits and fully trained soldiers whose pay differed accordingly. From reports of the historian Arib we may infer that the bodyguard of the caliph asked in 929 for $3\frac{1}{2}$ dinars per mensem (i.e. a lunar month). A cavalry man got at the same time $12\frac{1}{2}$ dinars a month. In 917, pay was reduced by two-thirds. But in 929 their monthly pay amounted to almost 42 dinars. The average pay of a soldier in the army of General Bedjkem, in 936, was $13\frac{1}{2}$ dinars.[15] That means that an infantryman serving in the bodyguard of the caliph demanded a pay amounting to double the wage of a skilled worker. The pay of a cavalryman was four or six times as much. The privileged situation of the soldiery in the Moslem world is even more striking if compared with their pay in the neighbouring Byzantine empire. There the average pay was, even in that period, apparently no more than 1–2 nomismata (equal to a dinar).[16] Further – and this is even more characteristic of the social standing of the soldiery in the Moslem world – their pay increased fairly steadily through the ages, whereas that of the Byzantine soldiers did not.

Regular pay was, however, only part of military income in the Moslem countries (as in Byzantium). They received additional payments, such as the accession money which the caliph had to pay at the beginning of his reign. The officers already had feudal estates. At the end of the ninth century and in the first part of the tenth, this was a general phenomenon in Irak and elsewhere, as in Egypt under Ahmad b. Tulun.[17]

In spite of their high pay the Moslem soldiery were never satisfied. It is true that there were often delays in payment, but, on the other hand, demands increased, and when the government could not meet them the troops rioted. The chroniclers tell us many stories of these riots. Time and again the troops attacked the vizier and the director of the financial administration, set fire to their houses, sacked palaces and interrupted the administration of justice. This happened both in Baghdad and in the provincial capitals. The caliph and his viziers had to give in. Once al-Muktadir was compelled to sell his cloth, carpets and other property in order to get money for a special payment to the troops.[18]

Perhaps the growing political influence of the army was a more serious phenomenon. The ever-increasing influence of the generals on the policy of the government and the appointment of the chiefs of the administration, on the one hand, and the grant of fiefs to the officers, on the other hand, paved the way for the establishment of a new order where all political and economic power would be concentrated in their hands.

Reading attentively the chronicles of the first half of the tenth century one becomes aware of the fact that most viziers were appointed by agreement of the commanding generals and that they could only remain in office as long as they had their support. The influence of a general like Munis was for a long time paramount. The role he and other generals played was a portentous indication of the forthcoming change.

However, the officers had not yet supplanted the civilian dignitaries at the head of the government. The foreign soldiery and the native capitalists shared power, the civilians being still predominant. The viziers were at the head of the government. The need of great sums to be paid to the troops and, on the other hand, the circulation of considerable quantities of gold and silver coins – these were two basic facts which determined the role of the ruling classes.

Riches in gold and silver coins are frequently mentioned in the chronicles of this period. People belonging to the upper classes possessed great sums of gold dinars and silver dirhams, payments were made in cash and there was a lively trade in bullion.[19] These phenomena are characteristic of any money economy. That of the Moslem Near East in the ninth and tenth centuries had other peculiar features. Money was kept in circulation by way of fines arbitrarily imposed on the rich, an expedient all Moslem governments used to get the money urgently needed for their expenditure. The caliphal government was even more than others inclined to have recourse to this method since its budget was always in deficit and its embarrassment ever growing. So the imposition of these fines – *al-musadara* – became a permanent institution of the Moslem state, one of its consequences being that great sums of money in the possession of rich men were put back into circulation. How important these fines were from the economic point of view may be gauged from a passage in Hilal as-Sabi's *History of the Viziers*. He says that he saw a document containing a list of the fines imposed by al-Muhassin during the third vizierate of his father Ibn al-Furat (923–4). The total was:

6,575,680 dinars

5,300,000 dirhams

6,955,000 dinars

The importance of these fines can be estimated from the fact that the total of the tax-revenue of the caliphate in 918 was 14,501,904 dinars. In extorting them the government used obvious pretexts, whether governors of the provinces or newly enthroned sovereigns. Usually even the relatives, employees and servants of a rich man would be fined together with him. The Ikhshid, when in need of money because of an impending campaign, would extort a fine from his secretary and other officials. The musadara system put great sums of money in circulation, but it had also a contrary consequence. For fear of these arbitrary fines people would hoard money, coins and bullion, jewels and precious products such as vessels and cloth, hiding them wherever they could, in stalls, privies and elsewhere.[20] The putting into circulation of considerable sums of money was, however, a far more important phenomenon.

Another method employed by the Moslem governments of those days with the same consequence was the confiscation of property left by deceased persons. A special diwan was created which had to apportion bequests and seize the property of those who died without heirs. This diwan, called diwan al-mawarith al-hashariyya and founded by the caliph al-Mutamid (870–92), was abolished in 896, but re-established about the year 920. Abolished again in 923, this ministry remained nevertheless an important institution which was adopted by almost all Moslem states. It obviously served the purposes of covetous rulers admirably. Sometimes they contented themselves with levying an inheritance tax, sometimes they used pretexts for confiscating illegally the whole of a rich bequest. The Ikhshid used this method in Egypt to appropriate great riches left by officials and merchants; Saif ad-daula appointed a judge in Aleppo who became famous for the tricks he employed to assign heritages to the ruler.[21]

Among the proceedings of the administration which gave the circulation of money a new impetus there must also be mentioned the sale of offices and the collection of fees for continuance in office (*istithbat*). Bribery was institutionalised. The vizier Ibn al-Furat, when reappointed in 917, established a 'secret profits bureau' (diwan al-marafik) to which dismissed officials had to refund a part of the bribes they had taken. After his subsequent downfall he was accused of having received during his first vizierate 400,000 dinars as 'secret profits' from the Syrian provinces, and altogether 1.2 million dinars in bribes. The officials levied also considerable sums as *istithna* – a fee for dropping a legal suit or the discharging of debts.[22] The same expression was used for the double sale of the products of crown lands: a purchaser was compelled to buy them at a low price in order that they should be resold on his behalf by the agents of the government. The first buyer had to pay the price immediately to the government, which in this way obtained the money it needed.

But this way of managing the administration made the situation of the ruling classes very precarious. As long as a man held office, he enjoyed the possibility of acquiring riches or adding to them. When he lost his post, he lost also a great part of his property. It was not riches that gave a man power, but the position that made him wealthy. That was a regular feature of Oriental social life and one diametrically opposed to what certain Western philosophers of history have deduced from the conditions known to them. The great Ibn Khaldun discerned it at the end of the fourteenth century.

At the summit of the social and political hierarchy of the Moslem state in that period were two groups which shared power, not as yet seized by the army. These were the tax-farmers and the heads of the administration, the viziers and high officials. In fact, these two groups were not necessarily different. On the contrary, the same people farmed taxes and occupied high posts in the administration. If a tax-farmer was appointed vizier he often retained his farming business.[23]

The system of tax-farming was considered the surest way to balance the budget of the government and to obtain in time the funds needed to pay the soldiery. So it prevailed everywhere, in Irak, Persia, Syria and Egypt. The great tax-farmers had sub-farmers who undertook the collection of the taxes in particular districts. The object of most farm contracts was the collection of the land-tax, the kharadj, the main source of income of the Moslem state. But very often the contract comprised also the management of the royal estates and in the same way other taxes were farmed, such as the so-called *mukus*, imposts on various branches of trade and commerce. Sometimes the royal estates and the private estates of the caliph were not farmed together with the kharadj of the province, but leased to other persons. In order to obtain a contract, one had to come to terms with the administration and give guarantees, a kind of bargain in which brokers were often instrumental. A chronicler reports that one day a man got a contract for the tax-farming of Khuzistan after he had paid 20,000 dinars to a broker.[24]

Most tax-farmers were wealthy businessmen who had enriched themselves in other fields of economic activity and could afford so large an undertaking. It was a symptom of the changing conditions in a period of transition that the commanders of the army were interested in the farming business. The great vizier Ali b. Isa imposed a veto on their endeavours and could thwart them. But as the tax-farmers could withhold the payment of the sums due to the government and in this way influence its policy, they became so powerful that they aspired to taking over themselves. Military campaigns were often dependent upon their goodwill, and if they wished they themselves equipped armies. But what is even more important – and a characteristic feature of the trend of development – they became governors of the provinces whose taxes they had farmed and in this way the real masters of the decaying caliphal régime. Ali b. Ahmad ar-Rasibi, who died in 913, farmed some districts in South-eastern Irak and Khuzistan which yielded the government 1.4 m dinars a year. The Arabic authors say that he ruled these districts with little or no interference from the caliphal government. The role played by Hamid b. al-Abbas, who was tax-farmer of the province of Wasit and later vizier, is another case. The Hamdanids too farmed the taxes of the province of Mosul. Abu l-Hasan Ali b. Khalaf b. Tayyab, who had been tax-farmer in various regions, became later governor of Diyar Modar. The Baridis, the sons of a postmaster in Basra, who played so great a role in the politics of

Irak and South-western Persia in the third and fourth decades of the tenth century, were tax-farmers before they became governors and military leaders.[25] As the administration of a province was usually conferred on the person who had farmed its taxes, this job was a step in the career of a future political leader.

The Arabic chronicles contain various details concerning the enormous profits of the tax-farmers. A man interested in obtaining a contract would not hesitate to offer some hundreds of thousands of dinars more than his predecessor had paid. In 919 Hamid b. al-Abbas offered 400,000 dinars a year more than the sum assessed for the taxes of Lower Irak, Fars and Isfahan, and in the course of the negotiations even added another 200,000. The taxes of the province of Isfahan alone were sometime before farmed to a man who had offered 100,000 dinars more than was paid by his predecessor. Yusuf Ibn Abi s-Sadj bid in 916 for the taxes of Rayy 700,000 dinars net, i.e. obliging himself to defray the charges of the officials in this province and other expenditure. But in 922 he was appointed to the government of Rayy and some other provinces, viz. Kazwin, Abhar, Zindjan and Adherbeidjan, for 500,000 dinars only. On the other hand, we find in the budget elaborated by Ali b. Isa for the year 918 the following figures for the taxes of the said provinces:

Rayy, Damawend	587,722 dinars
Kazwin, Zindjan, Abhar	174,000 dinars
Adherbeidjan, Armenia	226,370 dinars
Total	988,092 dinars

The province of Wasit, with the income from the royal estates therein, yielded, according to the same budget, 310,720 dinars. On the other hand, we read in a historical work that it was farmed, in 934, for 13 millions of dirhams, i.e. almost a million of dinars. The most striking sample of these outbidding offers is the deal over the taxes of Fars and Kirman in the year 910. al-Kasim b. Ubaidallah had been governor of these two provinces under the caliph al-Muktafi (902–8) for 4 m dirhams a year. His successor bid 7 millions. When the government was not ready to content itself with this sum, he offered 9 millions, undertaking to cover the expenses of the regiments garrisoned in these provinces. Finally he gave 10 millions.[26]

The considerable differences between the amounts for which the taxes were farmed can easily be explained. The applicants obtained contracts based on superannuated assessments which no longer corresponded to the actual yield and, on the other hand, they extorted from the taxpayers much more by heavily overcharging them. The riches and the power of the tax-farmers were still greater because often they did not pay the sums due to the government. We read, for example, in the chronicle of Miskawaih that Hamid b. al-Abbas was made liable for more than a million dinars excess due from the province of Wasit. The same author says that Yusuf b. Abi s-Sadj failed to pay the tribute he had undertaken to pay.

Powerful as the tax-farmers were, they did not enjoy security. Some of them were arrested and lost all their riches, whereas the property of others was confiscated after their death. The value of the estates of Hamid b. al-Abbas which were confiscated in 923 was no less than 2.2 m dinars. The brothers Abu Yusuf and Abu Abdallah al-Baridi were mulcted, in 933, of 12 m dirhams.[27]

The small group of directors of the great diwans (ministries) with the vizier at their head were, apart from the generals and the tax-farmers, the most influential in government. They too were wealthy people, for the centralisation of the imperial administration made it possible that they could accumulate great riches. Whereas the tax-farmers rose from business circles, these ministers came from the class of the kuttab, the higher officials. Their families belonged mostly to the class of rich landowners and were distinguished by their knowledge of Arabic language and literature. That was indeed what was required of them.

The social standing of the kuttab was reflected in their salaries. A subaltern official would get 6 dinars a month, while a katib who had more responsibilities would have from 8 to 20 dinars. The salaries of high officials, such as heads of departments, amounted to 20 dinars and more. This means that the middle officials earned 5 or 6 times as much as the skilled labourers, e.g. a mason or carpenter. The socio-economic stratification of Moslem society was, therefore, very similar to that of Byzantine society.[28]

Many of the kuttab belonged to families holding high posts in various departments through several generations. They formed real cliques with their friends and relatives in all government offices. From the accession of the caliph al-Mutamid in 870 to the death of ar-Radi there were altogether 37 terms of vizierate. But since 6 viziers were appointed twice and 4 held the post even three times, the number of persons holding the post was altogether 23. The share of some families is really astonishing. Let us sum up the data provided by the chroniclers:

Banu Wahb	5 viziers
	one of them 3 terms
Banu Khakan	3 viziers
Banu Djarrah	6 viziers
	two of them 3 terms
Banu l-Furat	2 viziers
	one of them 3 terms

That means that 16 viziers belonging to 4 families held the post for 30 terms out of 37.

The administration of the provinces too was monopolised, to a great extent, by oligarchic clans. A family of South Irakian officials was at the head of the financial administration of Egypt for almost the whole of this period, and often they held also that of Syria. Ahmad b. Ibrahim al-Utrush al-Madharai was appointed in 880 director of the administration of Egypt, and after his death his son Ali was vizier of Egypt. Ali's son Abu Bakr Muhammad was at the head of the Egyptian administration, with the usual ups and downs of dismissals and re-appointments, till 947. For part of the time he managed the adminis-tration together with his brother Abu t-Tayyib. From 905 his uncle Abu Zunbur b. Ahmad was director of the administration of Egypt and Syria for several terms.

All these ministers and chancellors of provincial treasuries were Moslems, although some of them were of Christian origin. There was, however, a great number of kuttab in government service who remained faithful to their Christian religion. Christians served as secretaries of many high-ranking dignitaries, generals and governors, or held high posts in the financial administration. This was a general phenomenon, both in Irak and in other provinces. From the reign of the caliph al-Mutadid (892–902) the number of Christian officials had considerably increased, and the vizier Ubaidallah b. Sulaiman, when asked about it, justified their employment. In spite of the protests lodged by zealous Moslems, the Christian kuttab also held posts in the War Office.[29]

A great number of these officials could easily live on the income from their estates, even without holding posts. The vizier Ali b. Isa had 80,000 dinars from his estates, when out of office. According to the reports of the Arabic historians, Ibn al-Furat had, before taking office, a yearly income of a million dinars. He was reputed to own in coins, estates and furniture, as much as 10 millions. When holding office the viziers, directors of departments, inspectors and other top-ranking officials not only received a high salary, amounting in the days of al-Muktadir to 5,000 or 7,000 dinars a month, but also had the income of the vizieral estates, yielding huge sums. Ali b. Isa, when holding office, had from his estates 700,000 dinars a year. Ibn al-Furat (in his second term) 1,200,000. Most of these estates had, however, been acquired by the viziers privately, and not granted to them as part of their payment. The crown land handed over to Ibn al-Furat for this purpose yielded only some tens of thousands. So the viziers acquired large estates, by making use of their position. According to one report the estates of Ibn al-Furat and his brother Abu l-Abbas yielded 200,000 dinars before his first appointment and 800,000 after his dismissal. Other high officials took advantage of their position to acquire large estates. Abu Djafar Muhammad b. Shirzad purchased from the crown lands estates yielding him a million dirhams a year. The directors of the financial administration of Egypt, Ibn al-Mudabbir and the Madharais, possessed many rural estates. Further, the vizier and the high officials were also engaged in manifold commercial activities, always profiting from their position. The story Hilal as-Sabi tells about the origin of the great fortune of Ibn Mukla is characteristic: he had been allowed by Ibn al-Furat, when vizier, to profit by a huge sum on a sale of grain in possession of the government.[30] The high officials were great businessmen, landowners and merchants. They pursued these activities always in close collaboration with certain cliques of high officers. A family of viziers or directors of departments would be allied with a general and his aides-de-camp. The viziers and high officials availed themselves also of their position to appropriate to themselves a great part of the fines and bribes. Often sums destined for the Treasury were simply paid to the vizier's private account. Ibn al-Furat had from this source, during his second vizierate, according to his enemies 1.2 millions a year.[31]

But in spite of its great wealth and power even this group of high dignitaries never lived in security. On the contrary, its situation was most precarious. Sooner or later a vizier would be dismissed, because he could not meet the demands of the soldiery. Then he would be arrested and fined. His relatives too would be put under arrest and his house searched, and when he refused to sign a bond for a considerable 'musadara', saying that the amount was beyond his possibilities, he would be beaten and tortured. The amounts of the fines imposed on the viziers and other high officials were really enormous. Here are some of them:[32]

Abu Bakr Muhammad al-Madharai, a. 923	1,100,000 dinars	
a. 935	1,000,000 ,,	
Abu Muhammad al-Hasan al-Madharai, a. 923	2,200,000 ,,	
Abu Zunbur al-Madharai, a. 923	1,700,000 ,,	
Ibn al-Furat, a. 912 (first dismissal)	7,000,000 ,,	(confiscated)
a. 918 (second dismissal)	700,000 ,,	(fined)
a. 924 (third dismissal)	3,000,000 ,,	(confiscated)
	2,000,000 ,,	(bond)
other account: from Ibn al-Furat, his clerks and dependants:		
a. 912	4,400,000 dinars	
a. 918	2,300,000 ,,	
a. 924	900,000 ,,	
Abu l-Khattab b. al-Furat, a. 933	300,000 ,,	
al-Muhassin, son of Ibn al-Furat, a. 933	3,000,000 ,,	
Ibn Karaba, a. 933	90,000 ,,	
al-Kalwadhani, a. 933	200,000 ,,	
Abdarrahman b. Isa, a. 936	70,000 ,,	
Ibn Mukla, a. 936	1,000,000 ,,	
Muhammad b. Kila, secretary of the Ikhshid, a. 944	300,000 ,,	

Even taking into consideration that these fines were only cashed in part, and allowing for a considerable margin of exaggeration in the reports on the wealth of these bureaucrats, we must conclude that they accumulated enormous riches. It cannot be maintained that the salaries paid to them were really intended to support them and their dependants. For the Arabic writers indicate *expressis verbis* the salaries paid to the secretaries and even the sons of the viziers who were still under age. So we must accept the reports of the Arabic historians as a clear proof that in this period the disparity between the socio-economic classes within Near Eastern society was very great.

It seems that the economic and social standing of the upper bourgeoisie was very high. This class was allied to the cliques in control of the caliphal administration, and was very rich and powerful. But, on the other hand, it was numerically weak and also easily vulnerable. The middle and lower bourgeoisie were oppressed by the ruling oligarchy. There was considerable economic and social disparity between the bourgeois classes themselves. The upper strata consisted, beside the rich landowners, of merchants and industrialists. These wealthy merchants, the *tudjdjar*, were a small class, mostly engaged in the trade in luxury goods, a characteristic feature of which was its very limited volume.

There was of course a group of wholesale dealers who traded in wheat and other grains and who had always to collaborate with the tax-farmers. In the pre-capitalistic régime of the caliphate the grain trade was still free, not yet being the business of feudal lords. Geonic responsa (juridical decisions) dating from this period refer to the wheat trade, and Arabic chroniclers mention rich grain and flour dealers. But very great quantities of grain were in possession of the government or, more precisely, in possession of the tax-farmers, to whom they had been delivered as taxes in kind. So big business could only be carried on in collaboration with the tax-collectors, the tax-farmers and the great capitalist owners of large estates. But these preferred very often to engage in profitable trade themselves. Royal princes and tax-farmers stored great quantities of wheat for speculative reasons. In 921 these speculations brought about a dearth in Baghdad. There were riots, the mob plundered shops, and finally the caliph had to intervene and compel the royal princes and the great merchants to sell wheat at reduced prices.[33]

There is good reason to suppose that similar conditions prevailed in other branches of the food trade, such as olive oil, a very important branch of commerce in Syria. In order to get orders for supplies for the army, the *marafik*, bribery money, had to be paid (or deposited with the brokers). This was the share of the high officials. Collaboration and the sharing of profits between the great businessmen and the bureaucrats was unavoidable, and therefore the profits which the traders could realise in this branch were limited.

The trade in textiles was much more lucrative. It was really free and he *bazzazun*, the cloth-merchants, were the richest and most esteemed group of merchants. They carried on the trade in precious and very expensive textiles, such as silk, Persian and Byzantine brocades, or cloth embroidered with gold. The cloth trade was to a great extent international, many articles being imported from other countries, Moslem or non-Moslem. For it was possible to import Egyptian linen products and Persian cotton stuffs in Irak, as the new Moslem states put up no obstacles to merchants crossing their borders as long as they were not induced by political conflicts to take measures against the export of their products. The riches of the *bazzazun* were notorious, as appears when Arabic chroniclers report the decease of rich cloth-merchants. When Affan b. Sulaiman al-Bazzaz, the richest merchant of Egypt in his time, died in 936, the Ikhshid confiscated 100,000 dinars from his property.[34]

The trade in precious stones and jewels was akin to the textile trade. Its articles were very expensive, its volume very small and the profits very great. Princes and viziers paid enormous prices for gems brought from India, Upper Egypt and elsewhere. Every species of precious stone had its customers, and the Arabic handbooks for merchants contain rules for distinguishing them. The traders in jewels were renowned for their riches, but also easily stripped of their fortune. The Arabic writers dwell on the case of Abu Abdallah Husain Ibn al-Djassas, a jeweller from Egypt who settled in Baghdad and was famous for his riches. In 914 he was arrested and made to deliver money and jewels to the value of 4 m dinars or even 6 millions. He boasted, according to the chroniclers, that he possessed far beyond 20 millions.[35]

Another small group of rich businessmen was the bankers. Banking activities were indeed intense in Oriental countries in that period, when their economies had reached an advanced state of pre-capitalism. Great sums of money were paid by cheque (*sakk*), guaranteed by bonds (*khatt*), and transferred by letters of credit (*suftadja*). The use of letters of credit made it possible to transfer funds to distant countries without the risks inherent in the political conditions of those times. The geographer Ibn Haukal speaks of a promissory note on the sum of 42,000 dinars sent from Sidjilmasa to a merchant in Audaghost. Even the government offices and the tax-collectors used this method too, transferring large sums by letters of credit.[36] The diversity of the coins struck in the various provinces of the caliphal empire and the fluctuation of the exchange rate also gave a strong impetus to banking. But in the first place it was the circulation of great quantities of money in gold and silver coins which induced people to have recourse to bankers.

Indeed, never before had the amount of money in circulation in this part of the world been so great. Huge sums were deposited with bankers, who invested them and gave loans on interest. Rich people were clients of bankers who administered their funds, received payments into their accounts and remitted funds to them. Ibn Shirzad, a high dignitary, had a Jewish banker – Ali b. Harun b. Allan; Abu Abdallah al-Baridi, the tax-farmer and governor of Khuzistan, had three bankers, two of them Jews and one probably a Christian. These bankers were indeed indispensable to high officials, for they required applicants to remit bribes to their bankers, who had orders not to keep accounts of these funds. In every town there were banking firms, but in the big towns there were bankers' streets. In Baghdad it was the Aun Street. In Isfahan in 1052 there were, according to the Persian traveller Nasiri Khosrau, no less than 200 bankers. These bankers were also engaged in commercial activities and traded in bullion and other goods.[37]

As the taxes were paid in different coins (insofar as they were paid in cash) and were transferred by letters of credit, the government itself had to use the services of bankers. Therefore it appointed royal bankers (those in Baghdad were called djahbadh al-hadra), whose tasks were somewhat similar to those of our modern National Banks. It goes without saying that the viziers, the Prime Ministers of the caliphate, chose the bankers whose clients they were.

From the chronicles of that period and from some Judaeo-Arabic documents we learn a good deal about a firm of Jewish bankers who fulfilled this task at the beginning of the tenth century and played a great role in the economic life of Irak and Khuzistan for several generations. Indeed, the Moslem government could not dispense with the services of Jewish and Christian bankers. When the caliph al-Muktadir, in 908, once more promulgated the ancient law forbidding the employment of non-Moslems in the government administration, he exempted the bankers and physicians.[38]

In 892 Netira, a merchant and banker, began to serve the caliph al-Mutadid, and was also in the service of his successors until he died in 910. One of his two sons, Sahl, inherited his post. But in the later years of the reign of al-Muktadir the role of this Jewish banker was eclipsed by that of another Jewish firm, Yusuf b. Phineas and Aaron b. Imran. One of these bankers was the grandfather of Sahl, for Netira had married a daughter of Yusuf b. Phineas. This firm served the vizier Ibn al-Furat as a private bank until it became a royal bank, both in

Baghdad and in al-Ahwaz, the capital of Khuzistan. Miskawaih and Hilal as-Sabi mention its activities from 908 to 924. The Jewish bankers administered considerable funds remitted to them by Ibn al-Furat, such as bribes and money obtained from fines. Ibn al-Furat confessed in 918 that he had deposited with them 700,000 dinars. Then, appointed royal bankers, they transferred the taxes of Khuzistan to Baghdad and supplied the government with great sums. According to the chroniclers the vizier Ali b. Isa obtained from them loans which enabled him to cover the normal monthly expenditure. The Arabic authors do not omit to indicate the rate of interest. Sahl b. Netira, on the other hand, is mentioned in texts referring to the fourth decade of the tenth century. He is probably identical with the Sahl b. Nazir who was one of the bankers of Abu Abdallah al-Baridi in al-Ahwaz, and was tortured in 941. The 'Sons of Netira' are mentioned in a text referring to the year 928, whereas in Judaeo-Arabic documents from the second half of the tenth century the 'Sons of Aaron' are spoken of as very active bankers. They were the descendants of Aaron b. Imran.[39]

Jewish court bankers

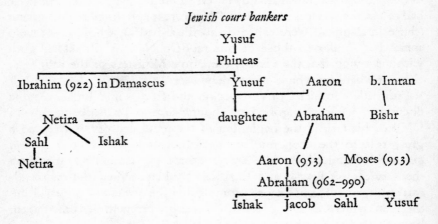

Having dwelt on the activities of a Jewish banking firm during four generations – and many Christian bankers in Irak and in Egypt could be mentioned – the question arises whether these bankers in whom was concentrated such great financial power were also strong enough to influence the course of political events. Could they be considered a political pressure group? The answer to this question must apparently be negative. They had neither the resources the tax-farmers had, nor could they aspire to political power as those other great financiers did.

The tax-farmers had become chiefs of the administration in their provinces, had guards and retainers, and, what is more important, their profits were much greater. For the revenue from the land-tax was the main source of wealth in the Moslem empire, even in that period of a flourishing pre-capitalism.

The data which we find in various Arabic sources of the end of the ninth and the first half of the tenth century indicate that commercial relations with India and the Far East had the same character as in the preceding period, as far as the articles are concerned. They consisted mainly in the import of perfumes – luxury goods destined for the upper classes. So the number of the merchants engaged in them was rather limited. The Indian and Chinese articles which are usually mentioned in the Arabic texts of this period are musk and ambergris. Dignitaries and rich landowners appreciated them very much, being ready to pay high prices for them and possessing considerable quantities of them. They hoarded them as they might gold and silver. Even in texts referring to the customs levied in the harbours of the Persian Gulf perfumes are listed as the most precious articles. Other articles imported from India and the Far East were camphor, aloes, spices such as pepper, cloves, cubeb, nutmeg and cardamom, and Indian woods, sandalwood and others.[40]

It is true that the Indian trade of the caliphal empire had always been a trade in precious products and that the number of the merchants engaged in it had never been great. But there is strong evidence for the supposition that at the end of the ninth century its volume was diminished. Arabic authors narrate how a revolt broke out in China in 878 with the result that anarchy reigned in the celestial empire, so that Moslem traders discontinued their travels to China. From that time the Arab and Persian merchants went only as far as Kalah, a port in Malacca, where they met Chinese traders.[41] Another change which took place in the Far Eastern trade of the Moslem empire was the considerable growth of the part taken in it by Siraf. This town took the place of Basra as the most important harbour on the Persian Gulf. In the stories of seafarers and other writings dating from this period the captains and traders of Siraf are mentioned time and again, and its inhabitants were famous for their great wealth. The rise of Siraf and the decline of Basra were probably the outcome of political changes, such as revolts which made the harbour at Basra less safe than before.[42] The ports of Oman and Aden, which also served as emporia of the trade with East Africa, were also busy harbours, though less important than Siraf. There was a regular traffic between all these ports and the trading towns in North-west India, such as Daibul, Saimur, Subara, etc. The stories of the seafarers of this period refer very often to travels to Ceylon, Sumatra and Java. On the other hand, trade with Malabar, the region from which the pepper was exported, is seldom mentioned. This is another indication of the character of Moslem trade with India in that period: it was mainly a trade in luxury articles. Moreover, we read in a history of the Ikhshid that at the time of his death it was difficult to find camphor in Damascus.[43] (Ikhshid was the title of the kings of Ferghana; the man commonly called 'the Ikhshid' was descended from them and became king of Egypt in 935, dying in 946.)

There was, however, in the tenth century another branch of international trade in which Moslem traders apparently made great profits – the import of furs from Russia and the adjacent countries. According to the Arabic authors various kinds of furs, such as sable-marten, ermine, fox-skin, mink, grey squirrel and beaver, were very much in vogue in the empire of the caliphs. The enormous quantities of Moslem coins which have been discovered in several provinces of Russia and in the countries bordering on the Baltic Sea bear evidence of the great volume of this trade, which was probably intensified after the embassy sent by the caliph al-Muktadir in 922 to the Bulgar kingdom on the river Kama. But what part did Near Eastern merchants take in this trade? The coin hoards unearthed in East and Northern Europe comprise overwhelmingly silver dirhams, struck by the Samanid kings of Bukhara.[44] According to the Arabic authors most of the traders were probably Khwarizmians and Persians as indicated by the Persian names given to articles imported from Russia. A great part of the furs remained in Khwarizm, Transoxiana and Persia, whose upper classes were fond of them. The furs imported into Irak and other Near Eastern countries were probably brought by Khwarizmian and Persian traders. al-Istakhri says that the Khwarizmians were the greatest travellers in East Iran, and al-Mukaddasi gives a long list of the articles exported from their country, which would have gone to Persia and Irak. Finally, attention should be drawn to the statements about the high prices fetched by furs in the Near East. al-Masudi says that a black fox-skin was worth about 100 dinars.[45] So we must conclude that even this trade was the business of a small group of rich merchants, most of them foreigners who came to the Near East to sell their merchandise.

All these merchants suffered very much from arbitrary imposts and other vexatious government measures, though the customs themselves were not high. al-Mukaddasi, it is true, complains about the tolls in Irak and about imposts on the trade in Syria, but usually the customs amounted to no more than 10%.[46] On the other hand, the authorities used to demand loans from the merchants which were sometimes compulsory, or simply imposed heavy fines on them. Rebels did the same. Another way of extorting considerable sums of money was by the compulsory purchase of goods at high prices fixed by the authorities and sometimes the army simply plundered the merchants' stores.[47]

The impact of these measures can be gauged from the fact that in the pre-capitalistic world of the caliphs no dynasties of merchant barons arose to remain rich and powerful for several generations, so that they could influence the policy of the ruling class. On the contrary, many merchants left Irak and emigrated to other countries where they hoped to find better conditions. Many texts in the Arabic chronicles and collections of biographies bear witness of this migratory movement, mainly directed to the Mediterranean countries. Even some members of the Jewish court bankers' families mentioned above emigrated from Irak. In a document dated in Damascus in the year 922, Ibrahim b. Phineas b. Yusuf appears as a vendor of an estate. He was probably a brother of the court banker Yusuf b. Phineas. Intellectuals who held positions in the government service and others emigrated too, most of them settling in Syria and Egypt, others going to the Maghreb and Moslem Spain.[48] Their situation was indeed even more precarious than that of the merchants, as they had no organisation whatsoever, in contradistinction to the later middle ages when they were backed by influential chief judges and enjoyed benefices of rich endowments. Although belonging to the upper classes as far as their income was concerned, for an esteemed professor would get 50 dinars a month,[49] they were completely dependent on the goodwill of the high dignitaries and were always compelled to comply with their wishes.

The great number of small traders (retailers), called *suka* or *baa*, belonged to the lower strata of society. They are clearly distinguished in the Arabic sources from the 'merchants' (*tudjdjar*), belonging to the high bourgeoisie. Many of them were craftsmen who sold their products, others perfumers or petty merchants who sold garments and vessels to the poor, home-made and of bad quality. The capital of such a small trader would be very limited, 100 or 200 dinars. Others were simple pedlars, selling their goods in the villages and hamlets. All these small merchants bore the brunt of the so-called *mukus*, the imposts on the various branches of trade and commerce. They were really crushed by these taxes and only few of them rose to the upper strata of society.[50]

The analysis of the copious information about the industries of the Near East during the period will result in similar, although not the same, conclusions. Since the textile industries were the most important, the discussion of the data provided by the Arabic authors must necessarily be focused on this branch.

Everywhere the royal factories constituted a very important sector of the flourishing textile industry. The royal factories, which were called in this period *tiraz khassa* (formerly *amma*), were often farmed to great businessmen, which means that they were managed on a purely capitalistic basis. In Khuzistan, where such factories existed in Tustar, Sus and Kurkub, and probably in the neighbouring province Fars, the putting-out system was employed. The same is true for Egypt, where the numerous tiraz factories were run by the government itself. For al-Mukaddasi says that the factories were in villages. In sources referring to this period there are mentioned royal factories in Tinnis, Damietta, Shata, Ushmum and Tuna in the Delta, Ansina, Fayyum and Ikhmim in Upper Egypt, and finally in Bansha, whose geographical situation is unknown to us. Not only the fact that the royal factories were located in small towns and villages, but also the reports about the weavers working in rented workrooms show clearly that the putting-out system was followed in all sectors of the Egyptian textile industry. In some Moslem countries the workers of the royal factories were slaves, or else corvée was imposed on free workers. A Persian writer who glorifies the Shiite caliphs reigning in Egypt in the eleventh century says that in this country all workers employed in the tiraz were free and paid for their work.[51] The royal factories, as a true capitalistic enterprise, at least sometimes sold their products to private customers. An Egyptian author writing in the second half of the tenth century mentions the high prices paid for the fabrics produced in the royal factories of Tinnis and Damietta. Speaking of the royal factories in the district of Fayyum, the geographer Ibn Haukal says that they are run by officials and that the merchants of many countries come thither to buy precious curtains at very high prices. So the fact that those robes of honour with an embroidered inscription which were manufactured in the royal factories for the court and its dignitaries were also in the possession of private persons need not be explained by the assumption that impoverished dignitaries sold them.[52] The Arabic sources leave no doubt that the factories themselves did so.

Besides the royal factories there was everywhere a flourishing private industry. The freedom of private enterprise was indeed a striking feature of the economic régime of the Moslem Near East in this period. Ibn Haukal distinguishes, when describing the textile industry in Upper Egypt, between royal and private factories, and al-Mukaddasi gives details about the division of labour and the imposts paid on the accomplishment of various stages of production and sale, both strictly controlled by agents licensed by the government. Probably the same brokers supplied the weavers with the raw material. They kept accounts of what each worker actually used so that he could not sell the products of his work himself. The Arabic writers of this period give a very interesting account of the scale of private industry in Southern Irak. It is contained in the biographical sketches of the tax-farmer Ali ar-Rasibi, mentioned above. There we read that he had 80 factories where garments were woven. Unfortunately some authors have added to this report that the garments were woven for his own use, and so they have misled modern scholars. Even supposing that these factories were small ones and that ar-Rasibi distributed great quantities of robes to his officials, it would be difficult to understand what he could do with the surplus products if he did not sell them.

Private industry was not only considerable in volume, but was expanding at the expense of the royal factories. A very interesting passage in the work of Ibn Haukal shows clearly how the private capitalists took over the management of royal factories. al-Istakhri, writing in the middle of the tenth century, mentioned the royal factories in various towns of Fars, such as Fasa, Siniz, Djannaba and Tawwadj. Ibn Haukal, who revised and simplified his work, extols the textile production of the province, but says that in all these towns the government *had* its factories.[53] So meanwhile the royal factories had been farmed out or sold to private capitalists.

In order to have a clear notion of the Near Eastern economies in that period it is necessary to know the volume of the industries, as compared with other sectors of the national economy. In the Arabic sources hints can be found which render it possible to make some conjectures. Miskawaih reports that in 985 the government of Irak had the intention to impose a duty of 10% on the price of silk and cotton cloth manu-factured in Baghdad. It was hoped to obtain a million dirhams every year, which means that the total volume of the textile production of Baghdad was assessed at 600,000 dinars. On the other hand, the total of the tax-revenue of Irak in the first half of the tenth century, when it must have been greater than in the second half, amounted to 1½ m dinars. These figures would indicate the great importance of the industry, as far as the value of its output is concerned. As to the output of the textile industry in the Nile delta, there is a reliable statement in Ibn Haukal's work, which has, however, been misunderstood by some scholars. The Arabic geographer says that before the vexatious impositions established after 971 the export of the linen products to Irak yielded a tax revenue (*himl*) of 20,000–30,000 dinars a year. A passage in al-Makrizi's Khitat where we read that the revenue from Tinnis, Damietta and Ushmum amounted sometimes to 220,000 dinars a day is surely exaggerated. A report included in a work of ath-Thaalibi (d. 1038) is more reliable. This author says that the taxes collected from the fine linen production of Egypt often amounted to 100,000 dinars a year. This figure would point to the fact that the output of the Egyptian linen industry amounted to almost a quarter of the national income. This conclusion would be in keeping, on the other hand, with a report on the size of the Egyptian textile industry in its most important centre: in Tinnis there would have been 5,000 looms.[54] But it goes without saying that from the value of the output no conclusion can be reached as to the number of workers employed. For the products of this industry, producing only for the rich, were very expensive.

The great industrial enterprises, both the royal tiraz and the private factories, could afford to try experiments and technological innovations, such as new methods of manufacturing old articles and the production of new ones. About the middle of the tenth century the textile factories in the Nile delta began to produce the so-called Abu Kalamun, a stuff which changes its colours. It seems also that the textile and other industries of the Near East were still expanding, although the great boom was over. There is good reason to believe that we have not gained any exaggerated notion of its size in the tenth century from the colourful descriptions of the geographers and other writers living in that period. The weaving of silk, richly embroidered brocades and scarlets, was developed in Baghdad in the tenth century, probably introduced by weavers from Tustar in Khuzistan. Authors writing at the end of the tenth century mention textile factories in towns where they had not existed before, such as Asyut in Upper Egypt. The flourishing of the indigo plantations in Palestine, reported by several authors of the tenth century, probably bears witness to this expansion. For this dye, so much needed in the textile industry, had otherwise to be imported from distant countries, such as Afghanistan. Much more sizable was the development of the paper industry in Syria and Egypt, where busy factories sprang up in provincial towns – Tiberias and others.[55]

The fabrics produced by all these industries were exported to both neighbouring and distant countries. The glass and fine cloth of Baghdad were esteemed everywhere and exported even to Spain. Fars exported silk, cotton and linen stuffs, Khuzistan was famous for its precious silk stuffs. Egypt supplied many countries with its linen fabrics, the dabiki produced in Dabik and elsewhere, the fine sharb* and others.[56]

But these were luxury goods. The number of the workers, in spite of the great value of the industrial output, was probably quite limited. Their economic situation was bad. According to the information we have on the conditions in tenth-century Egypt they owned their tools, but not the raw materials. It would be erroneous, however, to compare them with the craftsmen in medieval Europe. They were clearly distinct from the craftsmen, for they did not work for their own account. They were wage-earners, paid by the piece or by the day. From the indications found in the Arabic sources it is possible to compose a table showing the great difference between the salaries paid in that period to various classes.

Our table not only indicates the great difference between salaries but shows also the decrease in the wages of the workers. An Egyptian worker at the beginning of the eighth century could buy almost 400 kg bread with his monthly wage of 0.6 dinar, an unskilled worker in the middle of the tenth century with his dinar only 203 kg. The decrease in wages is also reflected by the discrepancy between the rise in grain prices and in the price of bread. Whereas the price of wheat had risen by 900%, that of bread had risen by only 230%. For a kilogram of bread probably cost 0.00147 dinar in Egypt (Fayyum) in 715, and in Cairo in 985 0.0049.[57] It is reasonable to assume that the decrease in wages was the consequence of the growth of the population and the surplus of manpower. On the other hand, it should be remembered that the decline of wages was slow and had begun a very long time before.

That was surely one of the reasons of the lack of revolutionary spirit among the working people. From time to time, however, the poor workers and others of the lower classes broke into revolt and riot – when prices suddenly rose or other causes provoked outbreaks of social discontent. In 917 there were riots in Basra because the

* see p. 95.

Monthly salary in the first half of the tenth century

	Irak	Egypt
Vizier or director of financial administration	5–7,000 dinars	3,000 dinars
Sons of vizier	500 ,,	
Judge, chief of market police	100 ,,	83 ,,
Professor	50 ,,	
High official	30 and more ,,	
Middle ranking government official	8–20 ,,	
Cavalryman	12–14 ,,	
Subaltern official, judge of lower rank	4–7 ,,	
Royal guardsman	$3\frac{1}{2}$,,	
Private clerk	3 ,,	
Skilled craftsman	2 ,,	2 ,,
Unskilled labourer	$1\frac{1}{2}$,, (or 91 kg bread)	1 ,, (or 203 kg bread)

government had imposed new taxes on the markets. In that case probably the small merchants were the most active and the most vocal. In 931 the lowest strata of society ('the wicked ones') rioted in Baghdad, but the government acknowledged that they had reason for complaint and satisfied them. When there was a dearth in Baghdad in 942 the people rose and sacked the houses of the rich. In a history of Ahmad b. Tulun riots in Tarsus are mentioned. Very often the discontent appears in disguised form, as usual in the middle ages, e.g. as orthodox fanaticism. For the supporters of the ultra-orthodox Hanbalite theologians were predominantly the poor, whereas the rich merchants in Western Baghdad and elsewhere were Shiites. The chroniclers narrate how the Hanbalites attacked the merchants and looted their shops or the banks in Aun Street.[58]

The common feature of all these riots was that they were more or less spontaneous outbreaks of popular discontent. It seems that they were not directed by revolutionaries aiming at the overthrow of the social order. What the rioters had in mind was the abolition of imposts or other measures taken by the authorities. However, the social tension in the towns was considerable, and it was perhaps greater in the rural population. As in any pre-capitalistic economy there occurred changes in production which increased the accumulation of capital, which means the rich became richer and the poor poorer.

Agricultural production and the conditions of the peasantry in that period were to a great extent determined by the growth of the latifundia and the freedom of selling and buying land. The royal princes, the rich merchants and high officials all had large estates. These estates belonged to different categories: some were private property (mulk), subject to the heavy land-tax (kharadj), others fiefs (ikta) liable to the tithe, or leases (idjara) against a fixed sum. The status of these lands was not only very different as far as the imposts are concerned, but also in other respects. Fief-holders were obliged to defray the costs of dyke repairs and had to maintain the irrigation system. Nevertheless the large estates yielded enormous profits, and rich people were very much interested in acquiring estates. Investment in agricultural enterprises was considered the most profitable and safe. High officials were especially eager to buy estates, because they did not pay the taxes. On the other hand, the Egyptian and Syrian estates of Muhammad b. Ali al-Madharai yielded 400,000 dinars a year.[59]

A great part of the estates held by high dignitaries was handed over to them by the government as part of their salary, or secured as appanages or obtained by unlawful methods. But there was also a lively free trade in estates. People belonging to the middle bourgeoisie and even poor town-dwellers bought rural estates. The caliphal government itself sold estates. In the course of four years, 929-32, it sold estates for 900,000 dinars. The vizier al-Khasibi established a special department for the sale of crown lands and there were many customers, since estates liable to the kharadj were fraudulently sold as ushr land (liable to the tithe). Sometimes the caliph was compelled to sell land to the military at very low prices and as ushr land. Even estates constituted as endowments were sold – against the law, but with the consent of the theologians. Another way of investing money in agricultural enterprises was to buy mills and to lease them.[60]

From the bourgeois who acquired rural estates there rose a class of *tunna*, wealthy landowners, who held a position ranking below the owners of latifundia and above the middle peasants, called by the Arabic authors *muzari*. Even they possessed different categories of land, kharadj-land and ushr-land, and did their utmost to increase their estates. They were strong enough to address themselves to the government, lodging protests against the tax-collectors. They tried also to evade payment of the heavy taxes by becoming tax-farmers themselves.[61] So the economic régime brought about the polarisation of the social classes.

Since many reports bear out the great interest of the rich in agricultural investment, the question arises whether the cultivated area increased in this period or not. Various passages in the writings of the Arabic authors show that the peasants, because of the heavy taxes, cultivated only the area necessary for the upkeep of their family. So some districts near Baghdad yielded at the beginning of the tenth century $\frac{1}{30}$ of what they had yielded a hundred years earlier. The neglect of the dykes and canals by corrupt officials and their destruction by fighting armies were other reasons for the fallowness of many fields. The geographer al-Istakhri says that some districts in Northern Irak were no longer cultivated in the first half of the tenth century and had become pasture land for the Bedouin and Kurds. The measures taken by the far-seeing and able vizier Ali b. Isa to protect the peasants brought relief and caused more land to be cultivated.[62]

The great landowners, on the other hand, undertook to turn marshy land into arable and to cultivate fallow land. The government itself was engaged in such activities, probably by means of contracts with capitalists. The diya mustahdatha – new estates administered by a special ministry – are often referred to in the Arabic sources of this period. al-Muwaffak, when regent in the days of al-Mutamid, colonised lands near as-Silh on the Tigris. The irrigation system, consisting of water-wheels and canals dug there by Khaizuran, the mother of Harun ar-Rashid, had been neglected, and the fields lay idle many years until al-Muwaffak invested 30,000 dinars in digging them out once more and providing the peasants with seed and cattle. The peasants settled there were partly tenants and partly independent farmers. But such activities were also undertaken by private landowners who possessed sufficient capital. Light is shed on the conditions of agriculture in tenth-century Irak by the statement of some Arabic authors that estates which had formerly been in the possession of the family of Ibn al-Furat and had been confiscated were no longer cultivated. The rich latifundists could afford to cultivate land which otherwise would have been neglected.[63]

The texts referring to the 'new colonisation' should, however, not mislead us. Besides the government only the tithe-paying landowners could afford and were interested in undertaking such enterprises, but their hold on the estates was not firm enough. The frequent changes of ownership, by confiscation and other methods, prevented great colonising activities, which would have considerably increased the cultivated area. The régime caused cultivation to decline in some regions. The number of the villages in Egypt at the time of its conquest by the Moslems is said to have been 10,000, whereas in 956 it had dwindled to 2,395. The former number is certainly very much exaggerated, but it shows that the Arabic authors were aware of the fact that since the Moslem conquest of Egypt the cultivated area had not increased but rather had declined. The tenth-century geographer al-Istakhri dwells on the decline of the oases west of the Nile. al-Makrizi lays stress on the devastation wrought on Egyptian agriculture in that period and the decrease of the revenue from the kharadj.[64]

On the other hand, the capitalist trend in tenth-century agriculture resulted in considerable changes in its structure and in the development of new branches. Enterprising owners of latifundia invested large amounts of capital in the commutation into rice plantations of estates growing other grains. They did so because there was a great demand for rice in the big towns, and because they alone could undertake this change of cultivation. Beside the districts of Lower Irak where rice had been grown in the second half of the ninth century, there were extensive rice plantations in some parts of the Great Swamp, as in the district of al-Djamida, and in Upper Mesopotamia. In Palestine rice was grown in the plain of Baisan, on the Golan heights near Baniyas, while in the northern borderland of Syria there were plantations in the district of Tarsus. In Egypt too the rice plantations increased considerably in the second half of the tenth century in the oases and in the province of Fayyum, where it became the most important of the grains produced.[65]

Another branch of agriculture which began to flourish in this period was sugar-growing. Like the planting of rice, that of sugar was an undertaking which only rich landowners could afford, all the more as the landlords had the sugar-refineries on their estates. In the tenth century the highest quality sugar was still produced in Khuzistan, but that of Yemen was also exported to Irak and elsewhere. But in that period sugar was grown too in Southern Irak, and it became one of the important agricultural products of Syria, where it was planted on the Mediterranean coast from Palestine to Tripoli in the north, in Galilee and in the Jordan valley. In Egypt sugar was grown in the Delta, east of the Rosetta arm of the Nile. Finally, the proprietors of big estates greatly extended the cotton plantations, the Hamdanids in Upper Mesopotamia for example.[66]

The latifundists who engaged in new colonisation and the introduction of new plantations suffered from insecurity and precariousness of possession, while the middle and small peasants were oppressed by the taxes. The average rate of the kharadj, collected according to the mukasama assessment, amounted to $\frac{1}{3} + \frac{1}{10}$ in Irak, in the first half of the tenth century, whereas the Hamdanids levied half or even $\frac{2}{3}$ of the crops. Mostly the taxes were paid in kind, both for grains such as wheat and rice, and fruits. But often the tax-collectors preferred to levy the tax in cash, and in that case they estimated the crops before the harvest in order to extort greater sums than were due. Complaints of their levying the tax in advance are often echoed by the chroniclers. It happened also that three times too much tithe was collected, and in Yemen this tax was commuted into a global sum. Often the tax-farmers introduced new taxes, seized the crops until the peasants paid them (when they were paid in cash), and tortured them to extort arrears. In addition to the land-tax (or the tithe), the peasants had to pay various customs, e.g. for using the mills. The wealthy peasants were also compelled to purchase the crops delivered to the government at arbitrarily fixed prices.[67]

It was not only because of the heavy taxation and the abuses and extortions of the administration that the period in which the caliphate declined was a very hard time for the peasantry. The first half of the tenth century saw a new expansion of the Bedouin, both in Northern Mesopotamia and in Syria, and the peasants suffered very much from their pillage. When the hold of the caliphal authorities was weakened, the Bedouin became more and more daring, as they knew that brigandage would not be punished. Many of these Bedouin, however, were no longer true nomads. They were to some extent already sedentary, or at least about to settle down. For part of the year they cultivated fields and for part they lived a roving life seeking good pasture land for their cattle. They encroached on the peasants' arable land, and even worse, they tried to supplant them. So there were frequent clashes between the peasants and the Bedouin. at-Tanukhi, a writer of the tenth century, has included in a collection of tales a lively description of the Bedouin's transition from nomadic to sedentary life. In a village in the district of Kutha, in Southern Irak, Bedouin had begun, at the beginning of the tenth century, to till land on the borders of the fields cultivated by the peasants. It was land which the peasants had no interest in tilling, and therefore the tax-collectors levied from the Bedouin only a part of the tax normally paid. But when another tax-collector imposed on them the full land-tax, there was an uproar and the Bedouin called other clans to join them in a revolt.

The Bedouin who became settled kept their tribal organisation, but were clearly distinguished from the true Bedouin. We are told that in 915 the army of the Hamdanid Husain consisted of 30,000 men 'from the tribes of the Bedouin and the ashira' (settled tribes). As these ashiras became more and more sedentary, their interests were opposed to those of their brethren who continued the pure nomadic life, and the antagonism resulted in acts of violence.

Many clans set out to occupy new pasture land and better fields. The main trend of this new migratory movement of the Bedouin was the advance of Kaisites from Upper Mesopotamia into Syria. Groups of the Banu Kilab left the Syrian desert, whereas both Northern Syria and the Djazira suffered incursions of clans of the Ukail, Numair, Kushair and Adjlan. These latter tribes supplanted sedentary Mudarites and Rabia in the districts of Harran, Araban, Kirkisiya and ar-Rahba. After the great defeat inflicted on the Bedouin by Saif ad-daula in 955, numerous clans of the Tayy and Kalb had to emigrate from their old sites to the Golan and leave them to the Banu Kilab. From that time the Dibab and Djafar, both Kilab, became the most important tribes in the province of Hims.[68]

The peasants who suffered more than all other classes from the taxation and the recrudescence of the Bedouin problem were the small farmers, the so-called *akara*. Many of these lost their property and became tenants and from that time always had to rely on advances of seed. Another consequence of the impoverishment of the small peasants was the abandonment of the villages altogether. The flight from the land which had already been a great problem in the days of the Umayyad caliphs became once more a burning question and caused the government much worry. When the Saffarids had conquered the province of Fars, they increased taxes so much that many peasants liable to the kharadj left the villages. That was the attitude adopted towards the peasantry by a new dynasty which owed its ascendancy to the support of the lower classes of society. When it had brought about massive flight from the land, the quota of the kharadj incumbent on the fugitives was imposed on the remaining peasants so that their situation became unbearable.[69]

These conditions, characteristic of the inner contradictions of a pre-capitalistic society, were surely pre-revolutionary. Great masses of direly oppressed and exploited petty craftsmen and small merchants, workers and peasants were ready to listen to a revolutionary call.

d) *The Karmatians*

For a long time the radical Shiite missionaries belonging to the Ismaili branch of the sect had been fomenting discontent and organising secret groups. These Ismailis strove for the establishment of the rule of the descendants of Ismail, considered as the seventh lawful heir of the caliph Ali. They addressed themselves to all classes, but many people identified orthodox Islam with the ruling plutocracy and military oligarchy. Nationalist Persians found in this movement a way to express their hatred of the Arabs. So the Ismailis, originally a religious sect, became a great revolutionary movement combining various tendencies. It would, however, be erroneous to believe that the original aim of this Shiite movement was thrust aside and that the overthrow of the social order became the real aim. But the Shia doctrine implied the re-establishment of social justice, as conceived in one way by the Moslems, and in another by Persians who knew about Mazdakite Communism. There were certainly some groups in the Ismaili movement for whom Shiism was only a superstructure, but in the ideology of the great majority all these ideas were interwoven, the dream of a true caliphate however superseding all other elements. The merger of the different tendencies was not complete, and therefore there were stages in the development of the movement in which it had a very different or even contradictory character.

When the revolt of the Zindj was at its height, the Ismaili missionaries had already begun their agitation among the peasants of Southern Irak, and the great slave revolt proved contagious. The first leader of the movement was a Persian, probably from the family of the oculist Abdallah b. Maimun. Then Hamdan Karmat, a carrier transporting corn or according to others a peasant in a village near Kufa, took over the leadership, and it was he who gave it its name – Karmatians. He went to live in Kalwadha, near Baghdad, and from there sent his emissaries to all the villages of Central and Southern Irak. The social-revolutionary tendency of their preaching was explicit: they promised their followers the goods of their masters. Hamdan Karmat's brother-in-law Abdan wrote tracts about this doctrine and their propaganda had great success among the peasants. At the beginning the emissaries levied certain contributions for the movement, then they asked for the fifth of a man's property, and finally they proclaimed the *ulfa*: they organised the villages in peasant communes, all the peasants delivering their goods to a local leader in order to use them collectively. The emissaries of Hamdan Karmat chose for this purpose a man who could be trusted; he collected cattle, furniture and jewels and, on the other hand, provided the peasants with cloth and took care of all their needs. The Arabic orthodox chroniclers, bitterly hostile to this movement, confess that thereafter there were no more needy among the peasants and that everybody worked assiduously, in order to be considered for his merits. The women delivered all that they earned by spinning. Private property was completely abolished. The orthodox historians say that even the women became common property, that the Karmatians abolished the Moslem prayers and allowed any immoral act such as murder. But these are false accusations, as is borne out by other reports saying that they imposed on their followers fifty prayers a day.

Although the number of the Karmatians had already become considerable in the district of Kufa in the years 882-8, the caliphal government underestimated the movement at first. At the same time it spread in Yemen, and according to an author writing before 899 it then had altogether 100,000 followers. In 897 there was the first Karmatian revolt in the province of Kufa. It was easily quelled, but the government was alarmed to discover that a high official in Baghdad was one of their secret leaders. Three years later the Karmatians rose in Djunbula, between Kufa and Wasit, set fire to the houses of the rich and killed their wives and children. It was a typical peasant revolt. Once more the rebels succumbed, but the government abstained from mass executions 'because it feared lest the countryside would be ruined, since the Karmatians were the tillers and workers'. In 901 there was a new revolt in the district of Kufa, and when it was quelled its leader was cruelly executed in Baghdad.[70]

The reports of the Arabic historians which we have quoted indicate clearly that these risings of the Karmatians were isolated revolts and did not develop into a general peasant rising. The rebels were not well armed and the superiority of the Turkish government troops was crushing. Attempts to bring about an alliance with the Zindj had failed, but, on the other hand, the Karmatians had partisans in the towns, among the intellectuals and other persons belonging to the upper strata of society. These were Shiites who supported them for their religious convictions. But as with the Zindj the town proletariat did not join them, not feeling that the Karmatians fought for their interests.

When the peasant revolt in Irak was crumbling, the Karmatian emissaries, looking everywhere for followers, had found a propitious audience among the Bedouin. They had addressed themselves to those who lived a true nomadic life and were at all times the enemies of the peasantry and eager for booty. As soon as the Karmatians had succeeded in stirring up these warlike tribes, there began a revolt which was much more dangerous for the existing social order, not consisting in isolated outbreaks, but aimed seriously at the overthrow of the régime.

The rebels had able leaders. The foremost was Zikrawaih b. Mihrawaih (or Zakaruya b. Mahruya), a Persian, but for a long time he lived in retirement and his sons led the movement. All of them claimed to have supernatural gifts, and the Bedouin sincerely believed them. The first converts were the Banu l-Ulais, a clan of Kalbites in the Samawa, a region between Kufa and the Syrian desert. Yahya, a son of Zikrawaih, became their commander in 902, claiming to be a descendant of the 'hidden' imam Ismail and covering his face, like so many Oriental prophets, with a veil. The rebels set fire to the mosque of ar-Rusafa in Northern Syria, sacked the little town and the neighbouring villages – true Bedouin as they were. When the news of these exploits spread, other clans joined the movement, and in 903 the Karmatians were strong enough to launch a general offensive in Central Syria. Troops sent against them by the governor of Syria were defeated, his own camp was sacked and the rebels laid siege to Damascus. The Tulunids sent reinforcements from Egypt, but even these well-trained regiments were beaten.

In the battle before Damascus Yahya had fallen and the Karmatians had made his brother al-Husain their leader. He had a mole on his face and pretended that it was a sign of his being a prophet (as Muhammad himself had had one). When he won more victories over the Egyptian troops, most of the Bedouin tribes of Syria joined him and he proclaimed himself the Mahdi, the Saviour who comes at the end of days to establish God's kingdom on earth. Success brought success. The Karmatians conquered the province of Hims, pillaging everywhere, and the town itself surrendered. Then Hamath, Maarrat an-Numan and other towns were taken and great numbers of their inhabitants killed, including women and children. In Baalbek almost the whole of the population was massacred. The same happened to the town of Salamiyya. Everywhere the villages were burnt and the peasants killed.

The townspeople, whatever their social standing, fought against the rebels, although the Karmatians had among them secret groups of partisans. When they besieged Aleppo in the autumn of 903 the inhabitants, aided by caliphal troops, offered valiant resistance and they had to retreat. Then the caliph sent against them a new army, which comprised a strong contingent of the Banu Shaiban. It crushed them at the end of 903 in a great battle near Hamath, and al-Husain, their leader, was caught and executed.[71]

A third son of Zikrawaih, Ali, emerged as a new leader. He made a raid into Palestine in 906, sacking Tiberias. When Zikrawaih's emissaries once more succeeded in stirring up the tribes which had retired to a peaceful life, the Karmatians made new incursions into Southern Syria and Palestine. After new failures Zikrawaih himself took over the command and won a victory over the caliphal army in Western Irak. But in a second battle, not far from Kufa, he was defeated and taken prisoner, dying some days later from his wounds. That was the end of the Bedouin revolt.

Why did it fail? It was crushed because the townspeople fought desperately against it and because the enmity of the peasants was similarly aroused by the Bedouin. al-Husain, the man with the mole, was caught and delivered to the authorities by the people of a small town, certainly living by agriculture.[72] Not even all the Bedouin supported the Karmatians. So they did not succeed in uniting all the revolutionary forces and setting up a powerful coalition, which alone could overthrow the caliphal régime. The particularism of the different classes was too strong. When Karmatism became a Bedouin movement, the peasantry changed its attitude, or more precisely the peasants who had property took the lead among the farmers.

The Karmatian missionaries meanwhile had great success in other parts of the caliphal empire. In Yemen, where they had begun their activities in 880, they had established control of the whole country by 906. But their success in Bahrain, a country near to the centre of the empire and situated on one of the main routes of international trade, seemed to be much more dangerous.

The towns of Bahrain had an active merchant population and every town was interested in increasing its share in the great Indian trade of the Persian Gulf. But in the countryside there were poor roaming Bedouin who envied the rich sedentary population. At one time the province had been a stronghold of the Khawaridj, then the leader of the Zindj had had some success. A Shiite party still existed in the towns and the antagonism between the province and the rich orthodox town of Basra was strong.

Like many other leaders of the Karmatians, the man who started the movement in Bahrain was a Persian, Abu Said Hasan b. Bahram al-Djannabi. According to some sources he was a flour dealer, according to others a weigher in Basra. His proletarian origin is not in doubt, as we read that people scoffed at him because he had once been mending sacks. He began his career in the province of Fars, where he roused the animosity of the Persians against the Arabs. Then he organised there a communist community which he administered. When this movement was suppressed by the government, Hamdan Karmat sent him to Bahrain. There he tried, without success, to win over the radical Shiites, and later addressed himself to the Bedouin. In 899 he conquered the town of al-Katif and a year later raided the environs of al-Hadjar, another town in Bahrain, and the district of Basra, where he defeated a body of caliphal troops. Then he took al-Hadjar, to whose inhabitants he guaranteed safety of life and property. The town was recovered by the government, but was once more conquered by the Karmatians, the inhabitants who remained in the town embracing their doctrine. Abu Said, however, established his headquarters in al-Ahsa.[73]

In the following years the Bahrain Karmatians were inactive, probably as a consequence of inner dissensions in the Ismaili movement. Hamdan Karmat and Abdan opposed Said b. Ubaidallah, an offspring of the Persian oculist Abdallah b. Maimun and the secret leader of the movement, who claimed to be a descendant of Ismail and the Mahdi, but the Bahrain Karmatians recognised him as such. In 909 Said b. Ubaidallah established his rule in Tunisia and founded a Shiite caliphate, and when his army invaded Egypt in 913 the Karmatians, the other branch of the movement, attacked Basra. In 919 Egypt was attacked again and Basra at the same time.[74] So the Abbasid caliphate found itself held by a pair of pincers threatening to crush it.

Meanwhile Abu Said had been murdered in his palace and his son Said had succeeded him, ruling together with his brothers. But later his younger brother Abu Tahir thrust him aside and embarked on a new policy. Whereas Abu Said had been supported at the beginning of his revolt by the Bedouin, Abu Tahir began to build up a powerful state, promoting the interests of the merchants, the most important group of the town-dwellers of Bahrain. Their interests were from then on a decisive factor in his policy, determining both the structure of the Karmatian state and its foreign policy. The successive changes of policy are clearly indicated by the accounts of chroniclers. Ibn Haukal, writing in the second half of the tenth century but certainly referring to the first half and the middle of it, says that the Karmatian leaders had got estates as appanages, which meant an end of communism. But whereas these estates yielded 30,000 dinars a year, the whole revenue of the state, from the customs levied on the merchants and other sources, amounted to 1.2–1.5 million. A fifth of it, after the deduction of the fifth for the imam, i.e. the caliph of the Ismailis, was assigned to the family of Abu Said, another fifth to the family of the vizier Sanbar and an equal part to the Ikdaniyya, the members of the state council. The Karmatian state had a democratic régime. There was a great council which deliberated on important matters and took decisions. So there had come into being institutions which were completely strange to the traditional Moslem world: a constitution (probably not written) and a democracy, although a guided one. For the Karmatian state was not a republic. What is, however, most characteristic of this stage in the development of Karmatism is the existence of private property.[75]

The first ten years of the reign of Abu Tahir, who made al-Ahsa his capital, were dedicated to the development of commercial relations with other regions of the Persian Gulf, such as the town of Siraf. This was accepted by Ali b. Isa, when at the head of the caliphal government, hoping that by allowing the Karmatians to develop their trade he would avert the danger of new invasions of Southern Irak. But when the Shiite anti-caliph of Tunisia decided in 923 to attack Egypt, once more the Karmatians had to comply with his orders. They conquered Basra, wrought great havoc on this rich city, and returned with immense booty, not before having destroyed the Great Mosque. Thereupon Abu Tahir began to ravage Irak with fire and sword. In 925 the Karmatians sacked Kufa. The story of this campaign, as told by the chroniclers, sheds light on one of the motives of Abu Tahir's policy: he had asked from the caliph the cession of al-Ahwaz and Basra, attempting in this way to get hold of Irak's seaborne India trade and the industry of Khuzistan. When his request was rejected, he invaded Irak.[76]

But the religious aims of the Karmatians were surely no less important. Abu Tahir decided to strike orthodox Islam at its most vulnerable point by cutting the pilgrims' route to Mecca, thus making impossible the holiest act of Moslem worship. For some years there was no pilgrimage from Irak. The caliphal government asked the ruler of

Aderbeidjan, Yusuf Ibn Abi s-Sadj, to equip an army and undertake the struggle against the Karmatians. But in 927, when Abu Tahir invaded Irak once again and occupied Kufa, Yusuf was defeated, and the whole of Irak seemed to be an easy prey for the valiant Karmatians. In spite of the resistance of the caliphal army they crossed the Euphrates and took the town of al-Anbar. With Baghdad already panic-stricken, the army succeeded in stopping the Karmatians by cutting a bridge, whereupon Abu Tahir retreated to the western shore of the Euphrates and finally to Bahrain. Next year the Karmatians returned and levied tribute on the Bedouin tribes of Northern Mesopotamia, while at the same time a new peasant revolt broke out. More than 10,000 peasants rose in the province of Wasit, seizing the crops of the rich landowners, and others revolted in the district of Ain at-Tamr. These rebels had white banners with the inscriptions: 'We fight for the oppressed, to make them masters and proprietors' (Koran 28[5]).

In 930 the Karmatians struck their most terrible blow against the caliphate. On the great holiday, when many thousands of pilgrims had flocked together, they conquered Mecca and sacked it throughout the following eight days. As a symbolic act they carried away the Black Stone, the holy of holies of Islam. The religion of Muhammad was stricken at its heart; the holy ceremonies lost their significance. And the Moslem world did not move – so the Karmatians maintained their assault. In the same year Oman was conquered, in 931 they again took Kufa, and other towns in Irak were abandoned by their inhabitants.

But in the years following the sack of Mecca the commercial interests of the Karmatians became again the primary factor of their policy. Two coastal towns in Fars suffered their ravages – in 933 Siniz, in 934 Siniz and Tawwadj. The intention was clearly to ruin those centres of the textile industry which competed with al-Ahsa. When the caliphal government negotiated with the Karmatians for the restitution of the Kaaba (the Black Stone), the Karmatians asked for freedom of trade with Basra. Once more they attacked and sacked Kufa, but in 939 a treaty was concluded in virtue of which the pilgrimage became possible, and in 950 the Kaaba was restored to Mecca.[77]

Meanwhile the Karmatian state underwent new changes. The Persian traveller Nasiri Khosrau, who visited Bahrain in the middle of the eleventh century, has left us a very interesting description of the Karmatian state as it had developed after the death of Abu Tahir in 944. It was a kind of welfare state where nobody paid taxes (in contrast with the conditions described by Ibn Haukal). The state owned 30,000 Negro slaves, who were occupied in agricultural work. A citizen in need was assisted by a government loan. Even foreigners obtained loans until their enterprises were established, so that a foreign craftsman could acquire the tools he needed. Everybody had the right to apply for help when he had to repair his house or his mill, state slaves being sent to do the work. Grain was ground in state mills free of charge.[78]

The régime described by Nasiri Khosrau was the last stage in a long development, something very different from the primitive communes of poor peasants which had been the first stage in the Karmatian movement. The later stages represented a form of socialism as the true Orientals conceived it.

However that may be, Karmatism was one of the most powerful and creative movements in the medieval Near East. It created a state which lasted for some generations, and would have been strong enough to overthrow the existing régime and to establish a new social order, had it not been for the particularism inherent in Oriental societies. Another reason for the failure was the religious fanaticism the Karmatians aroused against themselves. Everywhere devout Moslems fought against them, regardless of their social standing. Sometimes the fervour of the volunteers was considered excessive by the regular army, but so eager were the civilians to fight that the officers could not restrain them.[79]

CHAPTER V

The Beginnings of Feudalism

Although at the turn of the ninth and tenth centuries the Abbasids had lost their hold on many provinces, their régime lingered on. Irak was still a rich and flourishing country and the centre of the Moslem world. But in the middle of the tenth century the centuries-old caliphate collapsed, giving way to a new social order. Not only the Arabs but civilians in general lost their position at the top of the social hierarchy. There began the age of feudalism, as conceived by the Oriental armies. This upheaval was linked to a great change in the economic condition of Irak and the neighbouring countries. So the middle of the tenth century was in all respects a turning-point in the social and economic history of the old empire.

It was not a sudden change. The transition was slow, and it was a long time before the feudal lords tightened their grip on various sectors of economy. The bourgeois offered resistance to the overthrow of the old régime, and in the second half of the tenth century and the first half of the eleventh the Bedouin became even stronger than before.

Social and economic conditions in Egypt developed on the same lines although the change occurred later. The foundation of a Shiite counter-caliphate delayed the establishment of the new régime, but it could not prevent it.

a) *Economic decline of the central provinces*

The phenomenon most characteristic of the new trends in the social and economic life of Irak and the neighbouring provinces of the caliphal empire was the beginning of depopulation. The historian who tries to sketch the demographic development of Oriental countries in the middle ages cannot quote documents like those which have been preserved in the archives of Southern European towns from the end of the twelfth century. So we are compelled to make conjectures. But as far as the long-term trends of demographic development are concerned, their probability is strengthened by convincing evidence.

An Arabic geographer who was a keen observer recorded that at the end of the tenth century, when he wrote his work, the suburbs of Basra and Kufa had begun to decay. He speaks also of the decline of the small towns around Wasit, of Samarra, of al-Anbar and of Djardjaraya.[1] The decrease in the population of Baghdad must have been alarming. An Arab writer living in that period narrates that its population at the beginning of the tenth century was ten times as great as in the year 956. The geographer Ibn Haukal, writing at the end of the tenth century, says that most of the quarters of the town had fallen into decay.[2] According to this geographer the decrease of population was also a striking feature of social life in Upper Mesopotamia. He dwells on the progressive decay of many towns. He deplores the decline of Kirkisiya, ar-Rahba, as-Sinn, Mosul, Balad, Adhrama, Dara, Ras al-ain, Arzan and Mayyafarikin. The houses in these towns were empty, and only the poor who could not afford to emigrate remained.[3] The decrease of the population was progressive. A Persian traveller who visited Basra in 1052 says that most of its quarters were ruined.[4]

On the other hand, there can be no doubt that the peasants continued to leave the villages for the towns, at the very time when they were in decline. The number of villages certainly diminished, the abandonment of old ones not being counterbalanced by the foundation of new ones. The growth of the latifundia was undoubtedly an important cause of this phenomenon. It is a well-known fact, indeed, that the density of population in regions cultivated by freeholders is much greater than in those cultivated by tenants, the reason being the heavier burden imposed on tenants, which obliges them to cultivate larger areas.

There could be adduced negative proofs for the supposition of depopulation beginning in Irak in this period. The lack of any account of the enlargement of the areas of towns by walling in suburbs would be one of them. Silence as to the foundation of new ones would be another. But there are also facts which are considered by all economic historians to be clear evidence of declining population. Such a fact is the opposite trend of grain prices and wages. Whereas the average price of 100 kg of wheat had reached 1.36 dinar in Irak at the beginning of the tenth century, and in Upper Mesopotamia in 969 1.51 dinar, it went down in Central Irak to 0.75 dinar in the eleventh century. Speaking of average prices in a century may sound strange, but the Arabic sources reveal that long periods of stable or slowly changing prices were a characteristic feature of Oriental economies in the middle ages. Minimum wages rose, on the other hand, considerably. Although nominal wages had probably not increased, amounting to 1.5 dinar as before, in the first half of the eleventh century the unskilled worker who got this sum could buy 300 ratls of bread, against 227 at the middle of the tenth century.[5]

The decrease of the population of Irak had various causes. Certainly the chronic violence brought about depopulation. During the endless riots and many civil wars a great number of people were slain or impoverished or rendered homeless, whereas the growing insecurity prevented the increase of population or at least diminished the rate of its growth. Arabic chroniclers of the tenth century mention time and again the emigration of groups of merchants and other town-dwellers, who left for other countries in order to escape oppression by arbitrary taxation and to enjoy security under more stable governments.[6] Even if these groups were not very numerous, their emigration deprived many of their fellow-countrymen of their income. Craftsmen and shop-keepers, workers and servants remained without a livelihood. The lack of security had other sequels. Conditions for the transport of grain and other staple foods became very difficult, and local famines had disastrous consequences which otherwise could have been avoided. The spread of epidemics was another outcome of insecurity and the deterioration of sanitary conditions. The chroniclers narrate at length how water conduits were destroyed in Baghdad so that many people had to drink impure water from wells. Hence there were several outbreaks of pestilence in the middle of the tenth century. It appeared first in 941 and 943. According to the reports of the Arabic historians it spread again in Basra in the year 955 so that 1,000–1,200 died every day. At the same time there raged in al-Ahwaz, Wasit, Basra and Baghdad a disease which was probably spirochetosis icterohemorrhagica. In 957 swellings in the throat and other diseases were prevalent in Baghdad, causing many deaths. Other diseases resulted in sudden death. Three years later the plague spread in Upper Mesopotamia. In the first half of the eleventh century there were four heavy outbreaks of plague. In 1015–16 it spread in Basra and the neighbouring districts, in 1032 it raged in Irak, Upper Mesopotamia and Syria, as in other regions of the Near and Middle East. At the same time smallpox spread in Baghdad and Mosul and many thousands of adults and children died. Two years later a dangerous angina carried away countless people in Khurasan, Fars, Irak, Upper Mesopotamia and Syria. The chroniclers

say that it took a heavy toll in Baghdad and Mosul. Many houses were
shut up because there was no longer anyone to live in them. In 1048 a
dearth was followed by a new outbreak of plague.[7] Although the
epidemics became more frequent in this period than before,[8] it seems
that the victims of endemic diseases were even more numerous. It is,
however, sometimes futile to distinguish between epidemic and endemic diseases. Speaking of the plague in 1032 the chronicler Ibn al-
Djauzi says that 'it was heavier than usual'.[9] In any case there is good
reason to believe that wars, famine and worse sanitary conditions
aggravated the endemic diseases.[10] The interdependence between
periods of war and economic decay on the one hand and the rise of
the death rate on the other is a phenomenon well known in the social
history of medieval societies.

Besides depopulation the decrease of the cultivated area is frequently
alluded to in the Arabic sources. It would be an over-simplification to
say that it was the outcome of the flight from the land. It was another
aspect of economic decline and misgovernment. The agricultural
production decreased because demand diminished and there was no
pressure on the authorities to keep up the irrigation system. Since the
dykes of the Tigris and the Euphrates were not well maintained, they
were easily broken by inundations. The supervision of the dykes was
all the more important as the methods used for building and repairing
them were rather primitive. A chronicler emphasises that they were
made of thatch and mould and, on the other hand, according to a treatise
dealing with the problems of irrigation the holes in the dykes were
choked up with reed, branches and earth. Furthermore, canals were
not deep, some from $\frac{2}{3}$ to $1\frac{1}{2}$ cubits, others only $\frac{2}{3}$ to $1\frac{1}{4}$ kabda (equal to
8.3–9 cm). So the danger of new breaches and inundations was always
imminent, and when that happened, fields and villages came under
water. Sometimes the dykes were purposely broken by fighting princes.
Rebel forces destroyed the water-wheels which irrigated the fields.
Canals which were essential for the cultivation of extended areas, such
as the Nahrawan canal, were for long periods neglected, so that they
became silted up and useless.[11] Thus there is no doubt that the cultivated area decreased. Sometimes, as in the year 974, little seed was sown
because of the general anarchy.[12]

At the same time there was a continuous growth of latifundia, and
the situation of the peasants deteriorated. The geographer Ibn Haukal
vividly depicts the distress of the peasantry in his native province of
Upper Mesopotamia. He narrates how the Hamdanid princes appro-

priated estates, compelling the peasants by heavy taxation to sell them for ridiculous prices. The share of the crops left to the peasants was very small, not much more than was necessary for mere existence and for sowing. That the Arabic writer did not simply slander the dynasty which he hated is borne out by a source which is surely not suspect. R. Hai, head of a rabbinical academy in Baghdad, who died in 1038, says that some people have estates whose tenants keep a fifth of the crops. The growth of the rice plantations in Lower Irak in that period is established by a biography of Muhadhdhib ad-daula Ali b. Nasr, governor of the Swamp district, who died in 1018 after a term of 32 years. We read there that his yearly revenue consisted of 1.7 m dirhams, 9,600 kurr of wheat, 13,700 kurr of barley, and 8,000 kurr of rice.[13] Although Ibn Khurdadhbih, in his account of the revenues of the districts of Irak, lists the yields of barley and rice together, it seems that he indicates for only one district a greater portion of rice, i.e. Kaskar, a district comprising a big area east of the Tigris. On the other hand, the growing of rice remained an important branch of agriculture in the Swamp district, near Djawamid and west of Wasit, down to the present day. So we may conclude that there its great development, accompanied by the growth of latifundia, dates from this period, for the rice plantations were necessarily a capitalist enterprise undertaken by the owners of latifundia.

The decline of agricultural production was certainly the major trend in the economy of Irak in this period, and was one of the reasons for the decrease of the tax revenues. Although the varying efficiency of the tax-collectors played a great part in the fluctuations of the tax revenue, the volume of agricultural output must not be overlooked. The data which the Arabic authors provide are mostly copied from original documents, so that they can be considered authentic, and they point clearly to an almost progressive decline.

Tax revenue of Irak

819	5 m dinars	(108,457,650 dirh.)
870	3,120,000 dinars	(78,309,340 dirh.)
892	2,520,000 dinars	
918	1,547,734 dinars	
969	2,800,000 dinars	(42 m dirh.)
977–983	2 m dinars	(30 m dirh.)

These figures[14] prove that at the end of the tenth century even a very efficient administration could not raise 3 m dinars, as did the caliphs in the ninth century. The decline is even more conspicuous if we take into consideration that the figure indicated for 892 does not refer to the whole of Irak and that, on the other hand, the indication provided by Ibn Haukal for 969 is not reliable.

Some statements on the revenues from certain provinces and neighbouring countries substantiate the supposition of a progressive and general decline. In 918 the province of Basra yielded 121,095 dinars, with 22,575 dinars from the duties levied in the harbour. In 1040 this had dwindled to 70,000 dinars.[15] The accounts of the revenues from the provinces of Upper Mesopotamia are also very instructive.[16]

Tax revenue of Upper Mesopotamia

870	Mosul, Diyar Mudar, Diyar Rabia	692,000 din.	(17,300,000 dir.)
cca 900–905	Diyar Mudar, Diyar Rabia and Diyar Bakr	700,000 din.	(9,715,000)
918	Diyar Mudar, Diyar Rabia	1,094,295 din.	
959	Mosul, Diyar Rabia, ar-Rahba	200,000 din.	(2.9 m)
964–968	Mosul, Diyar Rabia, ar-Rahba	80,000 din.	(1.2 m)
967	Mosul, Diyar Rabia, ar-Rahba	80,000 din.	(1.2 m)

The same trend is perceptible in the accounts of the tax revenue of Syria. Even there the taxes collected in some of the provinces decreased very much in this period (see p. 174).

These statements[17] point on the one hand to the relative stability of the revenue from the province of Damascus and on the other hand to the tremendous decline of the provinces of Palestine and Jordan. The conditions of Khuzistan and Fars, the two provinces of Persia southeast of Irak, were different. The accounts which we find in the sources show that they flourished as before.[18]

The government in Baghdad was incapable of checking the downward trend of Irak's economy. On the contrary, as time went on, the decline became more perceptible. The fines imposed on high dignitaries were considerably smaller in that period than in the first half of the

Tax revenue of Syria
(all figures in dinars)

	Damascus	Palestine	Jordan	Hims	Kinnasrin
685–705			180,000		
786–809	420,000	310,000	96,000	320,000	400,000
819	110,000	159,000	109,000	108,000	360,000
cca 855	less than 140,000	175,000	175,000	180,000	
870	400,000	500,000	350,000	340,000	400,000
cca 890	300,000	300,000	100,000	220,000	
918	428,357	311,357	142,397	315,574	485,667

Tax revenues of South-West Persia

	Khuzistan	Fars
786–809	1.25 m din. (25 m dir.)	1.35 m din. (27 m dir.)
819	1.2 m din. (18 m dir.)	1.6 m din. (24 m dir.)
870	2 m din. (49 m dir.)	1.32 m din. (33 m dir.)
879–900		4 m din. (60 m dir.)
918	1,260,922 din.	1,634,520 din. + 253,000 din. duties
cca 969	2 m din. (30 m dir.)	2,010,200 din.
949–983		2,150,000 din.

tenth century. A vizier would be fined 100,000 or 200,000 dinars or even less, other high officials 20,000–40,000 dinars.[19] The stocks of gold and silver which were at the disposal of the mints and were put into circulation seem to have been rather limited, although there were great changes in this respect. In any case monetary conditions deteriorated. The chroniclers leave no doubt as to the shortage of gold coins in the second half of the tenth century. According to their reports payments of great sums were usually made in silver, i.e. in dirhams, in

Irak and South-western Persia. The taxes due from various provinces and the payments by the tax-farmers were made in dirhams. The army, both in Irak and in Upper Mesopotamia, got its pay in silver and the budgets were calculated in dirhams.[20] Monetary conditions in Syria were probably not different in the second half of the tenth century, for the treasures of Saif ad-daula consisted too in dirhams, and grants offered by him to the Bedouin were to be paid in silver.[21] Payments in dinars were in that period less frequent. As far as such payments are mentioned, it is in respect of wedding gifts.[22]

But at the end of the tenth century silver began to be rare, and in course of time it almost disappeared. Ghiyath al-umma Baha ad-daula, who ruled over Irak at the turn of the tenth and eleventh centuries, coined debased dirhams, which produced a rise in prices and consequently a mutiny of the army. The government had to revoke these dirhams and issue better ones. But as the silver stocks were rapidly shrinking, the dirhams coined at the beginning of the eleventh century were once more debased.[23] The great shortage of dirhams became a phenomenon characteristic of monetary conditions in all the countries of the Near East. It was brought about either by the draining of silver to India during the wars of Mahmud of Ghazna[24] or by its export to Russia in payment for furs. The rulers of Baghdad and those in other provinces tried from time to time to restore the coinage of silver dirhams but, to judge from the pieces preserved in numismatic collections, they encountered almost insurmountable difficulties. The reports in the chronicles of this period, contrary to those of the preceding period, mention almost exclusively payments in gold. Taxes and fines were paid in dinars, and the army received its pay in gold.[25] But it would be erroneous to believe that with the shortage of silver the old monetary stability had been re-established.

For a great change had occurred in the monetary system of Irak in the middle of the tenth century. Whereas at all times the stability of the gold currency had been a striking feature of the economy of the Moslem empire and moreover the basis of its prosperity, in the middle of the tenth century there was a forced debasement of the dinar. The chroniclers tell us that when the army clamoured for payment the princes had to break up their gold and silver vessels and hand over the metal to the mints.[26] But the mints were short of reserves and all the efforts to maintain the standard of the currency were in vain. Until the middle of the tenth century the standard of fineness of the dinars struck in Irak had been on the average 94–95%. In the second half of the tenth

century and in the first half of the eleventh century a great number of
the dinars had less than 90% gold. A. S. Ehrenkreutz arrived at the
following conclusions:[27]

*Standard of fineness of Iraki dinars before the middle
of the tenth century*

al-Mutamid	a. 872	94%
	a. 875	96%
	a. 877	96%
al-Mutadid	a. 901	90%
al-Muktadir	a. 917	85%
	a. 919	90%
ar-Radi	a. 938	97%
	a. 940	94%
Nasir ad-daula	a. 942	97%
	a. 942	94%
	a. 942	95%

The debasement of the Iraki dinars in the second half of the tenth
century is also very conspicuous if their standard is compared with those
struck in Syria in the tenth century.

Standard of fineness of Iraki and Syrian dinars

	below 90%	90%	91%	92%	93%	94%	95%	96%	97%	98%	99%	100%
Iraki after 946	7	1			1							
Syrian 891– 969	2	1	1	2	4	1	2	2	1			

The periods from which these Iraki and Syrian dinars date are not
congruous, but that does not impair the significance of the comparison
since the gold standard of coins struck in Syria after 969 was undoubtedly even higher. For its mints disposed then of greater quan-

tities of Sudanese gold. Arabic writers explain the debasement of the dinars which began at the middle of the tenth century in Irak and South-western Persia by the dishonesty of minters such as Ibn Kardam, farmer of the mint in al-Ahwaz.[28] But that is the medieval way of interpreting a phenomenon of economic life which was produced by objective causes and had far-reaching consequences.

b) *Buyid feudalism*

When the régime of the caliphs was on the verge of the abyss, a last attempt was made to save it by appointing the commander-in-chief of the army head of the civil administration, so that his jurisdiction should extend to the taxation and administration of all provinces. But the competition for this post soon resulted in civil war, and ten years after the first 'Amir al-umara' had been appointed Persian *condottieri*, hailing from Dailam, a borderland of the Caspian Sea, occupied Baghdad (in 946) and established the rule of their family over the central provinces of the caliphate. The rule of the dynasty of the Buyids (or Buwaihids) lasted 110 years and extended over Irak, Media, Khuzistan, Fars, Kirman and Oman. During their reign these countries were never united under the sceptre of one prince, although the rulers of the various provinces, at least in the tenth century, recognised the suzerainty of the oldest and most powerful member of the family. The Buyids did not even divide the countries which they had conquered so that certain branches of their family should reign over parts of their dominions. Time and again they redivided them according to political circumstances, the dynastic history of Irak and South-western Persia in that period thus becoming very complicated. The Buyids were Shiites, but ruled in the name of the orthodox caliphs and tried to keep up their empire.

Their reign meant the absolute supremacy of the army and the decline of the bourgeoisie. The princes of this dynasty, the first of whom in Irak was Muizz ad-daula (946–67), exercised full authority over all branches of the administration. They began to encroach upon the activities in which the bourgeoisie had been engaged without interference for many generations. It seems that the bourgeois no longer had full scope in commerce and in industry. The merchants suffered from the extortions of governors and the rank and file of the army. New taxes and arbitrary contributions diminished their profits, and woe to the banker or rich merchant who refused to grant a loan

to a prince. Worst of all, the military engaged themselves in commercial activities. They invested in them their pay, which had been a
charge upon certain districts, and enjoyed the privilege of carrying
their merchandise along the roads duty-free. Needless to say, that was
of great detriment to the merchants.[29] An attempt made by the greatest
of the Buyid princes, Adud ad-daula (who reigned from 949 in Fars
and from 978 to 983 also in Khuzistan and Irak), is most characteristic
of the new tendencies which were to become the maxims of the feudal
princes in the Near East. An Arabic historian narrates how this prince
instituted monopolies of manufactures such as silk 'of which the
manufacture and sale had previously been free to everyone'.[30] Even if
the Buyid government had later to abolish this monopoly, the measures
taken by Adud ad-daula were portentous. He had embarked on a new
policy which was contrary to the principles to which the preceding
rulers had adhered.

The troops of the first Buyids who had won fame in Persia as great
generals consisted of their fellow-countrymen, the Dailamites. But
already Muizz ad-daula had recruited many Turks, and his commander-
in-chief was the Turk Sebuktekin. Under the reign of Adud ad-daula
the Dailamites were still predominant, but the power of the Turkish
troops was steadily increasing and under the late Buyids they were the
mainstay of the régime. They were indeed indispensable, since they
formed the cavalry regiments, whereas the Dailamites were mostly
infantrymen. It goes without saying that the rivalry between the
Dailamites and the Turks caused the Buyids great difficulties. Frequently it brought about brawls and sometimes it degenerated into
civil war.[31] The troops of the Buyids, however, very often acted in
harmony against their princes when they were claiming an increase
of their pay or additional payment. The chronicles of the Buyid reign
comprise an almost interminable list of mutinies motivated by the
demands of the troops. Sometimes they revolted during a campaign,
sometimes they plundered the capital, not even refraining from
pillaging the palace of the prince.

The Buyid dominions in Irak and Western Persia being torn by civil
war and endless mutinies, powerful Bedouin clans, chiefs of influential
Arab and Kurdish families or even *condottieri* succeeded in setting up
as princes in various parts of Mesopotamia and the neighbouring
regions. The chieftains of the Banu Ukail, a strong Arab tribe, became,
at the end of the tenth century, the rulers of Upper Mesopotamia and
a great part of Northern Irak. One branch of this family ruled over the

districts of Mosul, Nasibin, ar-Rahba, Ana, Haditha, Hit, al-Anbar, Ukbara, Dakuka and sometimes even over Kufa, al-Madain and Kasr Ibn Hubaira. Another had its seat in Takrit. The Ukailids were still true Bedouin, living in tents, but when they became a princely family they recruited Dailamite and other mercenaries.[32] The chiefs of the Banu Numair, who ruled over Harran, Edessa and ar-Rakka, were another Bedouin dynasty. Much more powerful were the Kurdish Marwanids, whose dominions comprised at the end of the tenth century the provinces of Diyar Bakr and Mayyafarikin. In the districts on the middle Euphrates the Banu Khafadja, a strong Bedouin tribe, had the upper hand. Sometimes they were on good terms with the Buyid government, and their chiefs were appointed to the posts of governors, sometimes they sacked the towns in that region. South of the Banu Khafadja the Banu Mazyad, chieftains of the Banu Asad, established their rule over a region stretching as far as Kufa and made al-Hilla their capital. In South-eastern Irak, on the frontier of Khuzistan, the Banu Dubais had become effectively independent. In the region of the Swamp, which covered in that period a great part of Lower Irak, south and west of Wasit, there were governors in control who were to all intents and purposes independent.

Buyid power in Irak was more and more weakened and the dominions of the dynasty were shrinking, all the more that the rivalry between the princes of the ruling family frequently prevented a vigorous reaction against usurpers. The disobedience of the army, its covetousness and inclination to mutiny endangered the mere existence of their government even more.

Already the first Buyids, being unable to cope with these problems by employing the old methods, were compelled to embark on a new policy, and what emerged from the conditions created by their measures was a new social order, the feudal régime. When the Buyids encountered great difficulty in meeting the demands of their troops, they began to grant them estates instead of paying them in cash. The caliphs had used to grant tithe lands and estates against a fixed sum to be paid every year, regardless of the acreage or the size of the crop. The Buyids handed over the estates only for a certain period in order to provide the military with a livelihood by enabling them to collect their pay at the source. In spite of the fact that these estates were not tithe land, they were called *ikta* like the other kind of grants, i.e. of tithe land, which were given for ever. The Moslem jurisconsults distinguish, however, between the old *ikta* and the new ones, calling the first *ikta tamlik* (grant of possession) and the second *ikta istighlal* (grant of usufruct). It was indeed not the possession that was ceded, but the fiscal rights of the state over lands subject to kharadj. The grantee had no financial obligations whatsoever towards the state, and the officials of the government had no right of control on the spot. A striking feature of the new system of land tenure was the frequent changes in the estates given to the military. The real purpose of these changes was to prevent a close connection being formed between the grantee and his estate.[33] This was indeed a basic idea of the Turkish feudalism, and feudalism was introduced in the Near East by the Turks. Under their influence the new system was established everywhere. The idea of an army of mercenaries was alien to them, as is clearly stated in a passage of the great historical work of al-Masudi where he says that among all Oriental dynasties only the Khazars have a regularly paid army.[34] He probably meant to say that the Khazar khagans alone had not established the feudal system, for in his time mercenaries formed an integral part of all Near Eastern armies.

It goes without saying that the frequent changes in the estates had catastrophic consequences for agriculture. The grantees, who lived in the towns and knew that ere long the estates would be taken from them or that they themselves would ask for a change, did not look after their maintenance. They neglected the irrigation system, the dams and canals, and wrought havoc on the estates. There can be no doubt that this basic principle of Oriental feudalism was one of the major reasons for the economic decay of the Near East. The holding of a big area as the common property of a tribe or clan was a principle which proved most pernicious to Near Eastern agriculture, whose productivity depended upon the upkeep of a complicated irrigation system. But Turkish feudalism did not adapt itself to local conditions.

The prejudicial consequences of the new system of land tenure were perceptible from the day when it was established. The chronicler Miskawaih has left us a colourful description of the phenomenon. He narrates how the grantees farmed the estates with slaves and factors, kept no accounts of profits and losses and did nothing to further productiveness and improvement. The irrigation system was damaged and the peasants left the villages. When the revenue of the estates had diminished considerably, the grantees applied to the government to get others. The authorities charged with the furtherance of husbandry gave up their task when most of the estates in their districts had been given as fiefs to the military. They restricted their duties to calculating what was needed for this purpose and imposing the implementation on the fiefholders, who declined to pay for it.[35] The Buyid government could not ignore the damage done. Sometimes the princes gave special instructions to the governors to attend to the condition of agriculture, but more often they themselves gave orders to repair the neglected canals.[36]

The frequent changes of fiefs were one of the most characteristic features distinguishing Oriental from Western feudalism. The minor importance of fealty was another. The origins of the two systems were indeed completely different, and this basic difference had a decisive influence on their later development. Whereas European feudalism sprang up from personal dependence and subordination, the Oriental form of feudalism was a means of securing regular payment of the soldiery. In Western Europe the grant of fiefs was a subsequent, secondary phenomenon; in the Near East it was a primary one. Therefore the Oriental knights owed allegiance to the sultan himself, and the decentralisation and decomposition of the state was prevented. This was indeed the aim of the Moslem statesmen who outlined the principles of Oriental feudalism, and it may be said that it was to a great extent achieved. In the first age of Oriental feudalism the fiefholders, who got their estates from the government directly, had no liabilities to other, higher-ranking, feudal lords. Although knights belonging to the lower ranks committed their fiefs to powerful lords against a fee to be deducted from the income, there did not develop the hierarchy so characteristic of Western feudalism.

The role of the feudal régime in the history of the Near East was in other respects too very different from that of Western feudalism. Whereas the feudal régime in Western Europe was the concomitant of a contracting economy sunk to the lowest ebb of primitive self-sufficient economic units, the feudal régime in the Near East was established in a period of a declining but highly developed pre-capitalistic society, which was characterised by a punctilious division of labour. In some countries the economy was still flourishing. Furthermore the new régime in the Near East was introduced from abroad. Marx and Engels have maintained that feudalism was shaped by the productive forces of the countries where it was established. But here we have an example of a régime superimposed on a pre-capitalistic economy on which its effect was utterly pernicious.

Notwithstanding the great difference, the development of Oriental feudalism was similar to that of Western feudalism in various respects.

The fiefholders were also appointed governors of the districts where they had their estates (or vice-versa, the governor of a district was granted fiefs belonging to it), so that the judicial and financial authorities were united. Furthermore the clear distinction between the governorship and the financial administration, i.e. the levying or more correctly the farming of the taxes, which had been a basic principle of the caliphal government, was abolished. The two tasks were given to the same person. In most districts high-ranking officers held the position of tax-farmer-governor.[37] The civilians were ousted from this field of economic activity, which had previously for the high bourgeoisie been one of the most profitable.

The high officers obtained fiefs which yielded very great revenues. Muizz ad-daula granted fiefs yielding 50,000 dinars a year. The average revenue of a knight would have amounted to 1,000–1,250 dinars a year, a commander having from 1,300 to 2,000. The rich fiefholders also acquired estates, and in that way built up extensive latifundia. Lower ranks had fiefs in 997 which yielded no more than 10 dinars a month. These were, however, unusually small. For the Turkish soldiers who were patronised by Muizz ad-daula and were sent in 958 to collect the taxes of various districts allowed to them got as a provisional payment 20–40 dinars a month.[38] So there emerged a feudal aristocracy which appropriated the greatest part of the national income.[39]

The victory of the feudal system was, however, not yet complete. Not all the arable land had been given to the army as fiefs and not all the army had fiefs. Through the Buyid reign a great part of the army received its pay in cash.[40] On the other hand, the feudal system, as established by the Buyids, served as a model for most Near Eastern states. In course of time it was introduced almost everywhere, first in the neighbouring principalities in Upper Mesopotamia. So we read in the chronicles that the chiefs of the Ukailid clan had fiefs.[41]

The condition of the peasantry became very similar to that of its European counterparts. Theoretically the fiefholder had no judicial authority over the peasants, but in fact his position made him the patron in all respects. The peasants needed protection more than ever, as the pressure of the land-hungry Bedouin, keen to get arable land, became even stronger.[42] The land-tax, being amalgamated with the rent, was collected by the feudal lord. Many peasants surrendered their estates to them in order to redeem themselves from ever-growing extortions and new taxes, and became simple tenants. The estates of others who could not pay the high taxes were taken away by the fiefholders.[43] So the peasants, with the exception of freeholders in the districts near the big towns, were reduced to the same servile status as the peasants in medieval Europe. The régime of the feudal landlords had been established.

c) *Social unrest*

The new régime met strong resistance however in various sectors of the population. The opposition was directed against all the princes who had replaced the caliphs and who personified the new order. The princes who reigned in the second half of the tenth and in the first half of the eleventh century over Irak, Upper Mesopotamia and Northern Syria had armies consisting partly or wholly of foreigners or at least of Bedouin. Between their subjects and these armies there was sharp antagonism. The military were disliked for national reasons, and the fact that the greatest part of the taxes was destined for their maintenance increased the animosity.

The bourgeoisie, which was visibly losing ground, adopted a hostile attitude towards the new rulers, and when the circumstances seemed to be propitious it was always inclined to revolt. Everywhere its striking forces were the militia of the young people, called *ahdath*.[44] The chroniclers' accounts of the frequent riots and the revolts of some towns shed light also on the contrast between the upper and lower classes of the townspeople. The rich merchants were often more inclined to submit to the princes, notwithstanding the heavy taxes and extortions, than to endure the terror of proletarian rebellion.

In the second half of the tenth century and at the beginning of the eleventh there were revolts in several towns of Upper Mesopotamia and Northern Syria in which the higher strata of the bourgeoisie took the lead. In 963 the inhabitants of Harran revolted against the Hamdanid Hibatallah b. Nasir ad-daula, whose officers had brought them to despair by their tyranny and especially by compelling them to buy government stocks at arbitrarily fixed prices. When Hibatallah laid siege to the town they defended themselves valiantly, but later they made peace with Saif ad-daula, the suzerain of the Hamdanid dominions, who made them some concessions. The chronicler who tells us this story goes on to say that thereupon a group of proletarian rebels left the town. This account reveals clearly the contrast between the various classes: when the rich merchants had obtained concessions from Saif ad-daula, they submitted to him and had no regard for the proletarians

BLACK SEA

MEDITERRANEAN SEA

ARAXES

Malatiya
Amid
Mayyafarikin
Edessa
Dara
Harran
Nasibin
Balad
Aleppo
Sindjar
Mosul
Adhrama
Irbil
Antioch
Djabala
Tripoli
Hamath
ar-Rahba
Djubail
Hims
EUPHRATES
Saida
Takrit
Tyre
Ukbara
Bakub
Acre
al-Anbar
Nahi
Tiberias
Falludja
BAG
Damascus
Kasr Ibn Hubaira
al-Hilla
an-N
Damietta
Ascalon
Ramla
Kufa
Rashid
Gaza
Jerusalem
al
Alexandria
al-Farama
Tinnis
Cairo
Bilbais
Fayyum
Fostat
Bahnasa
Eilat
Ushmunain

TIGRIS

FATIMID
CALIPHATE

NILE

HIDJAZ

Ku

Assuan

Yanbu
Medina

RED SEA

Djidda

Mecca

Sana

⚬⚬⚬ ▬▬▬ ⚬⚬⚬ SAMANIDS

⚬⚬⚬ ▬▬ ⚬⚬⚬ BUYIDS

▬▬▬▬▬▬ HAMDANIDS

▬●▬●▬● FATIMIDS

0   100   200   300 MILES

BAER

THE NEAR EAST
AT THE END OF THE 10th CENTURY

who had fought with them. But some months later they supported Hibatallah against Saif ad-daula, and had to atone for it by a heavy contribution. The town was then left without a governor, and the chronicler mentions that the proletarian rebels came back and seized power.[45]

The revolt which broke out in 965 in Antioch was undoubtedly fomented by the upper bourgeoisie. Its leader was a rich tax-farmer, Muhammad b. Ahmad (or Hasan) Ibn al-Ahwazi. With the help of Rashik an-Nasimi, an officer, he rose against the governor, when Saif ad-daula was stricken with hemiplegia and was far away in Mayya-farikin. The upper classes of the townspeople sided with him, the revolt succeeded and the governor had to leave the town. Thereupon Ibn al-Ahwazi recruited some thousand mercenaries and addressed himself to the Byzantines, offering them a yearly tribute, if they would protect the rebellious town. The bourgeois families which were most influential in the town, such as the Ibn Manik, Ibn Diama and Ibn Muhammad, supported Ibn al-Ahwazi unhesitatingly, whereas the lower people, opposed to the betrayal of Islam, did it only grudgingly. Ibn al-Ahwazi tried to appease them by forging a letter of the caliph which contained the appointment of Rashik to the governorship of Northern Syria. Then the rebels set out to conquer Aleppo, the capital of Saif ad-daula. The troops which were sent against them deserted and at the end of October 965 they entered Aleppo. The governor, however, held the citadel, and after a siege of three months the rebels were compelled to retreat and Rashik, their commander, was killed. But they soon recovered. By squeezing the middle and lower classes they collected enough money to equip another campaign. A Dailamite officer, Dizbiri, was appointed commander, and Ibn al-Ahwazi recognised an Alid as suzerain. What really mattered for the leaders of the revolt was to establish the rule of a bourgeois oligarchy; the allegiance sworn to an overlord seemed to be quite secondary – he could be a Byzantine emperor, the Abbasid caliph or even an Alid pretender. In May 966 the rebels once more took Aleppo, but after pitched battles they had to give it up again. Yet they cherished hopes of imposing their rule on the whole of Northern Syria by enlisting the help of strong Bedouin tribes. The Banu Kilab, indeed, joined them, and some towns – Hims was one – paid them tribute. However in the meantime Saif ad-daula returned and crushed them in a battle near Aleppo. The partisans of Ibn al-Ahwazi were severely punished, many being executed and others heavily fined.[46]

In spite of their defeat and the subsequent suppression of the rebels of Antioch, the townspeople of Northern Syria shortly afterwards attempted to revolt once more against their rulers. It seems that in 967 or at the beginning of 968 the inhabitants of Tripoli rose against their governor because of his tyranny and expelled him from the town. When the mighty and energetic Saif ad-daula died in February 967 the malcontents hoped that the odds were in their favour. The people of Antioch revolted again, solemnly took the decision that no Hamdanid should ever be allowed to enter the town, and appointed themselves a governor.[47]

The rebellion spread to the towns of Upper Mesopotamia, where various dynasties were struggling for every district and town. In 982 the inhabitants of Nasibin rose against their governor and killed him. The revolt of ar-Rahba in 1009 which involved several potentates sheds light on the attitude and tactics of the upper classes. The town of ar-Rahba was a bone of contention between the Ukailids of Mosul and the Egyptians. Ibn Muhkan, a rich bourgeois, who had the support of a strong party, seized power there in 1009 after he had allied himself to the chieftain of the Banu Kilab, Salih b. Mirdas. An Arabic historian says that Ibn Muhkan courted the Bedouin chief, because 'he needed backing'. Some time later discord broke out between them and the Banu Kilab besieged ar-Rahba, but finally peace was made. Thereupon Ibn Muhkan subdued Ana, another town on the Euphrates. When the inhabitants of Ana rose against him, Ibn Muhkan undertook, together with Salih b. Mirdas, a campaign against the town, but the Bedouin chief used the occasion to kill him by treachery. Then he occupied ar-Rahba and confiscated the riches of Ibn Muhkan.[48] So the alliance of the rich bourgeois with the Bedouin had proved disastrous.

The bourgeois revolts were only sporadic outbreaks of discontent, but they endangered the rule of the new dynasts in several regions. The subversive activities of another class were continuous and troublesome, but less dangerous. The chronicles of the tenth and eleventh centuries contain long accounts of the activities of the so-called ayyarun, groups of proletarians who terrorised the towns of Irak during the reign of the Buyids.

The ayyarun, who are also called 'robbers' or 'brigands',[49] were more a phenomenon of social life than a revolutionary movement. They were proletarians without employment or regular income, living outside the society. But were they all simple robbers, as depicted by Arabic court historians and even by modern scholars who are influenced by them? It is true that many of them had no other aim. But we must beware of regarding the ayyarun as one monolithic group or even as an organised movement. There were undoubtedly many different and heterogeneous elements in this 'lumpenproletariat'. Many of them were eager to earn something by serving any who would pay them. Groups of ayyarun served both the orthodox Moslems and the Shiites, the two religious parties which carried on an endless contest in Baghdad and other towns of Irak. Others were happy when the authorities enlisted them in the police or as guards in the caliph's palaces. These were called 'ayyarun who repented'. Needless to say that the ayyarun were always ready to serve as auxiliary troops when civil war broke out; they did so in 945 and in 975.[50] But mostly they made a living from robbery, and the pages of the chronicles contain long accounts of their mischief: they plunder the residential quarters, break into the warehouses of the rich cloth merchants and set fire to them. Since thefts and burglary are their main activities, they carry on a stubborn fight against the police. They attack its chiefs, and demand from the government the disavowal of police captains who relentlessly persecute them and are sometimes so threatening that they retire or flee from Baghdad. The repression of the ayyarun by the police is cruel: they are hanged and drowned.[51]

Among the various groups of ayyarun there were, however, some who were influenced by the idea of the *fityan*, the freemasonic lodges of young people cultivating friendship and altruism. Apparently some of their leaders conceived the idea of establishing a new society. Disavowing the hypocritical régime of the lawful orthodox Moslem state, they opposed to its social injustice and its extortions the virtues of champions fighting for the poor and oppressed against the establishment. Their aim is a more moral society, unencumbered by the conventional lies of the old régime. Since they contest the morality of the establishment and even hold it in contempt, they no longer recognise rules laid down and sanctified by age-long tradition, and they despise Islam, the backbone of society. They publicly drink wine in the month of Ramadan. Being mostly illiterate, they probably did not write down their ideas, but unless certain groups of ayyarun are credited with such aims it is difficult to understand why people belonging to the highest strata of society supported them. Abbasids who later became caliphs, ruling princes and governors were connected with them.[52] Some of their leaders are described by the chroniclers as perfect gentlemen who never robbed the poor. That is how they describe Ibn Hamdi, who was their leader in the fifth decade of the tenth century, Aswad az-zabad, who was at the head of the ayyarun thirty years later, and al-Burdjumi, who won a great reputation in the years 1029–34. This latter chief of the ayyarun was a friend of the governor of Ukbara, that is to say he was on good terms with the ruling circles. Whereas the Arabic historians usually disparage the ayyarun, they extol the courage and faithfulness of al-Burdjumi. These were the typical virtues of the *fityan*. Characteristically enough he is called a *fata*! Ayyarun like these are said to have expressed their regret at being compelled to be robbers and to have severely criticised the injustice of the government, whose extortions according to them were worse and more immoral than robbery. These noble robbers never attacked a woman and were renowned for their chivalry.[53] The tales of the Arabic authors about these chiefs of the ayyarun remind us of the stories about Robin Hood and Candelas.

Some leaders of the ayyarun did not content themselves with this role. When the conditions seemed favourable, they tried to set up as authorities in some sectors of trade. Promising protection and security, a group of ayyarun would demand a fee (*khafara*) from the people living in a quarter or possibly from the shopkeepers of a market. Some chiefs of the ayyarun made a further step towards establishing their authority, collecting from some markets the taxes which were usually imposed on them, as was done by their chief Aziz in 994 and forty years later by al-Burdjumi.[54] So their aim was to get a part of the taxes levied by the government, so that the poor whom they represented should have a share of the wealth accumulated by the ruling classes. This was indeed the purpose of social revolutions in the medieval Near East.

One would like to know whether the ayyarun intended the overthrow of the régime and, secondly, whether they had any chance of achieving it. The accounts of their activities suggest on the whole a negative answer to both questions. According to these accounts the gangs of ayyarun mostly did not number more than some thirty to fifty men. They seldom attacked a whole quarter or fought with a corps of the army.[55] Only when the government was weak and anarchy prevailed did they become a force to be reckoned with. They were very active in the years preceding the establishment of Buyid rule, then in the years 972–5, under the reign of the incapable prince Bakhtiyar, and later when strife between Sunnites and Shiites in Baghdad resulted in street fighting and battles between various quarters, as in 990–1, 994, 1002–3, 1007, 1017, 1025–37 and 1049–53, or when the people rose against the army or at times of exceptional dearth. But when the government recovered, the ayyarun left the big towns or went into hiding.

Their great weakness was that they never had the solid backing of any class of the population. Their activities were usually directed indiscriminately against rich and poor as would be guessed from the fact that many of them were simply criminals. Therefore the people protested against the indolence of the government or even attacked them, just as it fought against the foreign mercenaries and the Bedouin. The merchants and craftsmen wanted to get rid of these troublesome elements.[56]

There is good reason to believe that the merchants and craftsmen who opposed the ayyarun were not an amorphous mass. Probably they had their associations, if not recognised unions or guilds. The development of these organisations has been connected with the propaganda of the Karmatians. Since the chroniclers are completely silent about the life of these classes of the population, contenting themselves with long accounts of the wars between Turkish and Dailamite generals, we are reduced to conjecture, which easily arouses opposition.[57] It is, however, a fact which cannot be denied that such organisations existed in the later middle ages, although their character must have undergone many changes. Whereas for a long period they were probably in control of the crafts or at least exercised great authority over their activities, they were later, when the feudal lords had established their rule over all sectors of public life, no more than workmen's clubs concerned with social activity or mutual help. So it is *a priori* very probable that the authority of the unions of craftsmen was at its peak when the power of the central governments was at a low ebb. On the other hand, there was a conspicuous change in the character of the Karmatian movement in the second half of the tenth century. It was no longer characterised by frantic hatred of orthodox Islam; the rulers of Bahrain had made peace with the government of Baghdad. So we may assume that the propaganda which they carried on among the craftsmen no longer met the opposition which Ismaili fanaticism and their alliance with the Bedouin had aroused before. Probably the groups of craftsmen and workers which had sided with them in the towns of Irak grew considerably under the reign of the Buyids. The attitude which the Ismailis adopted towards the crafts was favourable, in contrast to the mistrust and scorn of manual work shown by the orthodox theologians. The 'Letters of the Pure Brethren', an encyclopaedia composed by Ismaili circles in Basra and Baghdad in the tenth century, extolled the merits of the crafts. The authors of this encyclopaedia included in it a special treatise on the crafts in which they explained the importance for the welfare of the human society. Among the crafts which they praise there are weavers, tanners and well-diggers, who were held in contempt in the Oriental world from time immemorial.[58] Here is indirect evidence of the relationship between Ismaili propaganda and the development of the workmen's unions in the Near East. The propagandists of the Ismaili sect were instructed to dwell on the merits of the crafts, partly because of the sincere conviction of the leaders of the movement, partly in order to win the support of the craftsmen.

However that may be, the growth and prospects of the craft guilds were from the outset very different in the Near East from their counterparts in Europe, and since the feudal lords lived in the towns the possibility of their seizing power was decidedly limited.

d) *Bourgeois ascendancy under the Fatimids*

Whereas Irak lost the political hegemony of the Moslem world, Egypt became in the second half of the tenth century the seat of a strong and ambitious dynasty of Shiite caliphs who had already imposed their rule on the whole of North Africa. This dynasty, the so-called Fatimids, claimed to be the only lawful heirs of Mohammed, being the offspring of his daughter Fatima. The establishment of their rule was the outcome of the successful propaganda of Ismaili emissaries through several generations. It was the achievement of a religious movement, but many scholars have been misled by the interpretation of it given by medieval writers. The activities of the Ismaili emissaries alone cannot explain how this dynasty overran half of the Moslem world and built up so powerful an empire. The Ismaili propaganda of the Fatimids was the superstructure. Their real power depended on their alliance with a strong sector of the Egyptian population whose interests were linked to their rule. Nobody would deny the importance of the Ismaili propaganda in an environment so deeply religious as the Near East was in that age, and it would be erroneous to overlook the true aims of the Fatimids, but it seems that their strength was due to the support of the bourgeoisie.

Having conquered Egypt in 969, the Fatimids succeeded in the same year in annexing Syria to their dominions. North Syria remained under their sway until 1023, Southern Syria until the eighth decade of the

eleventh century, Palestine until the first Crusade. A little while after
the conquest of Egypt the Fatimids established their rule also over
the borderlands of the Red Sea, and sometimes even the princes of
Upper Mesopotamia recognised them as their suzerains. The golden
prime of their reign lasted 80 years, until the middle of the eleventh
century. In 1047 the Zirids, whom the Fatimids had appointed vassal
rulers of Tunisia, shook off their suzerainty, and not only North Africa
but also Sicily was lost to the caliphs of Cairo. But in Egypt they
maintained themselves for two centuries.

As with all Moslem dynasties the rule of the Fatimids was founded
upon a strong army. The army which invaded Egypt is said to have
numbered 100,000 men, and even in later times the Fatimids could
equip armies of some tens of thousands. The problems which they
encountered in recruiting and maintaining their army were the same
as those of the Abbasid caliphs. The army which conquered Egypt
consisted of Berbers, Kitama and Masmuda, for example, but already
under the caliph al-Aziz (975–96) many Turks were recruited and there
were also many Dailamites, Arabs from Barca and others, Slavs and
Negroes. Under al-Hakim (996–1021) the Berbers were still the most
powerful of the various nationalities represented in the army, but
under his successor az-Zahir the Turks supplanted them. When Tunisia
split away from the Fatimid caliphate, the recruiting of Berbers became
difficult and the Negroes became, apart from the Turks, the strongest
element in the army. They were infantrymen, whereas the Berbers
and Turks were horsemen. As usual, the rivalry between the various
contingents was strong, and already at the end of the tenth century
there were brawls between the Maghrebin and Turkish regiments.
The Fatimid military were paid in cash and estates, the officers acquiring
great wealth. But the rank and file were never satisfied and in times of
distress they made a living from pillaging.[59]

In order to defray the great expenses of the splendid court and the
army, the Fatimids had to increase considerably the taxes levied by
their predecessors and to impose new ones. The management of the
financial administration was the business of the Copts, who enjoyed the
favour of the Shiite caliphs. These Christian officials more or less
monopolised the various 'diwans', and some of them rose to the
highest posts, like Isa b. Nestorius, who became vizier under al-Aziz.
There can be no doubt that the favourable attitude of the Shiite
caliphs towards the Copts arose from their distrust of their orthodox

subjects. But the Christian officials represented also an important sector of the Egyptian bourgeoisie.

There were other bourgeois groups which derived great advantages from the system upon which the Fatimids built up their régime. As the Abbasids had done before, the Shiite caliphs of Cairo farmed out the land-tax and other taxes against a fixed sum. The surplus revenue was the profit of the farmers. An analogous institution was the bestowal of estates (*ikta*), which were granted to private undertakers by public auction against a sum comprising the rent and the taxes. Under the first Fatimids the allotment of these estates was for four years and everybody could make his offer in the public auction.[60] A striking feature of the Fatimid régime was freedom of enterprise. All sectors of economic life were free – crafts, industry and trade. The government interfered in the trade in victuals only so far as it had to in order to guarantee the supply of wheat to the big towns.

The Egyptian bourgeoisie enjoyed also the great prosperity which was produced, among other reasons, by the inflationary system of Fatimid economy. There is no reason to doubt the truth of the accounts of Arabic writers concerning the great quantities of gold which the Fatimids brought to Egypt. According to them the Fatimids possessed amounts of gold dinars unheard of and had acquired fabulous riches. As the first Fatimid caliphs of Cairo were in control of all the trade routes to Ghana, that Alaska of the middle ages, we can believe the statement that al-Muizz, the first Fatimid caliph of Egypt, came there with 500 camels bearing gold and other riches.[61] But even at the time when they had lost control over the North African coast, their mints disposed of great quantities of gold and could strike dinars the fineness of which was almost 100%. For the trans-Saharan trade routes remained open to them. The heavy strain upon the caliphs of Cairo at the beginning of the twelfth century led to a temporary debasement of the gold currency, but the caliph al-Amir (1101-30) overcame the shortage of gold and raised the fineness of the dinar once more to its old standard. So the purity of the dinar was one of the striking features of Egypt's economy down to the end of Fatimid rule. We should, perhaps, not too easily accept that they were always handled by numbers and not weight, a supposition which would be contradicted by many geniza documents, the specimens preserved in various collections testify to the maintenance of fixed weight standards. A. S. Ehrenkreutz, examining a great number of Fatimid dinars, found that about 70% weigh from 4.06 to 4.3 g. It seems that the standard was fixed under al-Aziz at 4.128 g, under al-Hakim at 4.188 g, and under al-Mustansir at 4.229 g. The dinars of al-Amir point to a standard of 4.186 g.[62]

Fineness of dinars of the later Fatimids

	under 90 %	90 %	91 %	92 %	93 %	94 %	95 %	96 %	97 %	98 %	99 %	100 %
al-Mustali (1094–1101)	1						1			1		4
al-Amir (1101–30)	10	1	2		1	3		8	3	9	8	40
al-Hafiz (1130–49)										1	2	22
az-Zafir (1149–54)												8
al-Faiz (1154–60)												2
al-Adid (1160–71)	1					1			1			1

Weight standard of Fatimid dinars
all figures in g

	3.5–3.6	3.6–3.7	3.7–3.8	3.8–3.9	3.9–4.0	4.0–4.1	4.1–4.2	4.2–4.25
al-Muizz				2	4	10	16	1
al-Aziz			1		2	4	31	
al-Hakim		2			2	3	36	5
al-Mustansir		1	2	9	12	18	38	24
al-Mustali					4	2	2	2
al-Amir	2	3	1	8	7	11	28	13
al-Hafiz		1	1	3	5	3	9	5
az-Zafir	1	1			1	4		
al-Faiz					1	3	1	1
al-Adid		1			2		2	1

The maintenance of a gold dinar being almost pure and of full weight was only possible because Egypt steadily received considerable quantities of gold from the Western Sudan, which must have been a strong stimulus for an expanding economy, for the rise in the prices of various goods and for the setting up of new enterprises. The great shortage of pure silver dirhams which was felt during the Fatimid reign in Egypt, as in other Near Eastern countries, did not check this trend.

Another major factor in the remarkable buoyancy of Egypt's economy in the Fatimid period and the enrichment of the bourgeois was the great development of its international trade.

Under the Fatimids the Red Sea supplanted the Persian Gulf as the main trade route from India to the Mediterranean. This change was brought about by various factors. Siraf, the great port of the Persian Gulf, declined after being destroyed by an earthquake, the robbery of the Shabankara deterred traders from visiting its shores, and the exactions of the rulers of the island of Kish had the same consequence. At the same time the iron curtain between the Moslem world and Southern Europe was removed by the enterprising and trustful Italian merchant republics, which based their economy on overseas trade. The Italian traders preferred to obtain Indian products in the emporia of Egypt and Syria, instead of visiting the distant and unsafe shores of the Persian Gulf. The Fatimids perceived the great advantages of increasing their countries' share in international trade, and made efforts to promote the change in the trade routes, i.e. to divert the Indian trade from the Persian Gulf to the Red Sea. For the Shiite caliphs this was not only an economic interest. Aiming at the establishment of their rule over the whole of the Moslem world, they hoped also to bolster up their politico-religious propaganda by their commercial relations. Missionaries followed the traders, and it is certainly not mere chance that the followers of the Ismaili sect in North-western India are called Bohora, meaning merchants. The great flourishing of Egypt's Indian trade was also connected however with a very important scientific advance – the use of the magnetic needle. According to the present state of research there is good reason to believe that Arab seafarers began to use it in the eleventh century.[63]

Aidhab, a small town on the Red Sea, became a great commercial port under the Fatimids and Kus, where the caravans coming thence arrived at the Nile, began to flourish. The Italian merchants regularly visited Alexandria and Damietta, and Tripoli and Antioch.[64] There began the close commercial relations between the Christian traders of Southern Europe and the Near Eastern countries which remained for four hundred years the main artery of international trade.

The merchants of Amalfi, Venice and Genoa were foremost among these Christian traders who came to the ports of Egypt and Syria. According to the account of a Christian Arabic writer there were not less than 160 Amalfitans in Cairo in 996. Even if the medieval author confused Amalfitans with other Italians, the number is impressive. The activities of the Amalfitans in Jerusalem in the seventh decade of the eleventh century, when they rebuilt an old hospice and a Latin church, testify too to their commercial relations with Syria. In 991 Venice sent embassies to the rulers of all the Moslem countries bordering on the Mediterranean. The Venetians carried on a very lively trade between Alexandria and Constantinople and, in the twelfth century, between the ports of Syria and Palestine held by the Crusaders and the seaports of Egypt. Genoa too was very active in the Levantine trade in the century preceding the first Crusade. An English pilgrim narrates how in 1065 a Genoese fleet came to Jaffa after having called at the Syrian ports and exchanged merchandise brought from the west. The Judaeo-Arabic geniza fragments too contain various references to the visits of Genoese traders in Alexandria and Cairo in the same period. By the end of the tenth century merchants of Bari and of Sicily visited the Near Eastern emporia, whereas the Pisans became prominent in the Levantine trade in the twelfth century. These commercial relations between Italy and the Fatimid dominions were continually increasing. The acts of the Genoese notary Giovanni Scriba disclose almost a hundred of his compatriots engaged in the trade with Alexandria in the years 1156–64.[65]

We know from European and Arabic sources the articles imported into Egypt and Syria by the Christian traders. They brought cloth, furs and timber, and metals, such as iron, copper, lead and tin, which were badly needed in the Near East, and even arms, armour and slaves.[66] The historians of the Levantine trade have dwelt on the policy of the Fatimids and their successors, who did their utmost to encourage European traders and to increase the import of the articles which they offered. The Judaeo-Arabic documents which have been discovered in the Cairo geniza enable us at the same time to gauge the great change which Egypt's Indian trade underwent in the Fatimid period, in both its content and its character. The many hundreds of documents referring to this trade, which date mostly from the eleventh century, show clearly that the spices – pepper, ginger, myrobalan, cinnamon cloves and others – and, secondly, dyes, such as brazilwood and gum-lac, supplanted the expensive perfumes which had been the main articles of the India trade in the days of the Abbasid caliphs. The spices were destined for mass consumption and consequently were cheaper, which means that the volume of the trade increased. The Europeans also began to acquire some products of the Near East which they needed for their developing industries, e.g. Syrian cotton and Egyptian alum.

Further, the geniza documents prove convincingly that in the Fatimid period many traders belonging to the middle class were active in the Indian trade. Merchants with only a small amount of capital went into partnership with others, that is to say they invested a certain amount by the commenda contract. Copper, lead and textiles were exported to India[67] in order to obtain in exchange a certain quantity of spices or other products.[68] Since the government did not monopolise the great Indian trade, either directly or indirectly, and freedom of enterprise prevailed, various classes of the bourgeoisie, exactly as in the Italian merchant republics, could take a share in international trade and enrich themselves. So from the economic point of view the Fatimid period was the golden age of the bourgeoisie. In fact, the government monopolised only those articles whose acquisition was indispensable for its military activities, such as iron, timber and pitch. These articles, when imported into Egypt, had to be delivered to the government's agents.

Similar conclusions will be drawn from the hundreds or perhaps thousands of geniza documents relating to the seaborne trade between Egypt and the Moslem West. Even this very lively trade remained free, and was not monopolised either by the state or by powerful companies of great capitalists. Although the Fatimid caliphs and other rulers participated in the Mediterranean trade, building and owning ships,[69] many hundreds and thousands of small traders commuted between the ports of Tunisia, Sicily and Egypt. S. D. Goitein has concluded from thousands of geniza documents he has studied that the value of goods exchanged between overseas traders in one season amounted on the average only to some hundred dinars.[70]

The main routes of the trade between the Moslem countries of the Mediterranean basin were those connecting Egypt with Sicily and Tunisia and Spain with Sicily and Tunisia. So Sicily and Tunisia were at the centre of a great network of commercial relations. Sicily also exported its own products, such as silk and silk fabrics.[71] From Spain and Tunisia precious silk was imported into Egypt, from Tunisia olive oil and soap. The articles which Egypt exported to the Moslem West were mainly spices and other Indian products and, secondly, raw flax.[72]

The great success of the merchants engaged in all these branches of international trade expressed itself in a strong consciousness of being an important group. Reading the *Merchants' Guide* written in the middle of the eleventh century by Abu l-Fadl ad-Dimishki, one becomes aware of the pride of the merchants in Fatimid times.[73]

The prosperity of various branches of industry was one of the most important of economic phenomena in Fatimid Egypt. The great luxury of the court, the needs of a big army, the construction of a war fleet, and last but not least the great development of Egypt's international trade with the opening of new markets, all these factors promoted the expansion of its industries. Those which existed in Egypt of old increased in volume and developed new branches, while others came into existence in this period. New methods were invented, old ones improved, or those employed in other centres successfully imitated, often by attracting foreign workmen. This prosperity must be at least partly explained by the economic policy of the Fatimid caliphs. They adhered to the principle of freedom of enterprise, and although they maintained royal factories, they abstained from establishing industrial monopolies.[74] A rich class of industrialists succeeded, in spite of heavy taxation, in building up new enterprises and conquering new markets for their products.

The textile industry enjoyed considerable prosperity. In the geniza documents there appear new centres of the linen industry, such as Katta and Munya (Munyat al-Khasib, Minyat Ghamr, or Minyat Zifta).[75] The industrial centres of Egypt began to produce articles which had been peculiar to other towns or regions. Tinnis and Dabik produced percale, Munya exported its dabiki. Egypt began to manufacture silk cloth, such as brocades imitated from the Byzantine fabrics in Tinnis and in Damietta,[76] and Tabaristan fabrics were imitated in Cairo and Ramla (in Palestine), whereas the Armenian type of manufacture was practised in Asyut.[77] The attabi cloth of Baghdad was copied in Damascus.[78] The new fashions introduced by the Fatimid court were a strong stimulus to the textile industry. Arabic authors narrate how at the end of the tenth century there began in the industrial centres of Lower Egypt the manufacture of turbans of sharb, a precious linen fabric embroidered with gold threads which were worth 500 dinars each. The availability of raw materials from other regions was another reason for the expansion of industry, for the states which had supplanted the Abbasid caliphate did not forbid their export. The gold threads were at least partly imported from Irak, and dyes came from Persia, such as the very expensive saffron grown in Media, or crimson from Armenia. The boom in Egypt's textile industry in the Fatimid period must have been conspicuous if the geographer al-Mukaddasi, a shrewd observer, could speak of Tinnis as 'Baghdad the lesser'.[79]

Most medieval writers dwell on the prosperous state of Egypt's textile industry under the Fatimids. But the development of other industries was not less considerable, although their products were not so expensive. The sugar industry undoubtedly became an important sector of Egypt's economy in the eleventh century. There is good reason to believe that the methods of refining the juice of the sugar cane were improved in the numerous sugar plants which existed in that period in many towns and villages of Egypt. The use of natron and alum, two rare materials found in the country, for the purification of various substances, such as honey, was known to the Egyptians of old. When the growing of sugar cane became common in the Nile valley, they apparently used these methods for the production of candy and, secondly, learnt to refine the sugar instead of repeated boiling by drawing off the mother-lye which remains between the crystals or even by separating it artificially (the so-called 'covering'). The fact that cube sugar became known in the Far East as 'Misri' (Egyptian) and Marco Polo's explicit report about the use of vegeto-alkali by Egyptian sugar refiners leave no doubt about that achievement. The use of purifying alkalis was the great innovation made in the Egyptian sugar plants. As long as only milk was used for refining the sugar, as mentioned in the long account of an-Nuwairi, the yield was only $\frac{5}{12}$, the rest being molasses.[80] Certainly the methods of refining the sugar juice were the result of long and patient experiments in the sugar plants, which were run by rich industrialists. The sugar industry in Egypt and in Syria under the Fatimids had indeed a capitalist character. The complicated methods of refining the juice of the sugar cane could only be employed in big factories. The geniza documents indicating the price of sugar plants show that they were big factories. Rich and enterprising industrialists had to make costly efforts to improve methods, the expected profits being the stimulus. Sugar production also enjoyed freedom of enterprise. The attempt to monopolise it made by the odd and whimsical caliph al-Hakim was not repeated. The same is true for the paper industry, which began to flourish after the extinction of papyrus production, both in Egypt and in Syria. The excellent paper of Damascus, Tripoli, Tiberias, Fostat and other towns was produced in capitalist enterprises.[81]

All these industries supplied not only the ever-increasing demands of the local market, but produced to a great extent for export to other countries. The profits of the industrialists must have been considerable. But the glowing accounts of the economic prosperity of Fatimid Egypt given by medieval writers should not mislead us. The data concerning the level of prices which are embodied in the geniza documents indicate that industrial products were still very expensive, whereas the real income of the workers was very low. As far as the economic situation of the working masses is concerned, these dusty documents contradict medieval and modern authors who describe the Fatimid reign as a happy period of Egypt's history. It was the golden prime of the bourgeois classes, but the workers were worse off than at any time before (or even after). That is the somewhat surprising

Prices		Wages (monthly)	
	dinars		*dinars*
garments for men:			
gown for poor	$\frac{1}{3}$–$\frac{1}{2}$	servant in academy of	
jacket of wool	0.4–0.5	al-Hakim a. 1005	1–1.25
overcoat of wool	0.5–1	servant in Azhar mosque	
average turban	2.5–3	a. 1010	1–1.29
garments for women:		water-carrier a. 1040	0.72
simple gown	1–2	water-carrier a. 1100	1.4
elegant gown	3–4	water-carrier, no date	1.04
simple ghilala dress	$1\frac{1}{2}$	journeyman mason	2.5
elegant ghilala dress	4	master mason	3–5
simple djukaniyya overcoat	$\frac{1}{2}$		
elegant djukaniyya overcoat	1–3		
simple mantle (mala)	1		
elegant mantle	3–4		
turban	2–3		

conclusion we must draw from the figures in the accounts of the geniza and in some reports of Arabic writers.

The table opposite sums up the data concerning prices of cloth in Fatimid Egypt, contrasted with the wages of unskilled and skilled workers. [82]

Many hundreds of inventories of dowries which have been found in the Cairo geniza bear out that ladies of the middle or lower bourgeoisie possessed many precious garments. Our table shows, on the other hand, that the workers could not afford to buy good cloth.

The situation of the workers had also deteriorated as far as the food basket is concerned. The quantity of staple food which workers could afford in the tenth century was considerably more limited than those which their forefathers could buy in the days of the caliphs. Their plight in the eleventh century was still worse. The following table comprises data concerning the nominal and the real wages of unskilled labour in Egypt. [83]

	Nominal wages	Real wages		
		bread	mutton	olive oil
beginning of eighth century	0.6 dinar	888 ratls	17.3 kg	30 kg
beginning of ninth century	0.75 dinar			
beginning of tenth century	1.00 dinar	454 ratls		
beginning of eleventh cent.	1.2 dinars	324 ratls	26.6 kg	43 kg

Although the quantities of mutton and olive oil which these workers could buy had increased owing to the insignificant rise in their prices, their dietary was much worse than before. For the quantity of meat they could afford was very limited, since they had to spend on bread the greatest part of their expenditure on food. [84] Skilled workers were better off, but suffered from compulsory employment. The Persian traveller Nasiri Khosrau, who was an enthusiastic admirer of the Shiite caliphs of Cairo, surely exaggerated when he contrasted the freedom of workers in the Fatimid dominions with the forced labour employed in the royal workshops of other Moslem countries. Once more the geniza documents contradict the literary sources. A geniza letter, written in Damascus around the turn of the tenth and eleventh centuries, reveals that weavers were forced to work in the caliphal workshops and that there was a special office to recruit artisans for this purpose. Further, we may infer from this document that work in these manufactures was very hard.[85]

That the Fatimid authorities had recourse to compulsory employment can easily be explained by the difficulty of meeting the requirements of the court. The deterioration of the economic situation of unskilled workers, on the other hand, was the result of the surplus of labour. The population of Egypt continued to increase at the end of the tenth and in the first half of the eleventh century. It is even very probable that the growth of the population was more conspicuous in that period than before. The upkeep of a big army and the supply of a splendid court provided work for many thousands of workers and artisans, and profitable jobs for various kinds of businessmen. The number of consumers who had to be supplied and fed greatly increased. A scholar who has made a thorough research into the history of Cairo has concluded that before the arrival of the Fatimids it had no more than 100,000 inhabitants. In the eleventh century, according to his calculations, the city reached the number of 300,000 inhabitants.[86] The great development of international trade had probably increased the population of the coastal towns, such as Alexandria and Damietta. Economic prosperity also attracted Bedouin tribes, some of them very numerous, to settle in the Nile valley. Other tribes, as the Banu Hilal and the Banu Sulaim, were forcibly settled in Egypt by the Fatimid caliphs in order to deprive their enemies in Syria of warlike allies. But more important than immigration, surely, was the natural growth of the population as a result of the general prosperity. The increase of the population is reflected in the steady rise of grain prices. That this cannot have been merely an inflationary phenomenon, i.e. a consequence of the influx of great quantities of Sudanese gold put into circulation by the first Fatimids, is proved by their fluctuation from the end of the eleventh century when Egypt still had a stable gold currency. The rise of the average price of wheat at the end of the tenth and in the first half of the eleventh century was continuous. Whereas 100 kg cost apparently 0.7–0.8 dinar at the beginning of the reign of the Fatimids, the price rose to 1 dinar at the beginning of the eleventh century.[87] The contrary movement of grain prices and minimum wages indicates clearly the progressive deterioration of the situation of the workers.

The prosperity of the bourgeois classes and the distress of the working masses had an outlet in various political movements – civil disobedience and resistance, revolts and civil war. The accounts of the medieval authors, unreliable and biased as they are, leave no doubt that in the flourishing period of the Fatimid empire the bourgeoisie sided always and everywhere with the caliphal government. But the other classes opposed it, in both Egypt and Syria.

The story of the conquest of Egypt by the Fatimids exemplifies the attitudes of the different classes. The final onslaught of the Fatimids on Egypt was made when, after the death of the efficient Ikhshidid ruler Kafur, the peasants had ceased to pay the land-tax and had begun to attack units of the army. An Arabic chronicler says that thereupon the 'notables' of Fostat, i.e. the leaders of the bourgeoisie, wrote to the Fatimids and asked them to occupy Egypt.[88]

Revolutionary tendencies were, however, much stronger in Syria. This difference may be attributed to the greater pliability of the Egyptians, but certainly it was also the reaction to the economic decline of Syria under Fatimid rule. This country had a lesser share in the economic prosperity brought about by the Fatimids, it benefited much less than Egypt from the shift of the trade routes and its silk industry apparently declined. So there must have been unemployment and great discontent. The ahdath, the town militia, was everywhere inclined to revolt against the Fatimid governors and to support other rebels.

The revolt which broke out in Tyre in 997 was a revolutionary movement of the lower classes, its leader being a sailor, al-Allaka. The political situation was seemingly propitious. There was a Bedouin outbreak in Palestine and the Byzantines had invaded Northern Syria. So the ahdath of Tyre, with al-Allaka at their head, rose against the Fatimids and the town constituted itself an independent republic, striking coins of its own. The rebels appealed to the Byzantines for help, but the flotilla sent by the emperor was defeated by the Fatimid navy. The caliphal troops which besieged the town addressed themselves to the upper classes of the townspeople, which promptly abandoned al-Allaka. Tyre fell in June 998, al-Allaka and his partisans were brought to Cairo and cruelly executed.[89]

The chroniclers' accounts of the vicissitudes of Damascus in the last third of the tenth century shed light on the great role of the ahdath, who fought stubbornly against the Fatimid governors. Undoubtedly they represented the lower classes of the townspeople, the crafts and the petty merchants, all of them bitterly hostile to the Fatimids. The upper classes called 'mashayikh' or 'akhyar' (or 'ayan', 'ashraf', 'shuyukh', all these appellations corresponding to the *majores* and *boni homines* of the Christian West) also suffered from the arrogance and exactions of the Maghrebin authorities and sometimes they made common cause with the ahdath, but mostly they were ready to come to terms with the Fatimid governors. Notwithstanding the burdensome taxation they had to bear, they preferred security and the normal course of trade and commerce to the excesses of the unruly proletarian town guards.

The bitter struggle between the ahdath and the Fatimid army began immediately after the conquest of Southern Syria by the Maghrebins. In 969 the ahdath had fought against the Fatimid army, but the rich bourgeois betrayed them and made peace with the conquerors. Then the ahdath rose against the Maghrebin garrison, which had committed acts of robbery and violence. The fighting between the ahdath and the Maghrebins went on throughout 974, and the town was rent by the hatred and the mutual fear of ahdath, bourgeois and Fatimid troops; whole quarters were set on fire. When in 975 the Turkish general Alptekin came to Syria, the leaders of the bourgeoisie offered him rule over Damascus so that he should protect them from the Egyptians and, on the other hand, from the ahdath, who terrorised them even more. Alptekin fulfilled their hopes and restored order. In 977, however, he was defeated by the Egyptians and taken prisoner, whereupon his officer Kassam al-Harithi took over. This Kassam had been a worker, a ditcher transporting on his asses' backs the earth he had excavated. Later he became the commander of the ahdath of Damascus, and characteristically enough the Arabic chroniclers call him – ayyar. When the Fatimids had subdued the Bedouin in Palestine his rule over Damascus was overthrown. As soon as their troops approached the town, the leaders of the upper classes split away from the ruling party and came to terms with the Egyptians. In July 982 the Fatimids were once more in control of Damascus, which had been independent for seven years. The bourgeois rejoiced, but they were soon utterly deceived by the heavy taxes imposed on the town and other measures taken by the Fatimid authorities. A year later the ahdath rose again and reestablished their power. Then a new governor, Bakdjur, attacked them, killing many, and thus secured his authority. Apparently the ahdath had to give in and keep quiet until the end of the reign of the caliph al-Aziz. After his death the inhabitants of Damascus revolted once more, in 997, and the governor was compelled to flee. At the beginning the upper classes took part in the revolt, but then they were thrust aside by the ahdath, whose leader was 'ad-Duhaikin' – a nickname indicating his proletarian origin. The revolutionary activities of the ahdath of Damascus came to an end, however, at least for some time, when in 999 the governor Djaish b. Samsama put to death 1,200 (or according to other reports 3,000) of them and imposed a heavy contribution on the town.[90]

The first Fatimids also had to fight another group of rebels who vigorously contested the hegemony of the ruling classes. These rebels were the powerful Bedouin tribes of Egypt and Syria. Most of them were apparently still true nomads who made a living from raising sheep, transporting goods or protecting caravans, and serving as auxiliary troops in the caliphal army. They were rich clans whose intelligent and ambitious leaders sought to substitute their own rule for that of the Fatimid caliphate. Their revolts were not the rising of exploited proletarians, but a struggle between classes belonging to the upper strata of society. In Egypt the provinces of al-Buhaira and the Said were strongholds of the Bedouin, in Syria they were particularly powerful in the province of Aleppo, and in Palestine, where they had castles of their own.

In the eighth decade of the tenth century al-Mufarridj b. Daghfal Ibn Djarrah, the chieftain of the Banu Tayy, was effectively the ruler of Southern Palestine. He was in control of Ramla, its capital, and his men could do any mischief without being punished. But in 980 the Fatimid caliph al-Aziz sent against him an army which put an end to his rule. However, al-Mufarridj, who fled to Northern Syria, came back after some years to lead another rising, sacked the villages of Southern Palestine and besieged Ramla. But after the suppression of the revolt of Tyre he had to submit.[91]

The reigns of the caliphs al-Hakim and az-Zahir were the most stormy. In both Egypt and Syria there were Bedouin revolts which brought the Fatimid caliphate to the verge of ruin. In 1005 Abu Rakwa, a foreign impostor, forged a powerful coalition of Berber and Arab tribes of Barca and Lower Egypt. Under his leadership the Berber tribes of Lawata and Mazata and the Arab Banu Kurra brought most provinces of Egypt under their control, and according to an account which is very characteristic of their designs they agreed upon the future partition of the Fatimid dominions: the Banu Kurra should rule over Egypt, their allies over Syria. In 1006 their revolt was, however, quelled by al-Hakim.[92]

Meanwhile the Banu Tayy had once more revolted in Palestine and occupied Ramla, then a rich commercial town. In the year 1000 the Fatimid governor of Damascus expelled Hassan, son of Mufarridj, from Ramla and took the tribe's castles in the district of ash-Sharat. But the ambitious Hassan, whose aim was the establishment of independent rule over Palestine, again rose and occupied Ramla once more. In order to legitimate his rule, in 1010 he appointed the sharif of Mecca (the descendant of Mohammed ruling over the holy towns of Hidjaz), Abu l-Futuh al-Hasan, caliph, invited him to live with him in Palestine, whereupon most provinces of Syria recognised him. The Banu Tayy defeated an army of the Fatimids and took the Egyptian general prisoner. At the same time the Banu Kilab, the strongest tribe in Northern Syria, conquered Aleppo. But two years later Hassan changed his mind, accepted al-Hakim's offer of a great sum of money, and sent the anti-caliph back to Mecca.[93]

It was in the reign of az-Zahir that the chiefs of the Syrian Bedouin made the greatest onslaught of the Fatimid caliphate. It was a well-concerted, general revolt aiming at the overthrow of Fatimid rule over Syria. In 1023 the most powerful tribes made an alliance, dividing among them the regions to be conquered and ruled by them. The Banu Tayy should have Palestine, the Banu Kilab Northern Syria and Sinan b. Alyan, a chieftain in Central Syria, the province of Damascus. Hassan b. al-Mufarridj, the chieftain of the Banu Tayy, indeed occupied Ramla, and Salih b. Mirdas, the chief of the Banu Kilab, conquered Aleppo and the whole of Northern Syria, from Baalbek to Ana on the Euphrates. His descendants held Aleppo, with short interruptions, until 1079. Temporary restorations of Fatimid rule were unsuccessful, since the ahdath sided with the Mirdasids and steadfastly withstood the Egyptian troops. Even in Palestine Hassan b. al-Mufarridj, after a crushing defeat sustained in 1029, re-established his rule in 1042.[94]

At about the same time, in the middle of the eleventh century, the flourishing period of the Fatimid caliphate ended. In the reign of the weak al-Mustansir (1036–94) rivalry between the Turkish and the Sudanese troops resulted in heavy fighting. The Negroes were several times expelled from Cairo and terrorised Upper Egypt, and the Turks exacted money from the caliph or plundered the capital. The Lawata Berbers occupied the coast. Then a terrible famine, caused by a low Nile, lasted seven years, from 1066 to 1072. It brought about an economic and social catastrophe. There followed a restoration when the Armenian general Badr al-Djamali was appointed vizier and commander-in-chief in 1073. But the crisis under al-Mustansir had far-reaching consequences.

During the long years of famine and civil war many peasants left

their villages and went to live in the towns.[95] Probably most of them
fell victims to the famine, and agricultural production diminished
through the abandonment of cultivation. It seems that this crisis was
a turning-point in the demographic history of Egypt. After many
centuries of growth, there began a contrary trend which was thereafter the most important phenomenon of its social history – depopulation. In the last third of the eleventh century grain prices were still
high, 100 kg of wheat amounting on an average to 1.79 dinar, against
1 dinar at the beginning of the century. This must mean that the profits
of the merchants were as high as before and that the prosperity of the
bourgeois classes was maintained. The volume of the great Indian
trade even increased after the end of the eleventh century, when commercial relations with the Italian merchant republics became closer,
owing to the establishment of many Italian traders in the towns
conquered by the Crusaders. But grain prices went down in the twelfth
century. In the year 1111 another epidemic took a heavy toll from
Egypt's population. Probably the average price of 100 kg was once
more 1 dinar as at the beginning of the eleventh century. Minimum
wages, on the other hand, began to rise. An unskilled worker probably
received 1.5 dinar a month, which means 405 ratls of bread.[96] These
data, conjectural as they are, indicate that a downward trend prevailed
in the demographic development of Egypt.

However, the natural fertility of Egypt's soil, its flourishing textile
industry and its foreign trade enabled Badr al-Djamali and his son and
successor al-Afdal to build up once more a very efficient administration.
The data which we find in various sources concerning the tax revenues
of the later Fatimids testify to this fact.

The revenue from the land-tax remained remarkably constant,
amounting to 3 m dinars on the average. The much higher amount

Tax revenue of Egypt under the Fatimids[97]

969	*3.4 m dinars
971	*3.2 m dinars
972	4 m dinars
996–1021	3.4 m dinars
1074	*2.8 m dinars
1090	*3.1 m dinars
1094–1121	5 m dinars

listed for the period of al-Afdal refers probably to the value of the military fiefs, calculated in fictitious units, the real income being about 20% less.[98]

Nevertheless a great change had occurred. The decrease of the population was so marked that the government united administrative units, creating bigger districts. Instead of 50–70 *kuras*, the country was divided into 26 *amal*. The structure of the Fatimid government itself was altered in that the hold of the military became much stronger. They replaced the civilians as tax-farmers and what had happened in Irak 100 years before now happened in Egypt. The villages farmed to the military became fiefs, the farmer paying less and less until the government gave up the attempt to exact sums due to it and handed the estates over to them as military fiefs. Whereas before they had been farmed for seven years, they were leased for thirty years in this later period of Fatimid reign.[99] The condition of the peasantry deteriorated more and more. The peasants were ground down with taxes. The land-tax had been considerably increased (or even doubled) by the first Fatimids, and under the later caliphs of the dynasty it became even more burdensome, as many peasants had left the villages.[100]

The way was paved for the establishment of the feudal régime.

CHAPTER VI

Feudal Knights and Bourgeois

The map of the Near East in the period of the Crusades was a very chequered one. The variety of dynasties, whether ruling over great kingdoms or small principalities, is really bewildering. Arabic chroniclers concentrate more than ever on the contests and vicissitudes of those princes, while the part played by the urban and rural classes is hardly alluded to. To extricate it from the lengthy accounts of the Oriental historians is the task of the modern scholar. Such an analysis will modify, to a certain extent, the generally accepted idea that the successive invasions of the Fertile Crescent by nomadic peoples from Central Asia were the decisive factor in its decay. Moreover, it may help us to find a solution of the main problem of Oriental history in the middle ages, namely the reason for the decay of Moslem power and of the once brilliant Arabic civilisation.

a) *The empire of the Seldjukids*

The migratory movement of the Turks and their establishment in the lands in and around the Fertile Crescent was certainly a major event in the history of Western Asia. In successive waves tens of thousands of Turkish tribesmen invaded Persia and thence Irak, Asia Minor and Syria. It was one of the greatest migrations in history and among other results it brought about the foundation of a new Moslem empire, that of the Seldjukids.

The migration of the Ghuzz tribes into Eastern Persia began in the third decade of the eleventh century, when many groups of these warlike Turks crossed the Oxus. A little while afterwards they began to raid all provinces of Persia and even Adherbeidjan and Upper Mesopotamia. When the news of their exploits spread in Central Asia new hordes joined them, so that in the course of some years several districts of Irak were fully occupied by them. The second wave of Turkish migration was connected with the establishment of the two brothers

Toghril Beg and Caghri Beg in Khurasan. They were grandsons of Seldjuk b. Dukak, a chieftain of the Kinik, a Ghuzz tribe, who at the end of the tenth century lived in the district of Djend, east of Khwarizm, and had become a Moslem. Toghril and Caghri came in about 1035 to Khurasan and settled near Nasa and Merw. The negotiations between them and the Ghaznewid sultan Masud for the peaceful settlement of the Turkish tribes in North-east Persia failed. Heavy fighting ensued and the Seldjukids began to invade every part of Iran and the adjacent countries. It was a series of splendid victories. In 1037 they captured Merw, in 1038 Nishnpur. An imperial army of the Ghaznewids was crushed in 1036, and in 1040 Masud himself was defeated at Dandan-akan. After this battle Khorasan was lost to the Seldjukids and there followed the invasion of Djurdjan, Tabaristan and Upper Mesopotamia.

Detailed as the reports about this great migratory movement are, the data to be found in the Arabic sources as to the composition of the Turkish invaders are few. The chroniclers mention the Döger, who settled in the provinces of Hulwan and Diyar Bakr and the Salghar, who lived later in Fars, Adherbeidjan and Kurdistan. Various tribes belonging to the Ivai established themselves in Adherbeidjan, Armenia and Upper Mesopotamia. The Yaruk, who played later a great role in Northern Syria, were one of these Turcoman tribes. The Avshar settled in Asia Minor, as did the Navuki, who also invaded parts of Syria.[1] It goes without saying that the details we have about the settlement of the Turkish tribes are even more scanty. The medieval authors describe the raids of great hosts, but there was probably, at the same time, a slow and continuous infiltration of small groups.

The campaigns of the two brothers Toghril and Caghri were not simple razzias, but real waves of conquest, and, in the course of some years, they changed the political map of Western Asia. In 1042-3 they conquered all that had remained of Khurasan; then Toghril Beg occupied most provinces of Media, and in 1047 it was the turn of Kirman and in 1054 of Adherbeidjan. There is good reason to believe that the great successes of the Seldjukids were partly due to the favourable attitude or even active help of the sunni theologians and other staunch supporters of Moslem orthodoxy. For from the beginning of the Seldjukids' career they appeared as supporters of orthodoxy and of the Abbasid caliphate, which could not vie with the strength of the shia and Ismaili movement. When Toghril Beg captured Baghdad in 1055, the caliph, liberated from the protectorship of the Shiite Buyids, seemed relieved and formally recognised him as the worldly ruler of all the Moslem countries. This solemn act had great historical significance: it sealed the alliance between the Arab caliph and the Turkish sultan, who represented the two classes – the native theologians and the Turkish officers. The new Seldjukid empire, born in 1055, was indeed based on the collaboration of these two classes, as were all the Moslem states which succeeded it in the Near East.

The establishment of Seldjukid rule was the final success of the Turkish army in the struggle for power in the Near East. The armies of the first Seldjukids were much greater than those of their predecessors, the standing army numbering 40,000 men, and forces mustered for an expedition swelling to much more than 100,000, most of them Turks. The commanders must have been very able generals. So the reign of the first Seldjukids was a succession of great military achievements. After the death of Toghril Beg, in 1063, Alp Arslan, son of his brother, became Great Sultan. During his reign there began the invasion of Syria, Armenia and Asia Minor. In 1071 Alp Arslan won a great victory over the Byzantines in the battle of Malazgerd and took prisoner the Byzantine emperor. This battle marked the beginning of Turkish rule in Asia Minor and indeed of the establishment of the Turks in that country, ever since known as Turkey. The reign of Malikshah, son and successor of Alp Arslan (1072–92), was the apogee of Seldjukid power. While Malikshah undertook great campaigns in Transoxiana, the conquest of the countries of the Near East made great progress. In 1076 Damascus was taken by the Seldjukids, in 1082 Aleppo (which was finally annexed to their empire in 1085), in Asia Minor one province after the other fell to them, and in 1089 even South Arabia recognised their rule. So at the death of Malikshah the empire of the Seldjukids stretched from the environs of Constantinople to the frontiers of China and from Aden to the Jaxartes. These great conquests were the achievements not only of the armies and their generals. To a great extent they were made possible by the very efficient administration built up by the able Persian vizier Nizam al-mulk. The first Seldjukid sultans apparently had great revenues and disposed of considerable sums in cash.[2] But, on the other hand, their empire remained a loose confederation of semi-independent kingdoms and autonomous tribes. In some regions of the Near East the Seldjukids left the ruling princes in their places as vassals, like the Mazyadids in Southern Irak and certain branches of the Ukailids in Upper Mesopotamia. In some countries the commanders who had conquered them set themselves up as virtually independent princes. Finally there was almost endless strife within the reigning family, whose members contended for the throne. So from the beginning the mighty empire bore within itself the seeds of dissolution.

Immediately after the death of Malikshah there began a long succession of wars and revolts which resulted in the dismemberment of the empire. When reading the story of these wars in the long chapters of the Arabic chronicles it is sometimes difficult not to lose the thread. According to the medieval writers the personal ambitions of the princes and their generals were the driving force in the dismemberment of the Seldjukid empire, and thus it surely was. All the princes of the royal family felt that they were entitled to the throne, and many generals tried successfully to carve out a principality for themselves. Revolt and the setting up of new principalities were relatively easy in this period because the Turkish migration had supplied the countries of Western Asia with great numbers of warlike young men who readily joined the armies of any who would pay them. The slave-markets were well supplied too. Evidence of these conditions is found in Arabic chronicles' accounts of armies whose numbers increased enormously within a very short time.[3] The Turkish princes could afford to enlist mercenaries and buy military slaves; they did not shrink from extorting great sums of money from their subjects. But the part played by the bourgeois in many insurrections should not be overlooked. Probably the upper bourgeoisie preferred the reign of weak princes, controlling a small territory and disposing of limited means. They rightly believed that these petty dynasts would have recourse to their collaboration, would be dependent on their goodwill and therefore would foster their interests.

The collapse of the Seldjukid empire ensued quite soon, in the generation of Malikshah's sons. From the wars of succession his son Muhammad emerged as the strongest and most able prince. But after his death in 1118 the empire collapsed. The descendants of Muhammad, whose capital was Hamadhan, ruled over Irak and Western Media until 1194, the Seldjukid dynasties in Syria became extinct at the beginning of the twelfth century, though Sindjar, a brother of Muhammad and lord of Khurasan, preserved the suzerainty of the Great Sultan until his death in 1157. The Seldjukid dynasty which had established itself in Kirman reigned till the end of the twelfth century, and that of Asia Minor even a hundred years longer.

The later Seldjukids were princes of quite modest resources. The armies they could mobilise numbered usually 10–15,000 horsemen.[4] So they had to acquiesce in the foundation of new principalities which sprang up in all parts of the Fertile Crescent and the adjacent countries. Kurdish princes ruled over districts of Eastern Irak, the Turkish Urtukids over Diyar Bakr, the Arab Munkidhits over Shaizar in Northern Syria. The most powerful of all these princes were the 'Atabeks', those governors who were appointed as tutors to young princes of the blood and usually supplanted them. One of these dynasties of Atabeks was that founded by Zengi who ruled over Upper Mesopotamia and Northern Syria from 1127 to 1146.

Though the great Seldjukid empire had broken into fragments, the migration of the Turks went on. In the first half of the twelfth century many Turcoman clans settled down in Syria. They lived near Aleppo and Aintab, in the plain of Amk, near Antioch, Harim, Tripoli and elsewhere on the frontiers of the Crusaders' principalities. When peace reigned they lived by sheep-breeding, and when the princes prepared military activities they supplied them with the necessary manpower.[5] At the end of the twelfth century there began a strong migration of Turcomans into Asia Minor, many of them coming from Upper Mesopotamia. It was in this period that some parts of Asia Minor such as Cappadocia became Turkish.

Another major result of the Turkish conquests was the consolidation of Oriental feudalism. It was the great vizier of the first Seldjukids, Nizam al-mulk, who gave the system its final shape and established it in regions where it had not existed before. The accounts of Nizam al-mulk's administration in Oriental chronicles are not very clear, whereas the rules laid down in his *Book of Politics* are something like a definite programme. In any case it seems very probable that he accomplished the amalgamation of the *ikta* – the assignment of the revenue of a certain estate – with the administration of the same area, which was undoubtedly a final step towards the establishment of a feudal régime. However, not all fiefs became also administrative units. Nizam al-mulk used to assign to the knights (sc. the low-ranking) fiefs consisting of estates in different districts. Furthermore, the government did not renounce the supervision of the administration of the fiefs. But, on the other hand, the great fiefs were assigned against the obligation to supply a certain number of horsemen.[6] In view of these different features it is not to be wondered at that scholars have expressed opposite views as to the character of Oriental feudalism, some assimilating it with Western feudalism and others scrupulously avoiding calling it by this name. But undoubtedly different forms of Oriental feudalism should be distinguished, some akin to Western feudalism, others different.

There were two phenomena which distinguished the feudal régime in certain periods of Oriental history from its European counterpart: the fiefs were not inheritable and there was no feudal hierarchy. Nizam al-mulk, indeed, lays down in his *Book of Politics* that every two or three years the fiefs should be changed 'lest the assignees become too securely established and entrenched and begin to cause anxiety'. The principle that a fief is nothing more than a right to an income and that its transformation into an inheritable estate should be prevented by all possible means was surely a basic and original precept of Oriental feudalism. It goes without saying that it proved fateful for the Oriental economy. Fiefholders had no interest in the maintenance and prosperity of their estates. But in certain periods the contrary tendency, namely to make the fiefs inheritable, was stronger. Notwithstanding the admonitions of Nizam al-mulk the fiefs, first and foremost the big ones, became inheritable in the Seldjukid empire and its successor states. This explains the accounts given by some Arabic authors who say that the régime of Nizam al-mulk brought about the prosperity of agriculture. Estates which had been neglected for a long time yielded good returns, since the fiefholders took measures to improve husbandry. Further, it emerges from various texts that the relations between the feudal lords and their vassals on the one hand and the sultan on the other hand were very similar in the Seldjukid empire to the feudal pyramid in medieval Europe. The great lords granted fiefs to knights, who owed them fealty. Although in the feudal chapters the rights and duties of the fiefholders were clearly defined, they have become the intermediates between the sultan and the small fiefholders. Under the rule of weak princes the great feudal lords became semi-independent.[7]

The consolidation of the feudal régime under the first Seldjukids had far-reaching consequences. Although not all the estates liable to the land-tax were allotted as fiefs to the military nobility, many estates remaining allodial property and whole provinces being farmed out to tax-farmers, the government had given up so great a part of its revenues that its financial difficulties were ever-increasing and it had to have recourse to various kinds of extortion. The feudal lords, who tyrannised over their subjects, became a powerful and rich class. Often they did not content themselves with the revenues they had from their estates and various duties, but engaged in trade and commerce and even monopolised it. An Arabic historian relates that Toghtekin, prince of

Yemen, made the great Indian trade a state monopoly. The situation of the peasants continuously deteriorated. Nizam al-mulk was aware of it. He avows in his *Book of Politics* that the peasants, having been impoverished by heavy taxation and extortion, are ruined and dispersed.[8] There is no reason to doubt his veracity.

b) *The civilian classes under the Seldjukids*

There can be no doubt that the feudal régime of the Seldjukids increased the difference between the bourgeois classes. Everywhere in the lands of the Fertile Crescent there was a small class of rich merchants and bankers who were the agents of the viziers and rendered them various services. A Jewish tax-farmer of Basra, Ibn Allan, known for his great wealth, gave Nizam al-mulk a loan of 100,000 dinars. Abu Sad Ibn Simha, also a Jew, fulfilled for a time the tasks of financial adviser and banker for Nizam al-mulk; 'ar-Rais' Abu Tahir Ibn al-Asbaghi acted similarly for his rival Tadj al-mulk. Without such financiers the viziers and governors of provinces could not manage; everywhere they had recourse to their help. But the Arabic chroniclers mention them only incidentally. We read, for instance, in the great chronicle of Ibn al-Athir, that Abu Talib Ibn Kusairat, who died in 1107, was the financial adviser of Djekermish, governor of Mosul. The Arabic author does not omit to emphasise that Abu Talib, a very rich man, belonged to an influential family which in his own days still held a prominent position.[9] Certainly we are not mistaken in conjecturing that these financiers often represented groups of bankers and merchants who shared in their business. The wars of the first Seldjukids, on the other hand, offered to enterprising purveyors possibilities unheard of during the reigns of their predecessors. The wars of Toghril Beg, Alp Arslan and Malikshah, were indeed campaigns on a very great scale, and the quantity of supplies needed was not to be compared with the requirements of the wars of the Buyids. So there can be no doubt that the class of entrepreneurs enriched itself considerably in the second half of the eleventh century.

However, weighing carefully the possibilities open to the rich bourgeois of that period, one arrives at the conclusion that they were more limited than in earlier periods. When the assignment of the land-tax to the military had become the usual way of paying them, the scope of tax-farming was much more limited than before. Further, it seems that new attempts were made by the feudal government to encroach

upon the freedom of industrial enterprise. Once more the production
of precious kinds of silk, such as the siklatun, was made a monopoly.
In 1118 it was abolished, but three years later was once more established.[10] Although this monopoly was in practice a kind of tax, it was
a heavy burden on the producers. Banking, on the other hand, probably
declined because of the shortage of silver money, a phenomenon
which remained a characteristic feature of all Near Eastern economies
throughout the twelfth century. So there was less necessity to change
money and less possibility of speculation on the fluctuation of exchange
rates. The supposition that large-scale business in Seldjukid times was
more limited than before is borne out by the accounts of the fines which
the government imposed from time to time on high dignitaries. The
sums are much lower than the *musadarat* extorted from the viziers and
other high officials in the tenth century. Usually such a fine or the sum
confiscated from a bequest amounted to 30–40,000 dinars, and it
seldom surpassed 100,000 dinars.[11]

The deterioration of the economic situation of the middle and lower
bourgeoisie was undoubtedly one tangible result of the feudal régime
of the Seldjukids. Many of the chroniclers' accounts point to it. One of
the methods employed by the government to obtain money when it
had renounced the revenue from the land-tax (or, indeed, had handed
it over to the military) was the imposition of new taxes collected from
various branches of trade and commerce or the increase of old ones.
Since these taxes, the so-called *mukus*, which are not established by the
Koran, were considered by the Moslem theologians unlawful, many
princes abolished them on certain occasions, mostly upon their accession to the throne. They were, however, re-established some time later,
a fact clearly indicated by the accounts of the chroniclers, who time
and again report their abolition. Certainly these taxes considerably
diminished the profits of the petty merchants and craftsmen. Their
frequent abolition brought relief only for a short time.

In 1087 sultan Malikshah abolished all the *mukus*, tolls and escort
dues in Irak, Khurasan and all the other provinces of his empire. They
had yielded 600,000 dinars a year. The caliph who shared with the
sultan in the government of Baghdad joined him in announcing
solemnly that the *mukus* should no more be collected. But apparently
they were re-established a short time later, for we read in a chronicle
that in 1108 sultan Muhammad once more took the same measures:
he announced the abolition of the *mukus* and tolls in all his provinces.
All these announcements were a sheer farce. The authorities oppressed

the people just as harshly as before by their grievous taxes. This is borne out by the long series of subsequent impositions and repeals of the *mukus*: according to the chroniclers they were imposed again in 1120 by sultan Mahmud, in 1121, when the brokers paid a large sum instead of the brokerage tax amounting to ⅔ of their profit, but some months later repealed altogether. They were, however, once more established and again abolished in 1138, but in 1147 a preacher had to admonish the sultan in a sermon to abolish a grievous commercial tax. The caliph al-Mustandjid repealed, upon his accession in 1160, the dues on sales of horses, camels, sheep, fish, leather and other articles. But a little while afterwards they were once more imposed, since his successor had to abolish them upon his accession in 1170. Most of these reports refer to the *mukus* in Baghdad, but some of them to the repeal of these taxes in the whole of the empire. There were, however, also many local taxes which were periodically abolished and re-established, e.g. in 1102 in Basra, in 1107, in 1170 and again in 1171 in Mosul. Nur ad-din, the pious king of Upper Mesopotamia and Northern Syria (1146–73), abolished all these taxes in his dominions, some of them amounting to as much as the tithe.[12] The great number of texts referring to the *mukus* bears evidence of their importance in the life of the lower bourgeoisie; probably they were in this period a much heavier burden than before.

Besides the *mukus* the merchants and craftsmen suffered very much from other extortions and frequent pillage by the Turkish army. The armies of the Seldjukid princes fighting with each other, the Bedouin of the Mazyadid rulers of Southern Irak and even the retainers of the Seldjukid governors plundered the towns and it goes without saying that the ruthlessness of the military was often disastrous. The countless passages where the chroniclers speak of the tyranny and the cruelty of the Turkish princes leave no doubt about the plight of Oriental townspeople in the Seldjukid age. There must surely have been a general decline of prosperity.

The consequence of misgovernment and poverty was a decrease of population. Various accounts in Arabic sources make it highly probable that the demographic decline was faster in this period than before. It was not an even, invariable regression, but differed in various periods and regions. The invasions of the Ghuzz and the Seldjukid wars of conquest wrought havoc on many provinces of Persia and the Fertile Crescent. It was everywhere a period of troubles and permanent warfare. Arabic authors say that in 1076 the population of Damascus had dwindled from half a million to 3,000. These figures are undoubtedly very much exaggerated, but they are suggestive. The reign of the first great Seldjukids, Alp Arslan and Malikshah, brought no relief. The construction of palaces by the new rulers was more than counterbalanced by the destruction of residential quarters. In the first half of the twelfth century conditions were very bad and the decline of population was resumed. ad-Daskara, east of Baghdad, once a flourishing town, in this period became a village. The reports of the Arabic authors are eloquent. They relate how people left their towns because of the tyranny of the governors and how the towns of Upper Mesopotamia and Northern Syria fell into ruins and were depopulated before the reign of Zengi. The decrease of the populations of Northern Syria at the beginning of the twelfth century must have been considerable. Owing to the imminent danger of occupation by the Franks and the frequent raids of the fighting armies, many people left the towns and villages which had remained in Moslem possession. In Aleppo there remained apparently only a few thousand inhabitants. The princes themselves were aware of these facts. The last great Seldjukid, Sindjar, accused Masud, the Seldjukid prince of Media and Irak, of having brought destruction on his countries. Some princes took measures to check depopulation. Ridwan, prince of Aleppo, sold uninhabited lots at very low prices so that people should build houses there and remain in the town.[13]

The copious information provided by the Arabic chroniclers makes it possible to discern various factors which brought about the decrease of population and the ruin of the towns. A great deal of destruction was done by the earthquakes which afflicted the lands of the Fertile Crescent in that period. It seems that nature joined man in the work of destruction. Earthquakes occurred in Irak in 1118, 1135, 1137, 1143, 1150, 1156, 1178, 1194, 1201 and 1204, and in Syria in 1094, 1114, 1137, 1157, 1170, 1201 and 1204. Some of these earthquakes caused the death of many thousands. At the turn of the eleventh and twelfth centuries there were famines in Irak – in 1099 and in 1108 – and other famines are reported from the years 1118, 1124, 1148 and 1194. But the main reason for the ruin of the towns and the decline of population was misgovernment and neglect of the public services, such as fire-brigades, water supply and scavenging. The consequences were very serious. The chronicles of this period report a great number of fires which destroyed parts of Baghdad. There can be no doubt that the same happened in other towns.

Epidemic and endemic diseases, which spread much more frequently than before, were, however, the most telling factor in depopulation. The accounts of the chroniclers are often ambiguous and they give only scanty details of the disease, but some conclusions can be drawn from their reports.

It seems that there were no outbreaks of bubonic plague or at least the reports of the Arabic historians do not mention it. The plague *stricto sensu*, i.e. the bubonic plague, is called in Arabic *taun*, whereas *waba* means any epidemic. But the chroniclers of this period sometimes report the outbreak of a *taun* and explain that people suffered from other diseases. So we must conclude that most epidemics were not plague, although some possibly were. It is probable that the Arabic authors who speak about plague without mentioning the buboes had in mind pneumonic plague or other diseases, the more so because they are apparently inclined to include in the pestilence many tumours and inflammations, such as meningitis. Some Arabic doctors say, indeed, that there are various kinds of *taun*. It is also a fact well known in epidemiology that often an epidemic begins with relatively light diseases, but at its height there appears actual plague, followed finally by curable though long-term diseases.[14]

Very often the epidemics followed a famine. In 1056–7 there were a famine and a heavy epidemic in Irak, Syria and Egypt, in 1075–6 there was a great inundation in Southern Irak followed by an epidemic, and in the year after there was pestilence in Syria. At the end of the eleventh century a succession of epidemics raged in Irak. According to Ibn Taghribirdi there was an epidemic of plague in 1082. In 1085 there spread in Baghdad and the surrounding districts a bile disease which caused trembling, falling on the face, a stiff neck, pleurisy and headache. The doctors said, according to Arabic chroniclers, that they had never heard of this disease (considering all the symptoms as due to one disease). A man would suffer five or six days and die. In one quarter of Baghdad all the inhabitants died and there were villages where nobody remained. This epidemic, called *taun*, raged also in Khurasan, Syria and Hidjaz. At the same time other diseases spread, such as smallpox, which afflicted the children, quinsy, tumours, diseases of the spleen, and sudden death. Under 1086 the historians once more register the outbreak of the *taun*, but an almost contemporary author says that mostly it was quartan fever with a fatal end. Intermittent fever sometimes appears, however, at the beginning of the plague. There were other epidemics in 1097 in Northern Syria, in 1100 in Irak, following a dearth, in 1105, when smallpox also raged in all the provinces of Irak and in other countries, in 1124, once more following a famine in Baghdad and Lower Mesopotamia, in 1137 in Baghdad, in 1142 in Central Syria, in 1146/47 in Baghdad, when people suffered from swelling of the throat and the victims were so numerous that the corpses were thrown into ditches. In 1149 pleurisy and meningitis (*sirsam*), normally fatal, spread in Baghdad, and under the year 1150 the chronicler Ibn al-Athir registers once more the spread of 'many diseases'. In 1157 various diseases raged in Baghdad, as a consequence of a siege, and among the children smallpox appeared. The plague appeared again in 1163 in Irak and in Syria, while in 1179 an epidemic of meningitis cost many lives in Syria, Upper Mesopotamia and Irak.[15]

The reports which we have quoted leave no doubt that these epidemics were much more frequent and more serious in the age of the Seldjukids than before. Probably the neglect of water conduits and irrigation canals, which became hotbeds of disease-carrying germs, and the general dirtiness were important causes of the deterioration of public health. Famines and wars were at all times followed by epidemics, and in this period they were rather frequent. Malnutrition was certainly a very important factor, particularly perhaps the disequilibrium between the great quantity of sugar which even the lower classes got from dates and the insufficient quantity of proteins obtained from the very scanty portions of meat they could afford. Hypoproteinemia may have weakened the resistance, first and foremost that of children. Calculating the quantities of bread and meat which minimum wage-earners could buy with their monthly wages in that period, we arrive at the following results:[16]

	Monthly wage	Portions of Bread	Meat	Other Expenditure
eleventh century	1.2 din.	60 kg–0.5 din.	8 kg–0.368 din.	0.33 din.
thirteenth century	2 din.	90 kg–0.855 din.	15 kg–0.66 din.	0.485 din.

If such a worker had to maintain a wife and three children, they could have had per diem:

	Calories	Proteins	Carbo- hydrates	Lipides
eleventh century	1087	41	196	14.87
thirteenth century	1682	65	294	26.2

Undernourishment (less than 2,000 calories!) and the lack of balance between carbohydrates and proteins probably made people an easy prey to epidemics. But it is highly probable that even more fatal than epidemics were endemic diseases. It is to these that the chroniclers apprently refer when they say that in a certain year 'there spread many diseases'.

The decrease of population was not only a quantitative decline. It was a permanent bleeding or indeed self-destruction of the ruling class. Reading the Arabic chronicles carefully one becomes aware of the really catastrophic consequences for the Turkish military of drunkenness. Innumerable passages deal with the excessive drinking of the princes and their courtiers. Time and again we are told that a prince died as a consequence of too much drinking or was murdered when he was drunk. A prince who abstained from drinking was considered exceptional. Sometimes whole armies were drunk.[17] Surely the caliphs and other Moslem rulers in former times drank too, but it seems that in this period it became a more general phenomenon, as far as the upper classes, the élite, are concerned. Undoubtedly the Turks had brought the custom of drinking from their homelands in the cold regions of Central Asia. One consequence was probably rather limited procreation.

The disappearance of the Turks, once so numerous in all regions of the Fertile Crescent, seems to prove that the supposition of self-destruction is not a mere conjecture. There is also clear evidence of the general decline of population. The reports of Arabic writers, travellers and geographers may be quoted. Time and again they speak of towns in Irak and Upper Mesopotamia which had fallen in ruins. The Spaniard Ibn Djubair, who travelled in Irak in 1184, says that the greatest part of Western Baghdad, Kufa and Samarra, were then depopulated. Yakut, writing in the third decade of the thirteenth century, laments the decay of Eastern Baghdad, where whole quarters had completely disappeared. Kasr Ibn Hubaira in Southern Irak, Djardjaraya and Djabbul on the Tigris, Kafrtutha and Barkaid in Upper Mesopotamia had in his days become villages, when once they had been populous towns. An Arabic author who served the prince of Northern Syria and Upper Mesopotamia and was sent by him in 1240-1 on a tour of inspection through certain districts of this latter country, reports that in the province of Harran 200 out of 800 villages had been abandoned.[18]

The slow but continuous decline of grain prices is certainly additional and convincing evidence of this phenomenon. The average price of one kurr, the usual measure of grain in Irak (2,925 kg), was in the eleventh century apparently 22 dinars on the average, in the twelfth century 18-20. The price of 100 kg wheat in the eleventh century was 0.75 dinar, in the twelfth century 0.68. In other words, it had fallen from the tenth to the middle of the eleventh century by 45%, and went down by 10% more in the following hundred years.[19] One would be tempted to connect the fall in grain prices with the scarcity of silver dirhams in the Seldjukid period, but the reports of the geographers quoted above induce us to explain this phenomenon by reduced demand, itself a consequence of depopulation. The contemporary chronicler Ibn al-Djauzi and other Arabic authors mention indeed quite often that the prices of grain were low, e.g. in 1066, 1083, 1091, 1102, 1161, 1163, 1165, 1166.[20]

Certainly the curve of grain prices was not the result of a larger supply. When the feudal régime had been consolidated, the condition of the peasantry deteriorated considerably. The chroniclers of Irak relate that they addressed themselves to the government with complaints of oppression by the fiefholders. They did so with good reason. The Seldjukid government imposed new taxes on the estates and in certain provinces changed the methods of assessment: instead of a certain share of the crop (the *mukasama*) fixed rates were collected once more (the so-called *misaha* system). In Southern Syria, on the other hand, the Seldjukids introduced the *mukasama*, but levied higher taxes than were due before according to the old kharadj assessment. Often the Turkish knights took estates from the lawful owners by way of usurpation.[21] In periods of dearth the peasants, having no provisions, left their villages and many of them died from starvation. This happened in 1148 when many peasants fell victims to a famine. In Upper Mesopotamia many peasants abandoned their villages in the reign of Zangi (1127-46) because they could not pay the taxes. In 1126 the caliph complained in a message to sultan Masud of the scarcity of victuals, which was the sequel to the abandonment of the villages.[22]

The flight from the land was, however, not the only reason for the decrease of the cultivated area. Because of neglect or bad maintenance the irrigation system deteriorated in many parts of Irak and probably elsewhere too. The chroniclers relate that the breach of a dam near al-Falludja left the Nile canal without water for four years until it was repaired. Consequently many peasants left the villages. The Nahrawan canal, which irrigated an extensive region east of the Tigris, broke in 1151 owing to a flood. As the water-wheels were made of wood, they were easily damaged by rain and mud, especially when they were not well maintained. This is what Ibn al-Athir reports under the year 1125. Sometimes the destruction of the irrigation system was not due to bad maintenance, but was done purposely by armies on campaign. They broke dams and destroyed water-wheels. Far-sighted rulers kept an eye on the system of irrigation, made tours of inspection and undertook to dig new canals, but they could not check the general decline. What could they do when the campaigning armies had cut down fruit trees, set fire to the crops and destroyed mills?[23] During the age-long wars between the Crusaders and the Moslem princes of Syria and Upper Mesopotamia it became a well-established custom to burn the villages subject to the enemy and to drive away the cattle. The destruction of the countryside sometimes caused an immediate dearth and scarcity of victuals,[24] but this was nothing to the warlike generals. From time to time the princes and their viziers took measures to rebuild the decayed or abandoned villages and to bring back the peasants. Atsiz, the Seldjukid conqueror of Southern Syria, did that in 1076; Toghtekin, the founder of the Atabek dynasty of Damascus, did the same at the beginning of the twelfth century. He sold abandoned lands in order to have them cultivated once more. A Seldjukid governor of Baghdad in the middle of the twelfth century built a village in the area irrigated by the Nahrawan canal, which he had undertaken to repair. He invested in this project for new colonisation the sum of 70,000 dinars.[25] But these undertakings being merely sporadic attempts, there can be no doubt that the cultivated area did not increase. In fact, it became smaller. The immigration of Turcoman tribes to the Fertile Crescent in the wake of the Seldjukid conquerors brought about in some regions a major shift from arable to pasture. That happened in Upper Mesopotamia and elsewhere.

So the fall in grain prices was not the outcome of an increased supply. Further, it should be taken into consideration that the cotton plantations probably increased in this period to a considerable extent, principally in Northern Syria. Various texts in contemporary Arabic sources point to this fact.[26]

The oppression and exploitation of the peasantry, and their exasperation and fury, brought about some revolts. But they were few and not of great momentum. Mostly they assumed the form of religious movements, i.e. heretical sects. Such a revolt took place in Syria in 1175, when a false prophet incited the peasants to rise against the government, first in the province of Damascus and later in that of Aleppo. The radical sect of Ismailis called Batiniya, whose founder had been Hasan-i Sabbah, was the most able group of agitators, carrying on a very efficient propaganda among the lower classes. In the third decade of the twelfth century they aroused among the peasants of Syria a strong revolutionary movement, inciting them against the rich and the rulers in the great towns. But the Batiniya was not a peasant movement, nor even one of the lower classes in general, although Hasan-i Sabbah and his emissaries often addressed themselves to the poor. Notwithstanding the fact that simple craftsmen, such as shoemakers, carpenters and others, appear sometimes as leaders of the Batinites, their attempts to stir up the lower classes were only aimed at bringing about the downfall of orthodox Islam and its social framework – the Seldjukid state. They addressed themselves, at the same time, to other classes and enjoyed the support of viziers and princes. Their religious tenets and their acts of terrorism, such as setting fire to mosques, aroused the hatred of the orthodox masses, by whom from time to time they were massacred.[27]

Class antagonism and discontent in the towns was no less evident. The authorities tried to canalise and supervise it by means of the guilds. In the Seldjukid empire and its successor states these organisations were under the control of the muhtasib, the chief of the market police. But the bitterness and rage of the lower classes resulted sometimes in pillaging and fighting with the army.[28] The most violent expression of the social unrest was given by the ayyarun, whose troublesome activities were never completely discontinued. Even under the firm rule of the first Seldjukids they sometimes collected 'protection fees' in the markets of Baghdad. After the death of Malikshah they became bolder than before, usually at the time of conflicts between the quarters of Baghdad, and the police were often helpless. Their activities were for the most part criminal; they robbed rich and poor alike. During the reign of the energetic sultan Muhammad the authorities succeeded in keeping order, but after his death the ayyarun once more caused great disturbance, committing many acts of robbery in the small towns and villages of Irak and fighting with the police. In the middle of the twelfth century their activities attained a new climax. It seems that through the weakening of the middle classes the harshness of class antagonism was more felt than ever. Probably many desperate and able-bodied men joined them in order to gain a livelihood and to express their feelings of bitterness and frustration. The Arabic chroniclers relate at length their activities in the years 1136–43, a time of civil war which the ayyarun turned to their advantage. They indulged in theft and robbery, attacking the rich and the poor. People of Western Baghdad who hated the Turks sided with them. At the peak of their activities the revolutionary tendency of some groups once more emerged. Highly-placed persons, such as the son of a vizier and a brother-in-law of the sultan, joined them, or at least protected them, either in order to win followers or to express their own discontent with the social order. The ayyarun became a power to reckon with in Irak and their leader Ibn Bukran even planned to mint money in the town of al-Anbar, i.e. to proclaim the ayyarun state. But they were no match for the Turkish feudal forces. Once more the movement of the ayyarun lost its force, although they are still mentioned in the chronicles of the second half of the twelfth century.[29]

c) *Bourgeois resistance*

Whereas the revolts of the peasants and the lumpenproletarians, for such were the ayyarun, were sporadic outbreaks of discontent and doomed to failure, the upper strata of the bourgeois became at certain periods a factor of some power in Oriental politics. When the feudal régime declined, the rich bourgeois tried to take its place and establish their own rule. These classes, mostly merchants and rich landowners, had economic interests opposed to those of the feudal nobility, and when they became aware of the weakness of the princes, they did not hesitate to avail themselves of the opportunity to rise against them. Most revolts took place in Syria, but also in many towns of Upper Mesopotamia and the adjacent provinces of Asia Minor the bourgeois were in control of the government for some time. In order to explain why there were not similar attempts in Irak and Egypt, it has been maintained that the Syrians were more warlike. But it seems that there was also another reason. The partition of the country between various powers and the foundation of small principalities made these revolts much easier than elsewhere.

However that may be, in the second half of the eleventh century and in the first half of the twelfth the bourgeois of Syria and Upper Mesopotamia everywhere aspired to independence, trying to establish urban republics or to camouflage its rule by leaving weak princes in their places as puppets. The character of the movement was different in different regions. On the Syrian coast, where it began about 1070 upon the decline of Fatimid power, its leaders were judges or mayors, who established their own rule as 'consuls' of urban republics. In Central Syria and in Upper Mesopotamia the movement began at the end of the eleventh century with the dismemberment of the Seldjukid empire. Here the mayors, who were called *rais* and were the commanders of the town militia, the *ahdath*, were almost everywhere in control of the administration. They were the leaders of the upper bourgeoisie, and fearing the rebellion of the lower classes they preferred to retain the princes, who became simple condottieri carrying on war with the Crusaders and other enemies.[30]

In the second half of the eleventh century the revival of commercial relations between the Syrian ports and the Italian traders was well on the way. Some towns had a relatively strong bourgeoisie, which felt that the Fatimids exploited them by heavy taxation to serve their political aims. These rich bourgeois were interested in taking advantage of the revival of international trade in the Eastern Mediterranean.[31] But there were in these towns also parties which adopted a different attitude. Either realising the advantages of protection by the Fatimid fleet or owing to social antagonism against the rich traders there was everywhere a strong pro-Fatimid party. So these commercial and industrial towns were torn by party strife. In addition there was widespread sympathy for the Shiite credo. Therefore the rebels and would-be rebels had a difficult task. But the economic interests were so strong that before long revolts broke out and the Fatimid régime was swept away.

In 1070 Ain ad-daula Ibn Abi Akil, judge of Tyre, rose against the Fatimids and established his rule. Badr al-Djamali, the powerful generalissimo of the Fatimid caliphate, laid siege to the town, but failed. Tyre and Saida remained for about twenty years an independent republic governed by Ibn Abi Akil and his sons, until the Fatimids succeeded in 1089 in once more imposing their rule.[32] The medieval chroniclers speak of the revolt of Ibn Abi Akil, but it emerges from their own accounts that he was the leader of an influential party of rich townspeople, whose interests he looked after. At the same time some towns south and north of Tyre had cast off the Fatimid yoke. For we read in the chronicle of Ibn al-Athir that in 1089 the Fatimid army also conquered the towns of Acre and Djubail.

It follows, however, from the writings of Arabic historians that the revolutionary movement in the towns of Palestine and Lebanon was not yet crushed. They report new revolts in Tyre in 1094 and in 1097. Once more these medieval authors speak of the insurrections of local governors which were suppressed with the help of the inhabitants. But their accounts of the contributions imposed on the town after the suppression of the revolts show that the rebels had strong backing from the population which was punished in this way.[33]

Tripoli, the main port of Central and Northern Syria in that period, revolted at the same time as Tyre. Here too the leader of the movement was the kadi of the town, Amin ad-daula al-Hasan b. Ammar, who belonged to a rich and esteemed family and had the support of the upper bourgeois. In 1070 he liberated Tripoli from Fatimid rule and from then on it was an independent republic whose 'consuls' were the Banu Ammar. After the death of al-Hasan his nephew Djalal al-mulk Ali ruled almost thirty years over Tripoli (1072–99). He succeeded in imposing his rule over a great part of the Syrian coast and its mountainous hinterland. When in 1081 he took Djabala from the Byzantines, the whole of the Syrian coast was free from foreign rule. Independent urban republics had been constituted everywhere. Their rulers cajoled both the Fatimids and the Seldjukids, offering them presents and, as a contemporary Syrian chronicler says, manœuvred between them as well as they could. Their recognition of the suzerainty of the Fatimids was mere lip-service, and on the other hand they enlisted mercenaries who were not Turks, lest they should be betrayed in case of a war with the Seldjukids. In 1092 Tutush, the Seldjukid prince of Central Syria, laid siege to Tripoli. Djalal al-mulk Ibn Ammar succeeded, however, in arousing discord among the Seldjukid generals and in bribing some of them, so that the siege had to be raised. The third ruler of Tripoli, Fakhr al-mulk Ibn Ammar (1099–1109), carried on a stubborn war with the Crusaders. In 1108 he left the town for Baghdad in order to win support from the caliph and the princes of Irak, whereupon a party of the inhabitants called in the Fatimids. But in 1109 the town succumbed to the stronger forces of the Crusaders.[34]

The town of Djabala had a long time earlier broken away from Ibn

Ammar's urban republic. The kadi of the town, Ubaidallah b. Mansur Ibn Sulaiha, rebelled against the ruler of Tripoli and made it an independent republic. When the pressure of the Crusaders became too strong, he decided, in 1101, to deliver the town to Toghtekin, the atabek of Damascus. But a party of inhabitants called in Ibn Ammar to take over the government. Eight years later the town fell to the Crusaders.[35]

The history of Ibn al-Kalanisi and other chronicles contain detailed accounts of the long and tenacious struggle which the mayors of Damascus carried on against its prince for about half a century. Although the medieval authors depict it as the outcome of personal ambitions, there remains not the slightest doubt that it was rather a contest between the rich bourgeois of the Syrian capital, whose leaders were the Banu as-Sufi, and the weak princes of Toghtekin's dynasty. As long as the capable and energetic mayors of the Banu as-Sufi family had the support of the town militia, the so-called *ahdath*, the striking force of the lower classes, they were a match for the princes.

The first mayor (*rais*) of this family was Amin ad-daula al-Hasan Ibn as-Sufi, who held the post at the end of the eleventh century. Owing to conflicts with the prince of Damascus he was twice imprisoned (in 1101 and in 1103) and died in 1104.[36] He was succeeded by his two sons, Abu l-Madjali Saif and Abu dh-Dhawwad al-Mufarridj. The latter played a great role in the politics of Damascus and held the post of mayor till 1130. He brought about the downfall of the vizier al-Mazdakani, who had sided with the Batinites, arousing a movement of social unrest among the lower classes. Undoubtedly al-Mufarridj had acted in this conflict as leader of the upper strata of the townspeople which feared the subversive activities of the Batinites. Shortly afterwards, in 1130, he was deposed and imprisoned by the prince of Damascus, but a year later he was once more appointed to the post, which he held five years. In 1136 he was killed by a son of the prince. Then a cousin of his, al-Musayyab Ibn as-Sufi, became mayor of the town. According to the reports of an Arabic chronicler he had obliged himself to periodical payments for the upkeep of the army. The bourgeois had thus entered an alliance with the prince. In 1144 al-Musayyab also became vizier, sharing power with the general Unur. After the latter's death in 1149 the courtiers incited the prince to get rid of al-Musayyab and to rule himself. Thereupon the mayor raised troops, revolted and besieged the prince in the citadel. This rising, which resulted in the victory of Ibn as-Sufi, was a revolt of the bourgeois. The prince had to give in and leave to al-Musayyab the posts of mayor and vizier. To all intents and purposes the bourgeoisie had achieved its aim: it was in full control of the principality's administration and pursued, together with the prince, a policy of resistance against Nur ad-din's scheme of annexing Southern Syria to a great unitary Syrian Moslem state.

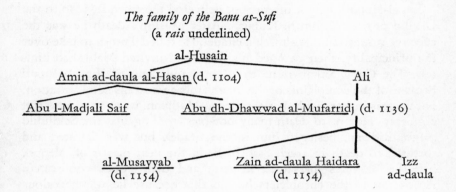

The family of the Banu as-Sufi
(a *rais* underlined)

al-Husain

Amin ad-daula al-Hasan (d. 1104)   Ali

Abu l-Madjali Saif   Abu dh-Dhawwad al-Mufarridj (d. 1136)

al-Musayyab   Zain ad-daula Haidara   Izz
(d. 1154)   (d. 1154)   ad-daula

The existence of the weak Damascene principality safeguarded the interests of the bourgeois. But in 1153 discord broke out in the family of the Banu as-Sufi. al-Musayyab was exiled and his brother Zain ad-daula Haidara took over his posts. A year later Zain ad-daula was killed by order of the prince and the townspeople plundered his house. The Damascene chronicler Ibn al-Kalanisi leaves no doubt about the reasons of the downfall of the Banu as-Sufi; he says explicitly why the lower people had changed their attitude: the Banu as-Sufi, he says, had only one thing in mind, namely to enrich themselves. They sold posts, and the property of the townspeople was no longer protected. So the lower classes withdrew their support from the upper bourgeoisie, which had turned to its own advantage the victory won with the help of the *ahdath*.[37]

The bourgeois of Aleppo pursued a policy similar to that of the Damascenes: they did not aim at the overthrow of the régime, but tried to use the princes as generals, while their own leaders would run the administration as mayors. This was indeed a clever policy and a scheme well adapted to the conditions. Aleppo was in great danger, being almost encircled by the principalities of the Crusaders. So the bourgeois of Aleppo treated the princes as condottieri. Within the town there were different parties whose leaders were the heads of influential families. The Banu Khashshab were the leaders of the Shiites, the Ibn Badi those of the Sunnites. For almost forty years these party leaders called in various princes to take over the princedom of Aleppo, hoping that they would be puppets and they themselves the men in control. But often they were disappointed, for the princes did not content themselves with the role assigned to them.

Ibn al-Hutaiti, mayor of Aleppo, delivered the town in 1080 to the Ukailid prince Muslim b. Kuraish. After Muslim's death he was the effective ruler and built himself a citadel. He called Tutush to take over the principality, then changed his mind and invited Malikshah himself. The Great Sultan came to Aleppo and deposed Ibn al-Hutaiti because of the complaints of the inhabitants against his administration. His successor, Barakat b. Faris, called al-Mudjann, was a very powerful dignitary. He put to death many notables, rose against the Seldjukid prince Ridwan, besieged him in the citadel, but was defeated and tortured to death in 1007. Said b. Badi, the next mayor of Aleppo, had the Batinites massacred in 1013 and their goods confiscated. According to the chroniclers he did this because he was a zealous Sunnite, but we shall not be mistaken in identifying his policy with that of the upper bourgeoisie, the bitter enemies of the sect.

In that stormy period of the history of Aleppo there were frequent changes in its government. Some time after the massacre of the Batinites Said b. Badi was exiled from Aleppo and the Banu Khashshab, their adversaries, got the upper hand in the town, torn as it was by party strife. In 1118 they delivered it to the Urtukid prince Ilghazi, who appointed Makki b. Kurnas as mayor. When the Urtukid left the town he entrusted the mayor with the government, together with his own son Sulaiman. Promptly they rebelled against him, whereupon he came back and had the treacherous *rais* killed. In 1123 another Urtukid, Balak, became prince of Aleppo, called in by the party of the Banu Khashshab. He exiled the leaders of the parties contending over the rule of the town. After his death in 1124 a son of Ilghazi succeeded him and handed the administration over to the Ibn Badi. He appointed Fadail, son of Said b. Badi, as mayor. Fadail held the post for some time, despite the frequent changes of the princes. Bursuki, called to Aleppo by the Banu Khashshab, left him the post, and when Kutlugh Abah mounted the shaky throne of Aleppo, thanks to the support of his own party his position became even stronger. In 1127 Kutlugh Abah was deposed and each party raised to the throne its own candidate, the party of the Ibn Badi called the Urtukid Sulaiman, the Banu Khashshab, the Seldjukid Ibrahim b. Ridwan. A short time later the mighty atabek Zengi annexed Aleppo to his dominions and put an end to the long party strife, which reminds us so strongly of the politics of an Italian city in the Trecento.[38]

Conditions in the towns of Upper Mesopotamia were very similar to those in the towns of Central Syria. The mayors, mostly belonging to influential families of notables, were in many towns in control of the government.

In Harran the *rais* Barakat Ibn Abi l-Fahm is spoken of in 1123. He was imprisoned by the Urtukid Balak. In Amid, now called Diyarbakir, the mayors were so mighty in the middle of the twelfth century that their relations with the princes of the town had become those of tutelage. The post was held by the family of Ibn Nisan, the son inheriting it from the father. When Murid ad-bin Ibn Nisan died in 1156 his son Kamal ad-din succeeded him. The *rais* of Amid was so great a personality that he could intervene with the prince of Mosul on behalf of his vizier. But he was also a petty despot who, according to a contemporary writer, oppressed his compatriots and caused many people to leave the town. In the small town of Sindjar the family Banu Yakub held the post of mayor for a long time. The capital of Upper Mesopotamia, Mosul, also had its *rais*. One of its mayors is mentioned on the occasion of its conquest by the Seldjukid sultan of Asia Minor, in 1107.[39]

The numerous reports we have quoted from the Arabic sources point to a remarkable synchronism: everywhere in the lands of the Fertile Crescent at the end of the twelfth century the bourgeoisie obtained its share in the government and urban republics came into existence. But the tide ebbed away. In some regions the feudal princes recovered their strength, in others a new régime was established.

d) *Revival of caliphal theocracy in Irak*

In Irak the waning power of the Seldjukids was replaced by a new caliphal state. Beginning with the reign of al-Mustarshid (1118–35), the caliphs had rebuilt their government step by step. But while the ambition of the caliphs was the driving force in the new development, the overthrow of the feudal régime corresponded also to the desires of the bourgeoisie. The lower classes which were antagonistic towards the Turkish military and considered them as foreign rulers only intent on exploiting them, readily joined the new army of the caliph. The rich bourgeois of Irak, who still carried on a great international trade with countries in Central Asia, such as Bukhara and Afghanistan, with the towns on the coast of the Black Sea and with Syria in the west, even they preferred the caliphal reign to that of the quarrelsome and bellicose Seldjukid princes. They resented the interference of the princes in their commercial and industrial activities and could not tolerate the frequent political crises resulting from their conflicts which interrupted the normal course of economic life. So they too lent a helping hand to the caliph.

The caliph al-Mustarshid, who first enlisted troops to protect Baghdad against the Bedouin king of Southern Irak and later defended it against Seldjukid princes, was formally recognised in 1132, by a treaty with sultan Masud, as independent ruler of Baghdad and the surrounding districts. His successors pursued the same policy with ever-increasing rewards. al-Muktafi (1136–60) re-established caliphal rule over most provinces of Irak. Under an-Nasir (1180–1225) the power and the influence of the new pontifical state attained its meridian. The dynasty of the Seldjukids reigning over Western Persia and Irak had become extinct. The attempts of the caliph to impose his rule on Media proved a failure, but he succeeded in conquering Khuzistan.

The revival of the caliphal state did not mean a complete break in the Seldjukid tradition. The caliphal army included a great number of Turkish slaves bought by the caliphs and called by their names, the 'mamluks of an-Nasir', 'the mamluks of az-Zahir', etc. Most of the officers were Turks, but there were also Irakis among them. The amirs (generals) had their own slave-guards, as in the days of the Seldjukids.[40] On the other hand, civilians, i.e. Irakis, were sometimes appointed commanders of the police or governors of large towns, and they and other civilians had Turkish mamluks.[41] The assignment of fiefs as payment of the military was not abolished. The Turks had their *iktas* as before. But it seems that tax-farming once more played a greater role than under the Seldjukids, or, in other words, that more land was administered directly by the Treasury. The tax-farmers were either Irakis or Turks.[42]

Whereas these facts indicate a generally moderate, conservative and cautious policy on the part of the caliphs, there are other data which show that the caliph an-Nasir had conceived the idea of a new theocracy, adapted to the conditions of the time, and that he made great efforts to realise his scheme. It appears that what he had in mind was a theocratic welfare state. an-Nasir once more abolished the mukus, the commercial taxes. An Arabic chronicler says that the revenue from the mukus abolished by the caliph in 1208 amounted to 200,000 dinars. This figure indicates that the measure taken by an-Nasir was a substantial relief of the tax burden. Under his successors the mukus were apparently once more collected till the caliph al-Mustasim abolished them, together with the *taksitat* (probably payments for certain government services), upon his succession to the throne in 1242. When new districts were annexed to the caliphal state, the local duties and mukus were abolished, as in the old provinces.[43]

an-Nasir also took other steps to promote social welfare. According to Moslem thinkers it was not incumbent on the state to take care of the poor. The functions of the state as conceived by them are limited to public security and safeguarding religion. The measures taken by princes in the fields of public education and assistance to the poor were considered highly meritorious acts, but not as their essential tasks. So the activities of an-Nasir were an innovation. It is true that other caliphs had embarked on similar activities, but it seems that those of an-Nasir were not regarded as philanthropy, since for him they were an integral part of public administration. Secondly, his activities fitted into a great scheme.

an-Nasir provided that every day portions of bread and meat and also alms should be distributed to the poor. In the month of Radjab the poor received additional payments. The caliph also had soup-kitchens opened in the month of Ramadan, when Moslems abstain from food during the day and sufficient meals in the night are badly needed to maintain physical strength. Further, an-Nasir offered the pilgrims going to Mecca or returning therefrom food, cloth and alms.[44]

Very characteristic of the far-reaching intentions and the boldness of an-Nasir's policy was his reform of the Futuwwa movement. Whereas the clubs of the *fityan* ('young men') had in the flourishing period of the caliphal empire been associations of pleasure-loving young gentlemen, their ideals had been permeated in the eleventh and twelfth centuries with religious and revolutionary tendencies. Some of these associations fought against the Shiites, others allied themselves to the ayyarun, intending to overthrow the existing social order and build up a new one, based on social justice and the idea of mutual help. But even when they were not mixed up with the criminal activities of the ayyarun, they were dangerous to the maintenance of public order. Their readiness to defend their reputation and their promptitude in retaliating when they considered themselves or their families offended very often resulted in acts of violence. an-Nasir decided to reform the futuwwa movement and make it an instrument of his policy. He himself became a member of one of their associations and later declared himself the leader of all *fityan*. On the one hand he sent emissaries to all Moslem princes urging them to recognise him as such and to mention his name during the chivalrous exercises and sporting activities cultivated by the *fityan*, while on the other hand he promulgated decrees forbidding the *fityan* to commit acts of violence. So he had two aims in mind: he tried to use the futuwwa as an order of knights, knitting together the Moslem nobility and imposing his suzerainty on the princes of the Moslem world; secondly, by suppressing people inclined to rioting and revolutionary activities, he used it as a means of realising his scheme of a new theocracy in the provinces governed by himself.[45]

Like many other reformers and visionary statesmen, an-Nasir was a despotic autocrat, but there can be no doubt that his subjects enjoyed a good measure of well-being. This, however, was not the only success of his policy. Both political and economic conditions were favourable to his endeavours. After a long period of silver famine, the mints of Irak and the adjacent countries once more in his time disposed of quantities of silver sufficient for the striking of great numbers of dirhams. The flow of silver from Central Asia towards the shores of the Mediterranean began once more at the end of the twelfth century, possibly in the wake of the Khwarizmian armies advancing to Western Iran. Its steady increase enabled the caliph al-Mustansir to issue many more silver coins than before and to forbid, in 1234, the use of fragments of gold coins, which for a long time had been substituted for dirhams. In the course of time the dirhams became so numerous that their exchange rate went down and had to be raised by a decree of the caliph.[46] Several passages in the contemporary chronicles testify to the fact that the Treasury possessed great funds. The caliph could spend considerable sums on his parties and make rich presents; he and his courtiers could build new mosques and other buildings. Apparently the population of the towns of Irak once more increased, for new quarters were built in Baghdad and probably elsewhere. Some enterprising aristocrats even engaged in projects of colonisation and founded new villages. an-Nasir and his successors themselves took measures to improve the conditions of agriculture; the caliph al-Mustansir, for example, dug canals. Under the stable rule of an-Nasir Irak's international trade prospered once more and a class of rich merchant capitalists sprang up, such as the Ibn Khurdadhi family in Baghdad, the

Ibn Suwaid from Takrit, and Asil ad-din Abbas al-Irbili – whose fabulous riches and high social standing aroused the envy and hatred of the poor.[47]

Although an-Nasir's aim was to establish a new Moslem theocracy, he was interested in enlisting the collaboration of all classes of the population. Both he and his successors readily employed Christian and Jewish officials. The Arabic chronicles of this period and the Hebrew diwan of a contemporary Iraki poet contain many particulars about these officials.[48]

The success of an-Nasir was not however complete. Class antagonism remained strong enough to induce people of the lower classes to attack the rich merchants and to fight with the police. Sometimes the vizier feared the lower classes so much that his home had to be guarded and he avoided walking unescorted in the streets of Baghdad. In the last years of the caliphal state, about the middle of the thirteenth century, prosperity was considerably declining. The advance of the Mongol hosts cast its shadow upon the countries of the Fertile Crescent. Their conquests in Iran had certainly repercussions in Irak. Once more international trade was often interrupted and economic difficulties ensued. The activities of the ayyarun, the characteristic phenomenon of periods of crisis, were once more renewed, and the fighting between the quarters of Baghdad offered them occasion for engaging in robbery and other crimes.[49]

e) The feudal régime of the Ayyubids

The Syro-Mesopotamian kingdom of Nur ad-din, son and successor of the atabek Zengi, and the Syro-Egyptian realm of the Ayyubids were offshoots and true replicas of the extinct Seldjukid empire. It was Nur ad-din (1146–73) who, after the integration of all the Moslem provinces of Syria, had sent Saladin to defend Egypt against the Crusaders and despatch the moribund Fatimid caliphate. The Ayyubid realm built up by Saladin (1169–93), after the elimination of Nur ad-din's descendants, was like the Seldjukid empire a confederation of semi-independent principalities. Its feudal régime was very similar to that of the Seldjukids.

The mainstay of the Ayyubid princes was a well-trained army, the core of which consisted of Turkish and Kurdish horsemen. The Arab (Bedouin) regiments were auxiliaries. Although the Ayyubids themselves were Kurds, the Turks were much more numerous in the armies of Saladin and his successors. The regular army of all the Ayyubid dominions in Egypt, Syria and Upper Mesopotamia numbered probably almost 20,000 horsemen. In time of war Saladin could mobilise approximately 12,000. When he set out to conquer Syria after the death of Nur ad-din he had only 7,000 horsemen with him. In the later years of Ayyubid rule, the prince of Aleppo could mobilise 1,500 horsemen for an important campaign, while a strong army of a Syro-Mesopotamian kingdom numbered 8,000 horsemen. But the military forces of these principalities increased considerably when the remnants of the once powerful Khwarizmian army joined them, for these Central Asian mercenaries numbered more than 10,000.[50] After the disintegration of the Seldjukid empire such armies were relatively strong forces.

The Turkish and Kurdish horsemen of the Ayyubids were feudal knights, holding fiefs and receiving payment in addition. Under the later Fatimids the system of land tenure in Egypt had become more and more similar to a feudal régime. Tax-farming had become inheritable and military fiefs numerous. So the establishment of the feudal régime by Saladin was not a complete break from the existing social order. But the accession of Saladin to the throne gave the development a strong impetus. The Egyptian historian al-Makrizi says that from his time all the cultivated land was assigned as fiefs to the army. The size of the fiefs varied very much. There was a great number of small fiefholders who were not vassals of generals (amirs). These knights, called al-halka al-khassa, fought in the centre of the battle line, being considered the core of the army. The amirs with their military slaves (mamluks) were the second part of the army. Their fiefs provided them with a considerable revenue, from which they had to give a share to their mamluks or else assign them regular pay. The mamluks of the sultan were the third part of the army. They seldom had fiefs comprising entire villages, but their fiefs were more productive than those of the halka. Faithful to the principles laid down by the founder of Oriental feudalism, the Ayyubids often assigned to their military *iktas* consisting of parts of estates situated in different places, to prevent the fiefholders winning a following in their districts. It is not easy even to guess the real income of an Ayyubid knight, since it is enumerated in arbitrary units, composed of payments in cash and in kind. Ibn Mammati, a contemporary author of a book on administration, speaks of fiefs producing from 600 to 1,000 dinars a year. Since he had in mind 'ghost' dinars, called 'dinar djaishi', these sums corresponded roughly to 480–800 dinars. On the other hand, we may conclude from the indications given by the vizier of Saladin that in 1181 the average income of a knight was 429 dinars a year. Fragmentary as our information is, we may venture to draw two conclusions from the scattered data: the pay of the Ayyubid knights was higher than that of the Buyid and Seldjukid military, which means that the revenue of the Moslem armies was in the course of centuries fairly steadily increasing; secondly, the data provided by the Arabic authors show that the greatest part of the state revenue was allotted to paying the army. According to the accounts of the vizier of Saladin, out of an expenditure amounting in 1189 to 4,653.019 dinars the Egyptian Treasury allocated not less than 3,462.096 dinars for the pay of the army. The strain on the Treasury was so heavy that from time to time the government had recourse to various expedients, on one occasion to the devaluation of the currency, on another to reducing the pay of the army. Saladin chose the former expedient, his successors the latter.[51]

Besides the increase in military pay the feudal régime of the Ayyubids was marked by two features: the inheritability of the fiefs and its transitional character. Nur ad-din used to leave the fief of a knight to his son, and the Arabic chroniclers emphasize that he did so even when a knight had been killed in battle and his son was still a child, in which case he appointed a trustee to look after his interests until he was grown up. The chroniclers say that owing to the inheritability of the fiefs the knights fought valiantly, since they were protecting their allodial property. Saladin adhered to the same principle; he even made fiefs hereditary.[52] That the Ayyubid reign was a transition period is evident from various data. Civilians were still admitted to a military career and could reach the position of commanders, they had mamluks of their own, and government officials received fiefs as payment. Neither in Egypt nor in Syria had all the cultivated land been handed over to the military, a considerable part of it remaining in private hands.[53]

The régime of the Ayyubids was undoubtedly less detrimental to the agriculture of Egypt and Syria than other feudal régimes in the Oriental world. The fiefholder was held responsible for the maintenance of dykes and irrigation canals, bridges and tracks, and had to see that the estates assigned to him were properly cultivated. Several passages in the Arabic sources show that the fiefholders supervised the harvest and also spent some time on their estates to pasture the horses in spring. Further, the peasants were not yet enslaved as in later periods, and were indeed still effectively protected by the government, their rents being strictly fixed so that they could not be overcharged. Sultan al-Malik al-Kamil (1218–36) made great efforts to raise Egypt's agricultural output. He personally supervised the maintenance of the dams, imposed the same duty on his amirs and punished them if they were negligent. An Arabic historian related that the agricultural output of Egypt increased considerably during his reign, but a change took place after his death. Many dykes were neglected and broken, and the cultivated area decreased once more. It seems, on the other hand, that independently of the efforts made by the government there was always a spontaneous colonisation, increasing the cultivated area. A report from the year 1181 refers to the confiscation of the harvest of the Bedouin in the provinces of ash-Sharkiyya and al-Buhaira. In general, however, it is more than probable that the reign of the Ayyubids was a flourishing period for Egypt's agriculture. Wheat was exported to the Hidjaz and sometimes to Syria. The problem of the nomadic tribes was in this period less serious than before for agriculture in Egypt and in Ayyubid Syria. The Bedouin tribes which immigrated into Central Palestine at the end of the Ayyubid period became peasants.[54]

But Egypt suffered at the same time from the consequences of a terrible famine and epidemic which had far-reaching consequences for its demographic development. In the second half of the twelfth century the chroniclers seldom mention outbreaks of pestilence. Apart from an epidemic in Damietta in 1150 they speak of pestilence in Cairo in the year 1179.[55] These few epidemics were apparently local ones, but that which raged through all the provinces of Egypt in 1201 and in 1202 was undoubtedly a major catastrophe. Following a terrible famine plague broke out, and countless people died. It may be that reports of three-quarters of Egypt's population being carried off are exaggerated. But the account of an eye-witness, the Arab doctor Abdallatif al-Baghdadi, is eloquent testimony to the terrible number of the victims. In many villages only empty houses remained. In some quarters of Cairo almost all the inhabitants had died. This epidemic was the second great demographic catastrophe in Egypt's medieval history. The famine of the days of al-Mustansir had been a turning-point in its demographic development, when the age-long expansion had come to an end. When the country had partially recovered in the course of the twelfth century there came the second blow which grievously reduced the population once more. There were additional epidemics in 1236 and in 1237. It is true that the decrease of population was not equal everywhere. The decline of the Fayyum was probably much faster than that of other provinces; it had 198 settlements in Byzantine times and only 100 in the year 1315.[56]

Apparently Levasseur's law did not operate after the famine and plague of 1201-2. Undernourishment and the disequilibrium between sugar and proteins in the food of the poorer classes was no less portentous a factor in Egypt than elsewhere. Both Abdallatif and al-Makrizi dwell on the malnutrition of the Egyptians. Abdallatif, an excellent observer, describes how the poor ate carcasses and reptiles, while al-Makrizi strangely enough was aware of their unbalanced diet. He knew that the inhabitants of Upper Egypt had plenty of sugar from the dates and sugar cane, those of Lower Egypt colocasia (arum lilies) – but almost nothing else.[57]

The development of prices and wages in the first half of the thirteenth century shows clearly how much the population had decreased. Prices of grain went down considerably, and the real wages of workers rose. The price of 100 kg of wheat which had been 1 dinar on the average in the twelfth century, was only 0.7 dinar after the great famine. But the price of bread rose. An Egyptian ratl of bread cost 0.0035-0.004 dinar (Cairene prices), in the eleventh century, its price under the last Ayyubids was probably on the average 0.0043 dinar – a consequence of the general rise of wages. We have no information on bakers' wages, but the evidence from the accounts of building activities is very clear. A journeyman who in the Fatimid period earned less than 2 dinars a month (when working 25 days) got 3 dinars in the first half of the thirteenth century.[58] These data demonstrate emphatically that the demand for grain had diminished and that the price of labour had risen because of the shortage of workers.

The Ayyubid period was a prosperous age for the merchants as well as for the workers. This was partly due to the revival of the bi-metallic monetary system. The mints had considerable stocks of silver, which came partly from Central Asia and partly from Europe. During the reign of Saladin the monetary system of Egypt underwent a crisis, owing to the great expense of the wars with the Crusaders. The dinars he issued were devalued and the dirhams contained (apart from a few specimens) only 50% silver. But the successors of Saladin struck good dinars, and al-Malik al-Kamil coined in 1225 the dirham called after him, 'al-kamili', which contained 66% silver. The dirhams put into circulation by the Ayyubids were so numerous that the thirteenth century may be called the age of silver in Egypt's medieval history. In the Judaeo-Arabic documents dating from the Fatimid period which have been found in the Cairo geniza, prices and values are indicated in dinars, whereas in those of the Ayyubid period they are fixed in dirhams. Several reports of Arabic authors point also to the great quantities of silver coins which the rulers of Egypt and Syria possessed in this period. Moslem Syria had even more silver than Egypt, both because of its being nearer to the Iranian and Central Asian regions whence the white metal came, and owing to its contacts with the Crusaders, who imported it from Europe. In Egypt there were even some temporary shortages of dirhams in that period, whereas the silver coins issued by the Ayyubid mints in Syria were of an excellent standard until the middle of the thirteenth century.[59]

Besides the change in the monetary system there were other reasons for the prosperity of the domestic and international trade of Egypt and Syria in the Ayyubid period. For Moslem Syria and Upper Mesopotamia the age of Nur ad-din and the reign of the Ayyubids spelt recovery and expansion. There was a demographic upsurge, notably in the big towns and probably also elsewhere. Outside the gates of Mosul, Damascus and other towns new quarters were built, and everywhere the princes founded new markets and caravanserais, schools and mosques. An anonymous copyist who lived in the twelfth century says that also the population of Maridin increased very much in this period.[60] So economic life acquired a new impetus and commercial activities were intense.

The volume of international trade increased owing to the growth of exchanges with the Italian republics. The activities of the Italian merchants in the Syro-Palestinian towns held by the Crusaders had intensified the commercial relations of the Near East with the Christian Occident and resulted in an ever-increasing demand for the spices and other products which the Moslem merchants obtained from Arabia and India. Italian merchants exported from Northern Syria great quantities of cotton, a raw material for the flourishing industries of Lombardy. The Ayyubid princes, who needed timber, iron and other materials for their numerous wars, gave readily granted privileges to the Italian 'merchant nations'. These privileges, or in some cases commercial treaties, granted them freedom of commerce, the reduction of duties and tolls, the right to have a *fondaco* (an inn with big storage space) and other facilities. Pisa concluded a treaty with Saladin in 1173 undertaking explicitly to import into Egypt iron, timber and pitch, articles on which the Church had imposed an embargo. A new treaty was concluded in 1215. Venice sent embassies to the sultan of Egypt in

1208, 1217, 1238 and 1244 and obtained various privileges. The Venetians also concluded treaties with the princes of Aleppo in 1208, 1225, 1229 and 1254. There was a steadily increasing number of European merchants who visited the ports of Moslem Egypt, Alexandria and Damietta, and penetrated from the coastal towns of Syria, still in possession of the Christians, to the emporia of the Moslem hinterland.[61]

The boom in domestic and international trade was, however, accompanied by a change in its structure which had far-reaching consequences for the social stratification of Egypt and Syria. In the first place the new lords of Egypt and Syria embarked on a policy similar to that of the Seldjukids or, more correctly, they were compelled to take similar measures. The need to obtain additional funds when the government had allotted a great part of the kharadj as fiefs to the military compelled them to extortion and the establishment of new taxes. The chroniclers of this period mention some cases of rich merchants who were terribly fleeced. But the consequences of the mukus-system were much more important. Although Saladin had solemnly abolished the mukus they were re-established, his son and first successor on the throne of Egypt, al-Malik al-Aziz, imposing them once more and even raising the rates. The Arabic authors relate that al-Malik al-Kamil imposed new and unheard-of taxes called *hukuk* (duties). His successor, al-Malik al-Adil II, reduced the rates of the mukus upon his accession to the throne, but did not abolish them. In Syria too these commercial taxes were everywhere a heavy burden. Sometimes a new prince would abolish them and a little while afterwards levy them again, as al-Malik al-Djawwad did when he became prince of Damascus in 1238. It goes without saying that the collection of the mukus considerably diminished the profits of the petty merchants,[62] who must have felt them more severely than the wholesale merchants.

In the great spice trade a group of rich merchants became so powerful in this period that they could monopolise it to a considerable extent. It is true that these 'Karimis' had already begun their activities in the reign of the Fatimids. But then the Indian trade of Egypt was still open to the numerous middle-class merchants. The Karimis in this period were shipowners who carried the Indian spices to the Near East. In the course of the thirteenth century they became wholesale traders. Apparently they seem to have been a rather loose company of rich merchants who associated from time to time or entered upon partnerships for a certain period or business. They had big warehouses in the principal emporia of Yemen and Egypt and enjoyed government protection. The families of the rich spice traders, such as the as-Samarri and at-Takriti, who had come from Irak and settled in Damascus, became a real merchant aristocracy. They corresponded with caliphs, sultans and Christian princes, who had recourse to their services.[63] But the middle-class merchants were hard pressed and edged aside. The feudal régime brought about social polarisation, the rich becoming richer and the poor poorer.

f) *Technological stagnation*

The age of the Seldjukids and the Ayyubids brought a great change in the structures and the output of Near Eastern industries. At the time of the Seldjukid conquests the industries of Irak, Syria and Egypt were still flourishing and their products were distinguished by their excellent quality. The West and South European industries, as far as such existed, could not compete with them. In the middle of the thirteenth century all this had completely changed. Many factories in the Near Eastern countries had been closed, some industries had very much shrunk or disappeared altogether, whereas the level of industrial production in the Occident had risen so much that a dumping of its products in the Near East was well on the way. An understanding of this development may serve as an approach to the solution of some major problems of Oriental history.

Many texts in the Arabic sources bear witness to the export of textiles from Irak through the Seldjukid period. In Baghdad and probably in other towns the attabi stuffs, the siklatun and other kinds of silk were produced as in earlier periods. As of yore, the famous linen manufactures of Tinnis, Damietta and the neighbouring towns of Lower Egypt produced those excellent products which were so much esteemed in all parts of the Near East and elsewhere. Many hundreds of inventories of dowries which have been found in the Cairo geniza show that down to the end of the Fatimid period no couple would miss having some pieces of Tinnis and Dabik cloth. Arabic authors mention the export of dabiki, dimyati and other Egyptian textiles to Irak. Most texts refer to the products of the major centres of the Egyptian textile industry, but there were in addition minor centres, some of them having home industries. In Bab, a small town in Northern Syria, muslin was produced, and in some villages of the Hauran carpets and robes.

The sugar industry of Khuzistan and other provinces of Persia was still flourishing and its products were the objects of a lively export trade, as indicated by accounts of the great quantities of sugar consumed in Irak. Apparently sugar was also produced in Upper Mesopotamia. The mention of the cheapness of sugar in Irak at certain dates is another indication of the great volume of this industry in various countries adjacent to it. The size of the sugar industry in Syria and Egypt had considerably increased through the Fatimid period, and as their products were renowned for their quality there was a demand for them everywhere. In the course of time there had been developed various kinds of sugar, which were strictly distinguished. The sugar of the Said (Upper Egypt) was for centuries famous for its purity, and known as al-Kifti. Great quantities of Syrian and Egyptian sugar were exported to other countries. A story told by an Arabic author bears evidence of the export of Egyptian sugar to Irak in the middle of the thirteenth century.

Another flourishing branch of Near Eastern industry was the manufacture of glass in Syria and Palestine. The glass vessels produced in the coastal towns of Lebanon, in Damascus, in Aleppo and other towns of Syria, but also in ar-Rakka in Northern Mesopotamia, were world-famous. In the twelfth century the glass workers in Northern Syria began to produce considerable quantities of enamel and gilded vessels which won great fame in all parts of the world. There is good reason to believe that the taste and the orders of the Seldjukid princes played a great role in the development of this industry. A story contained in an Arabic chronicle shows that at the beginning of the thirteenth century glass vessels from Aleppo were exported to Central Asia, where they aroused admiration.[64]

There is also clear evidence, both textual and archaeological, of technological progress in the Seldjukid period. Some passages in the chronicles of Irak mention mills which were not operated by water. It is a well-known fact that windmills were used in Sidjistan in the tenth century (and perhaps much earlier). The Iraki chronicler Ibn al-Djauzi speaks of mills which were turning and grinding grain on the earth without anybody knowing how they were operated. These reports refer to the years 1088 and 1152. If heat-power or gravity had been used, people would have perceived these devices. So it may be that magnetic power was used or that windmills are referred to. However that may be, it seems that windmills did not come into use in the Near East.[65]

The new styles of pottery and metalwork which spread in the twelfth century were technological innovations of considerable importance. Near Eastern potters learned to imitate the translucent Chinese porcelain by employing an artificial paste. Whereas they had for a long time counterfeited it by a surface glaze laid over crude, ordinary clay, they later used a composition of quartz-pebbles and melted potash, so that glaze and body were composed of the same materials. The new technique was used in Rayy, Kashan, ar-Rahba, and also in Egypt. In the first half of the thirteenth century the manufacture of metal vessels developed considerably in Upper Mesopotamia and elsewhere, as far as both the quality and the quantity of the products are concerned. The production of inlaid metalwork became in some towns, as in Mosul, a flourishing industry. The use of silver inlay was at least very rare before this period, all the more that for a long time there was a great scarcity of silver in Persia and other countries of Western Asia. In the second half of the twelfth century silver inlaid objects began to be produced in East Persia, while in the age of the Ayyubids ewers, basins, dishes and other inlaid vessels made in Mosul, and later in Syria and Egypt by workers who had emigrated from Mosul, were highly esteemed by rich people and exported everywhere.[66]

In contrast to the introduction of a new style in some of the artistic trades, there was in this period apparently a marked decline in some branches of technology while in others where there was no decline in technique there were no more innovations.

The attentive reader of the Arabic chronicles of the Seldjukid age becomes aware of these facts as time and again he comes across reports of bridges falling down and dams bursting. For often the chronicler reveals that it was not simply the consequence of negligence but of bad construction and ineffective repairs. Ibn al-Djauzi relates that bridges over the big canal of Nahr Isa crashed in 1036 and 1042 and that a floating bridge over the Tigris was carried away by high water in 1040. Reports of breaches of the dams are much more numerous. In the year 1062 the dam of the Tamarra canal, east of Baghdad, gave way, as did the dams of the Tigris, as the result of an inundation in 1069. The account of the hydraulic constructions of Bihruz, a Seldjukid governor of Baghdad, sheds light on these conditions. Three times he rebuilt the big dam of Nahrawan, the efforts lasting altogether seven years, from 1140 to 1146, when Bihruz died. His engineers undertook to dry out the old bed of the Nahrawan canal, in order to make it deeper and then by the construction of a very high dam, bring the water back to it.

Further, they dug a loop canal to bring in water from the Diyala canal. But the project proved a great failure. The water turned aside and the big dam remained amidst the dry land. The technological knowledge possessed in former times by Persian and Babylonian engineers was lost, and the Bihruz project was too much for the engineers of the twelfth century. In the second half of the twelfth century there were additional breaches of dams. In 1159 a dam near Baghdad crumbled away and some quarters of the town were inundated, and the same happened in 1174. At the end of the reign of the caliphs there was another such series of catastrophes. In 1248 the Tigris swept away the dams near Baghdad, in 1254 many dams of the Euphrates and the Tigris were broken and the fields flooded. In 1256 high water again caused an inundation of the fields on the banks of the Tigris and a contemporary Arabic chronicler says explicitly that the government services were incapable of repairing the breaches.[67] Neglect of the waterworks had diminished technological knowledge, for as the dams were seldom inspected and repaired people forgot how to do it.

The execution of great constructions in Egypt, at the end of the twelfth century, does not contradict the supposition of technological decline. For the citadel and the new walls of Cairo, which were constructed by order of Saladin, were built by Christian prisoners. The evidence for this is the report of a Moslem eye-witness, the Spanish traveller Ibn Djubair, who says that both the workmen and the overseers were Franks. He reports what he saw, but he did not know that even the architects were Christians, as is revealed by the Franco-Syrian style. The planning by foreigners of great military constructions in Egypt was not, however, a new phenomenon. Those executed by order of Badr al-Djamali, a hundred years earlier, had been designed by three Armenians of Edessa who imitated Byzantine fortification.[68]

There is strong evidence of technological stagnation in agriculture. The water-wheels were the same as those used for irrigation centuries earlier, and when cold weather caused the freezing of the rivers they did not operate. The attempts at improvement were probably proposed by engineers and mathematicians, but either they were unsuccessful or else they were not even tried. The irrigation canals in Irak were not well maintained, so that silting-up reduced the head of water which they could provide to the branches. The contrast between technological stagnation and even decline and the great progress achieved in the same period in European agriculture is striking.[69]

The decline of the Near Eastern textile industries in the first half of the thirteenth century is well known from the accounts of Arabic authors. Modern scholars have repeated them without analysing the true reasons for this phenomenon. Tinnis, the great centre of the Egyptian linen industry, was destroyed, by order of the sultan al-Malik al-Kamil in 1227, lest the town should fall into the hands of the Crusaders. Ever after it remained in ruins, and wherever al-Makrizi, in his great work on the topography of Egypt, mentions it he speaks of it as a town no longer existing, using the preterite.[70] He does the same when speaking about some other industrial towns in Lower Egypt, e.g. Tuna and al-Kais. The factories of Dabik and Shata too were closed, and according to the Arabic authors of the later middle ages they were in ruins. It seems that Dabik had already been destroyed by the end of the twelfth century, since Yakut in one passage uses the preterite when speaking about this town and in another passage explicitly says that in his days it was ruined. Even in Cairo old textile factories were used as colleges for theologians in the Ayyubid period.[71]

One must beware, however, of being misled by the accounts of the medieval authors. The evacuation of Tinnis and the subsequent decline of this and other industrial towns of Lower Egypt cannot have been the sole reason of the decline of the Egyptian textile industry. If their factories would have yielded adequate profits, they would have been re-opened in other places. They disappeared because they were no longer profitable enough to induce businessmen to re-establish them. The entrepreneurs preferred to import European textiles which were cheaper and more esteemed.

The textile industries of the Near East could not compete with the products imported from Western and Southern Europe because meanwhile there had appeared in the Christian world two technological innovations of major importance. One of them was the use of the treadle. This device, which was unknown to the Greeks and the Romans, was used in Northern France in the eleventh century and by English weavers at the end of the twelfth century. Treadle-looms appear frequently in illuminations of the thirteenth century. The second innovation was the automatic fulling mill. Mills operated by water were used for the fulling of woollen stuffs in Italy already at the end of the tenth century. They were well known in some provinces of France in the eleventh century. Then they were introduced into Germany and England. The use of the fulling mill meant a real 'industrial revolution' for the English wool industry,[72] and it goes without saying that once having learnt to employ water for driving mills (apart from those grinding grain) they were used not only for fulling but also for many other industrial activities. It seems that both the treadle-loom and this device remained unknown in the Near East, or more exactly did not come into use in industry. Even the mills driven by flowing water and used for grinding grain decayed as early as the tenth century. Ibn Haukal uses the preterite when speaking about these mills in some towns of Irak and Upper Mesopotamia. He says that those of Balad and Baghdad no longer operated, whereas in Mosul and al-Haditha on the Tigris some were still used. Further, he says that there were such mills in Takrit, Ukbara and also in Tiflis in Georgia. Those installed on the Euphrates, in Kalat Djabar and ar-Rakka, could not be compared with the mills of Upper Mesopotamia and in the towns on the Tigris, says the Arabic geographer.[73] So in the Near East technological stagnation had followed a period of great progress. Whatever the reasons for this phenomenon, it brought about the decline of many industries. The factories of Tinnis and the neighbouring towns were closed, not because of the danger of a Crusaders' invasion, but because they were technically inferior to the industries of Flanders and of Italy.

But why did the Near Eastern industries lag behind? Why did they not make progress as before? A main reason seems to be a change of industrial structures. The great technological progress had been made when freedom of enterprise prevailed and the tiraz system – factories which were great industrial enterprises – was flourishing. These great enterprises could afford experiments which resulted in technological innovations. In the age of the Seldjukids and the Ayyubids the princes curtailed freedom of enterprise, established monopolies and imposed heavy taxes on the workshops. This brought about a slow decline of private industry. The tiraz system too declined. The tiraz factories still existed everywhere, but they no longer had the funds they had disposed of in the days of the Abbasids and the first Fatimids. A passage in the *Topography of Egypt*, by al-Makrizi, sheds light on the decline of the tiraz system there. He says that the value of the annual production of the Egyptian tiraz factories for the royal court was 10,000 dinars, while according to other passages in the same work much higher sums were allowed for them in earlier times.[74] This figure surely refers to the late Fatimid period, and shows the tremendous decline of the production of the tiraz. In Irak the decline was without doubt more evident. Certainly in these circumstances experiments were beyond the possibilities of the tiraz.

Technological decline was the consequence of the rule of the feudal military. While private industry was hampered and even oppressed, royal industry was no longer urged to strive for technological innovation. This was surely a decisive factor in industrial decline.

CHAPTER VII

Irak Under Mongol and Turcoman Feudal Lords

From the middle of the thirteenth century Irak was under the rule of a foreign military class, for eighty years the Mongols and later the Turcomans. Feudalism reached its zenith and the conditions of the working class sank to their nadir. The population of Irak lived under a régime which intended only its merciless exploitation. In describing the consequences of this régime the historian must use time and again the expressions 'decline' and 'decay', but such was indeed the main substance of Irak's history in the later middle ages.

a) *The reign of the Ilkhans*

The revival of caliphal rule in Irak was a kind of Indian summer. In the middle of the thirteenth century a wave of Central-Asian nomadic tribes was sweeping over the Near East, whose weak rulers, wrangling with each other, could not offer a stout resistance. Most of the invaders were Turks, but the leaders were ruthless Mongols who had not yet come into contact with the refined Moslem civilisation or whose contacts with it had been at best superficial. The shrewd caliph an-Nasir had made a terrible mistake when he incited the Mongols against the shah of Khwarizm, who alone could bar Persia to the invaders. When his mighty kingdom had fallen, the Mongols overran the country and almost the whole of the Near East. Their armies were much stronger than those of the Near Eastern princes, that of Hülegü, which invaded Persia, Irak and Syria in 1256, numbering 70,000 men. Their military discipline was much better than that of the Moslems and, last but not least, they used Chinese artillery, which was considerably superior to the Near Eastern weapons.

After a short campaign in 1258 Hülegü conquered Baghdad, the seat of the caliph and the capital of the Moslem world. It was the first time it had been captured by a non-Moslem power. Irak became a province of the great Mongol empire, or rather of the Mongol kingdom of Persia which was part of it. In various provinces the conquerors left the princes on their thrones, the Salghurides in Fars, the Hazaraspids in Luristan, the Artukids in some districts of Upper Mesopotamia. But Irak was incorporated in their kingdom, which comprised also Afghanistan, Adherbeidjan and Asia Minor as far as the Kizil Irmak. Baghdad was no longer the seat of the government, as the Mongol kings of Persia, called Ilkhans, made Tabriz and later Sultaniyya and Udjan, other towns in Adherbeidjan, their capital.

The fact that Irak came under direct Mongol rule was of great consequence, for the establishment of Ilkhanid rule meant a complete change in the system of government. The new rulers were true nomads, alien to a settled life and eager to exploit peasants and town-dwellers to the utmost. For half a century the ruling class kept its national identity, its language, its pagan religion and foreign dress. It goes without saying that the Mongol army used to plunder the villages and carry away the cattle, but the new rulers also seized cornfields in order to use them for pasture. The tax burden became much heavier than it had been before. Beside the land-tax, the Mongols levied from the settled population a poll-tax (*kubchur*), various imposts for the expenses of the administration (*ikhradjat, awarid*) and extraordinary taxes (*shiltakat, shanakis*). As these taxes were usually farmed out, the profit of the farmers to be covered by the tax-payers, and were levied in the most arbitrary way, in advance and often several times a year, the lot of the population and especially of the peasants was sometimes insupportable. The townspeople suffered great losses by forced purchases (*tarh*) and had to pay commercial taxes (*tamgha*). But much worse than the tax burden was billeting. If we can believe the report of a contemporary Persian historian, the theft and robbery connected with it were disastrous for the subjects of the Ilkhans. The payment of the government's debts by giving drafts upon a district was an old custom in the Oriental empires, but in the days of the Ilkhans it became more grievous than ever. The taxation of the townspeople was also a merciless exploitation. The contemporary Arabic chronicler Ibn al-Fuwati relates how quite often heavy contributions were extorted from the inhabitants of Baghdad in various ways.[1]

Ghazan (1295–1304), the greatest of the Ilkhans, was a far-sighted ruler and tried to improve the system of government. He decided that henceforth the land-tax should be levied according to a fixed rate, he abolished the quartering of soldiers and officials in private houses and forbade the use of violence in the collection of taxes.[2] Another momentous change made by Ghazan was the establishment of the feudal system of land tenure. Even before his reign the military had been granted fiefs, but he distributed them to all of them and, secondly, he made the feudal estates hereditary, although they were not necessarily inherited by the sons of their former holders.[3]

The establishment of the feudal régime was certainly connected with the economic retrogression. For after the Mongol conquest the economies of Irak and the neighbouring countries had become predominantly natural ones. Most agrarian taxes in Irak were paid in kind, payments and salaries likewise.[4]

The most important phenomenon in the social history of Irak in that period was, however, depopulation. Although no detailed chronicles have come down to us from this period of Irak's history, there can be no doubt about that.

The havoc wrought by the cruelty of the Mongol conquerors was certainly beyond comparison with the consequences of previous invasions. The capture of several towns of Irak and Upper Mesopotamia was followed by horrible massacres. The number of inhabitants of Baghdad who were slaughtered after its conquest in 1258 may have amounted to 100,000. There were massacres also in Wasit, Irbil, Nasibin, Dunaisir, Harran, Urfa, ar-Rakka, Sarudj, Manbidj, Bira, Balis and Kalat Djabar. In Mosul, which was spared in 1258, there was a similar massacre in 1262. Contemporary Oriental writers may indeed have exaggerated in their accounts of the Mongol conquests, for many inhabitants of the towns of Irak and of Upper Mesopotamia fled before the Mongols approached and returned after their departure; but it is beyond question that the conquest of Irak by the Mongols was a demographic catastrophe. Many towns remained desolate and there was carnage in the countryside too. Rashid ud-din, the panegyrist of the Ilkhans, relates that the population of the frontier districts was extirpated and the land laid waste. He says that the same happened in some provinces of Diyar Bakr, such as Harran, Urfa, ar-Rakka, Sarudj and Abulustain. But he avows that also most of the towns on both sides of the Euphrates were devastated and deserted.[5]

The blood-letting that accompanied the Mongol conquest was followed by a certain recovery. The administration of Irak by Ata malik Djuwaini, who held his post for 24 years (1258–82), brought relief to the sorely afflicted country. Baghdad was the winter residence of the Ilkhans and that other towns must have recovered to some extent is indicated by the fact that there were mints in Wasit, al-Hilla, Basra and Sindjar. On the other hand, there were in the second half of the thirteenth century several periods of dearth, owing to various reasons including lack of rain or locust plagues. Sometimes victuals became scarce not because of a bad harvest but as a consequence of the fraudulent manipulations of merchants or of changes in the monetary system. Whatever the causes of these crises, bread disappeared and the poor suffered from undernourishment and subsequently diseases, as happened in 1270, 1279, 1285 and 1286. In the year 1285, according to a contemporary chronicler, the poor sold their children. In 1286 various diseases raged in Baghdad. In the first half of the fourteenth century famine recurred. In 1318 there was a dearth in all the provinces of Upper Mesopotamia and also in the districts around Baghdad. A chronicler relates that many people left the country, whereas others were reduced to selling their children or eating corpses. Then, in 1338, there was again a dearth in the same regions.[6]

The accounts of the globe-trotter Ibn Battuta, who visited Irak in 1327 and again in 1348, and of the Persian writer Hamdullah Kazwini, who wrote in 1339, provide valuable data on the demographic development of Irak under the Ilkhans. Baghdad as described by Kazwini is still very similar to the town as described by Ibn Djubair in the eighties of the twelfth century. According to returns of trade taxes, as reported by the same author, Baghdad was still the second town in the Ilkhanid kingdom (only Tabriz yielding more), whereas Wasit held the fourth place. On the other hand, both Ibn Battuta and Kazwini speak of the ruin of numerous towns in Irak and in Upper Mesopotamia, such as Abbadan, al-Madain, Hulwan, Khanikin, Nahrawan, Kufa, Karbala, al-Kadisiyya, Ukbara, Dara and Hisn Kaifa. Other towns may be added to this list. ar-Rakka, for example, was a flourishing town until the fourteenth century, then it decayed, according to the account of Abu l-Fida, who wrote at the beginning of the fourteenth century. He says also that a third of Mosul had fallen into ruins. But a comparison of the reports of the fourteenth-century writers with those of earlier authors, such as Ibn Djubair and Yakut, suggests that the decay of these towns was slow and progressive. It had begun a long time before the Mongol conquest. It was not always misrule that brought about the ruin of the towns. Some towns, like Karbala, had declined because of factional strife, others because the great land routes had changed. So Nahrawan decayed and Bakuba began to flourish when the great caravan route to Persia (the so-called Tarik Khurasan) was shifted to the north. According to Hamdullah Kazwini some towns grew considerably in that period, e.g. Djazirat Ibn Umar and Sirt in Upper Mesopotamia.[7] Reference could also be made to some reports which testify to the recovery of rural districts in Western Irak. Rashid ud-din gives an enthusiastic description of the district of Ana in the days of Ghazan, and Ibn Battuta too speaks in glowing terms of the Euphrates region through which he travelled in 1348.[8]

The overall picture which emerges from these reports is, however, that of a general and progressive decline of Irak's population under the Ilkhans. The decrease of population which had begun shortly after the dismemberment of the caliphate became rapid after the Mongol conquest. This conclusion from the literary evidence is convincingly borne out by the archaeological survey, based on surface reconnaissance, which has been made by R. McC. Adams. He has found that in the province of Diyala, east of the Tigris, the built-up area shrank from 414 hectares before the Mongol conquest of Irak to 190 after it. The decrease of the population of Irak and the consequences of the Mongol conquest were so catastrophic that a good observer like Hamdullah Kazwini inevitably perceived and recorded them. He says verbatim that 'there can be no doubt that even if for 1,000 years to come no evil befall the country, yet it will not be possible completely to repair the damage and bring back the land to the state in which it was formerly'.[9]

That a great number of rural settlements disappeared during the reign of the Ilkhans has been clearly borne out by the research of Adams. In many cases it was the consequence of inadequate maintenance of the irrigation system, in others probably the effect of depopulation, and sometimes both. When the number of inhabitants in a village had become too small the irrigation canals could no longer be properly maintained, harvests became insignificant, and finally the settlement had to be abandoned. Adams's results are summarised in the following table:

Late Abbasid sites continuing into,
or reoccupied in the Ilkhanid period

large towns	2 (28 ha)
small towns	12 (58 ha)
villages	35 (61 ha)

newly founded in the Ilkhanid period		*sites abandoned during or soon after the Ilkhanid period*	
large towns	1 (20 ha)		
small towns	1 (7.5 ha)	large towns	3 (48 ha)
villages	13 (16 ha)	others	51 (123 ha)
Total	64 sites (190 ha)	Total	54 sites (171 ha)

So 47·5% of the built-up area in the province of Diyala was abandoned during this period! The results of Adams's survey are even more striking in that the major settlements are not included in the table quoted above. Their decline was probably not less steep. Adams believes there was an immense decrease of population numbers in this province under Moslem rule. He estimates the following totals:

Population of the Province of Diyala (including Baghdad)

800 A.D.	870,000
1100	400,000
after 1258	60,000

The result of depopulation would have been that the number of the inhabitants of the Diyala basin had shrunk in the period to its size in the Cassite and Old Babylonian periods or even to less.[10]

The demographic decline must necessarily have had serious consequences for Irak's economy. It was one of the most important causes of its economic retrogression, and with it came a change in the monetary system. After the conquest of Persia, Irak, Adherbeidjan and East Anatolia by the Mongols, the mints of these countries were well supplied with Central Asian silver. Hamdullah Kazwini includes in his work a list of the rich silver mines in Turkestan, Ferghana, Bukhara and other provinces of the great Mongol empire, the output of which made it possible for all its mints to strike great quantities of silver coins. But there were also silver mines in those provinces of Asia Minor which were under the control of the Ilkhans, e.g. at Lulu and Kumish.[11] On the other hand, the mints of Irak and Persia got much less gold than in the period preceding the Mongol conquests. This was due to the interruption of regular trade with Egypt, from which Irak and Persia had in former times got their share of the Sudani gold. The decrease of the gold stocks in the mints of the Ilkhans was such that the monetary system had to be changed altogether. Whereas the currency of Irak and Persia had from the end of the ninth century been bi-metallic, based on the gold dinar of 4.25 g and the silver dirham of 2.97 g, the monetary system of the Ilkhans was mono-metallic. The basic unit of the currency was a silver dinar, weighing 12.9 g and called dinar raidj. This heavy silver dinar had the value of 6 depreciated dirhams weighing, as in the last days of the Abbasid caliphs, 2.15 g. The monetary system was, however, not uniform in all the provinces of the Ilkhanid kingdom. The mints of Irak issued dinars with the value of 10 dirhams (the so-called dinar mursal) or 12 dirhams (the so-called dinar awal). But the Ilkhans also struck gold dinars, the unit of which, the 'mithkal', was apparently 4.3 g. The value of 1 mithkal was 4 silver dinars.[12] In the early days of Ilkhanid rule the increase of good silver dirhams was the most characteristic phenomenon of monetary development. The chronicler Ibn al-Fuwati reports that in 1261 the 'black dirhams', equivalent to $\frac{1}{40}$ dinar gold, were withdrawn in Mosul and new dirhams, that is of pure silver, struck. The same author says that in 1283 an attempt was made to replace the small copper coins (the 'fulus') by silver coins. Under the reign of the last Ilkhans an ever-increasing number of lighter dirhams was issued, probably to supply coins for the demand resulting from the growth of trade.[13] In later times, when the international trade of the Ilkhanid kingdom began to flourish, gold was not at all rare. Ghazan had to forbid the lending of gold, as it was contrary to the precepts of Islam and he had become a Moslem. In that period the mints could strike heavy gold dinars. The increase of their gold stocks is clearly demonstrated by the results of research conducted by J. M. Smith and F. Plunkett, whose results are summarised in the table on p. 256.

The table shows the diversity of gold coins issued by the Ilkhanid mints. Although the number of those weighing 1 mithkal (4.3 g) and 2 mithkals (8.6 g) is conspicuous, there are many coins whose weight does not correspond to the standard. The underlying principle is, however, stated in a report by Ibn al-Fuwati on the monetary reform of Ghazan in 1298. There we read that he fixed the following exchange rate: 1 mithkal gold = 12 mithkal silver. So 1 mithkal gold (4.3 g) was equal to 4 dinars silver (of 12.9 g each) or 24 silver dirhams (of 2.15 g each).[14] This equation reveals the great change in the gold-

Weight of Ilkhanid gold coins (in grammes)

	1	1.01–1.25	2.01–2.25	2.51–2.75	3.01–3.25	3.76–4	4.01–4.25	4.26–4.5	4.51–4.7
Ghazan (1295–1304)				1		1	1	3	1
Öldjeitü (1304–1316)		1					2		
Abu Said (1316–1335)	3		2		2	2	3	1	

	5.26–5.5	5.51–5.75	6.01–6.25	6.26–6.5	6.51–6.75	6.76–7	7.01–7.25	7.26–7.5
Ghazan (1295–1304)								
Öldjeitü (1304–1316)				1				
Abu Said (1316–1335)	2	5	4	2		1	2	4

	7.51–7.75	7.76–8	8.01–8.25	8.26–8.5	8.51–8.75	8.76–9	9.01–9.25	9.26–9.5
Ghazan (1295–1304)				2	1			
Öldjeitü (1304–1316)		3	1		3	1	1	
Abu Said (1316–1335)	2	3	7	10	12	3	4	1

	9.51–9.75	9.76–10	10.01–10.25	10.26–10.5	12.76–13
Ghazan (1295–1304)			1		
Öldjeitü (1304–1316)					
Abu Said (1316–1335)	1	1	1	1	

silver ratio: whereas in the first half of the thirteenth century it had been 1:6 (1 dinar weighing 4.3 g gold being the equivalent of 12 dirhams weighing 25.8 g silver), under the Ilkhans it was 1:12. Persia and Irak had once more become 'silver lands', as they had been 500 years earlier.

During the long reign of the Ilkhans, of course, their monetary system underwent several changes and crises. In order to make good the deficiency of the Exchequer, the vizier of the Ilkhan Gaikhatu in 1294 issued paper money, modelled on the Chinese paper currency. The experiment was a complete failure, as the people refused to accept the banknotes. Economic activities came to a standstill, and the Persian historian Rashid ud-din speaks even of the 'ruin of Basra' which ensued upon the emission of the new money.[15] The description we find in the works of the medieval authors has a very interesting historical significance. They say that the 'chao', the paper money, was covered with the titles of the Ilkhan, the Moslem profession of faith and also Chinese words, proving that Chinese craftsmen had introduced block-printing in the Ilkhanid kingdom. Undoubtedly not only was the emission of paper money discontinued after the uproar which it aroused, but block-printing too. So the failure of Gaikhatu's vizier meant that his subjects had declined a technological innovation which could have been of paramount importance for the Near Eastern civilisation.

The information on prices in the historical records of Irak in the Ilkhanid period are very poor. Although conjectures based on these sporadic and 'isolated' data are therefore hazardous, they seem to fit very well into the picture of general economic retrogression. A reduced demand for victuals, in consequence of depopulation, and the substitution of gold by silver currency must indeed have resulted in the lowering of prices.

Shihab ad-din Ibn Fadlallah al-Umari, who wrote about 1340, says that in his day the normal price of a kurr of wheat in Irak was 39.5 awal dinars and that of a kurr of barley 15 dinars. Calculating the silver value of these prices and converting it into canonical gold dinars, one finds that 100 kg wheat amounted to 0.58 dinar and 100 kg barley to 0.26 dinar, which means that the price of wheat had fallen from the first half of the twelfth century by 15%. As to the price of bread we may quote a story told by Ibn Battuta. He says that in Baghdad he bought bread for 1 kirat, i.e. $\frac{1}{12}$ dirham. Supposing that the weight of the loaf was a ratl, one may conclude that it amounted to 0.003 canonical dinar, against 0.0035–0.004 in the first half of the thirteenth century. Some notes on the price of dates also seem to corroborate the conjecture of progressively falling prices. The Italian friar Odorico da Pordenon, says that in al-Ubulla one could buy 42 pounds for a Venetian grosso. According to Ibn Battuta 14 pounds cost a dirham ($\frac{1}{8}$ of the canonical dirham) when he visited Basra in 1327. These reports point to 0.0011–0.0012 (canonical) dinar being the normal price of a pound of dates. A hundred years earlier it had been 0.0015 dinar and two hundred years earlier 0.002 dinar.[16]

That the trend of prices did not result from the increase of agricultural production, at least as far as grains are concerned, is convincingly borne out by various accounts of agricultural conditions. In dealing with the situation of the peasants in successive periods of the middle ages, the historian of the Near East must stress time and again its progressive deterioration. But in the days of the Ilkhans the peasants of Irak were surely more oppressed than ever before. The rates of the land-tax were not equal in the various provinces of the Ilkhanid kingdoms which kept their old customs. In some provinces it amounted to a quarter or a third of the harvest, but in others, as in Khuzistan and in Irak, the peasants had to pay 60% or even 66%. In most provinces the tax was a proportional share of the harvest and was paid in kind (the 'mukasama' assessment), but in the districts around big towns like Baghdad it was paid in money and assessed on the cultivated area at a fixed rate (the 'misaha'). The owners of allodial land paid only the tithe, those holding their estates conditionally only a third of the harvest, but they levied from their tenants at least another third in addition.[17] As the rate of the taxes was not equal everywhere, so the situation of the peasants and the maintenance of the estates varied greatly. The exploitation of the peasants was much worse on state lands and fiefs than on private estates. This was partly the corollary of the Mongol idea of personal dependence. As the new rulers of Persia and Irak treated prisoners of war and even clients and retainers as slaves, the peasants were reduced to serfdom, tied to their villages and liable to corvée. What had in previous periods been a custom, under the Ilkhans became a law. A feudal lord was even forbidden to transfer peasants from one village to another. According to the law of Ghazan a peasant who had run away from a feudal estate even thirty years earlier was caught and sent back. The peasants were employed for the cultivation of fallow land and for other purposes. The enslavement of the peasants was, however, also the consequence of the shortage of labour, which itself resulted from depopulation. So there was a considerable change for the worse in the situation of the peasantry, and the antagonism between the ruling class and the peasants in this period seems to have been much greater than before.[18]

It goes without saying that the oppression of the peasants entailed another evil: desertion of the land became a characteristic of agrarian conditions throughout the Ilkhanid kingdom. Consequently there was a sizable decrease of the cultivated area. This was, however, also caused by the encroachment of nomadic tribes upon the activities of the settled population. The chiefs of the ruling Mongol class themselves and their viziers and other dignitaries had great flocks. The great increase of pasture land at the expense of the cultivated area was also due to the fact that the Mongol and Turkish tribes were accustomed to keep the cattle at grass through the whole of the year and so migrated from summer to winter quarters.

The decrease of the cultivated area was not equal in the various provinces of Irak. The figures of the tax returns in 1336, as quoted by Hamdullah Kazwini, shed light on the considerable difference. Whereas in some provinces a great number of villages yielded a rather small sum, less than a hundred settlements in another province paid a very great amount.

Tax returns of Irak in 1336

province	number of villages	tax return (in silver dinars)
Hulwan	30	6,100
Khanikin	20	12,200
Khalis	30	73,000
Tarik Khurasan	80	164,000
Dudjail	100	35,000
Nahr Isa	70	876,505
Nahr Malik	300	50,000

These figures are striking evidence of the tremendous decline of some provinces in East Irak and south of Baghdad (Nahr Malik).[19]

The Ilkhanid government made attempts to repair the irrigation system and to check the abandonment of the villages. Ata malik Djuwaini, governor of Irak under the first Ilkhans, dug a canal which irrigated the districts lying between al-Anbar and Nadjaf. According to Arabic authors he founded there 150 new villages and attracted settlers by lightening the tax burden. However, these activities cannot have had any notable success since Rashid ud-din, the historian who was minister of Ghazan, says that only a tenth part of the lands of the kingdom is under cultivation. Ghazan indeed took measures to bring about a change. In order to promote the cultivation of deserted lands he offered state lands to those who were prepared to colonise them and granted them tax reductions as incentives. He also had in West Irak, in the district of Karbala, a canal dug, which bore his name. Rashid ud-din designed projects for irrigation canals and dams in the provinces of Mosul and Malatiya, where new villages should be founded. For the realisation of his project in the district of Mosul the authorities of Upper Mesopotamia were ordered to provide 20,000 workmen. In the plain of Malatiya ten villages were to be founded. The peasants were to be brought from the neighbouring districts and given the necessary seed, agricultural implements and advances. The letters which Rashid ud-din wrote to the local governors included sketches of the canals and villages.

At the end of the thirteenth century and at the beginning of the fourteenth there must indeed have been a partial revival of agriculture in Irak. Ghazan's policy was followed by his successor Öldjeitü and later at the end of the reign of Abu Said (1316–35) by his minister Ghiyath ud-din, a son of Rashid ud-din. Hamdullah Kazwini speaks of the abundance of victuals in several provinces of Irak, of their low prices and of the export of grain. But the totals of the tax returns in 1336, as quoted by this author, leave no doubt that the policy of Ghazan and his successors had only partial success. The improvement in the conditions of the peasantry cannot have been substantial. Kazwini says himself that after the reign of Ghazan a new downward trend in agricultural production began. In order to show the general decline Kazwini provides his readers also with information about the sums which the same provinces yielded 100 years earlier. We reproduce his data together with their value in canonical dinars:

	reign of an-Nasir (1180–1225)	a. 1336
Irak	2.5 m (30 m dir.)	1,304,348 (3 m din. raidj)
Diyar Bakr, Diyar Rabia	833,333 (10 m dir.)	836,956 (1,925,000 din. raidj)

These data reveal the consequences of the Mongol invasion: the decline of Southern Irak was considerable, the two provinces of Upper Mesopotamia, which had suffered much less from the ravages of the conquerors, yielded the same amount as before. Kazwini does not give information about the tax returns of the third province of Upper Mesopotamia, viz Diyar Mudar, which had been thoroughly devastated.[20]

The age of the Ilkhans, however, not only saw a decline of Irak's agriculture. Their rule brought about a great change of its structures. After the conquest of Irak by the Mongols state lands had increased considerably, as a consequence of the extermination of the landowners or of confiscation. Even wakfs were seized by the new rulers. But later the government granted many estates as fiefs and began to sell land. These sales, which began as early as the eighties of the thirteenth century, resulted in the expansion of private ownership. It seems also that pious endowments increased once more, but the allodial lands (*arbabi* or *mulk*) became a very large sector of Irak's agriculture. As the purchasers of the state lands were often feudal lords or high dignitaries, a new class of latifundists came into being. Rashid ud-din left to his heirs 3,400 feddans (2.165 ha) of cornfields, besides palm groves, in Irak, and he had large estates in other provinces of the Ilkhanid kingdom. Beside the feudal lords and the high officials, the ulama apparently became an important group of landowners and consequently their interests were linked with those of the ruling class.

As the private estates were better maintained than those of the *diwani* (state lands), they took the lead in Irak's agriculture, as to both output and method of cultivation. The demand for grain decreased owing to depopulation, and the latifundists invested their capital preferably in cotton plantations and the growing of fruit trees. There is good reason to believe that among the cereals the cultivation of barley expanded at the expense of wheat, for barley could be grown on fields which owing to bad maintenance had become saline. Whereas Upper Mesopotamia produced beside wheat and barley mainly cotton, Irak had a great output of dates, which were exported to other countries, and of grapefruit. Southern Irak, the provinces of Basra, Wasit and al-Hilla, and also the districts around Baghdad were particularly rich in palm groves, and some districts of East Irak, such as Tarik Khurasan, in grapefruit.[21]

Just as the gross produce of Irak's agriculture decreased under the Ilkhans, so there was undoubtedly a considerable decline of its industries. As far as the number of people employed is concerned, they had never been an important sector of its national economy, even if compared with other Near Eastern countries. The reasons for their decay in the Ilkhanid period are evident: the massacres of workmen during the conquest, the loss of markets in the Mediterranean countries, and finally the rapacious fiscal policy of the new rulers.

The silk industry was particularly hard hit by the competition of the products of Persia, then united with Irak under the sceptre of the same dynasty, and by the increasing imports of Chinese silk in this period. Yet Baghdad still produced various silk fabrics and brocades, such as kamkha stuffs. These products were exported to Asia Minor and other regions. Silk was manufactured also in other towns of Irak and Upper Mesopotamia, e.g. in al-Karkh, north of Baghdad, and in Mosul. Probably Baghdad still produced its famous attabi stuffs, which in the second half of the thirteenth century were much in demand in other countries. The cotton manufacture, certainly a domestic industry, flourished in many small towns and villages of Irak and Upper Mesopotamia. Several passages in the geographical works of this period arouse doubts, as they are apparently copied from those of earlier writers. Perhaps a text referring to the production of coarse cotton in al-Hazira, north of Baghdad, is more trustworthy. Fine cotton stuffs were produced in Maridin and in Mush, in Upper Mesopotamia. Cotton was also manufactured in Ergani, Urfa, Arabgir and Erzindjan, as is borne out by the taxes collected in these towns and recorded in documents from the end of the middle ages.

Baghdad and other towns of Irak also produced paper, the quality of which was much esteemed. It was considered better than Syrian or Egyptian paper and therefore it was used at the court of the sultan of Cairo for correspondence with great potentates. Another industry of Irak exporting products to many countries was the glass industry. Precious glass vessels from Irak were sold in Asia Minor and Khwarizm in the first half of the fourteenth century. Finally, mention should be made of the production of preserves, which expanded with the great development of the fruit plantations. A Venetian ambassador who travelled in the Near East in the seventies of the fifteenth century dwells on the export of preserves from Baghdad to Persia.[22]

All these texts, however, do not invalidate the supposition of a considerable decline of Irak's industries in this period, which fits well into the general picture of shrinking towns and decreasing population. The technological stagnation of Near Eastern countries was surely another reason for industrial decline. Irak's most important industry had been the silk manufacture, but in the thirteenth century Lucca's silk manufacture had become famous, and the Europeans came to the Near East mainly to buy raw silk.

The development of the domestic and international trade of Irak in that period was closely connected with the great political and economic change brought about by the Mongol conquests. A short time after the atrocities of the Mongol invasion a lively trade was resumed everywhere. A class of rich merchants, engaged in international trade, had survived. Even before the conquest of Baghdad they had had connections with the Mongols and they continued their commercial and banking transactions afterwards. The Ilkhans were interested in the maintenance of regular trade and took measures to foster it. Ghazan made efforts to safeguard the merchants travelling by the great land routes of his kingdom. He also established control of commercial activities and a uniform system of weights and measures. The merchants of Baghdad and other towns of Irak took advantage of the new government's attitude. A contemporary historian speaks of Imad ad-din Ali b. al-Hasan al-Udhri, a rich merchant who lent money at interest to high dignitaries.[23] But the number of these rich merchants and the economic strength of this class – these are questions which the data we know leave open. Certainly the volume of commerce had shrunk, since Irak's economy had changed its character: it had become a predominantly natural economy, so there was much less scope for commercial activities. Irak was now a province of a great kingdom, Baghdad was no longer a capital and seat of a government where military expeditions were organised and a splendid court had to be supplied.

The international trade of Irak was even more upset. For half a century after its conquest by the Mongols there was no more regular trade with Syria and Egypt, the rulers of Tabriz and Cairo fearing lest commercial ties would be used for espionage. The trade between these countries was, however, not interrupted altogether. Sometimes, when the Ilkhanid government was opposed to it, the merchants of Irak travelled to the Christian kingdom of Little Armenia and from there to Syria. Some Ilkhans proposed to the sultans of Cairo that regular trade should be re-established. But only at the beginning of the fourteenth century was normal trade between the two states resumed. At the end of its first decade there was a special rate in Tabriz for duties to be paid by the 'merchants from Alexandria'. Characteristically enough it was a merchant, the slave dealer Madjd ad-din as-Sallami, travelling for many years between Egypt and Persia, who was instrumental in establishing peace between the two countries in 1320. Freedom of trade was agreed upon. In the third and fourth decades Syrian and Egyptian merchants made frequent journeys to Persia and beyond it, to Transoxiana, and Iraki traders visited the countries of the sultan of Cairo.[24]

On the other hand, the trade of Irak with Persia and the countries of Central Asia was considerably intensified after the Mongol conquests. Iraki merchants began regularly to visit Khwarizm and to travel through Turkestan to China. Others took advantage of the pax Mongolica to carry on trade with Kiptchak, the great Mongol kingdom north of the Caucasus. Ibn Battuta narrates that he met merchants of Karbala travelling on the great caravan routes from Khwarizm to China and other Iraki traders in Saray, the capital of Kiptchak.[25]

This new development was, however, balanced by the decline of Irak's share in the great Indian trade, which had formerly been a source of its wealth. Until its conquest by the Mongols a great part of the spices and other Indian articles had been shipped to Basra and thence carried via Baghdad and Antioch to the shores of the Mediterranean. After the establishment of Mongol rule, Tabriz became not only the capital of the Ilkhans but also a great emporium of international trade. Foreign merchants found there both the Indian spices and the products of the Persian manufactures. Tabriz itself produced precious silk stuffs – siklatun and atlas, and also attabi. Ten years after the conquest of Baghdad the sultan of Cairo captured Antioch, which had been the great commercial town at the other end of the overland route along which the Indian articles were transported from the Persian Gulf to the Mediterranean. The enmity between the rulers of Tabriz and Cairo, or rather the almost permanent state of war between them, was another reason for the shift of this great trade route. From that time a considerable part of the Indian articles which arrived on the shores of the Persian Gulf was sent to Tabriz and then on routes north of the Lake Van, via Erzindjan to Little Armenia. As the duties which the foreign merchants had to pay in the kingdom of the Ilkhans were much lower than those levied by the sultan of Cairo, the Indian trade of Persia began to flourish and Tabriz attracted ever-increasing numbers of Italian merchants. The trade of Tabriz developed necessarily at the expense of Baghdad, but the decline of Irak's share in the Indian trade was slow. W. Heyd arrived at this conclusion a hundred years ago, and his results are fully borne out by material which has been found since.[26]

Marco Polo, who travelled in 1272 from Trezibond to the Persian Gulf, describes Baghdad as a trading town. He was told that it traded with the island of Kish and that the Indian articles were sent from the Persian Gulf via Baghdad to Tabriz. He chose, however, to travel to the Persian Gulf by the new main route, viz Tabriz–Kashan–Yezd–Kirman–Ormuz. Other Oriental and European authors referring to the second half of the thirteenth century still speak of the old trade route. The Arabic geographers ad-Dimishki and Abu l-Fida and the Venetian Marino Sanuto Torsello describe Basra as the port where the Indian articles are discharged. According to several texts in the Arabic chronicles of the second half of the thirteenth century they were shipped on the Tigris from Basra to Wasit. We read that in 1272 the governor of Irak built a khan in Wasit which served the merchants engaged in the trade with Basra. The merchant ships coming from Basra to Wasit are mentioned in accounts from the years 1294 and 1299. Arabic biographical dictionaries contain biographies of merchants from Baghdad and other towns of the Fertile Crescent who travelled in the second half of the thirteenth century to India and to China. Sometimes the Arabic authors say explicitly that these merchants embarked in Basra, sometimes we can infer it from the context. On the other hand, there are the passages in the travelogue of Ibn Battuta mentioning the Iraki traders whom he met in Delhi. The merchants of Mosul must also have been very active in the Indian trade. They were renowned as traders in spices, pearls and silk. Iraki traders were often to be found at the other end of the overland route, at Lajazzo, the great port of Little Armenia. Abu l-Fida relates that when an expeditionary force of the Syrian army captured Lajazzo in 1335 many merchants from Baghdad were found there. We may safely conjecture that they were engaged in the spice trade. The acts of a Venetian notary show indeed that in that time many traders from Venice, Genoa, Ragusa, Crete and Cyprus sojourned there.[27]

There must, however, have been a sizable decrease of Irak's Indian trade in the first half of the fourteenth century, corresponding to the growth of the commercial activities carried on by the Italian traders in Tabriz and other towns of Adherbeidjan and Persia. The Ilkhans adopted a very favourable attitude towards the European merchants, allowed them to travel everywhere and, in contrast to the sultans of Cairo, let them continue their travels to India. In 1320 Venice concluded a commercial treaty with the Ilkhan, but also the Genoese, Florentines and even the Sienese had a share in the trade with Persia. From certain documents it can be inferred that it was a wholesale trade, although the articles which the Italians acquired in Tabriz and elsewhere were the lighter and more delicate spices, pearls from the Persian Gulf, and various silk fabrics. Some Genoese even devised schemes for interrupting the seaborne Indian trade of Egypt altogether, in order to divert it to the Persian Gulf. In the days of the Ilkhan Arghun (1284-91), under the auspices of his Jewish minister of finance Sad ud-daula, they sent engineers to Baghdad, where they built two warships to be sent to Aden.[28] These plans failed, but Ormuz, the great emporium of the Persian Gulf, at the beginning of the fourteenth century became the destination of the Indian ships.

It had already been an important harbour in the second half of the thirteenth century. But then the island of Kish was the great entrepôt of the international trade in the Persian Gulf and the principality of Ormuz tributary to it. At the end of the thirteenth century a rich merchant, Ibrahim as-Sawamili, became the lord of Kish. He was perhaps the greatest merchant of the Near East in that age, and the power he gathered into his hands was very great. He became tax-farmer of Fars and then also of Irak, while a brother (or son) of his was vizier of a king in Southern India. Kish, the centre of as-Sawamili's enterprises, was in his day a real merchant republic. But in opposition to the Italian merchant republics, the great trader-capitalists did not exercise power alone; they had to share it with the military.

as-Sawamili helped Ayaz, a Turkish officer of the prince of Ormuz, to revolt against him. Ayaz became the ruler of the principality and in 1300 transferred the capital to an island in the Persian Gulf. New Ormuz soon became a very busy harbour, and after as-Sawamili's death in 1306 the competition between his son Izz ad-din, who was also in control of Bahrain and Basra, and the prince of Ormuz, who ruled over a part of Oman, led to war. The two commercial states went on fighting for some years until Kish succumbed in 1327, so that New Ormuz monopolised the international trade of the Persian Gulf and the caravan road which connected it with Tabriz was the main route of the Indian trade in Persia.[29]

Some of the Indian articles which arrived in Ormuz were still shipped to Baghdad, but the greater part was transported to Tabriz. Consequently Basra and Baghdad declined. The Florentine Pegolotti, who in the fourth decade of the fourteenth century wrote his well-known *Manual of Trade*, does not mention Baghdad at all. Nasibin too, which was situated on the trade route connecting Irak and Mosul with Northern Syria, declined considerably in this period.[30]

b) *The reign of the Turcoman dynasties*

Abu Said (1316–35) was the last Ilkhan to reign over all the provinces of Persia, Adherbeidjan and Irak. After his death powerful generals set puppets on the throne, civil war ensued and within some years the mighty state of the Ilkhans fell to pieces. New dynasties carved out for themselves principalities on the ruins of the kingdom, the Karts and Sarbadars in Khurasan, the Muzaffarids in Fars, Kirman and Kurdistan. A time of troubles began in Western Persia, Irak and Adherbeidjan, political changes were frequent, princes and dynasties rapidly succeeded one another. It was an interregnum, which lasted 150 years and came to its end when the countries of the Fertile Crescent were annexed to new states on its northern and eastern fringes which had meanwhile become great powers.

After the collapse of the Ilkhanid kingdom the Near Eastern states revived once more. The old territorial units emerged as new states, the Arab-Persian administration functioned as of old, with a Mongol-Turkish military caste, living from its fiefs, superimposed on it. Irak and Upper Mesopotamia belonged to a state comprising Adherbeidjan and the neighbouring provinces. Misrule was worse than ever, the exploitation of the peasants and the town-dwellers merciless.

This period in the history of Irak and the neighbouring countries is divided into the reigns of three successive dynasties. The first was that of the Djalairids, a Mongol family. Its founder, Hasan 'the Tall', tried in vain to re-establish Ilkhanid rule by crowning one of the offspring of their family. His son Uwais, however, assumed sovereignty in 1356 and thereupon annexed Adherbeidjan to Irak, his possession of old. Uwais was an efficient ruler, made efforts to lighten the tax-burden of his subjects and abolished billeting. But the change brought about by his reforms cannot have been very considerable, the old taxes being after some time collected under new names.[31] Meanwhile Timur Lenk had built up a new Mongol empire, and neither the princes of Persia nor the Djalairids could withstand his onslaught. Ahmad b. Uwais (1382–1410) had to abandon Irak and fly to Egypt. From that time the Timurid armies cast their shadow on the politics of Irak. Whenever they approached its frontiers, its trembling rulers left their capital for the westernmost countries of the Near East. The great Mongol emperor took Baghdad twice, in 1393 and in 1401. But after his death Ahmad b. Uwais again occupied Irak in 1405.

The Djalairids were overthrown in 1410 by Kara Yusuf, chieftain of the Kara Koyunlu ('Black Sheep'), a federation of Turcoman tribes living north of Lake Van. In 1411 they also captured Baghdad and ruled for more than half a century over Irak, Upper Mesopotamia, Adherbeidjan and some provinces of Media. Their capital remained Tabriz, whereas Baghdad was the seat of a viceroy, usually a son of the reigning prince. Contemporary authors agree that the plight of Irak was never so wretched as under the rule of this dynasty. Ibn Taghribirdi says: 'The sons of Kara Yusuf altogether are the wildest people God has created, in their days the lands of Irak and Persia and the town of Baghdad have been ruined.'[32]

In 1467 another group of Turcoman tribes, the so-called Ak Koyunlu ('White Sheep') superseded this dynasty. The Ak Koyunlu had already, in the middle of the fourteenth century, taken part in the almost endless wars in East Anatolia. The seat of their chieftains, belonging to the Bayundur clan, had been Amid. In the fifties of the fifteenth century their prince Uzun Hasan became a powerful warlord. After his victory over the last of the Kara Koyunlu he conquered Baghdad in 1469 and then almost the whole of Persia (with the exception of Khurasan). So he was a mighty king and the Venetians, hard pressed by the rising power of the Ottomans, cherished hopes that he would check their advance. From the year 1463 there was a frequent change of embassies between Venice and the king of Persia, but also the sovereigns of Naples, Hungary and Poland sent embassies to him. His army probably exceeded 100,000 men, but it was not equipped with the new firearms. The Venetians decided to supply him with artillery. In 1473 they sent him 52 mortars, six of them big ones, 500 arquebuses, matchlocks and also the necessary ammunition. Two hundred musketeers were ordered to teach the Persian army how to use the modern weapons. But the consignment did not arrive in time. In July 1473 Uzun Hasan suffered a crushing defeat, because of the technological inferiority of his army. His men could not hold their own against the attack of the Ottoman artillery, which successfully used mortars and matchlocks.[33] This defeat did not, however, result in the loss of extensive territories, and even the son and successor of Uzun Hasan, Yakub Shah (1478–90), was a powerful king.

The end of the fourteenth century and the fifteenth were the apogee of feudalism in the history of Irak. Although the army was still partly paid in cash, the hold of the military on the feudal estates had never before been so absolute as then. The peasants and also the townspeople, however, suffered not less from the Bedouin and other nomadic and semi-nomadic tribes, which became very strong in this period of feudal anarchy. The Khafadja sacked al-Hilla, one of the important towns of Irak, in 1421. Basra was occupied by the Muntafik tribe at the beginning of the fifteenth century and remained under their rule till 1417, being captured again by these Bedouin at the end of the century. The rule of the Turcoman feudal lords, the Bedouin and the Kurdish clans in the north-eastern borderlands of Irak spelt destruction and extortion. Villages were plundered and set on fire, and the inhabitants of the towns had to pay contributions to ransom themselves from torture.

The burden of the townspeople was less heavy than that of the peasants. In some provinces the inhabitants of the towns paid lower taxes for their rural estates than the peasants. The régime of the feudal princes was nevertheless so oppressive that they were even looking forward to the invasion of foreign powers, whosoever they might be, as liberators. When Timur occupied Baghdad in 1393 the people, who hated Ahmad b. Uwais, gave him their blessing and subsequently collaborated with the new administration. In Shiraz too, where the people had suffered grievously from the Muzaffarids, Timur was received as a liberator.[34]

But the townspeople were incapable of offering the Mongol-Turkish feudal lords a strong resistance. They were not warlike, nor could they withstand the attacks of their cavalry. The same is true of the peasants. So there was only one class which could enter into a contest with the feudal lords – the Bedouin tribes. The age of the Kara Koyunlu saw indeed the birth of a revolutionary movement among the Bedouin tribes of Southern Irak, which became a factor to reckon with in the political life of the region of the Persian Gulf.

Not all the Bedouin of Southern Irak joined the rebels; many clans even fought against them. Probably the poorer tribes were the mainstay of the movement, and some groups of peasants possibly supported it too. The Arabic writers, most of them theologians or at least devout Moslems, describe the rebels as heretics, radical Shiites, who believed that the spirit of Ali had been incarnated in their leaders. Such was indeed the belief of the 'Hululiyya', the Ali Ilahi and other fanatic Shiites. That was the superstructure, the religious ideology which in the middle ages disguised so many social revolutionary risings. The leaders of the revolt are also decried as magicians who owe their success to witchcraft. However that may have been, their propaganda had much success among the Bedouin in South Irak, on the banks of the Lower Tigris, in the region of the Swamps and on the frontier of Khuzistan. These provinces were the same as had been the scene of the revolts of the Zindj and the Karmatians. The new revolt indeed bore a striking resemblance to those earlier revolutionary movements and contemporary authors were aware of this fact. The first leader of the revolt is called 'al-habith', the 'abominable', as the prince of the Zindj had been. The rebels are also explicitly compared, by Ibn Taghribirdi, with the Karmatians. Like the Karmatians they seldom succeeded in capturing large towns, and when they occupied one, they usually sacked it and abandoned it. But they founded a small commonwealth which existed for a long time, and at its heyday was a real state which exchanged embassies with powerful sovereigns.

The founder of the movement, Muhammad b. Falah, was apparently a Syrian, from Wadi t-Taym. Probably he came as a child to Wasit, or perhaps his parents had already settled there before he was born. He studied at al-Hilla under the guidance of a Shiite doctor, who was also a sufi and applied himself to the study of occult sciences. Muhammad b. Falah began his career in about 1420, pretending to be an Alid. By conjuration and magic he won a following among the Bedouin on the Lower Tigris and became known as 'al-Mushasha', the 'Radiated'. Later he proclaimed himself as the Mahdi, the Redeemer who according to the belief of the Moslems will come at the end of days. In 1440 he embarked on military activities, attacking Wasit. Two years later he made another onslaught on this town, but was driven back a second time and defeated in skirmishes with the government troops. His attempts to conquer Basra and other towns and fortresses proved a failure too. Nevertheless, Bedouin joined him in ever greater numbers. As the rebels constantly plundered villages and took plenty of booty, their activities appealed to the instincts of the poor nomads. Among those who recognised al-Mushasha as their leader were clans of the Banu Laith, Banu Hatit, Banu Sad, Banu Asad, Banu Salama (a tribe belonging to the Banu Muadi), Banu Raznan and Banu Tayy.

When al-Mushasha had succeeded in stirring up so many Bedouin, he retired and proclaimed his son Maula Ali leader of the movement. His leadership proved very successful. In 1453 he took Wasit, where he appointed a governor, and, still in the same year, he attacked the Iraki pilgrims' caravan on its way to Mecca. The rebels captured an enormous booty, and when after this heavy blow to the Moslem world an army was sent against them from Baghdad, they defeated it. Thereupon they sacked al-Hilla. In 1456 Maula Ali ravaged East Irak, in the district of Tarik Khurasan, plundering the villages and small towns and setting fire to them, and carrying off the women and children. When, at the end of 1457, the government of Irak sent an embassy to Cairo to inform the sultan of a victory over the rebels and to assure him that the pilgrims' route to Mecca was safe, that was pure vainglory. For many years there was no pilgrimage from Irak. When the Kara Koyunlu sent an army against the rebels, their leader retreated to al-Huwaiza, his seat near the frontier of Khuzistan. He also had ships and points of support on the islands of the Persian Gulf. In 1457 Maula Ali was killed, whereupon al-Mushasha, his father, once more took over the leadership. The parallel with the history of the Karmatians is striking indeed.

The power of the rebels was then at its apogee. A short time after the death of his son, al-Mushasha won a great victory over the government army, which was supported by many Bedouin clans. In 1462 al-Mushasha died and was succeeded by al-Muhsin, another son, who was as capable and bold as his predecessors had been. It is true that the rebels sometimes had to suffer setbacks. Djihanshah, the powerful prince of the Kara Koyunlu, sent a strong army against them and secured the passage of the pilgrims on the long-established route to Mecca. So in 1467 the hadjdj could once more be made from Irak, after an interruption of many years. But, on the other hand, al-Muhsin succeeded about the same time in conquering al-Hilla. His power was even greater than that of his father and brother. He ruled not only over the borderland of Irak and Khuzistan and the region of the Swamps, but also over the greater part of the province of Baghdad and some islands of the Persian Gulf. There were even some Kurdish tribes living on the eastern frontier of Irak who recognised him as their prince. His commonwealth became a state with all its appurtenances, including the minting of coins.[35]

In the days of the mighty Uzun Hasan al-Muhsin apparently abstained from razzias into the territories under the control of his officers. But immediately after his death in 1478 he launched new campaigns in several provinces of Irak – al-Hilla, Baghdad, Diyala and Khalis. In 1484 Uzun Hasan's son and successor Yakub Shah retorted by sending a strong army against the followers of al-Mushasha and had complete success. His army won a great victory. Characteristically enough, a contemporary chronicler says that Yakub Shah had been instigated to this campaign by the sultan of Cairo. So the revolt of the Bedouin in Southern Irak had frightened even the ruling class in Egypt and the kings of Persia-Irak and Egypt, otherwise bitterly hostile to each other, regarded the struggle with these rebels as a matter of common interest. However that may have been, the power of the rebels was not yet broken. For in 1487 they made preparations for a campaign against Tustar, a large town in Khuzistan. In order to re-assure Yakub Shah, they sent an embassy to him saying that the pre-parations were for the liberation of Basra from the Bedouin who had occupied it. According to a contemporary chronicler in 1492 an embassy came to the sultan of Cairo from al-Muhsin, 'the lord of the land of Basra'. So it may be that the followers of al-Mushasha actually occupied Basra for some time.

al-Muhsin died in 1508 and his offspring ruled for a considerable time longer over the Bedouin on the frontier of Irak and Khuzistan. They even struck coins, in this way proclaiming their independence.[36]

The hatred which the followers of al-Mushasha aroused among the theologians, both Sunnites and Shiites, was very great. Indeed, they had not only interrupted the regular pilgrimage to Mecca, but also desecrated the holy shrine in Nadjaf at the tomb of Ali, and that in Karbala, the place of martyrdom of al-Husain. Their adversaries maintained that they abrogated the precepts of Islam, allowing that which the Koran had forbidden. They were accused of sheer atheism and of allowing the marriage of a man with his daughter or his sister.

The imputation of libertinism was put forward against various heretical movements in the middle ages, both in the Moslem Near East and in the Christian world. It was very often a weapon against those heretics whose ideas were blended with a revolutionary programme.

It seems that the bulk of Irak's peasantry was not contaminated by the ideas of these rebels and heretics. The great masses of the peasants languished under the yoke of the Turcoman feudal lords, despairing of any change in their situation. Indeed, their conditions of life were in this period worse even than before, the feudal system of land tenure having now been completely established.

The taxes which the peasants had to pay were different in the various provinces ruled by the Kara Koyunlu and the Ak Koyunlu. Uzun Hasan undertook a codification of the local practice in every province, its purpose being to protect the peasants from arbitrary taxation. It seems that he enacted also a general reduction of the land tax. Since the

Ottomans used his fiscal code and the documents referring to it have therefore been preserved in some provinces of East Anatolia, the rates of various taxes are known. In the province of Diyar Bakr, for instance, the peasants had to deliver a fifth part of the crops, were liable to corvée (the non-Moslems to a greater amount) and had to pay many other taxes.[37]

The feudal system of land tenure in Irak was brought to perfection under the Turcomans. The new stage in its development had begun, however, in the days of the Djalairids. The expression *ikta* disappeared and was replaced by the Mongol term 'soyurghal'. This was not a mere change of name. The institution itself had undergone a great change. Whereas the fief of the Ilkhanid period had been a conditional grant, revocable upon failure of the fiefholder to meet his liabilities, the soyurghal was hereditary, even if this was not stated explicitly in the deed by which it was conferred. The grant was considered 'perpetual', although it had to be confirmed by the successor of the prince who had made it. Secondly, the fiefholders obtained administrative and judicial immunity. In the feudal charters of this period one reads that 'the feet of the officials are removed, their pens raised'. These expressions recall the wording of feudal charters in medieval Europe: *sine introitu iudicum*.

Both the Djalairids and the Turcoman princes of Irak and Adherbeidjan granted their military, and also civilians, large and small fiefs. Chieftains of strong tribes would get whole districts, lower ranking knights one or two villages. As the soyurghal was also an institution of the Timurid states, it became in the fifteenth century the most usual form of land tenure in Irak and in Adherbeidjan. Uzun Hasan, who tried to win the support of the clergy, granted many fiefs to people belonging to this class, although military service was still required from the fiefholders. His successors, Yakub Shah and Rustum, did the same.[38]

The increase of feudal estates necessarily led to disintegration, and the danger to the mere survival of the central authority was even greater since the military acquired so many estates that they became the majority of the owners of allodial land. So the last Ak Koyunlu made attempts to recover the fiefs and other lands granted to pious endowments, or at least a part of them. Just at the end of the reign of Yakub Shah such an attempt was made. But it encountered the opposition of the feudal lords and also of the theologians, and the death of Yakub Shah was followed by the downfall of the officials carrying out the reform. Ahmad, one of the last rulers of this dynasty, who reigned in

1487, had a more radical approach to the feudal system, which was not only dangerous for the régime itself but entailed the decline of agriculture by the oppression of the peasantry. Ahmad undertook to lighten the tax-burden and abolished altogether the 'ikhradjat' and 'shiltakat', those extraordinary imposts which were *eo ipso* arbitrarily assessed. At the same time he refused to confirm soyurghals granted by his predecessors, which suggests an intention to abolish the grant of fiefs. Once more the feudal lords opposed the good intentions of the prince and within a few months overthrew him.[39]

There can be little doubt that the feudal régime as built up by the successors of the Ilkhans proved detrimental to agricultural production and accelerated the decrease in output.

The reign of the Djalairids and the Turcomans also brought about a decline in the domestic and foreign trade of Irak. There were several reasons for this retrogression. One of them was certainly the overwhelming predominance of the barter economy. Never before, since the Moslems conquered Irak, had the country sunk to a natural economy of such a low level as under the Turcomans. Secondly, the general impoverishment of the population must have resulted in the shrinking of commercial activities. So the slow but progressive decrease of the volume of trade was an element in the general economic decline. The small number of Iraki coins which have come down to us from this period bear witness of these conditions. The Djalairids still struck gold and silver coins, such as dinars, awal and raidj dinars, and dirhams. They had mints in Baghdad, Basra, al-Hilla, Wasit, Irbil, al-Imadiyya and Mosul. The number of coins which have been preserved from the days of the Kara Koyunlu and the Ak Koyunlu is insignificant;[40] their paucity is a clear sign of economic decline. The rapaciousness of the feudal lords who ruled over Irak and Adherbeidjan in this period slackened the rhythm of commercial activities. Instead of taking measures to redress the downward trend of most branches of domestic and foreign trade, the Turcoman rulers increased the taxes on trade. According to Nasir ad-din Tusi, the adviser of Hülegü, the tamgha should amount to $\frac{1}{240}$, but the rate at which it was levied in Tabriz under Öldjeitü (1304–16) was 5%. Pegolotti, writing thirty years later, says that it was $4\frac{1}{2}$%. The first Djalairids, whose fiscal policy was more lenient, collected $2\frac{1}{2}$%. But in the fifteenth century the tamgha was much higher and rose to 10% in the second half of the century. Uzun Hasan wanted to abolish it altogether, but his advisers persuaded him to fix it at 5%. The exemption of the staff of the governor of Baghdad (and probably of other governors and feudal lords) from the payment of the tamgha was a characteristic feature of the feudal régime. It was undoubtedly very detrimental to the activities of private merchants. On the other hand, the last princes of the Ak Koyunlu dynasty and their vassals exploited the merchants in various ways or simply robbed them of their merchandise.[41]

Irak's foreign trade declined in the age of the Djalairids and the Turcomans together with that of the other countries formerly belonging to the Ilkhanid kingdom. The commercial ties between Irak and Syria, however, were probably closer than before. In the second half of the fourteenth century traders from Baghdad and Basra visited Egypt also, to which they exported textiles from Irak. But the share of Irak and Adherbeidjan in the Indian transit trade decreased considerably, mainly as a consequence of the general insecurity prevailing in these countries after the death of the Ilkhan Abu Said. In 1344 the rulers of Tabriz sent an embassy to Genoa and induced its traders to resume their activities in the Ilkhanid kingdom. But they sustained heavy losses, whereas the Venetians had adopted a more cautious attitude from the outset and had not responded to the invitation. The Djalairid Uwais repeated it in 1372. Addressing himself to the merchants of Venice with the invitation to return to his dominions, he promised their 'bailo' in Trebizond that he would in future repair any damage done to them. The deterioration of conditions in the former Ilkhanid dominions was, however, only one reason for the decline of their trade with the Italian republics. Another was the progressive decrease of Persia's overland trade with the Far East. In the age of the Ilkhans this country had been the starting-point for European and Near Eastern traders of their travels to China. But after the accession of the Ming to the throne of the Celestial empire its trade underwent a great change and the number of foreign merchants who travelled there through Central Asia dwindled more and more.[42]

The Italian traders, however, did not cut off all connection with Adherbeidjan and the neighbouring countries. In 1364 there were two tamgha offices in Tabriz, one for silk, Chinese spices and furs, the other for Persian, European and Egyptian textiles. Venetian documents give evidence of travel to Tabriz at the beginning of the fifteenth century and even much later, until about the first half of the sixteenth century. Other documents in the archives of Venice refer to the journeys of merchants in Central Asia in the sixties of the fourteenth century. But Tabriz and Sultaniyya remained the destination of most journeys.

There the Venetians and Genoese acquired various Indian articles which were preferably transported overland, and in addition pearls from the Persian Gulf, precious stones and silk, both raw silk from the Caspian provinces and costly silk fabrics from China and Persia. At the other end of the trans-Persian land-route Ormuz was still a flourishing harbour, and Oriental and European travellers dwell on the great volume of its trade with India. Among them are Abdurrazzak b. Ishak, who visited the island in 1442, the Russian trader Afanasij Nikitin, who was there in 1469, Giosafat Barbaro in the seventies of the fifteenth century, and Ludovico di Varthema at the beginning of the sixteenth century. The traffic in the harbour of Ormuz increased progressively. In the first half of the fifteenth century Chinese merchant fleets began to visit it, and its princes sent embassies to the emperor of China. Ormuz was indeed in this period a state ruled by an aristocracy of merchants and soldiers.[43]

The great prosperity of the trade of Ormuz and the revival of the trade between Irak and Syria caused some of the Indian articles arriving in the Persian Gulf to be shipped to Basra and thence to Baghdad. Italian merchants visited these towns and some of them stayed there a long time. The Venetian Dracone Zeno made a great overland journey in Asia in 1425 and lived some years in Basra.[44] The merchants of Baghdad took part in the Indian trade and were to be found in the great emporia of Ormuz and Tabriz. The main routes of the trade between Adherbeidjan and the ports of the Eastern Mediterranean were still those which crossed Armenia and East Anatolia, north of the frontiers of Irak. They connected Tabriz through Akhlat, Bitlis and Urfa, or through Amid, with Northern Syria. The destination of almost all the caravans was Aleppo, where the raw silk of Persia was handed over to the Venetian merchants. The assessments of the duties in Ottoman codes dating from 1518 shed light on the intense commercial movement on these trade routes. In Maridin duties were levied on the transit trade in silk from Yezd, on cotton fabrics from Balalbok, textiles from Damascus, Egypt and European countries, in Amid on textiles from Aleppo and Alexandria, in Kharput on silks and European textiles. Spices are not mentioned at all in these regulations. One is forced to conclude that the silk of Persia was transported to the shores of the Mediterranean by the caravan routes of Upper Mesopotamia and Armenia, the spices by other routes which connected Baghdad and Aleppo, to the south of the hill land of Upper Mesopotamia. That the transit trade of Upper Mesopotamia was still flourishing at the end of this period is borne out by the fact that in 1518 150 European merchants were staying in Amid.[45]

So the accounts of many travellers and various documents show that the shift of the trade routes from the Persian Gulf to the Mediterranean which had been a consequence of the Mongol conquests had changed trade relations between Irak and the Mediterranean countries during the later centuries of the middle ages. The main routes of the overland trade between Persia and Adherbeidjan no longer crossed Irak in post-Mongol times – a change that must have had a tremendous impact on the development of Baghdad and other towns of Irak. The progressive decrease of Irak's share in the transit trade of the Near East resulted necessarily in the shrinking of its towns.

The decline of trade was, however, only one cause of depopulation at the end of the middle ages. There were several others. At the beginning of the Djalairid reign, in 1342–3, there was once more a famine in Irak and Upper Mesopotamia. An Arabic author includes in the biography of Hasan the Tall, the founder of the dynasty, an account of an excessive dearth. According to him it induced many of the inhabitants of Baghdad to leave for other regions. Perhaps the author had the famine of 1342–3 in mind.[46]

Some years later Irak was visited by the terrible pestilence known as the Black Death. As in all other countries of the Near East, it was a real demographic catastrophe. This epidemic of bubonic plague took a heavy toll in the towns and villages of Irak and Upper Mesopotamia. The plague began in the province of Baghdad in the summer of 1347 and came to its climax in both Irak and Upper Mesopotamia in 1349.[47] The accounts of the pestilence in Irak which have come down to us are neither numerous, nor detailed, but its impact on the demographic development of Irak must have been tremendous.

The chroniclers report other subsequent epidemics which were certainly an important factor in the demographic development of Irak. In 1394 there was an epidemic and following it a famine in the province of Baghdad. In the first half of the fifteenth century these epidemics, some of which are called *taun*, meaning plague, were quite frequent. In 1416, when most other countries of the Near East were also haunted by the plague, it ravaged all the provinces of Irak and Upper Mesopotamia, apart from that of Mosul. In 1425 it appeared again in Upper Mesopotamia. In 1431, as a consequence of a war between the Kara Koyunlu and Shah Rukh, son of Timur Lenk, Irak was visited by dearth, famine and epidemics. They spread also in most provinces of Upper Mesopotamia. Then, in 1436, various diseases raged in Basra after a great flood. The year 1438 brought a heavy epidemic of the true bubonic plague, which spread at the same time through most countries of the Near East. It wrought havoc in Irak. The number of the victims was very great and in some places few inhabitants survived. One chronicle reports that in the town of al-Haditha only seven people remained. In 1470 there was a new outbreak of the plague. In Baghdad the number of victims reached 1,500 in one day. The plague spread also to Takrit, Shahrazur, Irbil and Mosul and everywhere took a heavy toll.[48]

Besides economic decline and the epidemics there were two other main causes of depopulation – frequent wars and misrule. The sieges and captures of towns by various armies often resulted in massacres. The worst was the carnage in 1401 following the second conquest of Baghdad by Timur Lenk. Some tens of thousands of the inhabitants were cruelly murdered. In the course of the fifteenth century there were several sieges of Baghdad and we shall probably not be mistaken in supposing that they accelerated the decrease of its population. The town was besieged in 1410–11, 1446, 1465 and 1467. After the siege and capture of the town in 1446 part of it was destroyed. The siege of 1465 lasted a year and was followed by a massacre. Arabic authors say that there remained only few people in the town.

Sometimes the inhabitants of a town preferred to abandon it when they despaired of withstanding an approaching army, as happened in Wasit and al-Hilla in 1453. The inhabitants of Wasit destroyed the town and abandoned it, seeing that they were incapable of offering resistance to the Bedouin of al-Mushasha. The exodus from al-Hilla was a true disaster, many of the fugitives dying from hunger, thirst and exhaustion. Then Maula Ali set fire to the abandoned town.

It seems, however, that among the factors which brought about depopulation misrule was not the least important. The contemporary chroniclers relate that in the days of Shah Muhammad, governor of Baghdad from 1411 to 1438, the emigration of its inhabitants became a major phenomenon in its life. But the people of other towns in Irak also left for Syria and other countries. The decay of the large towns was so obvious that even European travellers became aware of it. The Venetian ambassador Giosafat Barbaro writes in his travelogue that Baghdad 'which was once a famous town is now to a great extent destroyed'.[49]

So the centuries-long rule of the military had brought upon Irak destruction, economic decline and depopulation. At the turn of the sixteenth century the prosperity and culture of the land of the Euphrates and Tigris, the cradle of splendid civilisations, had sunk to the lowest level. The conquest of Baghdad by Ismail Shah in 1503 and the subsequent annexation of Irak to the new Persian state sealed the fate of a civilisation which was doomed to ruin a long time before.

CHAPTER VIII

Mamluk Feudalism

The conquest of Irak by the Mongols had far-reaching consequences also as far as the other countries of the Near East were concerned. One of them was the establishment of Mamluk rule in Egypt and in Syria. The regiments of military slaves who succeeded in repelling the Mongol invaders set up a government of their own, eliminating the civilians. For many centuries civilian dignitaries had shared the government with Turkish generals, but when the Mamluks took over officers were appointed to manage all the departments. Medieval feudalism in the Near East received its final shape from former slaves.

The Mamluks were foreigners ruling over millions of people who were excluded from the higher ranks of the feudal hierarchy. They had no interest in developing the economic forces of their countries. So their rule degenerated into reckless exploitation, which ruined once flourishing countries.

a) *The Mamluk régime*

After the conquests of the Mongols in the first half of the thirteenth century, their invasions of Eastern Europe and their long wars with the Khwarizm-shah, the slave markets of Western Asia were better supplied than ever. Countless prisoners of war were offered to the highest bidder. One of the Moslem princes who acquired great numbers of young able-bodied Turkish slaves for his army was the Ayyubid sultan of Egypt, al-Malik as-Salih Ayyub (1240–9). After his death the slave regiments, called in Arabic *mamluks*, deposed the Ayyubids and chose one of their generals to be sultan. This was the beginning of Mamluk rule which lasted more than 250 years, from the middle of the thirteenth century until 1517. After their great victory over the Mongols in the battle of Ain Djalut, in 1260, Syria fell to them and later they established their suzerainty also over Barca in the west, Hidjaz, Yemen and some provinces of Asia Minor, north of the Syrian frontier. The

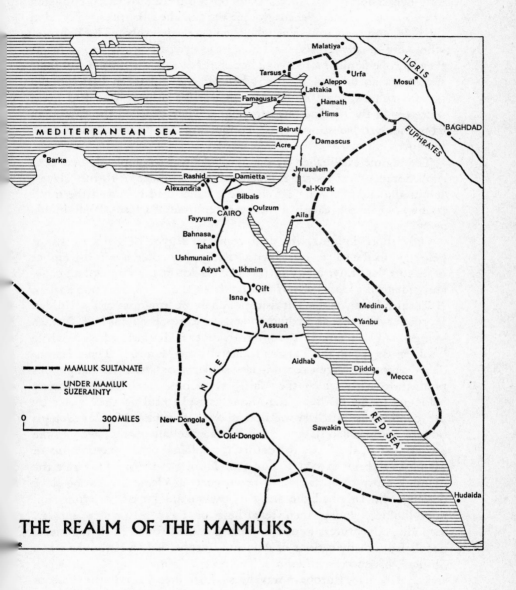

MALATIYA

TIGRIS

Tarsus • Urfa
Aleppo • Mosul
Lattakia •
Hamath •
Famagusta • Hims •

EUPHRATES

BAGHDAD

MEDITERRANEAN SEA

Beirut •
Acre •
• Damascus

Barka •

Jerusalem •
Rashid • Damietta • al-Karak
Alexandria •
Bilbais •
CAIRO Qulzum •
Fayyum • Aila •
Bahnasa •
Taha •
Ushmunain •
Asyut • Ikhmim •
Medina •
Qift • Yanbu •
Isna •

Assuan •

N
I
L
E
Aidhab •
Djidda • Mecca •

— — MAMLUK SULTANATE
- - - UNDER MAMLUK
SUZERAINTY

0   300 MILES

New Dongola •
Old Dongola • Sawakin •

RED SEA

Hudaida •

THE REALM OF THE MAMLUKS

long succession of Mamluk sultans on the throne of Cairo consisted
of two clearly distinguished groups: the so-called Bahrites, who ruled
till 1382, and the Circassians who then succeeded them. The Bahrites,
who were mostly Turks, maintained the dynastic principle insofar as
they left one family more than a hundred years on the throne, but their
successors abandoned it. But whatever the difference between the
various sultans, most of them were warlike princes who had great
successes in their numerous campaigns. They expelled the Crusaders
from the Syro-Palestinian coast, conquering Tripoli in 1289 and Acre
in 1291.

The régime established by the Mamluks was a completely new one,
a phenomenon *sui generis*: a Praetorian government of former slaves.
It was the end of a long development which had begun in the ninth
century when the caliph al-Mutasim enlisted Turkish slaves in his
army.

Only those knights who had come to Egypt or Syria as slaves
belonged to the ruling class, because only they could attain the higher
grades in the army. Many of them never learnt the Arabic language,
and remained a class entirely distinct from the indigenous population.
A Turkish koiné or the Turkish spoken in the kingdom of the Golden
Horde served them as a common language. Some sultans had Turkish
stories read to them. In the fifteenth century Turkish scholars wrote
books in Egypt on the Turkish spoken by the Mamluks. Their descendants were considered second-class subjects, as were the indigenous
population with which they fairly soon mixed. As their posterity
belonged to the civilians, the Mamluks had to fill up their ranks by
the continuous purchase of new slaves. The first Mamluk sultans
bought perhaps 800 slaves a year, the later sultans many fewer. In the
second half of the fifteenth century the sultans' yearly acquisitions of
Mamluks did not exceed 200 or 300. Throughout their long rule the
Mamluk army comprised very heterogeneous elements. As the slave
dealers, who supplied the army of the sultan, imported strong and
good-looking young men regardless of their nationality and as,
secondly, adventurers joined it, there could be found in its regiments
people from many nations of Asia and Europe. Sultan Kitbogha was a
Mongol, his successor Ladjin a Teutonic knight, sultan Khushkadam
was an Albanian. European travellers who visited Cairo in the fifteenth
century met there Mamluks who were of German, Hungarian or
Italian origin.

The Mamluks of the sultan, garrisoned in Cairo, were the core of the army. Their ranks were increased by the Mamluks of his pre-decessors and by those of dismissed or deceased amirs (officers). But the personal attachment of the Mamluks whom he had bought was the mainstay of the sultan. The royal Mamluks were the best trained corps of the army, and the bodyguard of the sultan, and the high officers and dignitaries of the court were recruited from them. The amirs who held the posts of provincial governors had Mamluks of their own. In the second half of the thirteenth and in the first half of the fourteenth century a rich and powerful amir would have 300, 600 or even 800 Mamluks. In the fifteenth century the amirs had no more than 200–300 Mamluks. A third part of the regular army was the 'halka', consisting of free knights, such as descendants of Mamluks, natives who had joined the army, Bedouin chieftains and Turcomans. In the days of the first Bahrites these non-Mamluk contingents were considered an important part of the army, but already at the beginning of the fourteenth century they were declining and later they lost any military value.[1] Altogether, the first Mamluk sultans could mobilise 40–50,000 knights, beside auxiliary troops who were mostly foot-soldiers.

Like the feudal armies which they succeeded the Mamluks lived on their fiefs, which corresponded to their military grades. This feudal system underwent, however, a great change about a lifetime after it came into being. Under the first Bahrite sultans the fiefs were heritable,[2] but later this system was abolished, and from then on the Mamluks practised the feudal system as conceived by Nizam al-mulk, drawing the logical conclusions from his precepts. The fief of an amir comprised usually some villages, that of a royal Mamluk one or even less. But the fiefs did not consist of contiguous estates. In order to prevent the rise of a feudal aristocracy based upon its estates and its following in a certain district, the Mamluk sultans granted their knights estates which were scattered in various regions. Further, when a Mamluk passed in the course of his career to another province, his fief was changed.[3] This policy achieved its purpose but it also had disadvantages. The knights, who held their fiefs only for a limited time, had no real interest in their maintenance or in improving or developing them. So the feudal system of the Mamluks proved, in the long run, really disastrous for the economy of the Near East.

The foreign slaves who had become the lords of Egypt and Syria did their utmost to enrich themselves as soon as possible. The revenue from their fiefs and other sources of income were much higher than those of the military who had ruled before them. At the beginning of Mamluk rule a royal Mamluk or a halka knight had a fief yielding 83–125 dinars a month, but by the middle of the fourteenth century an adult Mamluk had 40–60 dinars and in addition payments in cash and allowances in kind. The fief of an officer commanding ten Mamluks would have yielded him 45–130 dinars, and even the Mamluks of the amirs, whose revenue was lower, had 10–30 dinars a month. At the same time the salary of a subaltern official was 2–3 dinars a month and that of a middle-class official 6–7 dinars.[4]

The economic and political superiority of the military was the main feature of the Mamluk régime. Whereas the Ayyubids still left the bourgeois some shadow of self-government, appointing in Syrian towns those mayors who were called *rais*, the Mamluks abolished the last remnants of self-administration. The last *rais* of Aleppo is mentioned in 1260, just before the Mamluks occupied Northern Syria. When they seized the government town administration changed a great deal. The Mamluk knights lived in the towns and there exercised full authority. The chief of the police, the *wali*, who was a Mamluk, and the inspector of the markets, the *muhtasib*, administered the town. This latter official appointed the arifs, the syndics of the crafts. The associations of craftsmen lost much of their influence. They were not true trade-unions, but rather social fraternities. The syndicates of physicians and engineers, whose chiefs were appointed by the sultan, were not autonomous bodies. These corporations served the interests of the feudal government by supervising the activities of their members.[5]

The political decline of the Near Eastern bourgeoisie under the Bahrites was evidently associated with its economic dependence upon the feudal aristocracy. As the revenue from rural estates was the main source of wealth, the appropriation of the greater part of it by the military and the transition from tax-farming to enfeoffment reduced the bourgeoisie to a position of inferiority. The feudal knights disposed of the bulk of the grain crops, and they or their agents became the main dealers in victuals. They were also very active in economic life by investing large sums in the construction of market-halls and leasing shops.[6] The theologians, once a very influential class, became even more dependent upon the Mamluks. Either appointed by the government to the post of kadi, or teaching at the colleges (*madrasas*) which were endowed by the Mamluks, they had to collaborate with them. The protests which they lodged from time to time against the extortions of the government were no more than a gesture. The military, on the other hand, wooed them by championing orthodoxy, e.g. by promulgating decrees against Christians and Jews.

The detailed accounts of Arabic (native) chroniclers of the misgovernment of the Mamluks weigh heavily against their undoubted merits. Their reign was the rule of an élite, renovating or rather rejuvenating itself continuously with newcomers. Further, in their military hierarchy every member of the ruling class could attain the highest grade. So their régime was based on natural selection: the most capable (and most unscrupulous) seized power. This explains how they held their own during so long a period and how they could guarantee their subjects a large measure of security.

There remained in the Mamluk kingdom only one class which did not submit to them and continually rebelled against their rule. The almost endless revolts of the Bedouin sometimes looked dangerous, but the Mamluks always had the upper hand. One reason for the failure of these revolts was the heterogeneous character of the Bedouin tribes and their rather antagonistic interests. Some of them were still true nomads, others were half settled and a third group consisted of peasants who kept the tribal organisation of their ancestors.

The most powerful Bedouin in Syria throughout the later middle ages were the Yemenite Al Fadl. They lived near Salamiyya, Balis and in other districts of the provinces of Hims, Hamath and Aleppo. Their chieftains, who called themselves 'kings of the Arabs in the Eastern and Northern regions', were granted large fiefs from the sultans of Cairo, such as Tadmor, Sarmin and Maarrat an-Numan. Sometimes they went over to the Ilkhans, but before long they made peace with the Mamluks and returned to Syria. As true nomads they lived everywhere as sheep-breeders on the edges of the cultivated land. According to an Arabic author they numbered 24,000 combatants in the middle of the fifteenth century, whereas other Syrian tribes had no more than 1,000 or 2,000. There were, however, even in Northern Syria other tribes with whom the Mamluks had to reckon. One of them was the Banu Kilab, who were powerful all through the fourteenth century, another the Banu Khalid. The Al Fadl had come to Northern Syria from the Hauran. When they left this province other Yemenite tribes replaced them. The Al Mura became the most prominent tribe in the Hauran, the Al Ali in the districts around Damascus; the Zabid lived in both of these regions. In Transjordania the Al Ukba ranged from al-Karak to the borders of Hidjaz, other tribes which lived in this region were the Banu Lam and the Banu Sakhr. The strongest tribe in Cisjordanian Palestine was the Al Djarm, who lived in the province of Gaza and in the Judaean hill country. All these tribes continued the roving life of the Arabs of yore, breeding cattle and attacking peaceful peasants or caravans.[7]

On the other hand, the descendants of Bedouin who had become tillers of the soil were in certain regions of Syria and Palestine an important part of the peasantry. These free peasants (*ashir*), who kept their tribal organisation and had chiefs (*mukaddam*) appointed by the government, lived in numerous villages in the districts of the Mardj, az-Zabadani, the Bika, Wadi Taim and Central Palestine. In wartime they were called to service as auxiliary troops.[8]

The majority of the Bedouin in Egypt were in process of transition from a migratory to a settled life. They lived in *kufur*, hamlets outside the villages, sowing a little grain, but more inclined to cattle-breeding. In order to find good pasturelands they still wandered about for some part of every year. Their chieftains, who often lived in small towns or villages, were also responsible for security in certain regions. Some of these Bedouin clans were wealthy, possessing many thousands of sheep and camels, while others living on the southern border of Egypt carried on a lively trade with Nubia and enriched themselves, but many were very poor and eager to seize the grain crops. But whatever their economic situation, all of them were bitterly hostile to the Mamluks, whom they considered were usurpers. The animosity of the Bedouin in Egypt, where the social contrasts were sharper, was even greater than in Syria.[9]

When the Mamluks had deposed their Ayyubid masters, Hisn ad-din Thalab, chief of a strong tribe in Upper Egypt, rose against them and all over Egypt the Bedouin joined him. He proclaimed himself ruler of Egypt and for some years withstood the attacks of the Mamluks.[10] This was the most dangerous of the Bedouin revolts and the Mamluks never forgot it. They punished the Bedouin in the most cruel way whenever they tried to cast off their yoke. A Bedouin insurgent or even a simple robber caught by the Mamluks was sadistically tortured before being executed. Sometimes they were flayed, sometimes they were beheaded and their heads hung round the necks of their wives, who were paraded through the towns. Undoubtedly the Mamluks used these cruel methods in order to terrorise the Bedouin, for even after the defeat of Hisn ad-din they were a factor to reckon with. Their difficult economic situation or their warlike spirit spurred them time and again to new revolts. Sometimes they were joined by the peasants, but more often they were treated as their enemies. But the striking feature of their revolts was their isolation. Usually a single tribe rose against the Mamluk government without support from others. So they were no match for the Mamluks, whose military superiority was overwhelming.

It would be tedious to quote the almost innumerable accounts of the revolts of the Bedouin against the Mamluks. They began with the establishment of Mamluk rule and went on till the downfall of the sultans of Cairo. In 1262 they rose again in Upper Egypt, killing the governor of Kus, and in 1281 the ashir sacked Gaza and Nabulus. During the long and firm reign of al-Malik an-Nasir Muhammad (1309–41) there were no major outbreaks of Bedouin resistance, but in the middle of the fourteenth century there was again a great rebellion. In 1349 the ashir revolted in Palestine and in Southern Syria, and four years later the Bedouin of Upper Egypt rebelled under the leadership of Ibn al-Ahdab, chieftain of the Arak. The Al Fadl rose in 1368 and defeated and killed the governor of Aleppo.[11]

At the end of the fourteenth century the province of al-Buhaira in Western Egypt became the focus of Bedouin resistance. In this province there lived some tribes which led a partly settled life, such as the Banu Azala, who were rich cattle-breeders. But there were also the Banu Labid, a powerful tribe who lived mostly in the adjacent country of Barca, but often crossed its borders. The chroniclers list a long series of expeditions which the Mamluks had to undertake in al-Buhaira against the Banu Labid, who were sometimes joined by the other tribes living in the province. In 1379 the Bedouin took Damanhur, the capital of the province. There were other revolts in 1381 and in 1401. In the course of the fifteenth century the revolts became more frequent, so that almost every year the chroniclers had to mention a campaign against the rebels in some province or other. The intensity of the seditious movement was the corollary of the declining power of the Mamluks, for the rebels were often wealthy and powerful tribes. In Upper Egypt some tribes were so formidable that the Mamluk government had a great interest in being on good terms with them. Such tribes were the Hawwara, who had come from al-Buhaira at the end of the fourteenth century, the Banu Muharib, the Firada and the Arak. In the province of ash-Sharkiyya the Banu Wail and Banu Harram were very powerful, in the al-Gharbiyya the Sinbis, in the al-Manufiyya the Lawata. At the end of the period of Mamluk rule the

Egyptian Bedouins, who were aware of its growing weakness, were openly striving for supreme power. In Syria too there began a long series of Bedouin revolts in the middle of the fifteenth century. In 1449 the ashir rose in Palestine and killed the governor of Gaza, in 1478 and in 1480 the Al Fadl revolted in Northern Syria, and in 1501 the governor of Damascus had to proclaim a Holy War against the Bedouin.[12]

The accounts of the long struggle of the Mamluks against the Bedouin are an indication of social unrest and of the unsuccessful attempts of the tribal aristocracy to overthrow the rule of foreigners, for in spite of the frequency of Bedouin outbreaks the main feature of Mamluk rule was security.

b) *Economic prosperity*

One of the consequences of the stable régime and military strength of the first Mamluk sultans was a new demographic growth. It was clearly perceptible in both Egypt and Syria, although in the latter country the increase of population was slower.

In Egypt it was above all the consequence of a long period of peace. Whereas most countries of the Near East were invaded several times by the Mongols, who massacred the whole population of many small and larger towns, the Mamluks succeeded in repelling them before they approached the frontiers of Egypt. Secondly, the firm and efficient government of the first Mamluks brought both Egypt and Syria a hundred years of remarkable prosperity. Thus unhampered, natural procreation produced a considerable growth of the population.

There were, however, two other phenomena which explain the upward trend in demographic development. One of them was the immigration of many inhabitants of Irak and other countries into Syria and Egypt. When the Mongol armies advanced into Irak and then into Syria and news of their atrocities spread everywhere before them, many people, panic-stricken, left their towns and villages and fled west to Syria and Egypt. An Arabic author, for example, narrates that Balis, a town near the frontier of Syria and Irak, was completely abandoned by its inhabitants.[13] But even later this migratory movement continued. Pious Moslems who wished to live under Moslem rule left Irak for this reason. Theologians went to Syria and Egypt because these countries had become the intellectual centre of Islam. Others were attracted by the prosperity enjoyed by Egypt and Syria under the

Bahrites. Quite often individuals and groups of people emigrated from the kingdom of the Ilkhans to that of the Mamluks when they had been mixed up in political conflicts and feared the vengeance of their enemies. So the second half of the thirteenth century saw a steady stream of Irakian immigration into Syria and Egypt.

The Arabic historians mention mainly the theologians who came from Irak to the Mediterranean countries, being of course less interested in immigrants belonging to other classes. Further, their accounts are somewhat laconic. Nevertheless they convey some valuable hints as to the circumstances of this migratory movement. In some texts it is said explicitly that a man fled from Irak at the time of the Mongol invasion; in others we read that an immigrant from Irak succeeded in bringing with him his movable goods or that somebody went back to fetch what he had buried. From the reports of Arabic authors we learn also that people of all classes left Irak for Syria and Egypt: merchants, some of whom became agents or even viziers of the Mamluk rulers, physicians, theologians who were appointed judges and professors at *madrasas*. The famous Ibn Taimiyya, whose father fled from Harran to Damascus in 1268, belonged to these latter. The immigrants came from many towns and villages of Irak and Upper Mesopotamia, from Baghdad, Takrit, Irbil, Mosul, Dunaisir and Balis, but also from towns in the countries adjacent to Irak, such as Tabriz and Tiflis.[14]

The Arabic authors naturally say nothing about the immigration of craftsmen. But the Moslem works of art which have been preserved in various collections bear testimony to the immigration of many craftsmen (or artists) of Mosul. In the period preceding the Mongol conquests this town had become famous as a centre of specialists in inlaid metalwork. As many objects made in Syria and Egypt under the first Mamluks are characterised by the same technique of gold and silver inlay, there can be no doubt about the immigration of artists from Mosul.[15]

The chronicles of the Bahri period, on the other hand, contain several accounts of the immigration of groups of Mongols and other people belonging to the upper strata of Irakian society, the military and the bureaucracy. As early as 1258 remnants of the army of the last caliph of Baghdad had crossed the border of Syria and settled subsequently in Egypt. Then about 3,000 Kurdish horsemen appeared and were located in the district of Gaza. In the sixties of the thirteenth century groups of Mongols came to live in the Mamluk kingdom, some of them numbering hundreds of families. They were followed by people from Baghdad and Shiraz and Turkish knights. The most important group of these immigrants, as far as numbers are concerned, were the Oyarats (Kalmucks), who came in 1296 and numbered 10,000, or according to other accounts 18,000 families. Their chief was Targhai, son-in-law or husband of a granddaughter of Hülegü. Smaller groups of Tatars entered Syria and Egypt during the reign of al-Malik an-Nasir Muhammad. Some of these foreign soldiers settled in the capital of Egypt, others in various districts of Syria and Palestine.[16]

The growth of the population of Syria was certainly much slower than that of Egypt. The country was invaded by the Tatars several times in the second half of the thirteenth century, some coastal towns of Lebanon and Palestine were destroyed after their conquest by the Mamluks, and many neighbouring villages probably decayed in consequence of the loss of markets. Further, Syria lost many of its inhabitants in this period by their emigration to Egypt. Whenever the Mongols invaded Syria, a mass flight began and many people went to Egypt. Sometimes they did so by order of the authorities, sometimes against their will. Such mass flights are reported for the years 1259, 1260, 1261 and again from 1299. There can be no doubt that many of these refugees remained in Egypt. An account given by a Jew coming from Spain to Jerusalem in 1267 sheds light on these conditions. He mentions that when the Mongols approached the Holy City the people fled in all directions and did not return, so that seven years later the inhabitants numbered only 2,000. Moreover, many craftsmen and enterprising people went to Egypt rightly hoping to find there more scope for their activities.[17]

Besides the migratory movement there was another reason for the demographic growth of Egypt and Syria in that period. It seems that there was a considerable improvement of public health. This supposition is borne out by the fact that few epidemics are recorded in the histories of the Bahri Mamluks. The chronicles of the second half of the thirteenth century mention only two epidemics in Syria and Palestine, in 1258 and 1274, and two in Egypt, in 1274 and 1296. This latter epidemic, which followed a famine, was the only major outbreak of pestilence in that period.[18] There followed another half-century in which there are no reports of epidemics. It seems, however, that, as in Europe, the growth of the population slowed down in the first half of the fourteenth century or that the population remained stable.

However that may have been, the population of Egypt and Syria increased under the rule of the Bahrites during a long period, having previously declined for two hundred years. The conjectures of the late A. N. Poliak as to its numbers in the middle of the fourteenth century seem quite probable. He calculated 3 millions for Egypt and 900,000 for Syria.[19] The growth of large towns can be gauged from the development of suburbs. Contemporary authors speak of the great development of Cairo in the days of sultan Baibars, and a modern scholar calculates its population in the first half of the fourteenth century at 600,000. That of Damascus increased too, as new residential suburbs sprang up, such as as-Suwaika to the south-west and Suwaikat Sarudja to the north of the town.[20]

Another concomitant of the strength of the Bahri Mamluks was the stability of the monetary system of their kingdom. During a hundred and thirty years there was no monetary crisis to cause a sudden rise of prices or upset commerce. The mints were well supplied with precious metals and could coin sufficient quantities of dinars and dirhams, using alloys of excellent quality.

The stocks of gold came mainly from the countries which the Arabs still called Ghana and Takrur and which is now Mali. The relations between Egypt and the auriferous regions of Western Sudan were very close, pious Moslems coming from these countries to Egypt for their studies, Egyptian merchants going there to sell the products of the Egyptian textile industry, salt and cowries. The chroniclers narrate at great length the pilgrimage of Negro kings who passed through Egypt on their way to Mecca, but seldom mention the frequent journeys of the merchants. But the globetrotter Ibn Battuta and the sociologist Ibn Khaldun dwell on the commercial relations between Egypt and the Western Sudan. Ibn Battuta speaks of the Egyptians who lived there and the journeys of the people of Takedda, a town in Mali, to Egypt. Ibn Khaldun mentions the great caravan, numbering many thousands of camels, which came every year, on its way to Mali, to the town of Tadmekka, south-west of Ouargla. It seems that in this period the gold of Mali was carried to Egypt mainly by three routes. The first was the trans-Saharan route from Nyani to Taghazza and then to Touat; this was the way chosen by King Mansa Musa, who made the pilgrimage to Mecca in 1324. Another route led from Gao to Takedda, from there to the north and to Ghat. A third route, south of the Sahara, led from Gao to the northern shore of Lake Tchad, and through the lands of Kanem to Upper Egypt.[21]

The supply of silver to the Egyptian and Syrian mints was less regular, but quite sufficient. It came either from Europe or from

Central Asia. In the middle of the thirteenth century, just before the Mamluks became the rulers of Egypt, there was once more a shortage of silver in the Near East. The last Ayyubid sultan of Syria, al-Malik an-Nasir Yusuf, had to coin debased dirhams, and in Egypt there were mostly 'black dirhams', containing two-thirds copper, in circulation. But the French Crusaders who came with Louis IX brought great quantities of silver coins with them, and ten years later, in the wake of the Mongol conquests, a stream of Central Asian silver began to pour into Syria and Egypt as into the countries of the Near East. Sultan Baibars, the founder of Mamluk greatness, was able to raise the alloy of the dirham to 70% silver. On the other hand, the Arabic authors relate that the exchange rate of the dirham fell in his time so that 28.5 dirhams were given for 1 dinar, which means that the relation AU:AR had dropped from 1:6 in the Ayyubid period to 1:13.4. That there was a great abundance of silver in the Near East is also borne out by accounts of the presents made by or to high dignitaries: all of them comprised many thousands of dirhams.[22]

It is true that about 1290 the standard of the dirham was apparently once more lowered to 66%, but the supply of silver to Egypt's and Syria's mints was still sufficient. As the silver production in some European countries had considerably increased, its value went down, so that great quantities were exported to the Near East. From 1323 the kingdom of Little Armenia had to pay the sultan of Cairo a heavy tribute which consisted in silver trams (coins). New silver famines could have resulted from the hoarding of dirhams by the rich Mamluk aristocrats and by their melting down into vessels and jewellery. But when the demand for silver increased and its value rose, the Italian merchants once more imported great stocks of ingots and silver coins, which was always a profitable business, for the relation AU:AR was on the average 1:11 in Europe whereas it was 1:9.4 in Egypt during the reign of the Bahri Mamluks.[23] So the Mamluks were able to coin a great number of good dirhams whose value was stable – $\frac{1}{20}$ of a dinar – almost the regulation weight of 2.97 gr (if we take into consideration the incorrectness of medieval minting).

Demographic growth and the stability of the monetary system are clearly indicated by the movement of prices and the wages during the hundred and thirty years of the Bahri Mamluks' reign. There was in the middle and during the second half of the thirteenth century a progressive and considerable rise in grain prices and a decrease of nominal wages.

Average weight of dirhams of the Bahri Mamluks[24]

	weight	no. of specimens		weight	no. of specimens
Aibak	2.75 gr	18	Khalil	2.87 gr	15
Baibars	2.76	91	M. Nasir Muh.	2.93	43
Baraka Khan	2.77	21	M. Salih Ism.	2.63	27
Kalaun	2.82	46	M. Muzaffar Hadjdji	2.63	11

Ibn Fadlallah al-Umari, who wrote in 1340, says that an irdabb of wheat cost in his time on the average 0.75 dinars (15 dirhams) and the same quantity of barley 0.5 dinars. According to him there was no difference between the grain prices in Egypt and Syria.[25] So the price of 100 kg of wheat amounted to 1.07 dinars. The reports of the chroniclers confirm this statement, which certainly refers to grain prices in the big towns and during the autumn (when the size of the crops is already known). Furthermore, there is hardly any doubt that Ibn Fadlallah had in mind the second half of the thirteenth century.

Prices of grain (in irdabbs) in Egypt under the Bahrites

Date	Wheat	Barley
July 1264	2.25 din.	
July 1277	depression, 0.25 din.	0.15 din.
1277–79	depression, 0.25–0.3 din.	0.15–0.2 din.
1278–79		0.2 din.
April 1283	rise, 1.75, the sultan orders amirs to sell for 1.25; price goes down to 1 din., then to 0.9, and that is the price till the harvest	
December 1293	0.65 din.	
December 1296	0.8–0.9 din.	1.5, then 0.5 din.
January 1300	0.6–0.78 din.	0.6, then 0.48–0.6 din.
Spring 1300	1.35 din.	
Summer 1300	1 din.	
Autumn 1300	0.75 din.	

Date	Wheat	Barley
Autumn 1303	insufficient inundation, 2 din., then 1.25	
1305–06	rise from 1 din. to 2 din.	
Spring 1308	rise, 2.5 din.	
Autumn 1309	insufficient inundation, 2.5 din.	1 din.
January 1324	rise from 0.4 to 0.68 din.	
1326	depression in Upper Egypt, 0.36 or 0.225–0.27 din.	0.135–0.18 din.
early 1328	rise from 0.65 to 1 din.	
February 1336	rise from 0.75 to 2.5, then 3.5 din.	2.5 din.
December 1336	1.8 din.	
Winter 1337	in Upper Egypt 0.5 din., in Lower Egypt 0.4	0.3 din.
Summer 1338	Nile falling before the time, 1 din.	
May-June 1341	rise from 0.75 to 1.5 din.	
January 1342	depression, 0.54 din.	
Autumn 1343	excessive inundation, rise from 0.5 to 1 din.	
May 1346	rise, 2.75 din.	1.1 din.
end June 1346	rise, 1.5 din.	
September 1346	1.75, then 2.75 din.	
August 1347	rise, 3 din., then 1 din.	
November 1347	rise from 2 to 2.5 din.	
1348	0.99 din.	
Autumn 1350	irregular inundation, rise from 0.75 to 1 din.	
early 1352	rise from 1 to 1.85 din.	
Autumn 1358	depression, 0.5–0.75 din.	
1364	rise, 2 din.	
July-Aug. 1373	Nile falls before the time, 1.8–2 din.	
September 1373	1.5 din.	
Oct.-Dec. 1373	2.5–4.5 din.	1.25 din.
August 1374	rise, 5 din.	3 din.
November 1374	5.5 din.	3 din.
December 1374– January 1375	6.5 din.	4.5 din.

Date	Wheat	Barley
January 1375	5.25–5.5 din.	as much as 4 din.
April 1375	2.5 din.	0.83 din.
1375	after harvest, 1.25 din.	
end 1381	rise, 1.6 din.	
early 1382	2.4 din.	
April 1382	1.6 din.	0.88 din.

These figures show also that prices went down in the time of al-Malik an-Nasir Muhammad and rose once more under his successors. So the average grain prices were higher by 50% in the Bahri period than in the first half of the thirteenth century.[26]

The price of a ratl of mutton in Egypt (or more correctly in Cairo) in the first half of the fourteenth century was on the average 0.025–0.03 dinar, so that it had risen since the Fatimid period by 25–50%. Reports on the prices of sugar indicate a considerable increase in the second half of the thirteenth century, as compared with prices in the Fatimid period, and a progressive fall until the end of the fourteenth century. A kintar (djarwi, of 96 kg), which had cost under the Fatimids 6–7 dinars, was worth 12.5 in the second half of the thirteenth century. On the other hand, there was a continuous fall of the bread price from the beginning of Mamluk rule. The price of a pound of bread under the later Ayyubids was 0.0043 dinar, at the end of the thirteenth century 0.0041, and in the first half of the fourteenth century 0.003–0.0033 dinar.[27]

Price of bread in Cairo under the Bahri Mamluks

Date	Price of 1 ratl
early 1264	rise, 0.0166 din.
1273	rise, 0.0071 din.
June 1303	rise, 0.0125 din.
1326	depression, 0.0025 or even 0.0007 din.
February 1336	0.0009 din.
Winter 1373	rise, brown bread 0.2 din.
May-June 1374	rise, 0.0125, before 0.01 din.

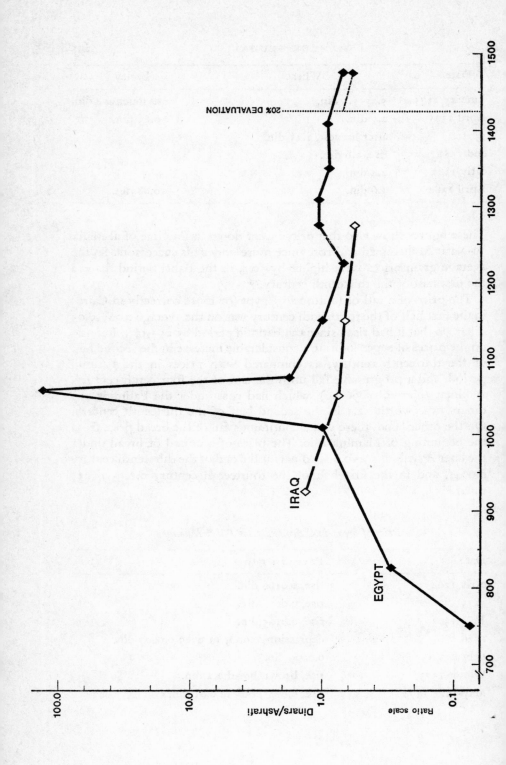

Date	Price of 1 ratl
October 1374	rise, 0.016–0.025, the authorities fix: 0.0125 din.
Winter 1374	rise, 0.033 din.
January 1375	rise, black bread 0.0234–0.0272 din.
April 1375	0.01 din.
May 1375	0.0071, the authorities fix: 0.005 din.
March 1378	dry bread 0.002 din.
March-April 1382	rise, 0.02 din.

So there is clear evidence of a general upward trend in the prices of victuals. The curve of the bread price, which seems to indicate a contrary trend, sheds light on the primary cause of the movement of prices under the Bahri Mamluks.

The prices of victuals rose because the demand increased. The upward movement of grain prices was to a great extent the effect of demographic growth. But this phenomenon also caused the price of labour to go down. When the number of working hands became greater, nominal wages decreased. The price of bread fell because the wages of the bakers, an important element in it, had been reduced. This is borne out by the endowment deeds of Egyptian and Syrian wakf establishments which fix the salaries of the staff. For a porter or a water-carrier (both full-time jobs) one would allow in the Bahri period 1–1.5 dinars a month, less than at the end of the twelfth century. These were the wages of unskilled workers; those of the skilled workers fell less steeply. The salaries of the lower Moslem clergy were also reduced, both in Egypt and in Syria. Calculating the wages of the workers in terms of bread they had nevertheless risen, but the quantity of meat such an unskilled worker could afford had diminished by almost 50%.[28] The small wage-earners had to suffer for the growth of population, whereas other classes enjoyed the benefits of economic prosperity.

The prosperity of the Syro-Egyptian economy would have been almost impossible without the continuation of the trade with Southern Europe. For the Christian traders supplied the Near East with great amounts of hard cash. These trade relations also provided a market for the products of agriculture and industry. But it was not only the rulers of Egypt and Syria who were interested in fostering them. The Italian merchants were no less eager to visit the Near Eastern emporia, in order to acquire the Indian spices for which there was such a great demand all over Europe. So international trade in the eastern basin of the Mediterranean went on, in spite of many difficulties.

The conquest of Acre by the Mamluks in 1291 was a heavy blow, which stirred up Latin Christianity against the sultans of Cairo. It was plain to everybody that the capture of this town meant the end of the Crusaders' possessions in the Holy Land. So the pope made great efforts to put an end to the close trade relations between the South European trading nations and the Mamluk kingdom. He did so not only to cut off its supply of arms, timber, iron and other articles badly needed for the sultan's army and the fleet, but also in order to weaken Mamluk economy. For the advisers of the popes convinced them of the great profits made by Egypt and Syria from the trade with Southern Europe. Immediately after the fall of Acre, Pope Nicholas IV prohibited the selling of arms, timber and similar articles to the infidels. This prohibition was repeated by his successors time and again. The urban republics of Italy, which had carried on trade with Egypt and Syria for centuries, were compelled to promulgate decrees forbidding their subjects to contravene the papal prohibition. In 1291 Genoa forbade all trade with the lands of the sultan. Jacob II, king of Aragon and Catalonia, did the same in 1302. Pisa, in its decrees of 1302 and 1322, forbade the sale of arms and war material only. But Philip the Fair, king of France, in 1312, and Venice, in 1323, adopted the more rigorous attitude, prohibiting any trade with Egypt and Syria. The Church did not content itself with the promulgation of these prohibitions, but sent out ships to capture transgressors and seize the ships and merchandise. But it proved impossible to stop the trade which was so profitable for both Christians and Moslems. The Europeans could not renounce the Indian spices, the Near Easterners needed the war material and the ducats. Experts like Marino Sanuto Torsello, who in 1306 wrote his *Secreta fidelium crucis*, tried to convince the Church and the princes of Europe of the necessity of breaking off trade with the Moslem Near East. But the appeal of the '*turpe lucrum*' was too strong and the pope had to give in, granting temporary permits for trade, except for the sale of war material. There can be no doubt, however, that the strenuous efforts of the Church had some success. They must have discouraged some of the Christian traders from visiting the ports of Egypt and Syria.

There was, however, another reason. The trade routes in the Eastern Mediterranean and those which connected it with the Persian Gulf and the adjacent regions changed considerably in the second half of the thirteenth century. After the fall of Acre and the pressure put on the trading nations by the Church, the two territories which remained in the possession of the Christians in the eastern basin of the Mediter-ranean, Cyprus and Little Armenia, became important centres of inter-national trade. In Famagusta and Lajazzo European merchants could buy all those Indian articles which they used to procure in Alexandria and Damascus. Moslem traders came there to offer spices and the products of the Near East. The rise of Lajazzo was also the outcome of the conquest of Irak by the Tatars. It became the terminus of one route of the trade which connected the Persian Gulf with the Mediter-ranean, Trebizond that of another. The establishment of flourishing Italian merchant colonies in some towns of the Crimea and on the Sea of Azov, the most important being Caffa and Tana, also had a great influence on the trade of Western Asia. For in the emporia of the Black Sea which were connected by caravan routes with Central Asia and Afghanistan, the Italians could obtain the products of India and the Far East, besides slaves and various products from Southern Russia.

But notwithstanding the prohibition by the Church and the develop-ment of other trade routes, commercial relations between the Southern European nations and the Mamluk kingdom, though diminished, were hardly ever interrupted. Marino Sanuto gives in his treatise a list of articles which the Christian merchants imported into Egypt, including those upon which the Church had laid an embargo.[29] We learn from other sources that the *fondachi*, the hostels of the trading nations, in Alexandria were seldom closed. Venice, Genoa, Pisa and Marseille kept their *fondachi* there and had their consuls. Even after the fall of Acre the trading nations sent embassies to the sultan of Cairo and concluded new commercial treaties, reducing imposts and acquiring new rights. The Venetians who carried on their trade in Alexandria, Damietta and Tinnis in 1302 obtained new privileges from the sultan, besides the concessions made by a predecessor which he confirmed. As they pursued their commercial activities both in Egypt and Syria, they also established contacts with provincial governors, e.g. that of Safed, to whom they sent an embassy in 1304. Owing to the measures taken by the pope, direct trade with Egypt and Syria had to be interrupted from 1323 to 1344, but that meant only that the exchange of the goods was transferred to Cyprus and to Crete. In 1345 direct trade was resumed, the galley service re-established and a new consul appointed in Alex-andria. Then, in 1355 and in 1361, Venice concluded new treaties with the sultan. It is true that the Genoese, who carried on a voluminous trade in their colonies on the coasts of the Black Sea, were less active in Egypt in that period, but on the other hand, other Southern European nations intensified their trading activities in Egypt. In 1350 the Catalans got from the sultan a privilege, reducing the imposts they had to pay. Marseilles, which from 1330 carried on a rather irregular trade with the ports of Egypt, increased it considerably from the middle of the fourteenth century. The merchants of Ragusa began at the same time to send their ships regularly to Alexandria. An attack by Peter I, king of Cyprus, on Alexandria in 1365 upset for some years the flourishing trade between Southern Europe and the Mamluk kingdom. In 1370 peace was made and there followed a new period of great commercial activity. Even Ragusa then obtained a privilege for its merchants.

The documents which provide data concerning the Levantine trade in this period leave no doubt that the Christian merchants were more active in Egypt than in Syria. Although Damascus was supplied with Indian articles not only from the Red Sea ports but also from the Persian Gulf, and Aleppo was called in contemporary sources 'little India', the trade of Syria with the European nations was rather limited. The measures taken by the Church and the destruction of the sea ports on the Palestinian-Lebanese coast had dealt it a heavy blow. Syrian merchants had to go to Famagusta and Lajazzo to sell their merchandise. But at the end of this period the Christian traders renewed their frequent journeys to Tripoli, Beirut and Acre, and even Damascus and Ramla, where they bought the Indian spices, Near Eastern textiles and great quantities of cotton, an important product of Syria and Palestine.[30]

So the trade with Southern Europe enriched Egypt and Syria and supplied these countries with large quantities of good gold and silver coins. But those who profited directly from this trade, besides the Mamluk Treasury, were the rich wholesalers. These merchants, the Karimis, carried on the great spice trade in Yemen, Egypt and Syria, but engaged also in other business and, last but not least, in banking. They apparently constituted a near-monopoly, almost excluding or at least seriously disadvantaging other traders. According to an Arabic chronicler there were about 200 Karimis in Egypt in the first half of the fourteenth century, and we know from other sources that people of all denominations belonged to them, Moslems, Christians and Jews. As they granted loans to the sultan of Cairo and other princes, their standing was very high and there were among them some families, such as the Kharrubi, the Ibn Kuwaik and the Ibn Musallam, who were reckoned the richest people of their time. But the fiscal system of the Mamluks made the growth of merchant dynasties impossible. The government could always expropriate them by imposing fines. The Karimi families and other rich merchants, such as those who carried on the trade with Turkish Asia Minor, remained wealthy for no more than three generations.[31]

c) Decline under the Circassian Mamluks

Both medieval chroniclers and modern scholars emphasise the great difference between the period of the Bahrites and that of the Circassian Mamluks. Whereas under the first Mamluk dynasty Egypt and Syria enjoyed economic prosperity, the age of the Circassians saw the decline of their economy and the decay of the Islamic civilisation in the Near East. But in fact these phenomena had already been perceptible long before the accession of the Circassians to the throne of Cairo.

The major fact of Near Eastern social history in this period was depopulation. It had begun in the middle of the fourteenth century. The Black Death ushered in the demographic decay of the later middle ages. As in many other regions of the ancient world this terrible pestilence swept off a great part of the population of Syria and Egypt. Undoubtedly the high mortality was to a great extent due to the undernourishment of large sections of the Near Eastern populations, exactly as the heavy toll taken by the Black Death in Europe has been explained by the same phenomenon. Arabic chroniclers describe the symptoms of the true bubonic plague, the pustules and buboes, the blood-spitting of the sick and death within a few days. Reading the detailed reports, we get a glimpse of the panic with which helpless people were stricken everywhere. The epidemic began in Egypt during the autumn of 1347, in April 1348 it had spread all over the country and at the end of the year it had reached its peak. It penetrated into Southern Syria during the spring of 1348, but at the same time spread from the north. As the pestilence had begun later in Syria, so it declined later. Whereas it came to an end in Egypt in February 1349, it was still taking a heavy toll in Syria during the early spring of that year.

The contemporary Arabic writers speak about thousands and myriads who died every day in the big towns. It goes without saying that the modern scholar will treat these figures with the utmost reserve. The total of 900,000 who, according to Ibn Iyas, died in two months in Cairo is certainly exaggerated. But the estimate of the contemporary writer Ibn Habib sounds probable: he says that the Black Death diminished the population of Egypt and Syria by a third.

From the long accounts of the Arabic historians we learn also that countless cattle perished during the plague. So the well-being of the survivors was to a certain extent delusive. In fact, the economy of the Mamluk kingdom had lost a considerable part of its potential.[32]

As in Europe, so in the Near East the Black Death was the beginning of a long period of demographic decline. The losses it had suffered by the terrible plague were not repaired by intensive procreation. Levasseur's law did not operate. On the contrary, there followed a series of epidemics. Many of them are called by the chroniclers *taun* – the name given to bubonic plague. As they seldom describe the symptoms of the disease, we cannot be sure whether they were, in fact, new outbreaks of the plague. But, as Kremer concluded ninety years ago, their number was certainly much greater in the later middle ages than in former periods. Reports found in unpublished chronicles considerably increase the list of epidemics compiled by Kremer. There were major epidemics in Egypt in 1363, 1367, 1381, 1416, 1430, 1438, 1444, 1449, 1459–60, 1468, 1469, 1476–7, 1492, 1498, 1505 and 1513, and in Syria-Palestine in 1363, 1369–70, 1373, 1381, 1385, 1411, 1437–8, 1459, 1460, 1468, 1469, 1476–7, 1492, 1497 and 1513.[33] The accounts of the chroniclers show that in the second half of the fourteenth century Syria suffered from epidemics much more than Egypt. In Egypt they were frequent in the second decade of the fifteenth century, and later in its seventh and eighth decades, and about 1500 they raged very often in both countries. The plague had then become so frequent that foreigners visiting Egypt were told that it broke out every seven years. As the plague and other epidemics infested the Near East so often in that period, Arabic authors dealt with the reasons for their spread or wrote special treatises about the subject. al-Makrizi concluded that the inhabitants of Egypt were easily liable to diseases because of malnutrition. The peasants, he says, nourish themselves with bread only, even that being bad.[34] There is good reason to believe that the medieval writer was right. The epidemics were the consequence of poverty and misery. On the other hand, it is true that many epidemics spread mainly among children, slaves and other foreigners (such as Mamluks), but nevertheless there can be no doubt that they diminished the population of the Near East considerably.

Medieval sources provide us with some data for statistical estimates of the demographic decline. Some Arabic writers give us the total of the numbers of the villages in Egypt, as it had been established by surveys made at different dates. Although the accounts are sometimes contradictory (or incorrectly transmitted by careless copyists), they leave no doubt as to the decrease in the later middle ages. These data[35] are summed up in the following table:

Number of villages in Egypt

A.D.	
956	2,395
reign of al-Hakim (996–1020)	2,390
reign of al-Mustansir (1035–94)	2,186
1210	2,071
1315	2,454
1375	2,322
1434	2,122

These data clearly reflect the changes in the demographic history of Egypt in the middle ages: after a long prosperity under the first Fatimids there began a downward trend in the second half of the eleventh century, and after the terrible famine in 1201–2 the number of villages had already decreased conspicuously; the stable government of the first Mamluks brought a new rise of population and new villages were founded or old ones rebuilt, while under the Circassians the number of Egypt's villages was smaller than five hundred years earlier. The demographic evolution of the Syrian countryside was probably similar to that of Egypt's villages. A Burgundian traveller, who visited Syria in 1432, says that near Hamath and Antioch several districts were uninhabited. According to Arabic authors, in some provinces hundreds of villages were abandoned at the end of the fifteenth century. On the other hand, the Turkish officials, taking a census in 1519–20, found that in the province of Tripoli the population of some villages had shrunk from 3,000 to 800.[36]

As to the demographic development of Near Eastern towns in that period, we may refer to many passages in the travelogues of Europeans, pilgrims and other travellers. When visiting Cairo and Alexandria they saw whole quarters which had fallen into ruins. Even in Damascus a part of the town which had been destroyed during the invasion by Timur Lenk was not rebuilt until the middle of the fifteenth century. It is true that Aleppo recovered in that period and that new suburbs sprang up outside the walls. In 1428 the area within the walls was enlarged, although the quarters added were only partially inhabited. But among the big towns of Syria and Egypt, Aleppo was an exceptional case owing to its flourishing trade. Contemporary Arabic writers too dwell on the decline of the towns of Egypt and Syria. al-Makrizi mentions in his Topography many mills which had been built in Cairo in the first half of the fourteenth century and, on the other hand, speaks of their destruction in his own day. In one district, according to him, eighty mills had been ruined. There was no longer any need for so many mills. Another Arabic author, Ibn Zuhaira, writes in 1438 that Cairo had shrunk to $\frac{1}{24}$ of what it had been formerly.[37]

The conclusions of Clerget, who estimates a decline of Cairo's population from 600,000 inhabitants at the beginning of the fourteenth century to 430,000 in the middle of the sixteenth century, are disputable. But the data found in the Turkish registers comprising the results of a census under Selim I and another under the reign of Soliman the Great are reliable. According to these documents Aleppo had less than 70,000 inhabitants in 1519, Damascus apparently the same number. The Turkish historian O. L. Barkan calculated from these registers that the total of Syria's population (including Palestine and the province of Adana) in the twenties of the sixteenth century amounted to 571,360.[38] Before the Moslem conquest it had been 4 millions.

So there can be no doubt about the considerable decrease of population in the Near East during the later middle ages. Whereas in Europe the demographic decline had begun some time before the Black Death and continued for 130 years, it was already a major phenomenon of Oriental history in the eleventh and twelfth centuries and lasted much longer at the end of the middle ages. The utter destitution of the lower classes of society and the sanitary conditions certainly helped to cause it. But they alone cannot explain why natural procreation did not make good the losses caused by the epidemics. Perhaps it was a psychological factor, the hopelessness of broad strata of Near Eastern society, which diminished procreation.

The Black Death was a turning-point in the demographic history of the Near East; at the beginning of the fifteenth century there followed another crisis which accelerated depopulation and economic decline. Contemporary Arabic writers provide us with the details of this economic crisis. What is left to us is to put it in a broader context of economic relations.

The striking feature of the economic life of Egypt and Syria at the turn of the fourteenth century was the disappearance of silver coins. The stocks of silver in the mints decreased progressively from about 1380 and consequently the silver content of the dirham had to be diminished. Whereas the exchange rate of the dirham had for 130 years been $\frac{1}{20}$ dinar, that of the debased dirham was $\frac{1}{25}$ and later $\frac{1}{30}$ dinar. Arabic writers explain the silver famine by saying that it was melted down to be used for the making of vessels and jewellery, but in fact the main reason was the great demand in Italy, where the value of silver had risen considerably at the end of the fourteenth century. al-Makrizi, who wrote a special treatise on this crisis, himself says that the Christian (i.e. the Italian) merchants exported silver from the Near East to Europe. On the other hand, great quantities of copper were imported. According to al-Makrizi this was done by a high dignitary at the court of Cairo whose greed induced him to enrich himself by the striking of copper coins. This, however, is the simplicity of the medieval mind. The increase of copper imports to the Near East was the consequence of the rise in the output of the mines in various regions of Europe. The Venetians could offer copper from the Netherlands, Hungary, Serbia and Bosnia.[39] At the beginning of the fifteenth century the striking of silver dirhams was discontinued altogether. The fulus and copper dirhams replaced them. Henceforth prices and values were indicated in amounts of copper coins, and payments were made in copper dirhams even when fixed in dinars or silver dirhams. In the monetary history of Egypt and Syria the copper era had begun.

The great change in the monetary system was accompanied by a social crisis which was the outcome of a dearth due to an insufficient inundation of the Nile and a long civil war. According to Arabic writers the dearth in 1403 and 1404 was a real catastrophe from which Egypt could not possibly recover for a long time. They say that half the population died during the famine, that many villages were abandoned and a great part of the cultivated area remained untilled. At the same time the Mamluk kingdom was riven by the war between the second Circassian sultan al-Malik an-Nasir Faradj and his amirs, who revolted time and again. In order to equip his armies the sultan had to collect high taxes from an impoverished and diminished population. Between the lines on the thick yellow paper of the old hand-written chronicles can be read the misery and despair which afflicted all classes. Syria was at the same time laid low and dreadfully ravished by the invasion of the Mongol army led by Timur Lenk, who wrought havoc in many towns and villages in 1400–1.[40]

The crisis in the reign of sultan Faradj brought not only a change in the monetary system and accelerated depopulation. Its impact was so great that it meant a change in ways of life. Since prices of victuals were indicated in dirhams which were more and more devalued, and great quantities of copper coins were put into circulation, there was a serious inflation resulting in a general rise in prices. The merchants used it to raise prices not only in terms of dirhams (that is, the debased ones) but in terms of dinars. All industrial products became even more expensive. So many people could no longer afford to buy products which they had been accustomed to use. Those who wore silk and other precious fabrics had to replace them by coarse woollen stuffs. The craftsmen who produced trinkets lost their customers, and al-Makrizi includes in his Topography a long list of markets in Cairo which had been closed or where only some shops remained. According to him, even most of the wax-dealers had closed their shops.[41]

The impoverishment of the Egyptians was, however, only one reason for this change. It resulted also from a phenomenon of much wider bearing – the decay of Oriental industries. Though the output and quality of their products had gone down considerably, the industries of Egypt and Syria were still an important sector of their economies in the fourteenth century. The textile industry of Egypt still produced great quantities of fine fabrics which were exported to all regions of North Africa. Alexandria was in that period the main centre of Egypt's linen and silk industry. Arabic authors say that there were still 12,000 or 14,000 looms working. Damascus and Hims exported their silk fabrics.[42] In both Egypt and Syria there was a flourishing sugar industry. This is borne out by the reports of Arabic authors about the great quantities of sugar consumed at festivities and by bills of consignment which provide indications of the shipping of Syrian and Egyptian sugar to Venice, Genoa, Aigues-Mortes, Marseilles and Barcelona. Arabic chroniclers speak about the caravans which exported Egyptian sugar to Irak. High dignitaries and rich merchants invested their capital in sugar factories, some possessing even twenty or more. Consequently the volume of this industry increased and the price of its products (various kinds of sugar) went down.[43] In Syria and Palestine there were many soap factories whose products were also exported to other countries. Further, there should be mentioned the paper mills of

Cairo, Damascus and Hamath and the glassworks of Aleppo and Damascus. These manufactures too marketed their products in many other countries.[44]

At the beginning of the fifteenth century most of these industries collapsed.

al-Makrizi narrates that after the economic crisis in 1404 people were compelled to dress themselves in the woollen stuffs imported by European merchants. But the import of European textiles was surely not the consequence of this crisis. Sometime earlier sultan Barkuk (1382–99) had ordered his courtiers to wear other fabrics than the customary silk. In fact, the prices of Oriental textiles had risen very much owing to the rise in wages, which was itself a consequence of the shortage of skilled workers. al-Makrizi bitterly complains about the difficulty of finding workers and the rise in wages.

The volume of the textile industry had shrunk considerably. According to Arabic sources there were no more than 800 looms working in Alexandria in 1434. In Cairo too many textile factories had disappeared. The decline of the sugar industry was no less conspicuous. Ibn Dukmak, a contemporary writer, lists sixty-six sugar factories which existed in Cairo in 1325. At the beginning of the fifteenth century about thirty of them had been closed. Some had become shops or dwelling-houses, others had fallen into ruins. al-Makrizi describes the decay of the sugar plantations in Upper Egypt and the ruin of the factories. But in this part of Egypt the downward trend of the sugar industry must have begun already before the middle of the fourteenth century, since al-Adfuwi (d. 1347) speaks of many factories which had been closed in some towns.[45]

But we must beware of exaggeration. The industries of Egypt and Syria had not disappeared altogether. In Damascus and Alexandria there existed until the end of the fifteenth century manufactures of silk and brocade which were exported to North Africa and to European countries.[46] Nevertheless the decline of Oriental industries was conspicuous both as to the volume of its output and to the quality. What was the reason?

Certainly it was not simply the consequence of a shortage of working hands nor of the faulty policy of the Mamluk government nor of the fact that the Mamluks no longer had sufficient funds to pay for costly fabrics. Even the forced emigration of many skilled craftsmen from Damascus whom Timur Lenk carried away to Samarkand cannot have been a decisive factor in the decay of Near Eastern industries. The competition of European industries had surely a greater bearing on it.

The superiority of the European textile industries, e.g. the Flemish and Florentine wool manufactures, was to a great extent brought about by the import of high quality raw material, for instance English wool. Furthermore, these industries could employ dyes produced in their own or neighbouring countries. The Near Eastern industries, on the other hand, used wool of incomparably inferior quality. Also the supply of dyes had probably become a difficult problem. After the conquest of Western Persia and Irak by the Tatars kermes and saffron from Armenia and Media could no longer be so easily obtained. The decline of the wool industry of al-Ushmunain in Upper Egypt was certainly a consequence of this change, for its products had been famous for the kermes colours. Saffron had to be imported from Central Italy and Catalonia, and as it was very expensive its use raised the price of Near Eastern textiles considerably. On the other hand, the saffron plantations which had been introduced into Southern Europe by the Arabs expanded there widely in that period, so that it became easily available. Consequently European textiles became cheaper than the Oriental products, both those of rather cheap quality and the costly fabrics.

Technological innovations also helped to establish the superiority of European cloths. The automatic mill, a great innovation in Western Europe, was not completely unknown in the Near East. The biography of a Mamluk dignitary who died in 1481 contains a note that he established on his estate in the province of Fayyum 'a Persian mill operated by water without animals'. We can reasonably infer from this account that such mills were quite exceptional in Egypt. A French traveller who visited Egypt in 1512 says explicitly that in this country there are neither water mills nor windmills. Windmills had been introduced by German Crusaders in Palestine, but they did not come into use elsewhere. As with other innovations they were not taken over by the conservative agriculturists. Besides the automatic mill and the treadle-loom, the introduction of the spinning-wheel was a very important innovation. It was used in Germany and Northern France in the second half of the thirteenth century, in England at least from the fourteenth century, and in Catalonia in its second half. Apparently it remained unknown in the Near East.

The reasons for the technological decline of Near Eastern industries in this period are evident. The role of the royal factories in all branches of industry had been overwhelming. They got the raw materials at cheaper prices, part of them being produced on the royal estates. The numerous sugar factories owned by the sons of the sultans and by high-ranking amirs surely enjoyed privileges which made competition for other industrialists difficult. The sultans and their amirs used their power to curtail the activities of their competitors by taxation or by the establishment of monopolies. The monopoly of sugar planting and refining by sultan Barsbay, established in 1423, was only one phase of this development. But when competition was strangled, there was little incentive to innovate. The royal factories themselves were ruined by corrupt managers whose maladministration induced the sultans in course of time to abolish the tiraz system altogether.[47] Industrial production sank to the level of small workshops which could not afford long and costly experiments.

It would however be unreasonable to claim that this change in industrial structures is a satisfactory explanation of technological decline. Sometimes great innovations are made by individuals without being helped by a powerful organisation. There are indeed historical questions which the historian can raise but not answer.

Whatsoever the reasons for the technological decline may have been, the phenomenon itself is illustrated by many symptoms. Ibn Khaldun (d. 1406) complains that the art of shipbuilding had declined in the Near East so much that in case of need the governments must have recourse to foreign help. Even skilled builders, such as lead roofers, had to be brought from abroad, e.g. from Anatolia, to repair the ravages of a fire in the Umayyad mosque in Damascus in 1479. A Lebanese author narrates how the engineers of the Mamluks were incapable of building a bridge over a river. Two attempts proved complete failures. The decline of some industries resulted in the actual dumping of foreign products in the Near East. Industrial products which during many centuries the manufactures of the Near East had exported to Europe and to India, such as glassware, inlaid work, paper and soap, had to be imported. The Venetians had learnt the production of fine glass vessels and inlaid work in Tyre from Jewish craftsmen. In the course of the fifteenth century the manufacture of glass in the Near East had so far declined that it was imported from Italy. Sultan Kaitbay (1468–96) ordered glass lamps in Murano. Whereas al-Makrizi deplored the decay of the art of silver inlay, it too had become a flourishing branch of the Venetian arts. That the Venetians had learnt it from the Jews in Syria is borne out by the names it was given – Jews' work or opus Salomonis. Chaucer writes of Sir Thopas:

> And over that a fyn hawberk
> Was al y wrought of Jewes work
> (ed. Robinson 1. 2050)

Even paper was brought from France and Italy, where the little town of Fabriano, in the province of Ancona, had become in the fourteenth century a world-famous centre of this industry. Soap was imported from Southern Italy and Chios. Another branch of Near Eastern manufactures which decayed in this period was pottery. Archaeological findings bear evidence of a great wave of import and imitation of Chinese porcelain. The Egyptian potters were incapable of duplicating the fine clay of the original, nor could they produce the transparent glaze.[48]

The dumping of European textiles became a major fact in the economic life of the Near East. In fact it was already well on the way at the beginning of the Mamluk period. According to the contemporary historian Ibn Wasil there were plenty of fine Venetian stuffs in Alexandria in 1263, and at the beginning of the fourteenth century European silk was imported into Egypt. At the end of this century the volume of the textile import in Egypt and in Syria increased steadily. The Florentine pilgrim Leonardo Frescobaldi narrates that textiles from Lombardy were loaded on the ship in which he sailed in 1384 to Alexandria. Documents in the archives of Bouches-du-Rhône testify to the export of the woollen fabrics of Languedoc to Egypt, and also of those of Malines. The rich archives of Francesco Datini, the famous merchant of Prato, yield many data concerning the prices fetched in Egypt and Syria by the stuffs of Perpignan and Reims, of the Florentines, and those of Flanders and Brabant. The export of Catalan textiles to the Near East became a lively trade at the end of the fourteenth century and was continued throughout the fifteenth century. Merchants' manuals and other treatises dating from the first half of this century show that Venice also exported great quantities of its textile products to the Levant. The treaties concluded in the middle and at the end of the century between Venice and Florence, on the one hand, and the sultan of Cairo on the other hand, the travelogues of European travellers and the reports of Venetian chroniclers throw light on the size of this trade. We read, for example, that in 1500 there arrived in Alexandria a Genoese ship with 4,600 pieces of European textiles and three French vessels with 13,000.[49]

The impact of depopulation and industrial decline is clearly reflected

by the movement of prices as reported by Arabic chroniclers of the late
fourteenth and the fifteenth centuries.

The following table comprises data which refer to 'normal prices'
or to periods of dearth (or depression) which were not excessive.[50]

Prices of grain (in irdabbs) in Egypt under the Circassians

Date	Wheat	Barley
Winter 1383–4	very low price, 0.24–0.5 din.	0.2–0.26 din.
1385	dearth, 1.66 din.	
1388	very low price, 0.24 din.	
September 1394	insufficient inundation, 1.6 din.	0.8 din.
Jan.-Feb. 1395	2.64 din.	1.32 din.
October 1395	2.4 din.	2 din.
March 1396	2 din.	1.2 din.
October 1396	2.0–2.4 din.	1.2 din.
June 1399	1.0–1.3 din.	
early 1400	1.16–1.33 din.	0.8 din.
1402	0.77 din.	0.38 din.
February 1403	rise, 1.16 din.	1.16 din.
August 1404	2 din.	1.1 din.
June 1408	depression, 0.5 din.	0.35 din.
early 1410	0.75 then 0.3 din.	0.57 din.
December 1410	0.54–0.64 din.	0.18–0.27 din.
October 1411	0.33 din.	
April 1412	0.62 din.	
April 1413	0.66 din.	rise, 0.54 din.
November 1413	0.5 din.	0.41 din.
March 1414	0.56 and less din.	
March 1415	0.5 din.	
April 1415	depression, 0.33–0.5 din.	0.27 din.
October 1415	0.58 din.	0.5 din.
May 1416	0.7–0.8 din.	
June 1417	rise from 0.72 to 0.8 din.	
January 1418	0.86 din.	as much as 0.7 din.
February 1419	1.3 din.	1.1 din.

Date	Wheat	Barley
October 1419	rise, 1.3 din.	
August 1420	1.3 din.	1.2 din.
January 1423	0.25–0.37 din.	0.25–0.27 din.
March 1423	very low price, 0.25 din.	
March 1424	0.9 din.	
late 1424	0.9 din	0.48 din.
Sept.-Oct. 1425	rise, 1.1 din.	1.24 din.
March 1426	1.33 then 0.9 ashrafi	
November 1426	0.66 and less ashrafi	0.44 ashrafi
May 1427	very low price, 0.35–0.53 ashrafi	0.28 ashrafi
November 1427	0.75 ashrafi	0.58 ashrafi
Mar.-Apr. 1428	0.71 ashrafi	0.4 ashrafi
September 1428	1.77 then 1.55 ashrafi	1.33 ashrafi
March 1429	1 ashrafi	0.48 ashrafi
August 1429	rise from 1.17 to 1.3 ashrafi	
October 1430	very low prices, 0.46 ashrafi	0.21 ashrafi
September 1432	depression, 0.5 ashrafi	0.3 ashrafi
Spring 1433	depression, 0.66 ashrafi	0.33 ashrafi
Sept.-Oct. 1433	rise, 0.63 ashrafi	0.49 ashrafi
May 1434	0.52 then 0.6 ashrafi	
October 1435	no fall of Nile, 1 ashrafi	
December 1436	depression, 0.38–0.53 ashrafi	
March 1440	0.87 then 0.7 ashrafi	
Autumn 1443	1.05 then 0.7 ashrafi	
April 1444	0.7 ashrafi	
October 1449	2.1 ashrafi	
February 1450	2.8 ashrafi	
October 1450	4.2 ashrafi	2.8 ashrafi
April 1451	2.8–3.5 ashrafi	2.4 ashrafi
May 1452	1.4 ashrafi	0.7 ashrafi
November 1452	1.1 ashrafi	0.8 ashrafi
late 1455	0.4 ashrafi	
March 1456	0.66 ashrafi	0.5 and less ashrafi
December 1456	1.2 ashrafi	

Date	Wheat	Barley
November 1459	1 ashrafi	
April 1460	2 ashrafi	
March 1464	rise, 1.2 ashrafi	1.06 ashrafi
Mar.-Apr. 1466	1.8 then 2 ashrafi	
May 1468	2 ashrafi	0.8 ashrafi
October 1468	2.66 ashrafi	1 then 1.5 ashrafi
April 1469	2 ashrafi	less than 1 ashrafi
June 1473	a bit more than 0.66 ashrafi	
June 1484	depression, 0.5 ashrafi	
June 1491	depression, 0.33 ashrafi	
1492	0.33–0.5 ashrafi	
April 1495	0.3 ashrafi	
early 1496	0.2 ashrafi	
November 1497	dearth, 3 ashrafi	
January 1502	dearth, 2.5 ashrafi	
Summer 1512	1 ashrafi	

Our table shows clearly that after the inflation at the beginning of the fifteenth century and the subsequent devaluation of the dinar grain prices were lower than in the period of the Bahri Mamluks. The data of the first half of the fifteenth century point to 0.5–0.7 dinar (then ashrafi!) as a 'normal' price during the fall. The fact that the devaluation of the dinar did not entail a rise of grain prices meant a decrease by 20%. In the second half of the fifteenth century they went down once more. For the anonymous author of the history 'Djawahir as-suluk' says that the usual price of an irdabb of wheat in the days of Kaitbay was ½ ashrafi (see p. 324).[51] So grain prices were going down throughout a long period. The secular trends are shown by the following table.

Price of 100 kg of wheat in Egypt

1250–1300	1.07 canonical dinar
1300–1350	0.85 ,, ,,
1400–1450 (after 1425)	0.74 ,, ,,
1450–1500	0.57 ,, ,,

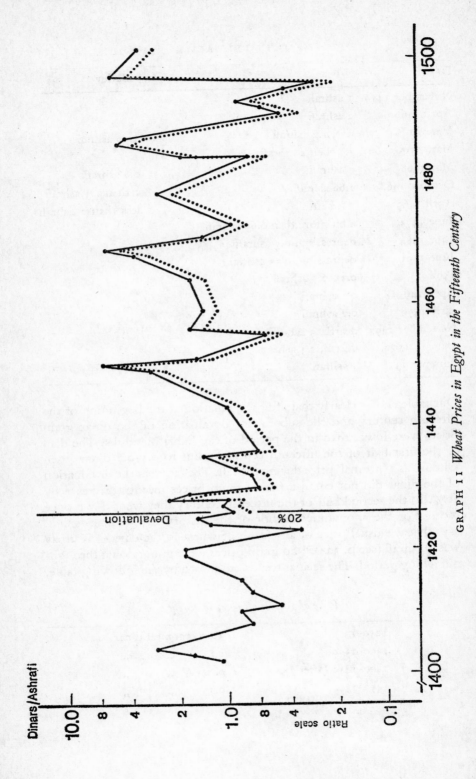

GRAPH 11 *Wheat Prices in Egypt in the Fifteenth Century*

As the Mamluks were great grain dealers and had the utmost interest in keeping prices high there cannot be the slightest doubt that the downward trend corresponded to lower demand, and was the result of depopulation.

The price of a ratl of mutton, the staple meat, rose during the crisis at the beginning of the fifteenth century to 0.03–0.04 dinar, but did not change after the devaluation. The price being then in canonical dinars 0.024–0.032, the rise was insignificant. That meat prices did not rise must have been because few could afford it. In Syria it even went down in price.[52]

The curve of the sugar price, on the other hand, reflects the considerable rise in the prices of industrial products. The monopolistic policy of the government, the decay of private industry and the rise in wages (mainly of unskilled workers) resulted in an enormous rise in the price of sugar of 200–300%. In Egypt a kintar (djarwi, of 96 kg) cost 55 dinars in 1396, in 1414 40 dinars and in the 1430s 35 dinars. In Syria too the rise was steep. It had begun in the eighth decade of the fourteenth century and advanced very much at the beginning of the fifteenth century. In mid-century a Damascus kintar (of 185 kg) fetched 50 ducats. The difference between the sugar prices in Egypt and in Syria probably points to the fact that wages in Syria had risen less than in Egypt.

The rise in the price of bread was slighter, because that of wheat, its main component, was going down. It rose in Egypt at the end of the fourteenth century to 0.004–0.0044 dinar the ratl, and at the beginning of the fifteenth century to 0.005 dinar, which meant a rise of 0.66%. The devaluation of the dinar, however, did not result in a further rise. A ratl of bread cost 0.005 ashrafi in the middle of the century. In Syria at the end of the fourteenth century the price of bread was more or less the same as in Egypt, but at the end of the Mamluk period it was lower.[53]

The downward trend of grain prices was certainly not the result of increased output. On the contrary, Arabic authors of the later middle ages complain bitterly of the decline of agriculture and the decrease of the cultivated area. Even descriptions of the golden prime of Mamluk rule include such complaints. Time and again the chroniclers report that the cultivated area had decreased, because the authorities had neglected the upkeep of irrigation canals and dams. The feudal lords collected taxes instead of enforcing on the peasants the duty of repairing the dams. So almost everywhere the ruin of the feudal estates was more conspicuous than that of others. The Fayyum had fallen into decay because of the destruction of a great dam. In 1389, out of 24,000 feddans of land held by the peasants of Luxor only 1,000 were cultivated. As in other periods of medieval history, pillaging by troops was responsible for the decay of many villages. From time to time the government took measures to repair the damage. Baibars, the first of the great Mamluk sultans, and al-Malik an-Nasir Muhammad had canals dug and others widened. In the reign of Barsbay the authorities once more made efforts to repair the dams in Egypt and the irrigation canals in Syria. The chroniclers of the second half of the fifteenth century and the beginning of the sixteenth century several times record such activities, as in the years 1469, 1480, 1487, 1491, 1507, 1511 and 1513. But they reveal also that the feudal lords offered opposition.[54]

The plight of the peasants who lived as villeins on the feudal estates was undoubtedly worse in that period than at any time before. New taxes and forced labour rendered their life almost unbearable. As always a flight from the land was the consequence of oppression. Those who could escaped from the villages, which had become forced labour camps. Many texts in Arabic works dating from the Mamluk period bear evidence of this phenomenon. They show that it had become a problem which the authorities had to deal with time and again. Already at the beginning of the Mamluk reign there were officials whose task it was to capture runaway serfs and bring them back to their lords. In Syria in the middle of the fourteenth century the authorities used to send back peasants who were caught within three years after their flight.[55]

The first Bahrite sultans did not content themselves with occasional repairs to the irrigation system, but tried by colonising projects to remedy the mischief done. These activities were concomitant with the demographic growth in the second half of the thirteenth century and the first half of the fourteenth. Landless peasants were to be settled, in order to increase the cultivated area and diminish the number of runaway serfs, who led a miserable life in the big towns. Baibars built a new village in Egypt and in Galilee restored to the previous proprietors the estates which had been abandoned as long as the Franks held Safed. These estates were brought under cultivation. Sultan Kalaun (1279–90) had a canal repaired in the al-Buhaira province, whereupon many estates lying fallow were once more tilled. Kitbogha, who reigned from 1294 to 1296, founded a village in Syria. al-Malik an-Nasir Muhammad embarked on the realisation of greater projects.

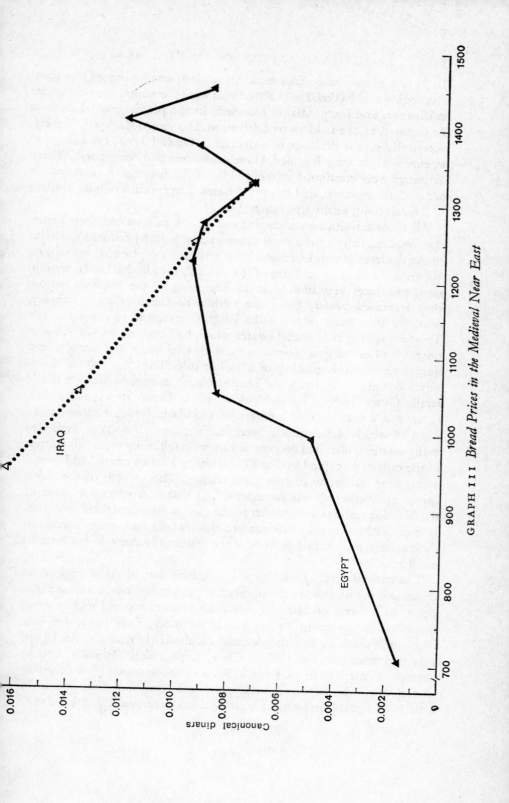

GRAPH III Bread Prices in the Medieval Near East

In 1310 he repaired a canal near Alexandria, employing 40,000 men. According to al-Makrizi 100,000 feddans were thereupon brought under cultivation and forty villages founded. In the province of al-Buhaira he restored 25,000 feddans to cultivation. His viceroy in Syria, Tenkiz, accomplished the drainage of a district in Central Syria, the Bika, and twenty villages were founded where once there had been marsh. These activities were continued in the middle of the fourteenth century. We are told, for instance, that in 1357 the emir Sarghitmish rebuilt Amman in Transjordan, settling peasants there.[56]

All these activities were carried out by the sultans and their emirs, the great majority of the rural estates being held by feudal lords. But under the later Mamluks a remarkable change took place in land tenure. Whereas the number and size of the 'amlak', the allodial lands, were in most provinces very limited at the beginning of the Mamluk period, they increased greatly from the middle of the fourteenth century. Many of the estates of the halka knights were sold to civilians. The Treasury readily sold feudal estates which had become vacant and also others. In Central and Northern Syria allodial lands had already been numerous at the beginning of Mamluk rule. Then the sultans themselves bought lands from the Treasury, such as several villages in the fertile Ghuta bought by al-Malik an-Nasir Hasan in 1359. Further, there was a considerable increase of wakf-land (pious endowments), most of which had formerly been feudal estates. But there were also many estates which had become family wakfs. The innumerable entries in the cadastrals copied by Ibn Djian, saying that an estate had become wakf, bear testimony to this great change. The growth of the aukaf (pious endowments) was so conspicuous that it aroused the anger of the Mamluks, and one pretender to the throne promised their abolition. It goes without saying that private landowners had more interest in their estates, and Arabic authors of the fifteenth century do not omit to emphasise it.[57]

The natural fertility of Egypt's soil, like that of some regions in Syria, and the increase in the number of private landowners meant that down to the end of Mamluk rule both countries could export great quantities of agricultural products. If the total of the cultivated area had diminished, so had the demand on domestic markets. So Egypt exported wheat to the Hidjaz, Crete, Cyprus and Dalmatia, and in periods of dearth to Syria. Even in Syria wheat was usually so abundant that it could be exported to Cyprus and elsewhere. But the main articles of agricultural export were Syrian cotton and Egyptian flax.[58]

The documents in the Italian archives which contain data concerning exports from Egypt and Syria point clearly to the changes in the agriculture of these countries during the later middle ages. These data are complemented by records in Arabic sources. The two major changes in the period of the Bahri Mamluks were the extension of sugar and of cotton plantations. Sugar was planted in Egypt in many regions where it had never been before, e.g. in the district of Alexandria and in the Fayyum. The increase of cotton plantations in all provinces of Syria and Palestine must have been conspicuous. Many passages in the travelogues of European travellers and evidence found in other sources testify to this fact.[59]

In the fifteenth century there took place another change, of the greatest significance in the economic history of the Near East – the decline of wheat, as compared with barley and other grains. Throughout the period of the Bahrites wheat had remained the staple food. Baibars and even Barkuk distributed wheat to the poor. But around the year 1490 people in Cairo began to eat millet and dhura bread. In Damascus civilians stored barley, and even the governor and the amirs used it. These accounts of Arabic chroniclers are complemented by the data found in the Turkish fiscal surveys made after the conquest of Syria. In many districts of Palestine the barley crops are equal or even superior to those of wheat, e.g. in Bethlehem, in a village of the sandjak of Gaza, in the district of Jaffa, and in five districts of the sandjak of Safed.[60] This is a clear proof of impoverishment as there is no evidence that this change came about through a growth of animal husbandry. The economic historian can also adduce other records which throw light on the decline of agriculture in the Near East at the end of the middle ages, namely the accounts of the import of olive oil from Southern Europe. Whereas Syria had been an exporter of olive oil, its output in the late Mamluk period scarcely sufficed for its own needs, and certainly not for those of Egypt. So olive oil was imported into Egypt and Syria from Dalmatia, Apulia, Provence and Catalonia.[61]

d) *The Breakdown*

All these data point to the fact that impoverishment was the major phenomenon of the Near Eastern economy at the end of the middle ages. Summing up accounts of the conditions of workers and bourgeois we arrive at the same conclusion.

As a consequence of the flight from the land there was in the big towns a real lumpenproletariat, thousands of wretched proletarians without permanent occupation, ready to hire themselves to rebels and to join warring factions. These paupers were an easy prey to epidemics, many of them suffering from chronic diseases. The lowest stratum of this class were the so-called harafish, beggars who were to be found near the mosques and elsewhere and who were allied to certain groups of dervishes. On the other hand, the situation of skilled workers had much improved after the Black Death and the subsequent epidemics, when their number had very much decreased. As always, shortage of manpower resulted in a rise of wages. Even a worker who had the minimum wage could henceforth afford 30 kg of meat (besides 90 kg of bread) a month. A skilled craftsman, who earned 6⅔ ashrafis, could offer his family 30 kg of meat (besides 120 kg of bread) and still spare more than 3 ashrafis for other expenses.[62] The stratum comprising these workers was, however, rather narrow.

The conditions of the petty bourgeoisie had considerably deteriorated. They were impoverished by the fiscal policy of the Mamluk government. At all times it had borne the brunt of the trade taxes, or suffered from them more than other classes, but the Mamluks also employed other methods to extort money from them. The most burdensome was apparently the 'tarh', the compulsory purchase of products owned or produced by the government. The merchants were compelled to buy, at high prices fixed by the authorities, wheat, rice, meat, sheep, goats, olive oil, dates, sugar, honey, spices, soap, textiles and even camels which had been taken as booty from the Bedouin. This was indeed a method used by many Moslem governments. Sometimes these compulsory purchases, which ruined the merchants, were abolished. But the Mamluk authorities employed this method of extortion time and again, even acquiring the goods by compulsory sale at cheap prices. According to Moslem law the authorities had the right to fix prices only in time of emergency, but the Mamluks did it at other times also. Often the merchants suffered severe losses through the arbitrary fixing of prices. Another way of curtailing the freedom of economic enterprise was the forestalling of the market by the agents of the government.[63]

Even the upper bourgeoisie had become less wealthy than in the days of the Bahri Mamluks. The monopolistic policy of the Circassian sultans and the participation of the Mamluk amirs in industrial and commercial activities brought about the decline of the upper bourgeoisie. Some of the Karimis became agents of the sultan, while other rich merchants co-operated with the amirs, who were the great wheat traders. Great shipments of wheat were brought from the Said, the granary of Egypt, to the 'corn shore' in Bulak, a suburb of Cairo, and stored in the barns of the amirs.[64] So the scope of enterprise for civilian merchants was decidedly more limited than before. In the chronicles of the fifteenth century one reads no longer, as in those of the Bahri period, of Karimis who were great capitalists and could lend sizable sums to the sultan and other princes.

But instead of the small group of great capitalists a relatively broad stratum of wealthy bourgeois had emerged. This was the great change in social stratification which had occurred in Egypt and Syria in the second half of the fourteenth and the first half of the fifteenth century. The great transit trade in Indian spices had not been monopolised by the Mamluk government, as some scholars still maintain. Although attempts were made to monopolise the pepper trade and the government wanted to fix its price, it remained free, as is borne out by many documents in the Italian archives. Further, it should be taken into consideration that the Italian merchants also bought great quantities of cotton in Syria, where there had never been a monopoly. The cloth merchants (bazzazun), the slave dealers and with them the grain dealers were a class of rich, influential bourgeois. They also traded with Turkey and other Near Eastern countries. But the wealth of the bourgeoisie originated probably just as much from its landed property. The progressive dissolution of the feudal system had enabled the rich bourgeois to acquire a great part of the rural estates which had been ikta. Perhaps the income that the bourgeois obtained from their rural estates was much more substantial than that from their commercial activities.[65]

There is plenty of evidence of the emergence of a new influential bourgeoisie. In the Arabic sources of the fifteenth century the rich merchants appear as one of the ruling classes, they have their corporative organisation, although in the loose Oriental way, with a chief called kabir at-tudjdjar at its head. Characteristically enough, the honorific title khawadja or khawadjaki which was bestowed upon them is not mentioned in the great manual of state administration compiled by al-Kalkashandi about 1410, though it appears in a similar work written in the later Mamluk period. This clearly shows the change in the social status of the new bourgeoisie, climbing up the ladder of the social hierarchy of the declining feudal state. These rich bourgeois have their Mamluks and found many madrasas, colleges for theologians. Sometimes they serve the Mamluk government as ambassadors.[66]

Besides the feudal aristocracy and the rich merchants there was a third influential class in the declining Mamluk kingdom – the theologians. At the end of the middle ages this class, from which the government recruited judges, professors and high officials, had become stronger than ever, as the numerous *madrasas* were training an ever-increasing number of young intellectuals. This class of ulama was clearly distinct from other strata of society, certain posts being held from generation to generation by the same families. These families of judges and professors were a real intellectual aristocracy which enabled the untutored Mamluk officers to carry on the business of the government. But they needed the Mamluks much more than the Mamluks needed them. The salaries of the theologians, whether they were judges or professors, came mostly from funds the Mamluks provided.[67]

So the conditions for revolutionary movements in the towns were not propitious, although the whole population had become poorer as a consequence of the Mamluk government's policy. The emergence of a new bourgeoisie, though less rich and powerful than the old one, and the improvement of the conditions of skilled workers militated against revolutionary tendencies. The skilled workers, the upper bourgeoisie and the intellectuals were essentially unfavourable to any attempt to overthrow the existing social order. Further, one must bear in mind that all classes of society were imbued with a spirit of rigid orthodoxy which made a social revolution allied to sectarian tendencies quite unthinkable.

The bitterness of the townspeople, who suffered from oppression by a foreign soldiery and the extortions of a corrupt bureaucracy, expressed itself in mob riots and ephemeral outbursts of popular resistance. But there were no real revolutionary movements.

The chronicles of the Circassian Mamluks contain many accounts of the activities of the so-called *zuar*, lumpenproletarians who formed real gangs, similar to those of the ayyarun in times of yore. They even demanded 'protection money' from the merchants and sometimes enjoyed the support of people belonging to the highest ranks of society. But contrary to the ayyarun they completely lacked any ideology; they were simply paupers interested in gaining a livelihood by any means. Often they hired themselves to fighting Mamluk factions or even enlisted in the expeditionary corps sent against rebels, such as the Bedouin, but usually they indulged in plainly criminal activities. The bourgeoisie hated them.[68]

The middle classes often lodged protests against heavy taxation and other measures taken by the Mamluk authorities. They demonstrated in the cathedral mosques or attacked officials. But one finds too in the Arabic chronicles many accounts of revolts in Syrian towns in which the bulk of the population participated. Such revolts broke out in 1397 in al-Karak, in 1399–1400 in Tripoli, in 1408 in Hamath, in 1413 in Aleppo, in 1418 once more in Tripoli, in 1439 in Damascus, in 1444–5 in Hamath, in 1448, 1456, 1480, 1484 and 1491 in Aleppo and in 1492–3 in Damascus. The revolts sometimes resulted in the expulsion of the governor or even in his murder. But the reports of contemporary historians leave no doubt that the rich bourgeois usually dissociated themselves from the rebellious populace.[69]

As there were no masses of industrial workers in the large towns of Syria and Egypt, these revolts were mainly sporadic outbursts of popular exasperation. But the bourgeois classes which opposed them suffered too from the rapacity of the Mamluks and were ready to support another dynasty which might replace them. They were interested in the existing social order without being faithful to the Mamluk government. Whenever the Mamluks were attacked by a strong army the bourgeois were ready to rally to them.

Meanwhile the resources of the Mamluk government diminished progressively and monetary difficulties began to shake the military power of the sultan of Cairo. At the beginning of the fifteenth century the mints of Egypt and Syria could not coin silver dirhams at all. In 1412 the governor of Syria, Nauruz, minted dirhams containing 50% silver and half-dirhams of pure silver. Probably he used Central Asian silver which was flowing to the Near East in the wake of the armies of Timur Lenk or through the strengthening of commercial ties after his conquests. Three years later, sultan al-Malik al-Muayyad Shaikh, who had subdued the revolt of the Syrian amirs, came back to Cairo with great stocks of silver and minted his half-dirhams, containing rather more than 90% silver. This half-dirham, called after his honorific title 'muayyadi' (pronounced by the Europeans 'maydin'), continued to be the silver coin of Egypt and Syria. All his successors struck such dirhams. The exchange rate of the muayyadi (also called nisf) even remained stable: 23–25 of these half-dirhams were given for one dinar of these sultans. The mints of Syria also continually issued silver coins, although these were mostly quarter-dirhams. The Mamluk mints were evidently regularly supplied with silver from the mines of Tyrol, Serbia and Bosnia and imported by Venetian merchants. This was rendered possible by the great advances made in European mining, both for separating the different metals mixed with silver and for preventing the inundation of the mines by subsoil-water.[70] But the coining of half- and quarter-dirhams instead of full-weight dirhams leaves no doubt that the stocks of the mints were not so rich as in earlier periods.

There are other symptoms of the general impoverishment, of the diminution of the imports of precious metals and the slowing down of their circulation. A comparison of the contributions imposed on high dignitaries in the second half of the fourteenth century and a hundred years later affords clear evidence of the great change that had come about. Even under the last Bahri sultans a high dignitary would often have been mulcted of 200,000 or 300,000 dinars, but in the fifteenth century such a musadara amounted only to 40–60,000 dinars.

The rising rate of interest was another symptom of the growing shortage of cash. Whereas in the period of the Crusades one could obtain in Egypt a loan for 4–8% per annum, the rate of interest rose in Egypt and in Syria in the fifteenth century to 18–24%.

The supply of gold to the Mamluk mints from the Western Sudan was never interrupted. Nevertheless sultan Barsbay undertook a reform of the dinar in 1425. For the first time in the history of the Moslem Near East the dinar was devalued. Instead of the canonical dinar weighing 4.25 g a lighter dinar weighing 3.45 g, like the Venetian ducat, was coined. The new dinar, called al-Ashrafi after the title of Barsbay 'al-Malik al-Ashraf', remained the gold coin of Egypt and Syria until the end of Mamluk rule. It has been maintained that Barsbay's intention was to supplant the ducat, a Christian coin which had become predominant in all the countries of the Near East, by a Moslem one having the same weight. However that may have been, the devaluation of the dinar points to the fact that the gold stocks of the Egyptian mints had diminished. Indeed, there can be no doubt that in that period a much greater part of the gold of the Western Sudan was going to Europeans, the Genoese and the Portuguese, than before. The Venetian traveller Alvise de Ca da Mosto, who travelled in 1455–6 in the Western Sudan, reports that the gold of Mali is divided into three parts, one transported by the caravans to Cairo and to Syria, a second to Timbuktu and thence via Touat to Tunis, a third to Oran, Fez, Marrakesh and Arzila, where the Italians acquire it.[71] As there is no clear evidence of a greater output of gold in the Western Sudan, the ever-increasing acquisitions of the Europeans must necessarily have diminished the supply to the Near East and weakened the sultan of Cairo.

The quantity of copper coins put into circulation in Egypt and Syria increased during the fifteenth century in consequence of the decrease of the gold and silver stocks in the mints and of the growth of the copper output in some European countries. In 1409 new copper mines had been discovered in Schwaz and Hall in Tyrol, and at the end of the fifteenth century the mines of Slovakia began to provide great quantities of copper. A considerable part of the output of all these mines was sold, via Venice, to the mints of the Mamluks. The great German merchant barons, the Fuggers, became the intermediaries. The chronicles of the late Mamluk period contain reports about the difficulties of the Mamluk government in maintaining the exchange rate of the copper coins in a climate of inflation. Whereas European governments tried to maintain the exchange rate of their silver coins, the Mamluks took measures to save their copper currency. Very often the government fixed an exchange rate much higher than the actual value of the 'fulus', or gave orders to exchange them by weight instead of number or vice versa. These measures often provoked economic crises and proved a complete failure. The chroniclers report the shortage of silver and the inflationary phenomena caused by the abundance of copper coins.

On the other hand there was from time to time a real coin famine. At the end of the third decade of the fifteenth century dinars (ashrafis) disappeared altogether. Even dirhams were scarcely to be found, and instead of coins people used wheat. The disappearance of dirhams was henceforth a frequent phenomenon. Consequently it often happened that the sultan could not make payments in gold as his predecessors used to do. Even copper coins sometimes became very rare, because they were re-exported to India, where their value was much greater.[72]

The great monetary difficulties of the declining Mamluk kingdom seem, at first glance, amazing, since the balance of payments of Egypt and of Syria must still have been very favourable. There is indeed clear evidence of a considerable increase of the volume of the Indian transit trade through the age of the Circassian sultans.

At the end of the fourteenth century some changes in politica conditions made the Red Sea once more the principal trade route between India and Southern Europe. No doubt the deterioration of conditions in Persia was the main reason for this change, but it was not the only one. In 1434 the Genoese took Famagusta, whereupon the Venetians had to leave Cyprus. Then, in 1375, the Mamluks conquered the kingdom of Little Armenia and put an end to the flourishing trade of Lajazzo and in the 1390s Timur Lenk destroyed Saray and Astrakhan, two emporia on the great land route from Central Asia to the Black Sea. So the Venetians, who were the most active in the great spice trade, had to return to the ports of Egypt and Syria, and from then on Alexandria and Beirut were the main centres of this trade. Once more the Venetians and other European 'trading nations' applied to the sultan of Cairo for commercial privileges and concluded advantageous treaties with him. Venice gained such privileges in 1415, 1422 and 1442. Venetian navigation in the Eastern Mediterranean became more and more intense. From 1422 the Serenissima had three regular galley lines to the Levant: from 1461 the line called Di Trafego connected Tunisia with Alexandria. Florence, which came into contact with the Mamluks at the beginning of the fifteenth century, in 1422 obtained the right to have consuls in Alexandria and Damascus and obtained new privileges in 1489, 1496 and 1497. But other Italian towns too had a share in the great Levantine trade. The Genoese had consuls and fondachi in Alexandria, Beirut and Damascus. They regularly sent their galleys and round ships to Egypt and Syria. Ancona and Naples had colonies and consuls in Alexandria at the end of the fourteenth and in the first half of the fifteenth century. The commercial activities of other nations were less regular. At the end of the fourteenth century the Catalans sent 3-5 galleys every year to Egypt and Syria, but later their commercial relations with the Mamluk kingdom declined. The merchants of Marseilles were also very active in the trade with Egypt and Syria in the eighties of the fourteenth century and, after an interruption, at the beginning of the fifteenth century and in its fourth decade. In the second half of the fifteenth century, however, traffic of the 'galleys of France' was quite regular. Even the Levantine trade of Ragusa was steadily increasing. The merchants of the Dalmatian emporium exported to Alexandria and Beirut silver, lead, textiles, corals, honey and other merchandise.[73]

The data which we find in Venetian sources concerning the trade of the Serenissima with Syria and Egypt illustrate the considerable increase of its volume. The doge Tomaso Mocenigo (1414-23) maintained in a speech made before his death that Venice sent 300,000 ducats in cash every year to the Levant. In the Cronica Morosini one finds a greater sum, 460,000 ducats, referring to the year 1433. But in that year the Levantine trade was resumed after an interruption due to a military conflict. Statistics of the end of the fifteenth century also mention the sum of 300,000 ducats.[74] The Venetians paid in cash, however, for only a part of the spices and cotton which they bought in Egypt and Syria, acquiring a great part of them by barter. From data on the most important articles they exported from Egypt and Syria a clearer pattern appears. The following calculations are made according to the data contained in the documents in the archives of Francesco Datini, who organised an excellent intelligence service at the end of the fourteenth century, in an account of the Venetian consulate in Alexandria, and in the Venetian *Diarii* of the late fifteenth century.

Value of the purchases of the Venetians in Alexandria and in Beirut

1382	pepper	Alexandria	40,800 dinars	
	ginger	Alexandria	7,080 ,,	
				total 47,880 dinars
1396	pepper	Alexandria	94,350 dinars	
		Beirut	42,090 ,,	
	ginger	Alexandria	24,000 ,,	
		Beirut	30,900 ,,	
				total 191,340 dinars
1404	pepper	Alexandria	90,720 dinars	
		Beirut	56,892 ,,	
	ginger	Alexandria	14,800 ,,	
		Beirut	46,000 ,,	
				total 208,412 dinars
1408	pepper	Alexandria	53,025 dinars	
	ginger	Alexandria	100 ,,	
				total 53,125 dinars
1419	pepper	Alexandria	114,770 dinars	
1496	pepper	Alexandria	101,840 ducats	
		Beirut	72,150 ,,	
	ginger	Alexandria	60,000 ,,	
		Beirut	14,987 ,,	
				total 248,977 ducats
1497	pepper	Alexandria	149,000 ducats	
		Beirut	32,175 ,,	
	ginger	Alexandria	90,016 ,,	
		Beirut	27,200 ,,	
				total 298,391 ducats

Value of the purchases of the Venetians in Alexandria and in Beirut

1498	pepper	Alexandria	130,218 ducats
	ginger	Alexandria	74,220 „
			total 204,438 ducats

The data concerning the quantities of pepper and ginger, the two most important spices, show even more conspicuously the great difference between the trade at the end of the fourteenth century and a hundred years later.

Export of pepper and ginger from Alexandria

	pepper	ginger
1382	679 sportas (of 225 kg)	472 kintar fulfuli (of 45 kg)
1396	1,258 „	800 „ „
1404	1,440 „	704 „ „
1408	707 „	20 „ „
1496	1,520 „	4,800 „ „
1497	2,000 „	6,208 „ „
1498	1,588 „	5,672 „ „

Since the prices of these great quantities of spices amounted to much more than the sums of money which the Venetians brought to the ports of Egypt and Syria, we must conclude that imports too increased very much in course of the fifteenth century. The Venetian chronicles compiled at the beginning of the sixteenth century contain valuable data on the export of one particular article – copper – which we reproduce in the following table, adding the value.[75]

Import of copper by the Venetians

1495	Alexandria	5,500 kintar djarwi	35,750 ducats
1496	Alexandria	10,000 „ „	65,000 „
	Beirut	1,500 „ „	9,750 „
1501	Alexandria	4,000 „ „	26,000 „

Our calculations,[76] which do not include the purchases of Syrian cotton, show convincingly that the balance of payments of the Levantine trade must have been favourable for the Mamluk kingdom, although less so than many scholars have believed. It is true, however, that the Mamluk kingdom spent every year a considerable sum of gold coins for the purchase of military slaves from the countries around the Black Sea and elsewhere and that it imported spices for the domestic market. But the acquisition of gold, exchanged in the Western Sudan for cheap products, such as salt and cowries, shifted the commercial balance of the Mamluk kingdom so that it was always in its favour.

But in spite of the uninterrupted supply of Sudanese gold and the favourable balance of payments the economy of the Mamluk kingdom crumbled in the second half of the fifteenth century. The collapse took place at a time when a new and vigorous military power was steadily expanding in the Near East and in Southern Europe and threatening the throne of the sultan of Cairo. The economic breakdown was one of the principal causes of political and military downfall.

The slow decay of Egyptian industry and the dumping of European and Far Eastern products certainly played their part in this collapse. The extravagant luxury of the ruling feudal class was another cause. Many accounts in the chronicles of the fifteenth century show that notwithstanding the great economic difficulties the amirs lavishly spent great sums on their households. The hoarding of gold and silver had always been a consequence of the musadara system of Moslem governments. There is good reason to believe that under the rapacious régime of the Mamluks people belonging to the wealthy classes were more inclined than ever to conceal their riches. This is borne out by accounts of confiscations.[77]

Another major reason for the breakdown was the military budget of the sultans of Cairo. The reports of the Arabic authors show that the sums the Circassian sultans had to give their troops, beside their income from the feudal estates, were continually increasing. The extraordinary payments due to the Mamluks on various occasions were in the fifteenth century much higher than before. In the first half of the century the sultan had to pay, before a military expedition, 400–600,000 dinars to his Mamluks. Sultan Djakmak (1438–53) spent 3 m dinars on his wars and the payment of his troops during the first three years of his reign.

Meanwhile the Portuguese had reached the island of Arguin in 1445, penetrated into the Senegal, and reached Cape Verde and the Gambia. Shortly after the middle of the fifteenth century they began to seize great quantities of Sudanese gold. The consequences were felt in Egypt. Several passages in the chronicles of this period mention the lack of gold in the Cairo Treasury.

At the same time the antagonism between the Ottomans and the Mamluks began to cast its shadow on the court of the sultan. For a long time the two Moslem powers had been on good terms. When the Ottomans began to extend their power to the southern provinces of Asia Minor, they bolstered up the Turcoman principality of Abulustain. Siwar-shah, the warlike prince of Abulustain, waged war against the Mamluks, and at the end of the sixties and the beginning of the seventies of the century armies had to be sent against him from Egypt time and again. According to an Arabic biography of sultan Kaitbay (1468–96) he spent from his accession to the throne to the end of January 1473 3,776,000 dinars on wars, on grants to the army and for the construction of various buildings. The regular pay of the military is not included in this sum. Already in 1472 Kaitbay had to take drastic measures to keep his budget balanced. He called the high dignitaries of the kingdom to a meeting and explained to them that he could no longer meet the demands of the army. As the military budget had been doubled, he said, there was no choice but to abolish the payment of pensions to several groups of soldiers and civilians. In the eighties of the century the sultan had once more to send troops against the Turcomans of Abulustain, who were supported by the Ottomans. Finally, the Mamluks and the Ottomans no longer fought by means of satellite states, but waged war between themselves. In the days of Kaitbay there were four wars between the two powers, in 1483, 1485, 1488 and 1490. Although these wars brought the Mamluks great military success, they put a heavy strain on their economy. A trustworthy Arabic historian relates that Kaitbay spent 7,065,000 dinars altogether on his sixteen wars. In order to cover these enormous expenses, his government had recourse to various expedients. Before even petty expeditions were undertaken it imposed contributions on certain classes of the population or on the quarters of the large towns. Often it collected extraordinary taxes from private property and pious endowments, and time and again there were reductions of the pensions of theologians, widows and others.[78]

The discovery of the sea route to India was indubitably a terrible blow to the economy of the Mamluk kingdom. What the sultans of Cairo had dreaded for many centuries and had tried to prevent had been accomplished by the daring and the ability of the Portuguese.

When spices became rare on the markets of Alexandria and Beirut and the Venetians had to go to Lisbon to buy them, the death-knell seemed to ring for the power of the Mamluks. Their efforts to wage war with the Portuguese in the Indian Ocean put an additional strain on the tottering economy of Egypt and Syria. It was the civilian classes who had to bear the brunt. So the emissaries of the Ottomans had an easy task when they came to arouse the population of Syria against the Mamluks. The Syrians were weary of their rule and listened readily to these suggestions. When the Ottoman army penetrated into Syria in 1516 and then into Egypt, it encountered no strong resistance. The decisive battle near Aleppo was won by the Ottomans through their technological superiority. They had numerous and well-organised artillery, whereas the Mamluks practised the old-fashioned Turkish style of fighting with archers, and had long despised the use of firearms. Later they had tried in vain to get from Venice the artillery badly needed to fight the Portuguese in the Indian Ocean. But apart from that their fleet could not withstand the Portuguese ships; it was technically inferior and its ships were easily sunk.[79]

The people of the Syrian and Egyptian towns, aware of the helplessness of the Mamluks, were looking forward to better days. The Ottomans took Cairo, Syria and Egypt became provinces of their great empire, and the last Abbasid caliph was carried off to Constantinople.

This was the end of what had once been the flower of civilisation in Western Asia and the Mediterranean world. The flourishing economy of the Near East had been ruined by the rapacious military, and its great civilising achievements had been destroyed through inability to adopt new methods of production and new ways of life.

Abbreviations

ASV   Archivio di Stato, Venice

BSOAS   Bulletin of the School of Asian and African Studies, London

JA   Journal Asiatique

JAOS   Journal of the American Oriental Society

JESHO   Journal of Economic and Social History of the Orient

JRAS   Journal of the Royal Asiatic Society

REI   Revue des études islamiques

ROL   Revue de l'Orient latin

RSI   Rivista Storica Italiana

RSO   Rivista degli studi orientali

SI   Studia Islamica

ZDMG   Zeitschrift der deutschen morgenländischen Gesellschaft

Notes

CHAPTER I

1. Caetani, *Annali* I, pp. 916, 961; P. K. Hitti, *History of the Arabs*, 6th ed. (London 1956), pp. 158, 161.
2. Caetani, *op. cit.* I, p. 834ff; C. H. Becker, *The expansion of the Saracens*, in *Cambridge Medieval History* II, pp. 333, 339.
3. Fr. Altheim-R. Stiehl, *Die Araber in der alten Welt* (Berlin 1964–9) I, pp. 139ff, 166, 289, 309ff, 313ff, 317ff; R. Dussaud, *La pénétration des arabes en Syrie avant l'Islam* (Paris 1955), pp. 23ff, 135ff; Fr. Nau, *Les arabes chrétiens de Mésopotamie et de Syrie* (Paris 1933), p. 15; Caetani, I, pp. 939, 946, 977, 993; Abu Yusuf, *Kitab al-Kharadj* (Cairo 1346), p. 170ff.
4. A. Müller, *Der Islam im Morgenu. Abendland* (Berlin 1885–7) I, p. 222; al-Makrizi, *al-Khitat* (Bulak 1270) I, p. 94; H. Lammens, *La Syrie* (Beirut 1921) I, p. 120; A. N. Poliak, 'L'arabisation de l'Orient semitique', *REI* 12 (1938), p. 43f.
5. al-Baladhuri, *Futuh al-buldan* (Leiden 1866), pp. 126f, 136, 150, cf. translation Hitti (New York 1916), pp. 194, 208f, 232; al-Yakubi, *Kitab al-Buldan*, pp. 309, 327, cf. translation Wiet (Cairo 1937), pp. 140, 178.
6. al-Yakubi, p. 327ff (tr. Wiet, pp. 177f, 180f); al-Baladhuri, *Futuh*, p. 127.
7. Ibn Haukal, *Surat al-ard*, ed. Kramers, pp. 215, 228 (tr. Wiet I, pp. 209, 222); al-Yakubi, pp. 324f, 326f, 329; C. H. Becker, *Beiträge zur Geschichte Ägyptens* (Strassburg 1902–3) II, p. 122ff; al-Kindi, *The Governors and judges of Egypt* (Leiden 1912), p. 76f; *al-Khitat* I, p. 80, II, p. 261.
8. Yakut, *Mu'djam al-buldan* IV, p. 757; A. N. Poliak, art. cit. *ibid.*, p. 48f; al-Djahiz, *Kitab al-Hayawan* (Cairo 1323–5) I, p. 143; *al-Khitat* I, p. 82, II, p. 261[8]; Becker, *Beiträge* II, pp. 125, 130; al-Baladhuri, p. 150.
9. A. Reifenberg, *The struggle between the desert and the sown* (Jerusalem 1955), pp. 98, 100; X. de Planhol, *Les fondements géographiques de l'histoire de l'Islam* (Paris 1968), pp. 45, 83, 90, 92ff; Poliak, art. cit., *ibid.*, p. 48.
10. L. Massignon, 'Explication du plan de Kufa', *Mélanges Maspero* III (Cairo 1935–40), p. 342f; Becker, *Beiträge* II, p. 122f; al-Yakubi, p. 326; S. D. Goitein, 'Jerusalem in the Arab period' (in Hebrew), *Jerusalem*, 1953, p. 87f; Ibn Haukal, pp. 215, 221 (tr. Wiet I, pp. 209, 215).
11. Becker, *Beiträge* II, p. 124; H. Lammens, 'La badia et la hira sous les Omaiyades', *Mélanges de la faculté orientale* (Beirut) IV, p. 91ff; another view is expressed by V. Strika, *Origini e primi sviluppi dell'architettura civile musulmana* (Venice 1968), p. 19f; Massignon, art. cit., *ibid.*, p. 344;

J. Sadan, 'Meubles et acculturation: Bédouins et sedentaires dans la civilisation califienne', *Annales E.S.C.* 25 (1970), p. 1361ff; E. Ashtor in *JESHO* VI (1963), p. 174f.

12. *al-Khitat* I, p. 98; Becker, *Beiträge* II, p. 130f; J. Schacht, *The origins of Muhammadan jurisprudence* (Oxford 1953), p. 238; N. J. Coulson, *A history of Islamic law* (Edinburgh 1964), p. 27ff; B. R. Foster, 'Agoranomos and muhtasib', *JESHO* 13 (1970), p. 128ff; J.-Cl. Vadet, 'L'"acculturation" des sud-arabiques de Fustat au lendemain de la conquête arabe', *Bulletin d'études orientales* 22 (1969), p. 11ff.

13. E. Ashtor, 'I salari nel Medio Oriente durante l'epoca medievale', *RSI* 78 (1966), pp. 341f, 346; id., *Histoire des prix et des salaires dans l'Orient médiéval* (Paris 1969), pp. 64f, 91, 533f; J. Wellhausen, *The Arab kingdom* (Beirut 1963), p. 174; H. Lammens, *Etudes sur le règne du calife omaiyade Mo'awiya Ier* (Beirut 1906–7), p. 235.

14. A. Müller, *Der Islam im Morgenu. Abandland* I, p. 241f; I. Goldziher, *Vorlesungen über den Islam* (Heidelberg 1910), p. 141; H. Lammens, 'Ziad ibn abihi', (in) *Etudes sur le siècle des Omayyades* (Beirut 1930), p. 33f; Wellhausen, *op. cit.*, p. 349; Ibn al-Athir, *Usd al-ghaba* (Cairo 1280) III, p. 315; Ibn Kutaiba, *Uyun al-akhbar* (Berlin 1900–08), p. 212; Lammens, *Etudes sur le règne du calife omaiyade Mo'awiya Ier*, p. 234.

15. Muh. b. Ali b. Tulun, *Rasa'il ta'rikhiyya* IV: al-Lum'at al-barkiyya (Damascus 1348), p. 10ff; al-Masudi, *Prairies d'or* IV, p. 253ff, cf. tr. Pellat III, p. 616; al-Yakubi, *Mushakalat an-nas bi-zamanihim*, ed. W. Millward (Beirut 1962), p. 13f; Ibn Sad, *Tabakat* III, 1, pp. 76f, 158; IV, p. 109; Ibn al-Athir, *Usd al-ghaba* III, p. 229; Ibn Hisham, *Sira* (Göttingen 1859), p. 968; Goldziher, *Vorlesungen*, p. 139ff; Yakut III, p. 700[21]; at-Tabari II, p. 1655; al-Baladhuri, p. 384.

16. Wellhausen, *op. cit.*, p. 180ff.

17. F. Løkkegaard, *Islamic taxation in the classic period* (Copenhagen 1950), p. 17.

18. Lammens, Ziad, p. 48; Massignon, 'Explication du plan de Basra', *Westöstl. Studien R. Tschudi* (Wiesbaden 1954), p. 159.

19. Wellhausen, *op. cit.*, p. 229f; T. Lewicki, art. Ibadiyya, in *Encycl. of Islam*, 2nd ed., III, p. 648ff.

20. at-Tabari II, pp. 634, 647, 689.

21. *Op. cit.*, pp. 609, 630, 634, 649f.

CHAPTER II

1. al-Baladhuri, *Futuh*, pp. 128, 148, 151, 267, 364, 366ff; *Chronique de Denys de Tell-Mahré*, 4e partie, publiée et trad. par J.-B. Chabot (Paris 1895), pp. 106, 130. Becker, *Beiträge* II, p. 129; Poliak in *REI* 12, p. 42; al-Kindi, *Governors and judges*, p. 346.

2. al-Yakubi, *Le livre des pays* (tr. Wiet), p. 164ff; Papyrus Erzherzog Rainer, *Führer durch die Ausstellung* (Vienna 1894), pp. 159, 166f, 186, 188.

3. Denys de Tell-Mahré, pp. 112, 133; Cl. Cahen, 'Fiscalité propriété, antagonismes sociaux en Haute-Mesopotamie au temps des premiers Abbasides', *Arabica* I (1954), pp. 142, 146, 151; Abu Yusuf, *Le livre de l'impôt foncier*, trad. Fagnan (Paris 1921), p. 76; Poliak in *REI* 12, p. 53.

4. al-Baladhuri, pp. 272, 368; Abu Yusuf, p. 56ff; at-Tabari I, p. 962f; C. H. Becker, *Beiträge* II, p. 116f; Fr. Løkkegaard, *Islamic taxation*, p. 122; Pap. Ezherz. Rainer, *Führer*, p. 199f; D. C. Dennett, *Conversion and the poll-tax in early Islam* (Cambridge, Mass. 1950), p. 62; Denys de Tell-Mahré, pp. 10, 113, 130, 133f, 159, 169f, 172.

5. al-Mukaddasi, *Ahsan at-takasim*, pp. 71, 136, 138, 160, 174f, 178, 180, 188, 203, 205, 264; tr. Guy Le Strange, in *Library of the Palestine Pilgrims' Text Society* III (London 1897), p. 91; Miskawaih, ed. Amedroz-Margoliouth, II, p. 318f; al-Baladhuri, p. 134; Kudama b. Djafar, *Kitab al-Kharadj*, p. 237f, cf. tr. de Goeje, p. 180; Ibn Khurdadhbih, p. 8ff, cf. tr. de Goeje, p. 6ff; E. Wirth, *Agrargeographie des Irak* (Hamburg 1962), p. 45; al-Masudi, *Kitab at-Tanbih*, p. 22; D. Müller-Wodarg, 'Die Landwirtschaft Ägyptens in der frühen Abbasidenzeit', *Der Islam* 32 (1957), pp. 17f, 21; E. Ashtor, 'The diet of salaried classes in the medieval Near East', *Journal of Asian history* IV (1971), p. 2f; B. H. Slicher van Bath, *The agrarian history of Western Europe A.D. 500–1850* (London 1963), p. 66.

6. Ibn Khurdadhbih, p. 10ff; Hilal as-Sabi, ed. Amedroz, p. 335; at-Tanukhi, *Nishwar al-muhadara* VIII (Damascus 1930), p. 66ff; M. Canard, 'Le riz dans le Proche Orient aux premiers siècles de l'Islam', *Arabica* VI (1959), pp. 115f, 123f, 131; H. Cohen, 'The economic background and the secular occupations of Muslim jurisprudents and traditionalists in the classical period of Islam', *JESHO* 13 (1970), p. 28; Müller-Wodarg, art. cit., *Der Islam* 32, p. 23f; Ibn al-Fakih, p. 187; al-Istakhri, p. 91; at-Tanukhi, in *Isl. Culture* IV (1930), p. 19f.

7. al-Istakhri, pp. 77, 80, 82, 85, 87; Ibn al-Fakih, p. 114; Ibn Haukal, *Surat al-ard*, p. 229; Cohen, art. cit., *ibid.*, pp. 29, 42.

8. al-Istakhri, pp. 58, 73, 78; Ibn al-Fakih, pp. 114, 117, 120, 122f; al-Mukaddasi, pp. 161ff, 174, 180f, cf. tr. Le Strange, pp. 71f, 90; A. Mez, *Die Renaissance des Islams* (Heidelberg 1922), p. 456f; Ashtor, 'Diet of salaried classes, etc.', p. 7; Cohen, art. cit., *ibid.*, p. 28; G. Tchalenko, *Villages antiques de la Syrie du Nord* (Paris 1953) I, p. 435ff.

9. Müller-Wodarg, art. cit., *Der Islam* 32, p. 35ff; al-Mukaddasi, pp. 160, 176f, 181, tr. Le Strange, p. 70; al-Yakubi, p. 324; cf. Guy Le Strange, *Palestine under the Moslems* (London 1890), p. 529.

10. On coffer dams, see Yakut IV, p. 16, and cf. E. Wiedemann, *Aufsätze zur arabischen Wissenschaftsgeschichte* (Hildesheim 1970) I, p. 288.

11. Abu Yusuf, tr. Fagnan, p. 167ff; al-Baladhuri, pp. 274, 290, 293, 356ff, 359ff, 367; Yakut I, p. 478, IV, pp. 16, 832ff (Nahr al-Ubulla), 835, 838, 840, 842, 994; G. Le Strange, *The Lands of the Eastern Caliphate*, p. 66f; Lammens, *Le califat de Yazid I[er]* (Beirut 1921), p. 424f; Jacobsen-Adams,

'Salt and silt in ancient Mesopotamian agriculture', *Science* 128 (1958), p. 1256f; at-Tabari II, p. 1655.

12. al-Baladhuri, p. 367, Glossary, p. 77; Yakut II, p. 331, IV, pp. 732, 830; art. Kanat in *Enc. Isl.* II, p. 708f; Ibn al-Athir IX, pp. 250, 253, 256; M. Streck, *Die alte Landschaft Babylonien* (Leiden 1901) I, p. 29; Ibn Khurdadhbih, p. 74; Ibn al-Fakih, p. 111; Ibn al-Adim, *Zubdat al-halab*, ed. ad-Dahhan I, p. 151; M. Canard, *Sayf al Daula* (Alger 1934), p. 268; al-Mukaddasi, p. 208; al-Makrizi, *as-Suluk* I, p. 409, II, p. 779; al-Yakubi, tr. Wiet, p. 67.

13. al-Makrizi, *as-Suluk* II, p. 692; al-Mukaddasi, p. 175 (the water-mills in Transjordan existed until the thirteenth century, see Yakut II, p. 61); al-Baladhuri, p. 294. On the water-wheels and similar engines in general see G. S. Colin, 'La noria marocaine et les machines hydrauliques dans le monde arabe', *Hespéris* 14 (1932), p. 22ff.

14. A. Reifenberg, *The struggle between the desert and the sown*, p. 58; Jacobsen-Adams, art. cit., p. 125, Abu Yusuf, tr. Fagnan, pp. 144, 150.

15. Jean Sire de Joinville, *Histoire de Saint-Louis*, ed. de Wailly (Paris 1874), p. 103; C. L. Woolley, *The Wilderness of Zin* (Palestine Exploration Fund, Annual 1914–15), p. 36; Ch. Parain, 'Evolution of agricultural technique', *Cambridge Economic History of Europe* I, pp. 144, 153f; Lynn-White, *Medieval technology and social change* (Oxford University Press 1962), p. 59ff; Slicher van Bath, *op. cit.*, p. 63f; *Kitab al-Aghani* (Bulak 1285) 15, p. 98; F. Wüstenfeld, *Geschichte der Fatimiden-Chalifen* (Göttingen 1881), p. 224; Müller-Wodarg, art. cit., *Der Islam* 32, p. 154f; *1001 nights*, ed. Habicht, I, p. 20.

16. Müller-Wodarg, art. cit., *Der Islam* 31, p. 216, 32, pp. 14ff, 20, 24; Parain, art. cit., *ibid.*, p. 219; Ibn Mammati, *Kawanin ad-dawawin* (Cairo 1943), p. 259; al-Makrizi, *al-Khitat* I, p. 101; G. Duby, *L'économie rurale et la vie des campagnes dans l'Occident* (Paris 1962) I, p. 187; Slicher van Bath, *op. cit.*, pp. 18, 172f.

17. N. Shalem, 'La stabilité du climat en Palestine', *Rev. Biblique* 58 (1951), p. 54ff; Cl. Vita-Finzi, *The Mediterranean valleys* (Cambridge 1969), pp. 101, 116ff.

18. W. C. Lowdermilk, 'Erosion at its worst', *Soil Conservation* V (1939–40), p. 157ff; id., 'The lost agriculture of Trans-Jordan', *ibid.*, p. 239; Tchalenko, l. c.; A. Reifenberg, *op. cit.*, pp. 39f, 44f; S. H. Shaw-N. A. Pharaon, 'Nablus-Tulkarm Valley', Government of Palestine, Soil Conservation Board, *Bulletin* No. 1 (Jerusalem 1941); A. E. Mader, *Altchristliche Basiliken u. Lokaltraditionen in Südjudaea* (Paderborn 1918), p. 6; P. L. O. Guy, 'Archaeological evidence of soil erosion and sedimentation in Wadi Musrara', *Israel Exploration Journal* IV (1954), p. 77ff; Y. Karmon, 'Geographical conditions in the Sharon plain' (in Hebrew), *Bull. of the Israel Exploration Society* 23 (1959), p. 130; M. Avi-Yonah, 'The economic past of the Negeb', *Palestine and the Middle East* IX

(1937), p. 440; N. Glueck, *The other side of the Jordan* (New Haven 1940), pp. 115, 122, 124f, 127, 149f, 160, 173; M. Evenari and others, *The Negev* (Harvard University Press 1971), p. 97.

19. D. Neev–K. O. Emery, *The Dead Sea* (Jerusalem 1967), pp. 30, 105.

20. Abu Yusuf, tr. Fagnan, p. 59f, Arabic text, p. 57 (tr. p. 74 erroneous); Yakut II, p.143; al-Masudi, *K. at-Tanbih*, p. 40; R. McC. Adams, *Land, behind Baghdad* (University of Chicago Press 1965), p. 98; Guy, art. cit.; Mader, 1. c.; Avi-Yonah, art. cit., p. 438; Planhol, *op. cit.*, p. 71; al-Makrizi, *al-Khitat* I, p. 99 1. 9; Omar Toussoun, *Mémoire sur les finances de l'Egypte* (Cairo 1924), p. 125f.

21. Ibn Rustih, *Les atours précieux* (tr. Wiet, Cairo 1955), p. 106f; E. Wirth, 'Landwirtschaft u. Mensch im Binnendelta des untern Tigris', *Mitteil. der geogr. Gesellschaft Hamburg*, 1955, p. 64ff.

22. Guy Le Strange, *The Lands of the Eastern caliphate*, pp. 42, 72f, 105; al-Masudi, *Prairies d'or* (tr. Pellat) I, p. 91; J. Wellhausen, *The Arab kingdom*, p. 252; al-Baladhuri, pp. 290f, 293f, 358, 361, 363; Kudama b. Djafar, p. 240f; Yakut II, p. 278, cf. I, pp. 864, 869, III, p. 208, IV, pp. 732, 835, 840f, 845; Denys de Tell-Mahré, p. 23f; C. H. Becker, *Papyrus Schott-Reinhardt* I (Heidelberg 1906), p. 19.

23. Abu Yusuf, tr. Fagnan, p. 99; Lammens, Ziad, p. 90; Wellhausen, *Arab kingdom*, pp. 332, 366; al-Baladhuri, pp. 127f, 133, 148, 152, 158, 358f, 362, 364; Yakut IV, pp. 830, 835, 838, 841, 844; Caetani, *Annali* II, p. 922. On the family Abu Bakra s. Lammens, Ziad, p. 45.

24. A. v. Kremer, *Culturgeschichte* (Vienna 1875–7) I, p. 258ff; id., 'Ueber das Budget der Einnahmen unter der Regierung des Harun alrašid', *Berichte des VII. Internat. Orient. Congresses* (Vienna 1889), p. 11f; Ibn Khaldun, *Muqaddimah*, tr. Rosenthal (New York 1958), I, p. 361ff; Ibn Khurdadhbih, tr., pp. 54, 68, 69; Kudama, *op. cit.*, p. 186f; Omar Toussoun, *op. cit.*, pp. 22ff, 58f, 126; Becker, *Beiträge* II, pp. 110, 117, 138, 140f.

25. See W. Popper, *The Cairo Nilometer* (Berkeley 1951), p. 221; C. E. P. Brooks, *Climate through the ages* (London 1950), p. 319ff; Duby, *op. cit.*, I, p. 142ff; K. W. Butzer, 'Quartenary stratigraphy and climate in the Near East', *Bonner Geogr. Abhandlungen* 24 (1958), p. 123f.

26. *Op. cit.*, pp. 92, 134, 156.

27. al-Baladhuri, *Anonyme arabische Chronik*, ed. Ahlwardt, p. 336f; Wellhausen, *Arab kingdom*, p. 285f; Denys de Tell-Mahré, pp. 105ff, 109f, 123f, 127, 134, 137, 191; H. I. Bell, 'Translations of the Greek Aphroditopapyri in the British Museum', *Der Islam* II (1911), p. 269f. (no. 1333), 274ff (no. 1343, 1344), 378ff (no. 1381, 1382, 1384); C. H. Becker, 'Historische Studien über das Londoner Aphroditowek', *Der Islam* II, p. 367f; id., 'Papyrusstudien', *Zeitschrift für Assyriologie* 22 (1908–9), pp. 139f, 141ff, 146; Poliak, in *REI* 12, p. 54.

28. Denys de Tell-Mahré, pp. 47ff, 172ff; al-Kindi, *The Book of governors and judges*, pp. 73f, 81, 94, 96, 102, 116f, 119, 190ff; al-Makrizi, *al-Khitat* II, p. 492ff; E. Quatremère, *Recherches critiques et historiques sur la langue et la*

littérature de l'Egypte (Paris 1808), pp. 152ff, 156ff; Becker, *Beiträge* II, p. 132f; at-Tabari III, p. 1319ff; Ibn al-Athir VI, p. 371f.

CHAPTER III

1. See Papyrus Erzherzog Rainer, *Führer durch die Ausstellung*, p. 159.
2. See Fr. Gabrieli, 'La successione di Harun ar-Rašid e la guerra fra al-Amin e al-Mamun', *RSO* II (1928), pp. 359, 371ff, 395ff; M. A. Shaban, *The Abbasid revolution* (Cambridge 1970), pp. XV, 156.
3. R. N. Frye, 'The role of Abu Muslim in the Abbasid revolt', *The Muslim World* 37 (1947), p. 31.
4. Gabrieli, art. cit., *ibid.*, p. 383f.
5. Denys de Tell-Mahré, pp. 27f, 42; Ibn al-Athir VI, pp. 38f, 52, 84, 114, 140; Weil, *Geschichte der Chalifen* II, p. 147f; B. Spuler, *Iran in früh-islamischer Zeit* (Wiesbaden 1952), pp. 197ff, 205f; Ibn an-Nadim, *Fihrist* (Leipzig 1872) pp. 65, 344; at-Tabari III, pp. 1075f, 1503ff,, 1510, 1552, 1563.
6. H. Lammens, *La Syrie* I, p. 116.
7. See Chapter II, p. 42ff; al-Bakri, *Description de l'Afrique septentrionale* (tr. de Slane), p. 15; ath-Thaalibi, *Lataif al-maarif* (tr. Bosworth), pp. 118, 126; Papyrus Erzherzog Rainer, *Führer*, p. 180; Ibn Haukal, p. 313.
8. M. Lombard, 'Les bases monétaires d'une suprématie économique: l'or musulman du VIIᵉ au XIᵉ siècle', *Annales E.S.C.* II (1947), p. 148; E. Ashtor, *Les métaux précieux et le balance des payements du Proche-Orient à la basse époque* (Paris 1971), p. 15f; R. B. Serjeant, in *Ars Islamica* 13-14, p. 107; Caetani, *Annali* III, p. 742ff; Chronique de Tabari, trad. Zotenberg, III, p. 416f; cf. also D. Sperber, 'Silver as a status-symbol in Sasanian Persia', *Persica* V (1970–1), p. 103ff.
9. Papyrus Erzherzog Rainer, *Führer*, p. 204; al-Yakubi, *Les pays*, trad. Wiet, p. 190; al-Masudi, *Les Prairies d'or*, trad. Pellat, II, p. 331.
10. E. Ashtor, *Les métaux précieux*, pp. 17, 20ff; Ibn Haukal, pp. 99f, 153; Ibn al-Fakih, p. 68; *The Itinerary of Benjamin of Tudela* (tr. Adler) (London 1907), p. 68f; Ibn Iyas I, p. 43.
11. Ph. Grierson, 'The monetary reform of Abd al-Malik', *JESHO* III (1960), p. 241ff, and see especially p. 248ff.
12. Ibn al-Djauzi, *al-Muntazam* VI, p. 118f; Ch. Pellat, *Le milieu basrien et la formation de Ğāhiz* (Paris 1953), p. 229.
13. G. C. Miles, *The numismatic history of Rayy* (New York 1938), p. 119f; R. N. Frye, *Notes on the early coinage of Transoxaina* (New York 1949), p. 39; Kudama b. Djafar, *Kitab al-Kharadj*, p. 237; A. v. Kremer, *Ueber das Einnahmebudget des Abbasiden-Reiches vom Jahre 306 h.* (Vienna 1887, SBAW, Phil.-hist. Cl. 36), p. 26ff.
14. Cf. Grierson, art. cit., *ibid.*, p. 258f; E. Ashtor, *Histoire des prix et des salaires dans l'Orient médiéval*, pp. 40, 77; al-Istakhri, pp. 280, 288.

15. A. S. Ehrenkreutz, 'Studies in the monetary history of the Near East in the Middle Ages', *JESHO* II (1959), pp. 135, 139, 141, 144ff, 148f; Grierson, art. cit., *ibid.*, p. 253; E. J. Holmyard, 'Maslama al-Majriti and the Rutbatu 'l-Hakim', *Isis* VI (1924), p. 304f; A. S. Ehrenkreutz, 'Extracts from the technical manual in the Ayyubid mint in Cairo', *BSOAS* 15 (1953), p. 443.

16. al-Baihaki, *al-Mahasin wa 'l-masawi* (Giessen 1902), p. 503; M. Lombard, *Monnaie et histoire d'Alexandre à Mahomet* (Paris 1971), p. 158f. As to the rate of interest, I deal with it in a paper to be published in *Miscellanea Franco Borlandi*.

17. *al-Fusul al-mukhtara*, p. 176, apud Lammens, *La Syrie* I, p. 120 (cf. my *Histoire des prix et des salaires*, p. 237); see also H. V. Mühsam, 'Fertility and reproduction of the Bedouins', *Population Studies* IV (1951), p. 354ff; id., 'Fertility of polygamous marriages', *Population Studies* X (1956), p. 3ff.

18. al-Khatib al-Baghdadi, *Tarikh Baghdad* II, pp. 73ff, 185f, 186, 226f, 273, 363f. III, p. 152. IV, pp. 76f, 171ff. V, p. 269. VI, p. 36; Yakut, *Irshad* (ed. Margoliouth) I, p. 37f; Nizam al-mulk, *Siyasat-nameh* (tr. H. Darke), p. 52.

19. A. v. Kremer, *Ueber die grossen Seuchen des Orients nach arabischen Quellen* (Vienna 1880), p. 41ff; Denys de Tell-Mahré, pp. 10, 32f, 178f; Ibn al-Athir VII, p. 177.

20. Ch. Pellat, *Le milieu basrien*, p. 6f; Guy Le Strange, *The Lands of the Eastern caliphate*, pp. 64, 72f, 90f, 101f, 120ff, 128ff; al-Mukaddasi, pp. 121, 139, 142; Yakut II, pp. 69, 764; Ibn Haukal, p. 225.

21. J. Lassner, *The topography of Baghdad in the early Middle Ages* (Detroit 1970), p. 160; R. McC. Adams, *Land behind Baghdad*, p. 115; E. Herzfeld, *Geschichte der Stadt Samarra* (Hamburg 1948), p. 137; id., Raqqah, in F. Sarre–E. Herzfeld, *Archäologische Reise im Euphrat- u. Tigris-Gabiet* II (Berlin 1920), p. 356; Mosul, *op. cit.*, p. 204; Ch. Pellat, *op. cit.*, l. c.

22. Adams, pp. 72, 98; J. Lassner, 'Massignon and Baghdad: the complexities of growth in an imperial city', *JESHO* IX (1966), pp. 1ff, 12f.

23. Le Strange, *op. cit.*, p. 130f; cf. Yakut IV, p. 287; Guy Le Strange, *Palestine under the Moslems*, p. 458f; E. Ashtor, 'Un mouvement migratoire au haut moyen âge', *Annales E.S.C.* 27 (1972), p. 198.

24. Kremer, *Seuchen*, pp. 41ff, 53; Denys de Tell-Mahré, p. 36, and see A. Sprenger in *Journal of the Asiatic Society of Bengal* (1843) II, p. 741; al-Baladhuri, *Futuh*, p. 158.

25. S. J. Sauvaget, *Alep* (Paris 1941), table (map) 53; K. Wulzinger–C. Watzinger, *Damaskus, die islamische Stadt* (Berlin 1924), p. 33 and table (map) 62; see also H. Lammens, *op. cit.* I, p. 119f; J. C. Russell, 'Late ancient and medieval populations', *Transactions of the American Philosophical Society*, N.S. 48, pt. 3, 1958, p. 89; Ph. K. Hitti, *History of Syria* (New York 1951), p. 484.

26. al-Kindi, pp. 49, 101; Quatremère, *Recherches*, p. 157; M. Clerget, *Le Caire* (Cairo 1934), I, p. 239.

27. Abu Yusuf, trad. E. Fagnan, p. 203; Papyrus Erzherzog Rainer, *Führer durch die Ausstellung*, p. 150; E. Ashtor, *Histoire des prix et des salaires*, pp. 42ff, 64, 78, 90ff.

28. R. B. Serjeant, 'Materials for a history of Islamic textiles up to the Mongol conquests', *Ars Islamica* 13/14 (1948), p. 88ff; H. Zayyat, 'The garments of fine linen' (in Arabic), *al-Mashrik* 41 (1947), p. 137ff; on the site of Dabik, see *an-Nudjum az-zahira* (ed. Cairo) IV, p. 81, note 3.

29. Serjeant, *op. cit.*, *Ars Islamica* 10 (1943), p. 81ff, 11/12 (1946), p. 138ff; Papyrus Erzherzog Rainer, *Führer*, p. 194.

30. Serjeant, *op. cit.*, *Ars Islamica* IX (1942), p. 60ff; C. H. Becker, *Beiträge* II, p. 114.

31. See my lecture, 'Les lainages dans l'Orient médiéval, emploi, production commerce', in *Atti della 2a Settimana di storia economica* (Prato 1970), p. 11f, and also Ibn Rustih (tr. Wiet), p. 182; J. Karabacek, *Die persische Nadelmalerei Susandschird* (Leipzig 1881), p. 53ff.

32. Serjeant, *op. cit.*, *Ars Islamica* 13/14, pp. 92f, 109; 10, p. 90f.

33. A. L. Oppenheim, *Ancient Mesopotamia, portrait of a dead civilization* (Chicago University Press 1964), p. 323f; id., The 'cuneiform texts', reprint from his *Glass and glassmaking in ancient Mesopotamia* (Corning N.Y. 1970), p. 22ff; A. v. Kremer, *Culturgeschichte des Orients* II, p. 281; C. J. Lamm, *Mittelalterliche Gläser und Steinschnittarbeiten aus dem Nahen Osten* (Berlin 1930), p. 14ff.

34. J. Karabacek, 'Das arabische Papier', *Mittheilungen aus der Sammlung der Papyrus Erzherzog Rainer* II/III (1887), pp. 108ff, 141f, 147; A. F. R. Hoernle, 'Who was the inventor of rag-paper?', *JRAS* 1903, p. 663ff; Th. F. Carter, *The invention of printing in China*, 2nd ed. (New York 1955), p. 7f; al-Istakhri, p. 288; al-Kalkashandi, *Subh al-asha* II, p. 476; G. Awwad, 'Paper or kaghid' (in Arabic), *Rev. Acad. Arabe* 23 (Damascus 1948), pp. 415, 420, 422f, 427ff; al-Yakubi (tr. Wiet), p. 195; on paper-makers see al-Khatib al-Baghdadi, *Tarikh Baghdad* I, p. 290. II, pp. 91, 152, 236f, 291. III, p. 61f. IV, pp. 63, 91f, 101, 193f. V, pp. 126f, 233. 11, p. 233. 12, pp. 3, 151. 13, p. 45; Ibn al-Djauzi, *al-Muntazam* VI, pp. 210, 385; on the paper market of Baghdad see Yakut, *Irshad* I, p. 153.

35. al-Masudi, *Les Prairies d'or* (tr. Pellat) I, p. 159f; Defrémery, 'Fragments de géographes et d'historiens arabes et persans inédits', *JA* 1849, II, p. 462.

36. al-Bakri, *Description* (tr. de Slane), pp. 300f, 322f, 325, 327, 335, 343; Ibn Haukal, p. 101; on Kugha see J. Sp. Trimingham, *A History of Islam in West Africa* (Oxford University Press 1962), p. 88f; Benjamin of Tudela, p. 69; E. W. Bovill, *The Golden trade of the Moors*, 2nd ed. (London 1968), p. 82.

37. al-Bakri, pp. 300, 328, 335, 342.

38. The English edition of Pirenne's *Mohammed and Charlemagne* was first

published in London in 1939 and several times reprinted; a selection of
critical views of it has been published by A. F. Havighurst, *The Pirenne
thesis* (Boston 1958); see also Br. Lyon, *The origins of the Middle Ages,
Pirenne's challenge to Gibbon* (New York 1972); a selection in the original
languages: P. E. Hübinger, *Zur Bedeutung und Rolle des Islams für den
Übergang vom Altertum zum Mittelalter* (Darmstadt 1968).

39. See O. v. Falke, *Decorative silks*, 3rd ed. (London 1936), p. 7; al-Masudi,
Les Prairies d'or (tr. Pellat) II, p. 332; for other data see E. Ashtor,
'Quelques observations d'un orientaliste sur la thèse de Pirenne',
JESHO 13 (1970), p. 166ff; 'Nouvelles reflexions sur la thèse de Pirenne',
Revue suisse d'histoire 20 (1970), p. 601ff.

40. P. Adams, 'A propos des origines de la voile latine', *Mediterraneo e oceano
indiano*, Atti del sesto colloquio internazionale di storia marittima,
Venezia 1962 (Florence 1970), pp. 212, 215.

41. See E. Ashtor, 'Che cosa sapevano i geografi arabi dell'Europa occidentale?' *RSI* 81 (1969), p. 453ff.

42. See L. Rabinowitz, *Jewish merchants adventurers* (London 1948); Cl. Cahen,
'Y a-t-il eu des Rahdanites?' *Revue des études juives* 123 (1964), pp. 499–
505, and cf. my 'Quelques observations d'un orientaliste sur la thèse de
Pirenne', *ibid.*, p. 181ff.

43. See Quelques observations, etc., *ibid.*, p. 174ff.

44. Travelbook of Sulaiman apud J. T. Reinaud, *Relations des voyages faits par
les Arabes et les Persans dans l'Inde et à la Chine* (Paris 1845), pp. 13, 32, cf.
I, p. CIXff; W. Heyd, *Histoire du commerce du Levant au Moyen Age* (tr. F.
Raynaud, Leipzig 1885–6) I, pp. 27, 28 (Chinese sources), 30; A. Lewis,
Naval power and trade in the Mediterranean A.D. 500–1100 (Princeton
1951), p. 132ff; G. R. Tibbetts, 'Early Muslim traders in South-East
Asia', *Journal of the Malayan Branch of the Royal Asiatic Society* 30 (1957),
p. 9; T. Lewicki, 'Les premiers commerçants arabes en Chine', *Rocznik
Orientalistyczny* 11 (1935), p. 178f; R. R. di Meglio, 'Il commercio arabo
con la Cina dalla Ğahiliyya al X secolo', *Ann. 1st Univ. Or. Napoli*, N.S.
14 (1964), pp. 532, 534, 541f, 547; al-Baladhuri, *Futuh*, pp. 341, 435; al-
Masudi (tr. Pellat) I, p. 327.

45. Ibn Haukal, p. 11; J. T. Reinaud, *Géographie d'Aboulfeda*, Introduction
(Paris 1848), p. CCCLIII; Abu Zaid, apud Reinaud, *Relations*, pp. 113f,
123, 142; al-Istakhri, pp. 19, 25, 33, 53, 245, 280; Ibn Khurdadhbih, pp.
59, 61, 70f, 170, trad. de Goeje, pp. 40ff, 51, 132; Travelbook of Sulaiman,
apud Reinaud, *Relations*, pp. 13f, 17, 60; al-Masudi, trad. Pellat, I, p. 142;
Reinaud, 'Mémoires géographiques, historiques et scientifiques sur
l'Inde', *Mémoires de l'Académie des inscriptions et belles-lettres* 18, pt. 2
(1848), pp. 216, 220ff; R. R. di Meglio, art. cit., *ibid.*, p. 548; G. F.
Hourani, *Arab seafaring in the Indian Ocean in ancient and early medieval
times* (Princeton 1951), pp. 71, 74f; on Kalah see P. Wheatley, *The Golden
Khersonese* (Kuala Lumpur 1961), p. 216ff; J. Sauvaget, 'Sur d'anciennes
instructions nautiques arabes pour la mer de l'Inde', *JA* 236 (1948), p.

16; Tibbetts, art. cit., *ibid.*, pp. 18, 34; see also R. R. di Meglio, 'Arab trade with Indonesia and the Malay peninsula from the 8th to the 16th century', in D. S. Richards (ed.), *Islam and the trade of Asia* (Oxford 1970), p. 109.

46. Sulaiman, *op. cit.*, pp. 4, 7, 8, 12, 30, 35; Abu Zaid, *op. cit.*, pp. 93f, 125ff, 135f, 139, 143ff, 146ff; Ibn Khurdadhbih, pp. 66, 70f; al-Masudi (tr. Pellat) I, pp. 136, 148, 151f; al-Yakubi, *Les pays*, p. 237f; al-Istakhri, p. 154; Tibbetts, art. cit., *ibid.*, p. 16f; di Meglio, 'Arab trade with Indonesia', pp. 108, 123.

47. al-Mubarrad, *al-Kamil* (Cairo 1927–30) VIII, p. 12; H. J. Cohen, 'The economic background and the secular occupations of Muslim juris-prudents and traditionalists in the classical period of Islam', *JESHO* 13 (1970), pp. 36, 40; C. H. Becker, 'Grundlinien zur wirtschaftlichen Entwicklung Ägyptens in den ersten Jahrhunderten des Islam', in his *Islamstudien* I, p. 205; Ch. Pellat, *Le milieu basrien*, p. 228f.

48. A. L. Udovitch, 'Credit as a means of investment in medieval Islamic trade', *JAOS* 87 (1967), p. 260ff; id., *Partnership and profit in medieval Islam* (Princeton University Press 1970), p. 77f; al-Baladhuri, *Futuh*, pp. 361 1. 13f, 367 1. 5; Chronique de Denys de Tell-Mahré, pp. 92, 156; A. Mez, *Die Renaissance des Islams*, p. 358; C. H. Becker, 'Steuerpacht u. Lehnwesen', in his *Islamstudien* I, p. 236; W. Björkman, 'Kapitalsentste-hung und -anlage im Islam', *Mitt. Sem. f. Or. Sprachen, Westasiat. Studien* 32 (1929), p. 92.

49. S. D. Goitein, 'The rise of the Middle-Eastern bourgeoisie in early Islamic times', in his *Studies in Islamic history and institutions* (Leiden 1966), p. 239; Björkman, art. cit., *ibid.*, pp. 82ff, 86f; A. K. S. Lambton, 'The merchant in medieval Islam', in *A locust's leg*, Studies in honour of S. H. Taqizadeh (London 1962), p. 122 (quoting al-Djahiz); Ibn Kutaiba, *Kitab al-Maarif* (Göttingen 1850), p. 283f; copied by Ibn Rustih (tr. Wiet), p. 254; H. J. Cohen, art. cit., *ibid.*, pp. 36, 40. The physicians were a class apart, s. Ibn Abi Usaibia I, p. 185f, about their dislike of the sons of merchants.

50. A. L. Udovitch, 'Theory and practice of Islamic law, some evidence from the geniza', *SI* 32 (1970), pp. 291, 303; id., 'The "law merchant" of the medieval Islamic world', in *Logic in classical Islamic culture*, ed. G. E. v. Grunebaum (Wiesbaden 1970), pp. 115ff, 122f.

51. Caetani, *Annali* IV, p. 109; at-Tabari III, pp. 1103, 1194f, 1204ff, 1234ff, 1254, 1303, 1350, 1435, 1436, 1509, 1550 (misunderstood by Goitein, art. cit., *ibid.*, p. 237); D. Sourdel, *Le vizirat abbaside* (Damascus 1959) I, pp. 246ff, 253, 254ff. See also at-Tabari III, p. 1661, on Salih b. al-Haitham, the son of a weaver, who became head of the intelligence service.

52. Max Weber, *General economic history* (tr. F. H. Knight) (New York 1961), p. 207; cf. M. Rodinson, *Islam e capitalismo* (Turin 1968), pp. 51, 56, 72, 75f.

53. L. Massignon, 'L'influence de l'Islam au Moyen Age sur la fondation et l'essor des banques juives', *Bulletin d'études orientales* I, (1931), p. 3ff; Rodinson, *op. cit.*, p. 60.
54. Becker, *Islamstudien* I, pp. 185, 215; Ibn Khaldun, *The Muqaddimah* (tr. Fr. Rosenthal) (New York 1958) II, p. 93f.
55. Becker I, p. 205; at-Tabari III, pp. 1330f, 1376; Denys de Tell-Mahré, pp. 124, 193, and see also pp. 108, 122f.

CHAPTER IV

1. J. Walker, 'A rare coin of the Zanj', *JRAS* 1933, p. 651ff.
2. at-Tabari III, pp. 1742ff, 1834ff; al-Masudi, *Prairies d'or* VIII, p. 31ff; Th. Nöldeke, 'A servile war in the East', (in) *Sketches from Eastern history* (London 1892), p. 146ff; see also H. Halm in *Die Welt des Islams* N.S. 11 (1967–8), p. 241, who believes that the Zindj represented the mawali and, on the other hand, A. Popovic, 'Les facteurs économiques et le révolte des Zang', in *Proceedings of the Conference on Economic history of the Near East* (Princeton 1974).
3. at-Tabari III, pp. 1687, 2208f, 2220f; Ibn al-Athir VII, p. 364f.
4. al-Istakhri, p. 273ff; al-Masudi VIII, p. 41ff; Th. Nöldeke, 'Yakub the coppersmith and his dynasty', in *Sketches*, etc., p. 176ff; W. Barthold, 'Zur Geschichte der Saffariden', in *Orientalische Studien Th. Nöldeke zum 70. Geburtstag* I, p. 171ff; B. Spuler, *Iran in früh-islamischer Zeit* (Wiesbaden 1952), p. 69ff.
5. at-Tabari III, p. 1523ff; A. S. K. Lambton, *Landlord and peasant in Persia* (London 1969), p. 48, note 1.
6. al-Makrizi, *al-Khitat* I, pp. 313, 318[17]; II, p. 268; Ibn Iyas I, p. 37, and cf. C. H. Becker, *Beiträge* II, p. 147.
7. See my *Histoire des prix et des salaires dans l'Orient médiéval*, p. 77ff.
8. 'Studies in the monetary history of the Near East in the Middle Ages', *JESHO* II (1959), p. 149.
9. C. H. Becker, *Beiträge* II, p. 138; *al-Khitat* I, pp. 99, 315.
10. Ehrenkreutz, 'Studies', *JESHO* II, p. 151.
11. Art. cit., *ibid.*, p. 153.
12. Miskawaih I, p. 255.
13. *Op. cit.*, pp. 16, 38f; Ibn al-Djauzi, *al-Muntazam* VI, p. 326; Hilal as-Sabi, ed. Amedroz (Leiden 1904), p. 11; M. Canard, *Sayf al Daula*, p. 267f.
14. Abu 'l-Mahasin, ed. Juynboll-Matthes (Leiden 1851–5) II, pp. 155, 157; *al-Khitat* I, pp. 94, 314[19]f; Ibn Iyas I, pp. 37, 43; al-Balawi, *Sirat Ahmad b. Tulun* (Damascus 1358), p. 349; on the officers in the army of Ibn Tulun see al-Balawi, pp. 70, 93, 101, 103f, 244, 267f, 315, 320, and on those of the Ikhshid's army see Ibn Said, *al-Mughrib*, ed. Tallquist (German text), p. 38.
15. Hilal as-Sabi, p. 17, and see *Histoire des prix*, p. 71, and also Miskawaih I, p. 261.

16. S. H. Antoniadis-Bibicou, *Etudes d'histoire maritime de Byzance* (Paris 1965), p. 142f.

17. Arib, *Tabari continuatus* (Leiden 1897), pp. 23, 144; Miskawaih I, p. 258; al-Balawi, p. 294; cf. Becker, *Beiträge* II, pp. 195, 197.

18. H. Bowen, *The Life and times of Ali Ibn Isa* (Cambridge 1928), pp. 261, 271; Ibn Said, p. 28.

19. at-Tanukhi, *The Table-talk of a Mesopotamian judge*, pt. I (tr. Margoliouth), p. 19; Ibn Said, p. 42; *Sheelot u-teshubhot mi-hageonim* (Mantua 1597), no. 165.

20. Hilal as-Sabi, p. 223ff; Arib, p. 127f; Ibn Said, pp. 38, 39, 51; at-Tanukhi, p. 15f.

21. E. Tyan, *Histoire de l'organisation judiciaire en pays d'Islam* (2nd ed.), p. 547; at-Tanukhi, p. 24; Ibn Said, pp. 25, 36, 66; Ibn al-Adim, *Zubdat al-halab* I, p. 112.

22. Miskawaih I, pp. 25, 42, 44, 61, 64; Hilal as-Sabi, p. 93; Ibn Said, p. 29; Bowen, *op. cit.*, p. 153; Irshad al-arib III, p. 184; Amedroz in *JRAS* 1908, p. 429.

23. Miskawaih I, p. 62.

24. at-Tabari III, p. 1838; Miskawaih I, pp. 52, 59f, 150, 158. II, p. 213; al-Balawi, p. 179.

25. Miskawaih I, p. 75; Yakut II, p. 617; Arib, p. 44; Canard, *Histoire de la Dynastie des Hamdanides* I (Paris 1953), p. 490; Bowen, pp. 335, 342f.

26. Miskawaih I, pp. 18f, 46, 60, 70, 83, 246; Kremer, *Ueber das Einnahmebudget des Abbasiden-Reiches vom Jahre* 306 h., p. 33f; Bowen, 1. c.

27. Miskawaih I, pp. 25, 32, 62, 65, 249, 273; Bowen, p. 228.

28. *Histoire des prix*, p. 66, to which should be added Hilal as-Sabi, p. 140; see also my paper, 'I salari nel Medio Oriente durante l'epoca medioevale', *RSI* 78 (1966), p. 346.

29. D. Sourdel, *Le vizirat abbaside* II, p. 727f; H. Gottschalk, *Die Madaraijjun* (Berlin 1931), p. 29ff; Hilal as-Sabi, pp. 95, 140; Arib, pp. 112, 145; Miskawaih I, pp. 257, 299. II, p. 199, and cf. Canard, *Sayf al Daula*, p. 248; Abu 'l-Mahasin II, p. 158; Bowen, pp. 216, 302; Assemani, *Bibliotheca Orientalis* III, pars 2, p. XCVIf.

30. Hilal as-Sabi, pp. 23, 199, 139, 322; Bowen, pp. 103, 133; Arib, p. 128; Miskawaih I, pp. 64, 250, 270; Becker, *Beiträge* II, p. 161; *Histoire des prix*, p. 66.

31. Miskawaih I, p. 64.

32. *Op. cit.*, pp. 66, 246, 250, 337, 338; Hilal as-Sabi, pp. 8, 39f, 54, 56, 103; Ibn Said, p. 39; Gottschalk, pp. 72, 108.

33. *Shaare sedek* (Salonica 1792), f. 77b, 78a no. 5; Miskawaih I, p. 72ff (cf. Arib, p. 84); Ibn al-Djauzi VI, pp. 156, 268.

34. *Teshubhot hageonim*, ed. Harkavy, no. 556; Ibn al-Adim I, p. 167f; Pellat, *Ǧāhiziana*, *Arabica* I, pp. 155, 158; Canard, *Sayf al Daula*, p. 219f; on the high prices see *Histoire des prix*, pp. 55, 85f; at-Tanukhi, p. 31; Ibn Said,

p. 40; see also Abu 'l-Mahasin II, p. 167. On an embargo on exportation (of wheat) by Ibn Tulun see Becker, *Beiträge* II, p. 167.

35. Miskawaih I, p. 35; at-Tanukhi, p. 16ff. (Ibn al-Djauzi VI, p. 127, surely a mistake: 16 for 6 millions!) Cf. G. Wiet, 'Un homme d'affaires mésopotamien au X*e* siècle', in *Mélanges E. Tissérant* (Città del Vaticano 1964) III, p. 475ff.

36. N. Levtzion, 'Ibn-Hawqal, the cheque, and Awdaghost', in *Journal of African History* IX (1968), p. 223ff; Miskawaih I, p. 43; E. Ashtor, 'Banking instruments between the Muslim East and the Christian West', *Journal of European Economic History* I (1973), p. 557.

37. Miskawaih I, p. 247; *Sefer Nameh* (tr. Schefer), p. 253; W. J. Fischel, *Jews in the economic and political life of medieval Islam*, p. 32f; Hilal as-Sabi, p. 79f; *Shaare sedek*, f. 96b no. 12; *Teshubhot hageonim*, ed. Harkavy, no. 386, 424, cf. Mann, 'Responsa of the Babylonian Geonim', *Jew. Quart. Rev.* N.S. X (1919–20), p. 330ff.

38. Abu 'l-Mahasin II, p. 174.

39. Fischel, p. 8ff, and cf. Arib, p. 74; Mann, 'Responsa', *Jew. Quat. Rev.* N.S. VIII (1917–18), p. 341f, IX, p. 153; *idem*, 'Gaonic Studies', *Hebrew Union College Jubilee Vol.* (Cincinnati 1925), p. 231, and see below note 48.

40. Miskawaih I, pp. 66, 244, 295; at-Tanukhi, p. 18; Ibn Said, pp. 22, 65f; Abu 'l-Mahasin II, p. 166; al-Makkari, *Analectes* I, p. 229ff; al-Masudi, *Prairies d'or* I, pp. 334f, 341; A. S. Ehrenkreutz, 'al-Buzajani (A.D. 939–997) on the Mā'sīr', *JESHO* VIII, p. 92; *Koheleth Shelomo*, ed. Wertheimer (Jerusalem 1899), f. 71a.

41. al-Masudi I, p. 302ff, and cf. Heyd, *Histoire du commerce du Levant* I, p. 31f.

42. *Livre des merveilles de l'Inde* par Bozorg, fils de Chahriyar (Leiden 1883), pp. 2f, 5, 12, 14, 38f, 63f, 103f, 121ff, 124, 125, 126; al-Masudi II, p. 52; al-Istakhri, pp. 127f, 154 et cf. Heyd I, p. 36, note 5; S. M. Stern, 'Ramisht of Siraf, a merchant millionaire of the twelfth century', *JRAS* 1967, p. 10ff.

43. *Merveilles de l'Inde*, pp. 7, 8, 12, 38f, 66, 67, 114f, 118, 119, 121f, 124ff; travels to Malabar, pp. 94, 120f; Ibn Said, p. 59.

44. G. Jacob, *Der nordisch-baltische Handel der Araber im Mittelalter* (Leipzig 1887), p. 46ff; Markow, *Topografiia kladov vostochnykh monet* (Petersburg 1910), *passim*; T. J. Arne, *La Suède et l'Orient* (Upsala 1914), p. 62ff; T. Lewicki, 'Nouveaux travaux russes concernant les trésors russes de monnaies musulmanes trouvés en Europe orientale et en Asie centrale (1955–63)', *JESHO* VIII, p. 81ff, and especially p. 89; A. Lewis, *The Northern Seas, shipping and commerce in Northern Europe A.D. 300–1100 A.D.* (Princeton 1958), p. 217.

45. al-Istakhri, p. 304f; Jacob, *op. cit.*, p. 121; al-Masudi II, p. 14; idem, *at-Tanbih*, p. 63; al-Mukaddasi, p. 324f. See also Ibn Haukal, p. 392.

46. pp. 133f, 189; Ehrenkreutz in *JESHO* VIII, p. 91.

47. al-Balawi, pp. 61, 249; Abu 'l-Mahasin II, p. 159; Canard, *Sayf al Daula*, p. 247; Miskawaih I, p. 254f; Arib, pp. 127f, 186.

48. J. Sourdel-Thomine–D. Sourdel, 'Trois actes de vente damascains du IVe/X siècle', *JESHO* VIII, p. 164ff; see further my paper, 'Un mouvement migratoire au haut moyen âge', *Annales E.S.C.* 27 (1972 , p. 185ff.

49. *Histoire des prix*, p. 67f.

50. Miskawaih I, pp. 28, 74; Hilal as-Sabi, p. 335; L. Ginzberg, *Geonica* (New York 1909) II, p. 80.

51. al-Istakhri, p. 93; Ibn Haukal, p. 256; al-Mukaddasi, pp. 202, 410; Ibn Abd Rabbihi, *al-Ikd* (Bulak 1293) III, p. 362; al-Kindi, 'Fadail Misr, apud Youssouf Kamel', *Monumenta cartographica* II, p. 638; *al-Khitat* I, pp. 181, 226; J. v. Karabacek, *Die arabischen Papyrusprotokolle*, SBAW 161 (1909), p. 38f; Grohmann, in *Enc. Isl. s. v. Tiraz* IV, p. 789f; al-Kazwini, *Kosmographie* (Göttingen 1848–9) II, p. 129; Nasiri Khosrau tr. Schefer (Paris 1881), p. 113; Becker, *Islamstudien* I, p. 183f; Goitein, in *Jew. Quart. Rev.* N.S. 45 (1954–5), p. 30ff.

52. Ibn Haukal, p. 159 (misunderstood by Serjeant, 'Materials for the history of Islamic textiles', *Ars Islamica* 13/14, p. 108, and in the translation of Wiet I, p. 157).

53. al-Mukaddasi, p. 213, and cf. Becker 1. c.; Arib, p. 44f; Miskawaih I, p. 191; Ibn al-Djauzi VI, p. 126; Abu 'l-Mahasin II, p. 192, and cf. Yakut II, p. 616ff; Kremer, *Culturgeschichte des Orients unter den Chelifen* II, p. 293f; al-Istakhri, p. 153; Ibn Haukal, p. 299.

54. Miskawaih III, p. 117f; Ibn Haukal, p. 152; *al-Khitat* I, p. 177[36]/[37] (misinterpreted by Serjeant in *Ars Islamica* IX, p. 83 , and see on the meaning of himl al-Khwarizmi, *Mafatih al-ulum* (ed. Van Vloten), p. 62, II, p. 6[6]; ath-Thaalibi, *Lataif al-maarif* (ed. Van Jong), p. 97, tr. Bosworth, p. 120; Becker, 1. c.

55. See al-Muhallabi writing about 985 (cp. HKh V, p. 512) as quoted by Yakut I, p. 882; *Hudud al-alam*, p. 138; *Lataif al-maarif*, p. 132; J. v. Karabacek, 'Uber einige Benennungen mittelalterlicher Gewebe', *Mitteilungen des Österr. Museums f. Kunstgewerbe* 1880, p. 28; Ibn Zulak (al-Hasan b. Ibrahim, d. 998), on Asyut, quoted by Yakut I, p. 272; al-Mukaddasi, pp. 180, 186.

56. al-Makkari I, p. 229ff; *Hudud al-alam*, p. 138; al-Istakhri, p. 153; Serjeant, in *Ars Islamica* X, p. 72ff; *Lataif al-maarif*, p. 95 (tr. Bosworth, p. 118), 132; at-Tanukhi, p. 190.

57. Cf. *Histoire des prix*, p. 81: 680 kg (8 artabes of Fayyum, 140 l each).

58. Arib, pp. 66, 157f; Miskawaih II, p. 24; Ibn al-Djauzi VI, p. 326; al-Balawi, p. 312; as-Suli, *Akhbar ar-Radi wa 'l-Muttaki* (Cairo 1935), p. 198.

59. Arib, pp. 128, 129; at-Tanukhi, pp. 19, 22; Miskawaih I, p. 254; Hilal as-Sabi, pp. 94, 257; Ibn Said, p. 36.

60. Mann, 'Responsa of the Babylonian Geonim', *Jew. Quart. Rev.* N.S. X, p. 314; Miskawaih I, pp. 199ff, 240, 245, 273; at-Tanukhi, p. 42f; Sourdel-Thomin–Sourdel in *JESHO* VIII, p. 164; *Teshubhot ha-geonim* (Lyck 1864), no. 64 (cf. Mez, *Die Renaissance des Islams*, p. 117, on Fars).

61. Hilal as-Sabi, p. 337.

62. Bowen, *Ali Ibn Isa*, p. 123; Miskawaih I, p. 30f, II, p. 9; al-Istakhri, p. 87; Ibn al-Djauzi VI, p. 315f; Yakut IV, p. 849, and cf. Rogers, Samarra in A. H. Hourani–S. M. Stern, *The Islamic City* (Oxford 1970), p. 153.

63. Hilal as-Sabi, p. 314; Miskawaih I, pp. 59, 71, 295; at-Tanukhi, tr. by Margoliouth, in *Islamic Culture* IV, p. 232ff, and I, p. 40.

64. Ibn Abdalhakam, *Futuh Misr*, p. 156; *al-Khitat* I, pp. 73, 98; Ibn Dukmak, ed. Vollers, V, p. 43; al-Istakhri, p. 52.

65. Ibn Haukal, p. 213; al-Mukaddasi, pp. 162, 176, 180; at-Tanukhi, in *Islamic Culture* IV, p. 235. Müller-Wodarg, 'Die Landwirtschaft Aegyptens in der frühen Abbasidenzeit', *Der Islam* 32, p. 23.

66. al-Istakhri, p. 91; Hilal as-Sabi, p. 318; Ibn Rustih (tr. Wiet), p. 125; Cahen in *JESHO* 13, pp. 29, 42; al-Mukaddasi, pp. 145, 162, 180; Yakut I, p. 201; Nasiri Khosrau, pp. 40, 46; Müller-Wodarg, art. cit., *Der Islam* 32, p. 47f; Ibn Haukal, pp. 213, 215.

67. at-Tanukhi, in *Islamic Culture* IV, pp. 233, 235; Ibn Haukal, p. 213; Miskawaih I, pp. 30f, 42f, 70, 74, II, p. 213; Hilal as-Sabi, pp. 72, 335, 336ff, 359; Ibn Rustih (tr. Wiet), p. 126.

68. *al-Faradj bad ash-shidda* (Cairo 1938) I, p. 112; Miskawaih I, p. 37; Canard, *Histoire des Hamdanides* I, pp. 136, 137, 240.

69. See *Islamic Culture* IV, pp. 25, 233, 540; Hilal as-Sabi, pp. 338, 339ff.

70. M. J. de Goeje, *Mémoire sur les Carmathes du Bahrain et les Fatimides* (Leiden 1886), p. 29f; at-Tabari III, pp. 2124ff, 2179, 2198, 2202, 2206; Ibn an-Nadim, *Fihrist*, p. 187; Ibn Khaldun IV, p. 84f; Silvestre de Sacy, Introduction (to his) *Exposé sur la religion des Druzes* (Paris 1838), p. CLXVIf; al-Masudi VIII, p. 203ff.

71. at-Tabari III, pp. 2188, 2192, 2193, 2196f; al-Masudi VIII, pp. 191, 193f; Silvestre de Sacy, p. CCXVI; de Goeje, *op. cit.*, p. 33ff.

72. Abu 'l-Mahasin II, p. 115.

73. *Op. cit.*, p. 126; Ibn al-Athir VII, pp. 340f, 344f; Ibn Khaldun IV, p. 88.

74. There is considerable disagreement among the Arabic authors as to the date of the Karmatian attack of Basra in 913, see al-Masudi VIII, p. 280; Miskawaih I, p. 33f; Ibn al-Athir VIII, p. 49; Arib, p. 38; the texts published by de Goeje, p. 213f, and see p. 69. In fact it is very probable that the raid was not so simultaneous with the invasion of Egypt as it had been planned. About the campaign in 919, see Ibn al-Djauzi VI, p. 153; Abu 'l-Mahasin II, p. 207.

75. S. W. Madelung, 'Fatimiden u. Bahrainqarmaten', *Der Islam* 34, p. 63f; Ibn Haukal, p. 25f.

76. Arib, pp. 59, 110f, 123f; Ibn al-Athir VIII, p. 114f; Abu 'l-Mahasin II, p. 219. Once more the Arabic historians give different dates. Ibn al-Djauzi VI, p. 196, says that the conquest of Basra took place two years later.

77. Arib, pp. 132f, 137, 162; Ibn al-Athir VIII, pp. 124ff, 132f, 136f, 220f, 232, 249f; Ibn al-Djauzi VI, pp. 208ff, 215f; Hamza al-Isfahani ed. Gottwaldt, p. 313; Miskawaih I, p. 284; de Goeje, pp. 140, 145.

78. p. 227f.
79. Ibn al-Adim I, p. 88f.

CHAPTER V

1. al-Mukaddasi, pp. 117ff, 122f.
2. at-Tanukhi, *Table-talk*, pt. 1 (tr. Margoliouth) (London 1922), p. 71; Ibn Haukal, p. 241f.
3. Ibn Haukal, pp. 216, 220ff, 225, 227.
4. Nasiri Khosrau, p. 235ff.
5. *Histoire des prix*, pp. 45, 102 (grain prices), and cf. pp. 50, 105 (bread prices), 65, 112 and cf. 465.
6. See my paper, 'Un mouvement migratoire au haut moyen âge', *Annales E.S.C.* 27 (1972), p. 185ff.
7. Ibn al-Athir VIII, pp. 282, 384, 389, 397, IX, pp. 184, 290, 299, 370; Hamza al-Isfahani, p. 195f; Miskawaih II, pp. 167, 406; Ibn al-Djauzi VI, pp. 331, 384, VII, p. 276, VIII, pp. 62, 69, 77, 79, 132; as-Suyuti apud A. v. Kremer, *Ueber die grossen Seuchen des Orients*, p. 88f.
8. Kremer, *op. cit.*, p. 55.
9. VIII, p. 79.
10. See *op. cit.* VI, p. 319, and cf. p. 326.
11. Miskawaih II, pp. 296f, 406; Ibn al-Djauzi VI, p. 315f, VII, pp. 114, 252, VIII, p. 105; Ibn al-Athir VIII, p. 518, IX, p. 159; Guy Le Strange, *The Lands of the Eastern Caliphate*, p. 59; Cl. Cahen, 'Le service de l'irrigation en Iraq au début du XIe siècle', *Bulletin d'études orientales* (Damascus) 13 (1949–51), pp. 137, 141f; see also H. Busse, *Chalif u. Grosskönig* (Beirut 1969), p. 380ff.
12. Miskawaih II, p. 201.
13. Ibn Haukal, p. 210ff; J. Mann, 'The Responsa of the Babylonian Geonim', *Jew. Quart. Rev.* N.S. X, p. 313f; Ibn al-Djauzi VII, p. 290.
14. The sources are: Kudama b. Djafar, p. 239; Ibn Khurdadhbih, summed up by Kremer, *Culturgeschichte* I, pp. 291, 373; Hilal as-Sabi, p. 11; Kremer, *Einnahmebudget*, p. 32; Ibn Haukal, p. 247; Mez, *Renaissance des Islams*, p. 123. The statement of al-Mukaddasi, p. 133, is based on an account in dirhams whose value we do not know.
15. Kremer, p. 33; Ibn al-Athir IX, p. 318.
16. The following data are taken from: Ibn Khurdadhbih, pp. 73f, 94, 95; Ibn al-Fakih, p. 135f; Kremer, p. 37; Miskawaih II, pp. 174, 206 (where 6.2 million should be corrected into 1.2 million), 239. According to Ibn Haukal, p. 217, the province Diyar Rabia yielded in 969 1,086,000 dinars, but this figure is certainly very much exaggerated.
17. al-Baladhuri, p. 193; Kremer, 'Ueber das Budget der Einnahmen', *ibid.*, p. 11; Ibn Khurdadhbih, p. 75ff; al-Yakubi, p. 327ff; Kremer, p. 35f; the data provided by al-Mukaddasi, p. 189, are without value, being

copied from older sources; Le Strange, *Palestine under the Moslems*, p. 45ff.

18. Kremer, 'Ueber das Budget der Einnahmen', *ibid.*, p. 9; Kudama, p. 242; Ibn Khurdadhbih, pp. 42f, 48; Kremer, p. 33; Ibn Haukal, pp. 259, 304; Ibn al-Balkhi, 'Description of the province of Fars', *JRAS* 1912, p. 889; at-Tanukhi, in *Islamic Culture* IV (1930), p. 540.

19. Miskawaih II, pp. 157f, 185f, 263; Ibn al-Djauzi VII, p. 222; Ibn al-Athir IX, p. 412.

20. Miskawaih II, pp. 143f, 170, 205, 206, 239, 244, 265, 321; ar-Rudhra-wari (Amedroz-Margoliouth, *The Eclipse of the Abbasid Caliphate* III), pp. 11, 45, 71, 202.

21. Ibn al-Adim I, p. 138; Miskawaih II, p. 215.

22. Miskawaih II, pp. 274, 283; ar-Rudhrawari, p. 254.

23. ar-Rudhrawari, pp. 250f, 254, 293; Ibn al-Djauzi VII, p. 172; Hilal as-Sabi, pp. 468, 484.

24. R. P. Blake, 'The circulation of silver in the Moslem East down to the Mongol epoch', *Harvard Journal of Asiatic Studies* II, p. 310.

25. Ibn al-Athir IX, pp. 157, 233, 273f, 318, 412; Ibn al-Djauzi VII, p. 222, VIII, p. 25.

26. ar-Rudhrawari, pp. 151, 253; Ibn al-Djauzi VIII, p. 35; Ibn al-Athir IX, p. 257f.

27. 'Studies in the monetary history of the Near East', *JESHO* II, p. 144ff, VI, p. 256.

28. at-Tanukhi I, p. 78.

29. Miskawaih II, pp. 152, 158, 173f, 294, 308f; ar-Rudhrawari, pp. 71, 272, 282; Ibn al-Athir IX, p. 233.

30. ar-Rudhrawari, p. 71.

31. Miskawaih II, pp. 138, 157, 159, 162f, 166, 236, 311, 329; ar-Rudhra-wari, p. 41; Dailamite cavalry, see *op. cit.*, pp. 184, 283; Ibn al-Djauzi VIII, pp. 51, 104, 119, 128; Ibn al-Athir IX, pp. 254, 257f. Cf. C. E. Bosworth, 'Military organisation under the Buyids of Persia and Iraq', *Oriens* 18/19 (1965–6), pp. 148ff, 154f, 158.

32. ar-Rudhrawari, pp. 280, 300.

33. Cl. Cahen, 'L'évolution de l'iqta du IXe au XIIIe siècle', *Annales E.S.C.* VIII (1953), p. 30ff.

34. *Prairies d'or* II, p. 11.

35. H. F. Amedroz, 'Abbasid administration in its decay', *JRAS* 1913, p. 823ff.

36. Miskawaih II, p. 165; ar-Rudhrawari, pp. 69, 177; Ibn al-Djauzi VII, p. 260; Ibn al-Athir IX, p. 130; Ibn al-Balkhi, 'Description of the province of Fars', *JRAS* 1912, p. 889.

37. Miskawaih II, pp. 293, 294.

38. *Op. cit.* II, pp. 150, 241; ar-Rudhrawari, p. 173; Cahen 'L'évolution de l'iqta', *Annales E.S.C.* VIII, p. 33; *Histoire des prix*, p. 71f.

39. See Miskawaih II, p. 242; Ibn al-Athir IX, p. 235.

40. C. E. Bosworth, 'Military organisation under the Buyids of Persia and Iraq', *Oriens* 18/19, p. 164; Miskawaih II, pp. 114, 173f, 236. (Many fiefholders, at least the officers, get an additional payment in cash, see Miskawaih II, p. 157f. Further, the soldiers get rations which are sometimes replaced by payment in cash, see ar-Rudhrawari, p. 283.)

41. ar-Rudhrawari, p. 30f.

42. *Op. cit.*, p. 213.

43. Amedroz, art. cit., p. 825; Miskawaih II, pp. 173f, 175f; ar-Rudhrawari, pp. 47f, 71, 174.

44. See Ibn al-Djauzi VII, p. 237f, VIII, p. 89.

45. Ibn al-Athir VIII, p. 405f. The proletarian rebels are called *ayyarun*, see below.

46. The most complete account is given by Ibn al-Adim I, p. 148ff, another by Miskawaih II, p. 214f, followed by Ibn al-Athir VIII, p. 415. See also Yahya b. Said (Beirut 1906), pp. 123f, 126f; Canard, *Sayf al Daula*. p. 265ff; Ibn Kathir, *al-Bidaya wa'n-nihaya* II, p. 255.

47. Yahya b. Said, pp. 127, 131.

48. ar-Rudhrawari, p. 83; Ibn al-Athir IX, p. 148.

49. Ibn al-Djauzi VII, pp. 219, 237; Ibn al-Athir VIII, p. 311.

50. Ibn al-Djauzi VII, p. 287, VIII, pp. 59f, 62, 73, 78f; Miskawaih II, p. 91; Ibn al-Athir VIII, p. 477.

51. Ibn al-Djauzi VII, pp. 174, 237, 252f, VIII, pp. 22, 56, 75, 79, 82, 88.

52. *Op. cit.* VII, p. 220, VIII, p. 83; at-Tanukhi, *Table-talk* I, p. 53; al-Hamadhani, 'Takmilat tarikh at-Tabari', *al-Mashrik* 51 (1957), p. 408; as-Suli, *Akhbar ar-Radi wa 'l-Muttaki*, p. 262.

53. Ibn al-Athir VIII, p. 311, IX, p. 298f; Dozy, *Mémoire sur les Carmathes du Bahrain*, pp. 112, 221ff; as-Suli, p. 243; Ibn al-Djauzi VII, p. 74f, VIII, p. 72; *an-Nudjum az-zahira* (ed. Cairo) IV, p. 107f.

54. Ibn al-Djauzi VII, pp. 74f, 78, 174, VIII, p. 76f.

55. *Op. cit.* VIII, pp. 24f, 47, 57, 88 (they are 100 together with Kurds and Bedouins!), 154.

56. *Op. cit.* VIII, pp. 44f, 54, 75f, 82, 91.

57. See B. Lewis, 'The Islamic guilds', *Economic History Review* VIII (1937), p. 20ff, and cf. S. M. Stern, 'The constitution of the Islamic city', in *The Islamic City*, p. 36ff, and Cl. Cahen, 'Y a-t-il eu des corporations professionelles dans le monde musulman classique', in the same volume, p. 51ff.

58. B. Lewis, 'An epistle on manual crafts', *Islamic Culture* 17 (1943), p. 142ff.

59. Ibn Taghribirdi, *an-Nudjum az-zahira* (ed. Cairo) IV, pp. 118, 119; Wüstenfeld, *Geschichte der Fatimiden-Chalifen* (Abhdl. der Kgl. Ges. der Wiss. zu Göttingen 26/27), pp. 168, 181, 208, 209, 231, 232f, 264f, 301, 303, 309, 312; id., *Die Geographie u. Verwaltung von Ägypten nach el-Calcaschandi* (Göttingen 1879), pp. 180, 206f; Becker, *Beiträge* I, p. 48f.

60. *al-Khitat* I, p. 82.

61. *an-Nudjum az-zahira* IV, p. 71.

62. A. S. Ehrenkreutz, 'The standard of fineness of gold coins circulating in Egypt at the time of the Crusades', *JAOS* 74 (1954), pp. 164, 166; id., 'The crisis of dinar in the Egypt of Saladin', *JAOS* 76 (1956), p. 178ff; geniza documents: Cambridge N.S. J 27 dating from 1140, and see my paper in *SI* 21 (1964), p. 109.

63. J. Aubin, 'La ruine de Siraf et les routes du Golfe Persique aux XIe et XIIe siècles', *Cahiers de civilisation médiévale* II (1959), p. 259f; B. Lewis, 'The Fatimids and the route to India', *Revue de la faculté des sciences économiques de l'Université d'Istanbul* II (1949–50), p. 50ff; A. Mieli, *La science arabe* (Leiden 1966), p. 160ff.

64. Ibn Khallikan, *Wafayat al-ayan* (Cairo 1299) II, p. 158; Ibn al-Athir II, p. 184; Sibt Ibn al-Djauzi, *Mirat az-zaman* (ed. Jewett), p. 235; Nasiri Khosrau, pp. 41, 112, 177ff, 285ff; Heyd, *Histoire du commerce du Levant* I, pp. 380f, 383f; Italian traders in Damietta: T.-S. 10 J 16²; R. Morozzo della Rocca–A. Lombardo, *Documenti del commercio veneziano nei secoli XI–XIII* (Turin 1940) I, no. 15, 24, 41, 73, 74, 75, 77, 134, 164, 179.

65. See Cl. Cahen, 'Un texte peu connu relatif au commerce oriental d'Amalfi au Xe siècle', *Archivio Storico per le Provincie Napoletane, Nuova Serie* 34 (1953–4), p. 61ff; A. Schaube, *Handelsgeschichte der romanischen Völker* (München 1906), pp. 21, 29, 36f, 65; *Morozzo della Rocca-Lombardo* I, no. 90, 148, 149, 155, 159, 167, 181, 183; *Famiglia Zusto*, ed. L. Lanfranchi (Venice 1955), no. 14, 16, 19, 27; for the trade of the Genoese see also T.-S. 10 J 16⁷, T.-S. 10 J 16¹⁷; Goitein, *A Mediterranean society* I (University of Californian Press 1967), p. 45; for Pisa: M. Amari, *I diplomi arabi del R. Archivio Fiorentino* (Florence 1863), p. 241ff; K.-H. Allmendinger, *Die Beziehungen zwischen der Kommune Pisa und Ägypten im hohen Mittelalter* (Wiebaden 1967), p. 45ff; E. H. Byrne, 'Genoese trade with Syria in the twelfth century', *Am. Hist. Rev.* 25 (1919–20), p. 202.

66. Ibn Abi Usaibia II, p. 53 (import of copper); S. M. Stern, 'An original document from the Fatimid chancery concerning Italian merchants', *Studi orientalistici in onore di Levi della Vida* (Rome 1956) II, p. 529ff (timber); Byrne, art. cit., *ibid.*, p. 217; id., 'Easterners in Genoa', *JAOS* 38 (1918), p. 181.

67. *Morozzo della Rocca-Lombardo* I, no. 11; Byrne in *JAOS* 38, p. 181; Bodl. Cowley 2878⁶⁴ (of 1098), 2878¹⁰⁸, Cambridge T.-S. N.S. J 1.

68. T.-S. 18 J 5¹, T.-S. 12.416, T.-S. 24.64, T.-S. 24.66, T.-S. 28.22.

69. Nasiri Khosrau, pp. 41, 112; E. Strauss, 'Documents for the economic and social history of the Jews in the Near East' (in Hebrew), *Zion* VII (1941–2), p. 152; Goitein in *Tarbiz* 36 (1967), p. 378; id., *Mediterranean society* I, p. 310.

70. *Mediterranean society* I, p. 216.

71. *Op. cit.* I, p. 102; id. in *JESHO* IV, p. 174; *Jew. Quart. Rev.* N.S.X., p. 330, and see also *JESHO* VI, p. 168; T.-S. 13 J 19²⁷, T.-S. 13 J 20¹⁹,

T.-S. 12.367, T.-S. 12.656, T.-S. 20.2, T.-S. 20.7, T.-S. 20.69, T.-S. 20.180, Oxford MS. Heb. b 3[19], Bodl. 2806[18], 2621[16] f. 47b; Nasiri Khosrau, p. 122; cushions from Sicily, T.-S. 12.12, T.-S. 16.32, T.-S. 24.80, T.-S. J 1[48,50]

72. Goitein, *Mediterranean society* I, p. 102; Bodl. 2805[20], T.-S. 12.5, T.-S. 12.251, T.-S. 12.794, T.-S. 12.339, T.-S. 13 J 8[5], T.-S. 13 J 23[18], T.-S. 13 J 25[8], Oxford MS. Heb. c 28[61].

73. See Cl. Cahen, 'A propos et autour d'"Ein arabisches Handbuch der Handelswissenschaft",' *Oriens* 15 (1962), p. 160ff.

74. See, for instance, al-Idrisi, *Description de l'Afrique et de l'Espagne*, ed. Dozy–de Goeje (Leiden 1866), p. 50. The account on the structure of the tiraz factories given by Nasiri Khosrau (see above p. 150) should be accepted *cum grano salis*. It would be erroneous to infer from it that the Royal factories were working for the court only. Geniza documents dating from the Fatimid period prove that they also had private customers, see Goitein in *Jew. Quart. Rev.* N.S. 45, p. 35.

75. T.-S. 12.41, T.-S. 16.86, T.-S. 16.147, T.-S. 20.1, T.-S. 20.48, T.-S. J 1[26], J 1[28], T.-S. 8 J 9[7b], T.-S. N.S. J 226, Bodl. 2821[16] f. 45b, 54b.

76. T.-S. 12.12, T.-S. 16.86, T.-S. 20.116v, T.-S. 13 J 13[10d]; Cambridge Miscell. 8[97], Bodl. 2821[16] f. 48a; Serjeant, 'Islamic textiles', *Ars Islamica* 13/14, pp. 93, 98; al-Barawi, *The economic conditions of Egypt in the Fatimid period* (in Arabic) (Cairo 1948), p. 136.

77. *al-Khitat* I, p. 104f; *JESHO* VI, p. 174f; Serjeant, *op. cit., ibid.,* p. 109.

78. Oxford MS. Heb. d 75 f. 14.

79. *al-Khitat* I, pp. 226, 469; al-Istakhri, p. 199f; Serjeant, *op. cit., ibid.,* p. 96; *Ahsan at-takasim*, p. 201.

80. See Mez, p. 410; al-Barawi, p. 178; an-Nuwairi, *Nihayat al-arab* IX, p. 264ff; E. Wiedemann, 'Zur Geschichte des Zuckers', in his *Aufsätze zur arabischen Wissenschaftsgeschichte* II, p. 137ff, and especially p. 143, note 3; E. O. v. Lippmann, *Geschichte des Zuckers* (2nd ed. Berlin 1929), pp. 168, 221ff. On sugar growing in Syria see an-Nuwairi, p. 271, and Nasiri Khosrau, p. 40.

81. See *Histoire des prix et des salaires*, pp. 190, 235; Goitein, *Mediterranean society* I, p. 81.

82. *Histoire des prix et des salaires*, pp. 147, 149, 151, 173.

83. See *op. cit.,* p. 465f. The ratl is the Egyptian, equal to 450 g.

84. See my paper, 'The Diet of salaried classes in the medieval Near East', *Journal of Asian History* IV (1970), p. 11.

85. S. D. Goitein, 'Petitions to Fatimid caliphs', *Jew. Quart. Rev.* N.S. 45, p. 32ff.

86. M. Clerget, *Le Caire*, p. 239.

87. *Histoire des prix et des salaires*, pp. 80, 124.

88. Ibn Iyas I, p. 44.

89. Ibn al-Kalanisi (Leiden 1908), p. 50f; Yahya b. Said, p. 181f; Ibn al-Athir IX, p. 84; ar-Rudhrawari, p. 226; Ibn Khaldun IV, p. 56f.

90. Ibn al-Kalanisi, pp. 5ff, 10, 11f, 21ff, 25ff, 49f, 53f; ar-Rudhrawari, p. 209; Ibn al-Athir VIII, pp. 472, 483f, 512f, IX, pp. 5f, 12; Ibn Khaldun III, p. 430, IV, p. 56; Ibn Taghribirdi, *an-Nudjum az-zahira* IV, p. 114f; Wüstenfeld, *Geschichte der Fatimiden-Chalifen*, pp. 111f, 124, 126, 141, 145f, 171f.

91. Ibn al-Athir IX, p. 5; Ibn al-Kalanisi, p. 50f; Wüstenfeld, pp. 140f, 145, 170.

92. Wüstenfeld, p. 181ff.

93. Ibn al-Athir IX, pp. 86f, 159f, 233. For the dates see adh-Dhahabi apud Ibn al-Kalanisi, p. 64. Ibn al-Athir (IX, p. 86f) confounds two revolts, that of 997 (cf. above) and that of 1010, cf. Wüstenfeld, p. 196.

94. Ibn al-Athir IX, p. 162ff; Wüstenfeld, pp. 221ff, 229, 232f, 248f.

95. al-Makrizi, *Traité des famines* (tr. of G. Wiet) (Leiden 1962), p. 23.

96. Ibn ad-Dawadari VI (Cairo 1961), p. 476; *Histoire des prix et des salaires*, pp. 128, 455, 465.

97. For the sources see Omar Toussoun, *Mémoire sur les finances de l'Egypte* (Cairo 1924), p. 28ff. The figures marked by an asterisk indicate what was apparently the amount of the kharadj, the others the total.

98. See my paper in *JESHO* 12, p. 407.

99. *al-Khitat* I, pp. 72, 82; al-Barawi, p. 326.

100. al-Barawi, p. 332ff. The data quoted by the Egyptian scholar from Ibn Mammati refer to the Ayyubid period when the kharadj was reduced, see below. Consequently we may suppose that the tax burden was much heavier under the Fatimids.

CHAPTER VI

1. Cl. Cahen, 'Les tribus turques d'Asie Occidentale pendant la période seldjukide', *Wien. Ztschft. f. Kunde des Morg.* 51 (1948–51), pp. 178–87.

2. Ibn al-Djauzi IX, pp. 63, 150, 228; A. K. S. Lambton, 'The internal structure of the Saljuq empire', *Cambridge History of Iran* V (Cambridge 1968), p. 223.

3. Ibn al-Athir X, p. 461; Ibn al-Djauzi X, p. 252.

4. Ibn al-Djauzi IX, p. 134, X, pp. 25, 45, 124; Ibn al-Athir X, pp. 210, 227, 384, 396; 11, p. 22.

5. Ibn al-Kalanisi, pp. 114, 203, 213, 242; Kamal ad-din in *ROL* III, p. 217, V, pp. 42, 95; Abu Shama, *Kitab ar-Raudatain* I, p. 43f; id., *Dhail ar-raudatain* (Damascus 1947), pp. 81, 89; al-Kalkashandi, *Subh al-asha* 13, p. 36; Cl. Cahen, *La Syrie du Nord à l'époque des Croisades* (Paris 1940), pp. 185, 407.

6. Lambton, 'The internal structure, etc.', *op. cit.*, p. 231f; Imad ad-din quoted by al-Bundari, ed. Houtsma: *Textes relatifs à l'histoire des Seldjoucides* II, p. 58; the passages in the 'History of the Atabeks of Mosul' quoted by Cl. Cahen, 'L'évolution de l'iqta du IX*e* au XIII*e* siècle', *Annales E.S.C.* VIII (1953), p. 42f.

7. *The Book of government or rules for kings* (tr. H. Darke) (London 1960), p. 43; Cahen, 'L'évolution de l'iqta', *ibid.*, p. 44; al-Bundari l.c. Cf. on this argument Cl. Cahen, 'Reflexions sur l'usage du mot de "féodalité",' *JESHO* III (1960), p. 4ff.

8. Ibn al-Athir 12, p. 51; Nizam al-mulk, *Book of government*, p. 132.

9. Ibn al-Djauzi IX, pp. 61, 63; Ibn al-Athir X, pp. 14, 23f, 79, 293f.

10. Ibn al-Athir X, p. 382; Ibn al-Djauzi IX, p. 228. On the silk industry of Baghdad see Serjeant in *Ars Islamica* IX, p. 82ff.

11. Ibn al-Djauzi IX, pp. 112, 250, X, pp. 27, 227; Ibn al-Athir X, p. 203.

12. Ibn al-Kalanisi, pp. 118, 235, 329, 353; Ibn al-Athir X, pp. 105, 233, 235, 239, 266, 295, 317, 369, 420, 425; 11, pp. 42, 47, 170, 238; Ibn al-Djauzi IX, pp. 35, 72, 218, 228, 232, X, pp. 78f, 120, 194, 233; Abu Shama, *Kitab ar-Raudatain* I, pp. 5, 7, 16; cf. Lambton, art. cit., p. 250.

13. Sibt Ibn al-Djauzi, quoted by Amedroz in the notes to Ibn al-Kalanisi, p. 111; J. Lassner, 'Massignon and Baghdad', *JESHO* IX (1966), p. 26f; Yakut II, p. 575, and cf. Ibn Rustih (tr. Wiet), p. 190, and see also on Iskaf Bani Djunaid Yakut I, p. 252; Ibn al-Athir II, pp. 40, 72f; Ibn al-Djauzi X, p. 138; Kamal ad-din in *Recueil des historiens des Croisades*, *Hist. Or.* III, p. 598; J. Sauvaget, *Alep* (Paris 1941), p. 107.

14. Ibn Sina, *al-Kanun* (Rome 1593) IV, p. 67; Thabit b. Kurra, *adh-Dhakhira* (Cairo 1928), p. 168, and cf. T. Fr. Pearse, *Report on plague in Calcutta* (Calcutta 1907), p. VII; G. Sticker, *Die Pest* (Giessen 1908–10) II, p. 255. See also Ibn Hadjar apud Ibn Iyas I, p. 348, and cf. J. Sublet, 'La peste prise aux rêts de la jurisprudence', *SI* 33 (1971), p. 141f.

15. Ibn al-Djauzi IX, pp. 14f, 27, 113, 249, X, pp. 68, 120, 138, 176; Ibn al-Athir IX, p. 434, X, pp. 69, 204, 273, 435; 11, pp. 35, 100, 142, 299; Ibn Taghribirdi, *an-Nudjum az-zahira* (ed. Popper) II, p. 272; A. v. Kremer, *Ueber die grossen Seuchen des Orients*, pp. 55, 59, 61, 89; cf. Sticker, *op. cit.* I, p. 38, and on the sirsam Ibn Sina, *op. cit.* II, p. 302, and Ibn Hubal, *Kitab al-Mukhtarat fi 't-tibb* (Haydarabad 1362–3) III, p. 23ff.

16. See my paper, 'The diet of salaried classes in the medieval Near East', *Journal of Asian History* IV (1970), p. 11. These calculations refer to Egyptian workers, but the basket of their Iraki and Syrian fellow was similar or rather poorer.

17. See in the same paper, p. 16f, and further Ibn al-Athir 12, pp. 48, 314, 341; Sibt Ibn al-Djauzi, *Mirat az-zaman* (ed. Jewett), pp. 32, 230, 307; Usama b. Munkidh, *L'autobiographie d'Ousama* (ed. Derenbourg), p. 88; Abu Shama, *Kitab ar-Raudatain* II, p. 229; *Dhail ar-Raudatain*, pp. 220, 229; Ibn Khallikan, *Kitab al-Wafayat* II, p. 389; Ibn Kathir, *al-Bidaya wa 'n-nihaya* 13, p. 164.

18. Ibn Djubair, *ar-Rihla* (Leiden 1907), pp. 211, 225, 232; Yakut II, pp. 23, 54, III, p. 194; Guy Le Strange, *The Lands of the Eastern Caliphate*, pp. 71, 97, 99; Cl. Cahen, 'La Djazira au milieu du XIIIe siècle': *REI* 1934, p. 111.

19. See my *Histoire des prix et des salaires*, p. 100ff.

20. VIII, p. 241, IX, pp. 49, 132, 200, 205, 212, 218; Ibn al-Athir X, p. 85.

21. Ibn al-Djauzi IX, p. 132; Ibn al-Athir X, p. 382; 11, p. 427; Ibn al-Kalanisi, p. 219. On the *mukasama* introduced by feudals see Cahen in *Arabica* I, p. 145.
22. Ibn al-Athir X, p. 448; 11, p. 90; Ibn al-Djauzi X, p. 134.
23. Ibn al-Djauzi X, pp. 145, 169; Ibn al-Athir X, pp. 69, 442; 11, p. 103.
24. Ibn al-Djauzi X, pp. 78, 95, 145, 165, 176, 181; Ibn al-Athir X, p. 207; 11, p. 103.
25. Ibn al-Kalanisi, pp. 109, 219, cf. 145; Ibn al-Djauzi X, p. 95.
26. Kamal ad-din in *Recueil des historiens des Croisades* III, p. 646; Usama b. Munkidh, p. 112; Bustan al-djami (ed. Cl. Cahen) in *Bulletin d'études orientales* VII–VIII (1937–8), p. 153.
27. Abu Shama, *Kitab ar-Raudatain* I, p. 251f; Kamal ad-din in *ROL* IV, p. 147f; Ibn al-Kalanisi, pp. 215, 221ff; Ibn al-Athir X, p. 445f.
28. See Ibn al-Fuwati, *al-Hawadith al-djamia* (Baghdad 1351), pp. 8, 216; Ibn al-Athir X, p. 232; 11, p. 287.
29. Ibn al-Djauzi IX, pp. 103, 113, 137f, 216f, 224, X, pp. 58, 59, 67ff, 86, 95f, 105f, 226f, 230, 275; Ibn al-Athir X, pp. 204, 232, 259, 383; 11, pp. 26f, 40ff, 59, 63.
30. On the *rais* see my paper, 'L'administration urbaine en Syrie médiévale', *RSO* 31 (1956), p. 108f.
31. See my paper, 'Quelques observations d'un orientaliste sur la thèse de Pirenne', *JESHO* 13, p. 172ff.
32. Ibn al-Kalanisi, pp. 96, 98, 112, 120; Ibn al-Athir X, p. 40; see also Nasiri Khosrau, p. 47.
33. Ibn al-Kalanisi, pp. 124, 133f; Ibn al-Athir X, p. 180.
34. Ibn Taghribirdi (ed. Popper) II, pp. 267, 271; Ibn al-Kalanisi, pp. 97f (note), 139, 160f; Ibn al-Athir X, pp. 48, 136, 328; cf. G. Wiet, 'Une inscription d'un prince de Tripoli de la dynastie des Banu Ammar', *Mémorial H. Basset* (Paris 1928) II, p. 279ff.
35. Ibn al-Athir X, p. 211ff; Ibn al-Kalanisi, p. 139; Cl. Cahen, *La Syrie du Nord*, p. 233f.
36. Ibn al-Kalanisi, p. 140; Cl. Cahen, 'La Chronique abrégée d'al-Azimi', *JA* 1938, p. 374, and see my paper, 'L'administration urbaine', etc. *ibid.*, p. 93f.
37. See my paper, pp. 94f, 122ff, 127.
38. See art. cit., pp. 95ff, 100.
39. Art. cit., p. 101f; the additions of the copyist to Ibn Haukal, p. 223; Ibn al-Athir X, p. 295f.
40. Ibn as-Sai, *al-Djami al-mukhtasar* (Baghdad 1934), pp. 82, 144, 147, 149; Ibn al-Fuwati, pp. 16f, 23, 27, 33, 44, 45, 72, 168f, 189.
41. Ibn as-Sai, pp. 116f, 226, 265.
42. *Op. cit.*, pp. 22, 46f, 150, 200f, 215f, 219f; Ibn al-Fuwati, p. 17.
43. *Op. cit.*, p. 227; Ibn al-Fuwati, pp. 162f, 182.
44. *Op. cit.*, pp. 230, 258f; Ibn al-Fuwati, pp. 2, 14f, 44; Abu Shama, *Dhail ar-Raudatain*, p. 64.

45. See Ibn as-Sai, p. 221ff; G. Salinger, 'Was the futuwwa an Oriental form of chivalry?' *Proceedings of the American Philosophical Society* 94 (1950), p. 490; Cl. Cahen, 'Bagdad au temps de ses derniers califes', *Arabica* IX (1962), p. 301.

46. Ibn al-Fuwati, pp. 71, 223f.

47. *Op. cit.*, pp. 129, 230f. Guy Le Strange, *The Lands of the Eastern Caliphate*, p. 50; Ibn al-Fuwati, p. 259; id., *Talkhis madjma al-adab* IV (Damascus 1962–3), p. 364; Ibn Kathir 13, p. 262, and see M. Djawwad in *Madjallat ghurfat tidjarat Baghdad* VI (1943), pp. 439f, 601f.

48. Ibn as-Sai, pp. 161, 219, 229; Ibn al-Fuwati, pp. 11, 48, 94, 198; *Diwan of Eleasar ben Jaakob ha-Babli* (ed. H. Brody) (Jerusalem 1935), nos. 1, 8, 171, 172, 185, 186, 189, 200, 207, 223, 300, 302, 319.

49. Ibn as-Sai, p. 228; Ibn al-Fuwati, pp. 162f, 254, 276, 278, 298, 304.

50. H. A. R. Gibb, 'The armies of Saladin', in Gibb: *Studies in the civilization of Islam* (Boston 1962), p. 76ff; Kamal ad-din in ROL III, p. 560; Sibt Ibn al-Djauzi, p. 486; al-Makrizi in ROL X, pp. 257, 285f, 297.

51. A. N. Poliak, 'The Ayyubid feudalism', *JRAS* 1939, p. 429ff; *al-Khitat* I, p. 97[13]; Gibb, *op. cit.*, p. 75ff; H. Rabie, 'The size and value of the iqta in Egypt 564–741 a. h. 1169–1341 A.D.', in *Studies in the economic history of the Middle East* (Oxford University Press 1970), p. 129f; my paper, 'I salari nel Medio Oriente all' epoca medioevale', *RSI* 1966, p. 343; Cl. Cahen in *Annales E.S.C.* VIII, p. 46f; Bustan al-djami, *ibid.*, p. 155.

52. Sibt Ibn al-Djauzi, pp. 151, 194; Abu Shama, *Kitab ar-Raudatain* I, p. 8; Kamal ad-din in ROL III, p. 535; *al-Khitat* II, p. 216[24-26].

53. al-Makrizi in ROL X, pp. 293f, 299; Abu Shama, *Kitab ar-Raudatain* II, pp. 58, 195; *Dhail ar-Raudatain*, pp. 29, 117, 172; Ibn Abi Usaibia II, p. 176.

54. Ibn Mammati, *Kitab Kawanin ad-dawawin* (ed. Atiya), p. 343; Ibn al-Athir 12, p. 102; Poliak, 'La féodalité islamique', *REI* X (1936), p. 261, note 5; al-Makrizi in ROL VIII, p. 537, X, pp. 293, 298; Sibt Ibn al-Djauzi, p. 214; Ibn Kathir 12, p. 299; Imad ad-din al-Isfahani, *al-Fath al-kussi* (Cairo 1322), pp. 346, 357; Poliak in *REI* 14, p. 55.

55. Ibn al-Kalanisi, p. 316; al-Makrizi in ROL VIII, p. 535.

56 See the sources quoted in ROL IV, p. 221; Abdallatif, *Relation de l'Egypte*, trad. Sylvestre de Sacy (Paris 1810), pp. 360, 412; al-Makrizi in ROL X, pp. 277, 284; as-Suyuti apud Kremer, *Seuchen*, p. 89; Planhol, p. 72.

57. Abdallatif, *op. cit.*, p. 314; *al-Khitat* I, p. 44.

58. *Histoire des prix et des salaires*, pp. 128f, 131, 224f, 454.

59. A. S. Ehrenkreutz, 'The crisis of dinar in the Egypt of Saladin', *JAOS* 76 (1956), p. 178ff; id., 'The standard of fineness of gold coins circulating in Egypt at the time of the Crusades', *JAOS* 74, p. 164; al-Makrizi in ROL X, pp. 252, 277, 290; P. Balog, 'History of the Dirham', *Revue Numismatique* 1961, p. 129.

60. See Ibn Haukal, pp. 216, 234; the autobiography of Abdallatif apud Ibn

Abi Usaibia II, p. 207; *Répertoire de l'épigraphie arabe*, no. 3284, 3292; Abu Shama, *Kitab ar-Raudatain* I, pp. 5, 9.

61. W. Heyd, *Histoire du commerce du Levant* I, pp. 374ff, 397ff, 410f; M. Amari, *I diplomi arabi del R. Archivio Fiiorentino*, p. 257ff.

62. Kamal ad-din in ROL III, pp. 530, 536; Abu Shama, *op. cit.* II, p. 64; *al-Khitat* I, p. 104f; al-Makrizi, *as-Suluk* I, p. 85f; al-Makrizi in ROL X, pp. 293, 296, 301.

63. See my paper, 'The Karimi merchants', *JRAS* 1956, p. 52f; S. D. Goitein, 'New light on the beginnings of the Karim merchants', *JESHO* I (1957–8), p. 175ff; *as-Suluk* I, p. 735f; Ibn Kathir 13, pp. 262, 351.

64. Ibn al-Djauzi IX, pp. 85, 184, 216, 228, X, pp. 4, 24, 30, 37, 45, 170, 212, 233, 235, 244; Ibn as-Sai, p. 144; Yakut I, pp. 316, 437; Ibn al-Hadjdj al-Abdari, *al-Madkhal* (Cairo 1929) IV, p. 154; Sibt Ibn al-Djauzi, p. 523; Ibn Kathir 13, p. 120; E. Kühnel, *Die Kunst des Islam* (Stuttgart 1962), p. 88f.

65. Ibn al-Djauzi IX, p. 38, X, p. 149; cf. E. Wiedemann, 'Zur Mechanik und Technik bei den Arabern', *Aufsätze zur arabischen Wissenschaftsgeschichte* I, p. 217ff; Lynn White, *Medieval technology and social change*, pp. 86f, 161f.

66. A. Lane, *Early Islamic pottery* (London w.d.), p. 32; *Islamic pottery from the ninth to the fourteenth centuries A.D. in the collection of Sir Eldred Hitchcock, with an introduction of A. Lane* (London w.d.), p. 13f; D. Barrett, *Islamic metalwork in the British Museum* (London 1949), pp. VIIIf, XIf, XIV.

67. Ibn al-Djauzi VII, p. 289, VIII, pp. 88, 104, 108, 225, 254, X, pp. 84, 95, 189f, 244ff; Ibn al-Athir 11, pp. 43, 51; Ibn al-Fuwati, p. 232, cf. 229ff, 273, 317.

68. Ibn Djubair, *Rihla*, p. 51; Lane-Poole, *The story of Cairo* (London 1902), p. 180; K. A. C. Creswell, 'Fortifications in Islam before A.D. 1250', *Proceedings of the British Academy* 38 (1952), p. 113.

69. Ibn al-Djauzi VIII, pp. 25, 31; Jacobsen–Adams, 'Salt and silt in ancient Mesopotamian agriculture', *Science* 128 (1958), p. 1257; see also I. Imberciadori, 'Agricoltura italiana dall 'XI al XIV secolo', *Rivista di storia dell'agricoltura* (1971), p. 220ff.

70. *al-Khitat* I, p. 181[25] (but not in 1192, as says Serjeant in *Ars Islamica* 13/14, p. 97f, misunderstanding a passage in al-Makrizi's *as-Suluk*, but see in his paper, p. 100!), and cf. p. 177ff; *as-Suluk* I, p. 224.

71. *al-Khitat* I, pp. 181[25, 31f], 182[2f], 226[13], 464, II, p. 104. Perhaps Samnay and Bura should be added, see 1. c.; Ibn Dukmak, *al-Intisar* (Cairo 1893) V, p. 79; Yakut II, p. 548, cf. 546.

72. Lynn White, pp. 83f, 89, 117; E. M. Carus-Wilson, Haberget; a medieval conundrum, *Medieval Archaeology* 13 (1969), p. 165f; id., 'An industrial revolution in the thirteenth century', *Econ. Hist. Rev.* II (1941), p. 39ff.

73. Ibn Haukal, p. 219f; on the use of 'Persian mills', i.e. driven by water,

in Monastir in the eleventh century see al-Bakri, *Description de l'Afrique septentrionale* (French text), p. 79.

74. *al-Khitat* I, pp. 398, cf. 361, 452.

CHAPTER VII

1. Ibn at-Tiktaka, *al-Fakhri* (ed. Ahlwardt), p. 31; I. P. Petrushevsky, 'The socio-economic conditions of Iran under the Il-Khans', in *The Cambridge History of Iran* V, pp. 490ff, 529ff; W. Hinz, 'Steuerinschriften aus dem mittelalterlichen Vorderen Orient', *Belleten* 13 (1949), p. 750ff; Barthold in *ZDMG* 101 (1951), pp. 261ff, 267f; A. K. S. Lambton, *Landlord and peasant in Persia*, p. 82; Ibn al-Fuwati, pp. 398, 424, 430, 454, 482ff; Rashid ud-din, *Tarikh-i Mubarak-i Ghazan-i* (ed. Jahn), p. 348f.

2. Petrushevsky, *op. cit.*, p. 494f.

3. Rashid ud-din, *op. cit.*, p. 303ff; B. Spuler, *Die Mongolen in Iran* (Berlin 1968), p. 408.

4. Rashid ud-din, *op. cit.*, p. 264; id., *Mukatibat-i Rashidi* (Lahore 1945), p. 37ff, cf. Petrushevsky, pp. 513, 517.

5. See A. A. Duri, s. v. Baghdad in *Enc. of Islam*[2] I, p. 902; Rashid ud-din, *Histoire des Mongols de la Perse* (tr. E. Quatremère) (Paris 1836), pp. 310, 330f, 388; id., *Tarikh-i Mubarak-i Ghazan-i*, p. 350; Barhebraeus, *Syriac chronicle* (tr. A. W. Budge), p. 435; id., *Arabic Chronicle* (Beirut 1890), p. 486. On the exaggerations cf. my paper, 'The Mongol storm and the Jews', *Zion* IV, p. 63 note 98.

6. Ibn al-Fuwati, pp. 366, 408, 446, 447, 449; A. al-Azzawi, *Tarikh al-Irak bain ihtilalain* (Baghdad 1935 ff) I, p. 335, II, p. 28; Ibn al-Wardi, *Tarikh* (Cairo 1285) II, p. 266.

7. G. Le Strange, 'Baghdad during the Abbasid caliphate', *JRAS* 1899 p. 886; *The geographical part of the Nuzhat al-qulub* (tr. cf. Le Strange) (Leyden 1919), pp. 43, 47ff, 52, 103f; *The Travels of Ibn Battuta* (tr. Gibb) (Cambridge 1962), pp. 281, 322, 326, 352; *Géographie d'Aboulfeda* (tr. Reinaud) II, 2, pp. 54, 61. Cf. *The Travels of Ibn Jubayr*, p. 211; Yakut II, pp. 79, 277, 317, 393, 516, III, p. 705, IV, p. 447, and see also G. Le Strange, *The Lands of the Eastern Caliphate*, pp. 35, 50, 61, 62, 76, 114, 191; R. McC. Adams, *Land behind Baghdad*, pp. 90, 92, 94.

8. *Tarikh-i Mubarak-i Ghazan-i*, p. 144f; Ibn Battuta (ed. Defrémery–Sanguinetti) IV, p. 314.

9. *Land behind Baghdad*, pp. 96, 107; *Nuzhat al-qulub*, p. 34.

10. *Land behind Baghdad*, pp. 108, 109, 115.

11. *Nuzhat al-qulub*, p. 193f; Ibn Battuta (tr. Gibb), p. 436.

12. Ibn Fadlallah al-Umari, quoted in al-Kalkashandi, *Subh* IV, p. 422; A. Z. Validi, 'Mogollar devrinde Anadolunun iktisadi vaziyeti', *Türk hukuk ve iktisat tarihi mecmuasi* I (1931), p. 6f; W. Hinz, 'Ein orientalisches Handelsunternehmen im 15. Jahrhundert', *Die Welt des Orients* I (1949), p. 326.

NOTES 361

13. Ibn al-Fuwati, pp. 348, 430. J. M. Smith, 'The silver currency of Mongol Iran', *JESHO* 12 (1969), p. 16ff.
14. *Tarikh-i Mubarak-i Ghazan-i*, p. 312ff; J. M. Smith–F. Plunkett, 'Gold money in Mongol Iran', *JESHO* 11 (1968), p. 285; Ibn al-Fuwati, p. 498.
15. K. Jahn, 'Das iranische Papiergeld', *Archiv Orientalni* X (1938), p. 308ff.
16. See my *Histoire des prix et des salaires*, p. 451f (with some corrections); 'Odorico da Pordenone' in H. Yule, *Cathay and the way thither* (Taipei 1966) II, p. 111f, and see p. 112, note 2. Supposing that the dirham which Ibn Battuta had in mind when he mentioned the bread price was also a debased one, it would have been rather improbably low.
17. *Nuzhat al-qulub*, p. 31; Rashid ud-din, *Tarikh-i Murabak-i Ghazan-i*, pp. 262, 346; id., *Mukatibat-i Rashidi*, pp. 33f, 121f; cf. I. P. Petrushevsky, *Zemledelie i agrarnie otnosheniya v Irane XIII–XIV vv.* (Moscow–Leningrad 1960), pp. 348, 354; id., 'The socio-economic conditions of Iran under the Il-Khans', in *Cambridge History of Iran* V, pp. 526, 531f.
18. Rashid ud-din, *Histoire des Mongols de la Perse* (tr. Quatremère), p. 130ff; id., *Tarikh-i Mubarak-i Ghazan-i*, pp. 305f, 355; *Djami ut-tawarikh* (ed. Alizade) (Baku 1957) III, p. 558; Petrushevsky, *Zemledelie*, pp. 238f, 329f; id., 'The socio-economic conditions', etc., *ibid.*, p. 523f; Lambton, *Landlord and peasant*, p. 99.
19. *Tarikh-i Mubarak-i Ghazan-i*, pp. 249, 306; *Nuzhat al-qulub*, p. 33; Petrushevsky in *Cambridge History of Iran* V, p. 490; id., *Zemledelie*, p. 107.
20. al-Yunini, *Dhail mirat az-zaman* (Haidarabad 1954–61) IV, p. 225; *Tarikh-i Mubarak-i Ghazan-i*, pp. 203, 349ff; Lambton, p. 91; *Mukatibat-i Rashidi*, p. 244; Petrushevsky in *Cambridge History of Iran* V, pp. 495f, 498; *Nuzhat al-qulub*, pp. 33, 36, 41, 47, 102 (in the Persian text the totals of the period preceding the Mongol conquest are not given in gold dinars. So there was not such a tremendous and general decline of the tax revenues as some scholars have inferred from this author's figures. Further, many data from pre-Mongol times have been misunderstood or incorrectly transmitted by Kazwini, cf. Barthold in *ZDMG* 101, pp. 254f, 269.)
21. *Mukatibati-i Rashidi*, pp. 225f, 233f; Petrushevsky in *Cambridge History of Iran* V, p. 521; *Nuzhat al-qulub*, pp. 46, 48, 49, 53, 102ff, and cf. Petrushevsky, 'Feodalnoe khozyaystve Rashid addina', in *Voprosi istorii* (1951), no. 4, pp. 90, 94, and id., *Zemledelie*, pp. 110, 217, 219f, 237f; Lambton, *Landlord and peasant*, p. 98; E. Wirth, *Agrargeographie des Irak* (Hamburg 1962), p. 46.
22. Marco Polo (ed. Yule–Cordier) (London 1921) I, pp. 60f, 63; Ibn Battuta (tr. Gibb), pp. 335, 420, 446, and ed. Defrémery–Sanguinetti, III, pp. 8, 11; al-Kazwini, *Athar al-bilad* II, p. 248; al-Yunini IV, p. 145; *Marasid al-ittila* (ed. Juynboll) I, p. 309; W. Hinz, 'Das Steuerwesen Ostanatoliens im 15. und 16. Jahrhundert', *ZDMG* 100 (1950), p. 195; *as-Suluk* I, p. 497; *Subh* II, p. 476; al-Azzawi II, p. 88; *Viaggio di Giosafat Barbaro, Il Nuovo Ramusio* VII (Rome 1973), p. 148.

23. *Tarikh-i Mubarak-i Ghazan-i*, pp. 225ff, 286ff; Ibn al-Fuwati, *Talkhis madjma al-adab* IV, p. 779.

24. al-Yunini III, p. 254, and see also IV, p. 121; M. Djawwad, 'Tidjarat al-Irak fi usur al-hukm al-mughuli', *Madjallat ghurfat tidjarat Baghdad* VI (1943), p. 440, VII (1944), pp. 64, 263; Ibn Kathir 14, p. 142f: Iraki merchants who go to Syria in the second half of the thirteenth century; see also al-Azzawi I, p. 465; Ibn al-Fuwati, p. 424f; *an-Nudjum az-zahira* (ed. Cairo) VIII, p. 138f; W. Hinz, 'Das Steuerwesen Ostanatoliens', etc. *ZDMG* 100, p. 196; *ad-Durar al-kamina* (Haydarabad 1348–50) I, p. 381f; *as-Suluk* II, pp. 128, 175, 209, 211, 366; Shihab ad-din Ibn Fadlallah al-Umari, in *Notices et Extraits* 13 (1838), p. 238; M. Djawwad, art. cit., in *Madjalla* VII, p. 259.

25. Ibn Battuta (tr. Gibb), p. 516; ed. Defrémery–Sanguinetti III, p. 16f; R. R. di Meglio, 'Il commercio arabo con la Cina dall'avvento dei Mongoli al XV secolo', *Annuario Ist. Univ. Or. di Napoli* N.S. 16 (1966), p. 144f; M. Djawwad, art. cit., *Madjalla* VII, p. 259f.

26. al-Kazwini, *Athar al-bilad* II, p. 339f; Heyd, *Histoire du commerce du Levant* II, pp. 78, 107f, 112f. On merchants from Piacenza in Tabriz see R.-H. Bautier in *Sociétés et Compagnies de commerce en Orient et dans l'océan indien*, 'Actes du huitième colloque international d'histoire maritime' (Paris 1970), p. 325f, and cf. p. 279f; *La Persia e la Repubblica di Venezia, mostra di documenti* (Tehran 1973), no. 24ff.

27. Marco Polo I, pp. 60, 63, 75; ad-Dimishki, *Cosmographie* (tr. Mehren) (Amsterdam 1964), p. 113; *Géographie d'Aboulféda* (tr. Reinaud), p. 72; Marino Sanuto, 'Secreta fidelium crucis', in Bongars, *Gesta Dei per Francos* (Hanover 1611) II, p. 22; Ibn al-Fuwati, pp. 372, 476; al-Mufaddal b. Abi l-Fadail (ed. Blochet), p. 460; Ibn Rafi as-Sallami, *Tarikh ulama Baghdad* (Baghdad 1938), p. 165ff; Ibn Hadjar, *ad-Durar al-kamina* I, p. 338f; E. Ashtor–Strauss, *History of the Jews in Egypt and in Syria under the Mamluks* I, p. 281, and cf. A. Lane–R. B. Serjeant in *JRAS* 1948, p. 113f; Ibn Battuta (ed. Defrémery–Sanguinetti, III, pp. 404f, 425; Abu 'l-Fida, *al-Mukhtasar* (Istanbul 1286) IV, p. 119; *Felice de Merlis, prete e notaio in Venezia ed Ayas* (ed. A. Bondi Sebellico, Venice 1973), no. 72ff.

28. G. M. Thomas–R. Predelli, *Diplomatarium Veneto-Levantinum* (Venice 1880–99) II, no. 85, 93, 111; R. Morozzo della Rocca, 'Sulle orme di Polo', *L'Italia che scrive* 37 (1954), p. 120 and note 28; G. Ferrand, 'Une navigation européenne dans L'Océan indien au XIVᵉ siècle', *JA* 1922, 2, p. 307ff; G. I. Bratianu, *Recherches sur le commerce génois dans la mer Noire au XIIIᵉ siècle* (Paris 1929), pp. 188f, 320ff; L. Petech, 'Les marchands italiens dans l'empire mongol', *JA* 250 (1962), p. 560f; Guglielmo Ada, 'De modo Sarracenos extirpandi' (ed. Ch. Kohler), *Rec. Hist. Crois., Doc. arméniens* II, p. 551. Cf. Bautier, art. cit., *ibid.*, p. 279.

29. Marco Polo I, p. 107; *ad-Durar al-kamina* I, p. 59f; M. Djawwad in *Madjalla* VII, pp. 66f, 264f; J. Aubin, 'Les princes d'Ormouz du XIIIᵉ au XVᵉ siècle', *JA* 241 (1953), pp. 89ff, 100ff, 120; 'Odorico da Porde-

none', in Yule, *Cathay* II, p. 112; ad-Dimishki (tr. Mehren), pp. 215, 239; Ibn Battuta (tr. Gibb), p. 400.

30. Ibn Battuta (tr. Gibb), p. 275, and cf. on al-Ubulla, *op. cit.*, pp. 281, 351, and see Yakut IV, p. 787.

31. Petrushevsky, *Cambridge History of Iran* V, pp. 531, 535f.

32. *al-Manhal as-safi*, MS. Cairo 1113, vol. III, f. 333r.

33. V. Minorsky, 'A civil and military review in Fars in 881–1476', *BSOAS* X (1940–2), p. 169; Viaggio di Giosafat Barbaro, *Il Nuovo Ramusio* VII, p. 103; Angiolello, 'Vita et fatti del signor Ussuncassano', *Ramusio* (Venice 1559–65) II, f. 67a; G. Berchet, *La repubblica di Venezia e la Persia* (Torino 1865), pp. 3–18, 135f.

34. al-Azzawi, *Tarikh al-Irak bain ihtilalain* III, pp. 43, 65, 272f; W. Hinz, 'Das Steuerwesen Ostanatoliens', etc. *ZDMG* 100, p. 186; Ibn Arabshah, *Adjaib al-makdur* (Cairo 1305), p. 47; Nizam ud-din Shami, *Zafar nameh* (ed. Tauer) (Beirut 1937), pp. 135, 141.

35. al-Azzawi, *History of Iraqian currency for the post-Abbasid periods* (in Arabic) (Baghdad 1958), p. 87.

36. Ibn Taghribirdi, *Hawadith* (Berkeley 1930–42), pp. 199, 249f, 305f, 524, 549, 592f; Ibn Iyas II, pp. 45, 54, 60; al-Azzawi, *Tarikh al-Irak*, etc. III, pp. 107ff, 111, 142ff, 147, 149ff, 160, 174f, 186, 250, 258f, 261, 268, 472f; as-Sakhawi, *ad-Dau al-lami* (Cairo 1353–5) VIII, p. 280; id., *Dhail duwal al-islam*, MS. Bodl. 853, f. 194b; Abdalbasit b. Khalil, *Nail al-amal*, MS. Bodl. 812, f. 336a; W. Caskel, 'Ein Mahdi des 15. Jahrhunderts', *Islamica* IV (1931), p. 48ff.

37. al-Azzawi, *op. cit.* III, p. 254; W. Hinz, 'Das Steuerwesen Ostanatoliens', etc. *ibid.*, pp. 179, 181ff; Lambton, p. 102f.

38. I. P. Petrushevsky, 'K istorii instituta soyurgala', *Sovetskoe Vostokovedenie* VI (1949), p. 228ff; id., *Cambridge History of Iran* V, p. 520f; V. Minorsky, 'A soyurghal of Qasim b. Jahangir Aq-qoyunlu', *BSOAS* IX (1937–9), p. 927ff; Lambton, pp. 102, 104.

39. V. Minorsky, 'The Aq-Qoyunlu and land reforms', *BSOAS* 17 (1955), p. 451ff.

40. al-Azzawi, *History of Iraqian currency*, pp. 58f, 80ff.

41. Hinz, art. cit., *ZDMG* 100, p. 191ff; id., 'Steuerinschriften aus dem mittelalterlichen Vorderen Orient', *Belleten* 13, p. 757f; Minorsky, art. cit., *BSOAS* 17, pp. 450, 452; Marino Sanuto, *Diarii* IV, vol. 354, VI, col. 94.

42. M. Djawwad, art. cit., *Madjalla* VII, p. 262ff; Heyd, *Hist. du commerce du Levant* II, p. 128ff; Thomas–Predelli, *Diplomatarium* II, no. 97; R. R. di Meglio, 'Il commercio arabo con la Cina dall'avvento dei Mongoli al XV secolo', *Ann. Ist Un. Or. di Napoli* N.S. 16, pp. 146, 155f.

43. Hinz in *ZDMG* 100, p. 193; ASV, Cancell. Inf. Notai, Busta 232, Nicolo, prete di S. Silvestre, protocollo V; F. Lucchetta, 'L'affare Zen in Levante nel primo Cinquecento', *Studi Veneziani* X (1968), pp. 148, 152; R. S. Lopez, 'Venezia e le grande linee dell' espansione commerciale nel

secolo XIII', *La civiltà veneziana del secolo di Marco Polo* (Florence 1955), p. 52f; *Narrative of the embassy of Ruy Gonzalez de Clavijo to the court of Timour* (tr. C. R. Markham) (New York 1970), pp. 89f, 93; 'Relation du voyage d' Abdarrazzaq', *Notices et Extraits* 14, pt. 1 (1843), p. 429; Afanisiy Nikitin, *Il viaggio al di là dei tre mari*, pub. C. Verdiana (Florence 1963), pp. 9, 43; 'Viaggio di Giosafat Barbaro', *Il Nuovo Ramusio* VII, p. 147f; *The Itinerary of Ludovico di Varthema* (tr. J. W. Jones) (London 1928), p. 38; see also 'Sommario di tutti li regni', etc. in *Ramusio* I, f. 326a; J. V. Mills, 'Notes on early Chinese voyages', *JRAS* 1951, pp. 13f, 19ff; J. Aubin, 'Les princes d'Ormouz', etc. *JA* 241, pp. 115ff, 126f; the Portuguese sources quoted by di Meglio, 'Arab trade with Indonesia, and the Malay peninsula from the eighth to the sixteenth century' in *Islam and the trade of Asia*, pp. 120, 122.

44. 'Lettera di Andrea Corsali', *Ramusio* I, f. 187b; cf. the routes traced by Antonio Tenreiro, as quoted by V. Rau, 'Les Portugais et la route terrestre des Indes à la Mediterranée aux XVIe et XVIIe siècles', *Mediterraneo e Oceano Indiano*, 'Atti del VI Colloquio int. di storia marittima' (Florence 1970), p. 93, and see there p. 94; 'Relation du voyage d'Abdarrazzaq', *Not. et Extr.* 14, pt. 1, p. 429; 'Viaggio d'un mercante che fu nella Persia', in *Ramusio* II, p. 83b; G. Berchet, *Le repubblica di Venezia e la Persia*, p. 6.

45. *Itinerary of Ludovico di Varthema*, p. 8; *Viaggio d'un mercante*, 1. c.; Marino Sanuto, *Diarii* IV, col. 192, V, col. 339, 779, 821, 943, VI, col. 58, 487; O. L. Barkan, 'Osmanli devrinde Akkoyunlu Hükümdari Uzun Hasan Begi ait kanunlar', in *Tarih Vesikalari* I (1941), pp. 96ff, 185ff, and cf. Hinz in *ZDMG* 100, pp. 188, 193.

46. *as-Suluk* II, pp. 622, 657; Ibn al-Imad, *Shadharat adh-dhahab* (Cairo 1950–1) VI, p. 183.

47. *as-Suluk* II, p. 774; *an-Nudjum az-zahira* (ed. Popper) V, p. 64; cf. al-Azzawi, *Tarikh al-Irak*, etc. II, pp. 53f, 56, 60.

48. *Inba al-ghumr* I, p. 488, III, p. 481; *as-Suluk* IV, p. 1034f; al-Azzawi II, p. 224, III, pp. 42, 72, 80, 98, 99, 239.

49. J. Aubin, 'Tamerlan à Baghdad', in *Bagdad* (Leiden 1962), p. 308; *as-Suluk* IV, p. 1029; Ibn Taghribirdi, *Hawadith*, p. 523; al-Azzawi II, p. 309f, III, pp. 91, 100, 135, 143f, 170, 186; Barbaro, *Il Nuovo Ramusio* VII, p. 147.

CHAPTER VIII

1. B. Atalay, *Ettuhfet-üz-zekiyye fil-lugat-iltürkiyye* (Istanbul 1945), introduction; D. Ayalon, 'Studies on the structure of the Mamluk army', *BSOAS* 15 (1953), pp. 203–28, 448–76; id., *L'esclavage du mamelouk* (Jerusalem 1951).

2. al-Makrizi, *as-Suluk* I, p. 509, II, p. 216; Ibn Fadlallah al-Umari, *at-Tarif* (Cairo 1312), p. 93⁶⁻⁷.

3. A. N. Poliak, *Feudalism in Egypt, Syria, Palestine and the Lebanon* (London 1939), p. 18ff.

4. A. N. Poliak, 'Some notes on the feudal system of the Mamluks', *JRAS* 1937, p. 103; D. Ayalon, 'Payment in Mamluk military society', *JESHO* I, pp. 5off, 56ff, 257f; E. Ashtor, 'I salari nel Medio Oriente durante l'epoca medievale', *RSI* 78 (1966), pp. 329, 333, 343f.

5. E. Ashtor, 'l'urbanisme syrien à la basse-époque', *RSO* 33 (1958), pp. 189f, 201f; on the corporation of the engineers see Abdalbasit b. Khalil, *Nail al-amal*, MS. Oxford 812, f. 220b, and cf. his *ar-Raud al-basim*, MS. Vaticana 729, f. 249b. So the existence of such corporations cannot be denied altogether, as it has been by some scholars.

6. I. M. Lapidus, *Muslim cities in the later Middle Ages* (Harvard University Press 1967), pp. 51ff, 59f.

7. Ibn al-Wardi, *Tarikh* (Constantinople 1325) IV, p. 140; Khalil b. Shahin az-Zahiri, *Zubdat kashf al-mamalik* (ed. Ravaisse), p. 105; Ibn Khaldun, *al-Ibar* V, pp. 436–40, VI, pp. 6–11; *Nail al-amal* 812, f. 335a, 350b; Ibn Tulun, *Mufakahat al-khillan* I (Cairo 1962), pp. 98, 104, 225f, 264, 344, 385; Mudjir ad-din al-Ulaimi, *Continuation of his History of Jerusalem*, MS. Bodl. 853, f. 219a f.; Gaudefroy–Demombynes, *La Syrie a l'époque des Mamlouks* (Paris 1923), p. 183ff; A. S. Tritton, 'The tribes of Syria in the fourteenth and fifteenth centuries', *BSOAS* 12 (1947–8), pp. 567–73.

8. *Ibn Kathir* 14, p. 195; Ibn Tulun, *op. cit.*, pp. 93, 94, 96, 110, 200, 212, 213, 217, 256, 337; cf. Poliak, *Feudalism*, p. 12f; al-Ulaimi, *Tarikh*, MS. Br. Mus., Suppl. 488, f. 143a.

9. On the Bedouin tribes of Egypt see al-Kalkashandi, *Subh al-asha* IV, p. 67ff.

10. *as-Suluk* I, p. 386ff; *Subh* IV, p. 68; cf. A. N. Poliak, 'Les révoltes populaires en Egypte a l'époque des Mamelouks et leurs causes économiques', *REI* 1934, p. 259f.

11. *as-Suluk* I, pp. 471, 689f, 699; al-Kutubi, *Uyun at-tawarikh*, MS. Cambridge 699, f. 109b, 110b, 111b; Ibn Iyas I p. 200; Ibn Khaldun VI, p. 10.

12. *Nail al-amal* 812, f. 67b, 124a, 167a, 236a, 270a; Ahmad al-Bairuti, MS. Bodl. 712, f. 123b; Ibn Iyas I, pp. 249, 256, 348, II, p. 346; Ibn Taghribirdi, *an-Nudjum az-zahira* (ed. Popper) VII, p. 142; Ibn Tulun I, p. 240.

13. Ibn ash-Shihna, *ad-Durr al-muntakhab* (Beirut 1909), p. 159.

14. al-Kutubi, *Fawat al-wafayat* (Cairo 1283) I, p. 83; *an-Nudjum az-zahira* (ed. Cairo) VII, p. 181; Brockelmann, *GAL²* II, p. 125; al-Yunini, *Dhail mirat az-zaman* III, p. 434; *as-Suluk* I, pp. 613, 739, 818; *al-Khitat* II, p. 22; Ibn Hadjar, *ad-Durar al-kamina* II, p. 406, cf. 410, III, p. 327f, IV, pp. 12ff, 23, 257; as-Subki, *Tabakat ash-shafiiya* (Cairo 1324) VI, p. 23; as-Safadi, *al-Wafi* (Istanbul 1931 ff) IV, pp. 187, 262; Ibn Kathir, *al-Bidaya* 13, p. 310; Ibn al-Imad, *Shadharat adh-dhahab* V, pp. 332, 359, 427, 428, 441.

15. E. Kühnel, *Islamic art and architecture* (London 1966), p. 121. Surely it is possible that some of these craftsmen came to Syria and to Egypt even

before the conquest of Irak by the Tatars, see D. T. Rice, *Islamic art* (London 1965), p. 137.

16. al-Yunini III, p. 30; Ibn al-Furat, *Tarikh ad-duwal wa l-muluk* (Beirut 1936–42) VII, p. 203ff; *as-Suluk* I, pp. 407, 411, 468, 473f, 477, 500, 501, 511, 515; *al-Khitat* II, pp. 22f, 117; Abu 'l-Fida, *al-Mukhtasar* (Cairo 1325) IV, p. 33; K. V. Zettersteen, *Beiträge zur Geschichte der Mamluken-sultane* (Leyden 1919), p. 38f; A. N. Poliak, 'Le caractère colonial de l'état mamlouk', *REI* 1935, p. 235; D. Ayalon, 'The Wafidiya in the Mamluk kingdom', *Islamic Culture* 25 (1951), p. 89ff.

17. *as-Suluk* I, pp. 416, 423, 473; al-Mufaddal b. Abi 'l-Fadail, *an-Nahdj as-sadid* (ed. Blochet), pp. 537, 539ff, 543f; *an-Nudjum az-zahira* (ed. Cairo) VIII, p. 131f; A. Yaari, *Iggroth Eres Yisrael* (Tel Aviv 1943), p. 85.

18. *as-Suluk* I, pp. 410, 612, 814; al-Yunini I, p. 91; Ibn al-Wardi II, p. 199; Ibn al-Furat VII, p. 10; adh-Dhahabi, *Tarikh al-islam*, MS. British Museum, Suppl. 468, f. 117a f.; Ibn Kathir 13, p. 204. What Kremer says, *Seuchen*, pp. 62, 67ff, is mistaken. According to him there was also an epidemic in Egypt in 1258, whereas he does not mention that in 1274 the population of Palestine suffered from various diseases.

19. 'The demographic evolution of the Middle East', *Palestine and Middle East* X (1938), p. 202. Calculating according to the number of feddans which were cultivated at the beginning of the fourteenth century, J. C. Russel arrived at a higher estimate, viz. 4–4.2 millions, see 'The population of medieval Egypt', *Journal of the American Research Center in Egypt* V (1966), p. 76.

20. al-Yunini III, p. 261; M. Clerget, *Le Caire* I, pp. 159, 240; J. Sauvaget, 'Esquisse d'une histoire de la ville de Damas', *REI* 1934, p. 466.

21. E. Ashtor, *Les métaux précieux*, p. 21ff.

22. *Op. cit.*, p. 36ff.

23. *Op. cit.*, p. 47ff. The essays made by P. Balog show that the dirhams of Baibars range between 62% and 77% AR and those of al-Malik an-Nasir Muhammad between 65.2% and 78%, see 'History of the Dirham in Egypt', *Revue Numismatique* ser. VI, t. 3 (1961), p. 139. But in another work Balog indicates a higher silver alloy for the dirhams of Baibars, viz. 66–77%, against 68–72.5% of those of al-Malik an-Nasir Muhammad, see *The coinage of the Mamluk sultans of Egypt and Syria* (New York 1964), p. 44f. The results arrived at by Bacharach–Gordus are different; they indicate a much lower alloy of silver, viz. 56.2% of the dirhams of Baibars, 66.5% of those of Sulamish, 66% of the dirhams of Kalaun, and 65.4% of those of al-Malik al-Ashraf Khalil, see 'Studies on the fineness of silver coins', *JESHO* II (1968), p. 314f. The differences in these findings certainly is due to the fact that these scholars assayed a rather limited number of coins.

24. See Balog, 'History of the Dirham', *Revue Numismatique* 1961, p. 137.

25. *Subh* III, p. 447.

26. E. Ashtor, *Histoire des prix et des salaires*, pp. 283ff, 295ff, and cf. pp. 128f,

454f. The table (and also the following) does not carry indications of exceptionally high prices, as at the times of famines, etc.

27. See *op. cit.*, p. 313 and cf. p. 133f; p. 316f and cf. p. 134f; p. 309f and cf. p. 131.

28. *Op. cit.*, p. 373f and cf. p. 224; pp. 262f, 376, 443f, 447, 465f; E. Ashtor, 'I salari nel Medio Oriente', etc. *RSI* 78, p. 334ff.

29. 'Secreta fidelium crucis', in Bongars, *Gesta Dei per Francos* (Hanover 1611) II, p. 24.

30. Heyd, *Histoire du commerce du Levant* II, p. 25ff; *Histoire du commerce de Marseille* II, par E. Baratier–F. Reynaud (Paris 1951), pp. 35, 219ff; B. Krekić, *Dubrovnik (Raguse) et le Levant au moyen âge* (Paris 1961), no. 74, 235, 241, 257, 304, 312, 318, 319, 320, 332, and cf. pp. 113f, 115f.

31. G. Wiet, 'Les marchands d'épices sous les sultans Mamlouks', *Cahiers d'histoire égyptienne* VII (1955), pp. 81–147; letter of Mr. Naura in *JESHO* I, p. 333; E. Ashtor, 'The Karimi merchants', *JRAS* 1956, pp. 45–56; E. Strauss (Ashtor), 'A private letter of the Mamluk period', *Kiryath Sepher* 18 (1941–2), p. 199ff. On the trade with Turkey see Ibn al-Wardi IV, p. 146, on the riches of India traders see al-Kutubi, *Uyun at-tawarikh*, MS. Cambridge 699, f. 159b f.

32. See the Arabic texts translated by G. Wiet, 'La grande peste noire en Syrie et en Egypte', *Etudes d'orientalisme à la mémoire de Lévi-Provençal* (Paris 1962), pp. 367ff, 384; *Orientalia* (ed. Juynboll–Roorda–Weijers) (Amsterdam 1840–6) II, p. 388. M. W. Dols, 'The general mortality of the Black Death in the Mamluk empire', *Proceedings of the Conference on Economic history of the Near East* (Princeton 1974).

33. A. v. Kremer, *Ueber die grossen Seuchen des Orients*, p. 72ff; Abdalbasit b. Khalil, *Nail al-amal*, MS. Bodl. 803, f. 71a f., 86b f., 139a; Bodl. 812, f. 125b, 128a ff., 202b, 207a, 209a f., 210a ff., 215b, 274b, 275b, 276b ff.; id., *ar-Raud al-basim*, MS. Vaticana 729, f. 20a ff., 202a f., 208b; Ibn Habib, *Durrat al-aslak*, MS. Bodl. 739, f. 17b, 60a, 181a f., 214b; al-Bairuti, MS. Bodl. 712, f. 37a; *Muntakhabat Ibn Kadi Shuhba*, MS. Br. Mus. 1240, f. 75b; Ibn Hadjar, *Inba al-ghumr* II, p. 482; al-Makrizi, *as-Suluk* IV, pp. 1025, 1027f, 1031, 1041, 1046f, 1048; Eliyahu of Ferrara, in E. Carmoly, *Itinéraires de la Terre Sainte* (Bruxelles 1847), p. 333; as-Sakhawi, *Dhail duwal al-islam*, MS. Bodl. 853, f. 12a, 36b, 198b ff.; Mudjir ad-din al-Ulaimi, *Tarikh*, MS. Br. Mus. Suppl. 488, f. 138b; MS. Vaticana, Arab. 273, f. 48b, 79a f., 102b f.; Marino Sanuto, *Diarii* I, col. 756, 845; 17, col. 155; 18, col. 155; Felix Fabri, *Evagatorium* (ed. Hassler) III, p. 102f.

34. *Cosmographia* of an unknown author, MS. Laurenziana, Cat. Bandini, Suppl. III, col. 354; *al-Khitat* I, p. 44.

35. *al-Khitat* I, p. 73; Ibn Taghribirdi, *Hawadith*, p. 333; O. Toussoun, *Mémoire sur les finances d'Egypte*, p. 129ff; Ibn Mammati, K. *Kawanin ad-dawawin*, p. 30; total of the figures given by Ibn Djian, *at-Tuhfa as-saniya* (Cairo 1898) for the provinces of Egypt; *op. cit.*, p. 3 (for 1375); *an-Nudjum az-zahira* (ed. Popper) VI, p. 717.

36. *Bertrandon de la Broquière* (ed. Johnes) (Hafod 1807), pp. 154, 160; Lapidus, *op. cit.*, pp. 39, 255; R. Mantran–J. Sauvaget, *Règlements fiscaux ottomans, Les provinces syriennes* (Paris 1951), p. 80.

37. *Voyages et ambassades de Guillebert de Lannoy* (Mons 1840), pp. 75, 80; *Bertrandon de la Broquière*, p. 113; Stephan v. Gumpenberg, in *Reyssbuch* (Frankfort 1609), p. 451; Bernhard v. Breydenbach, in *Reyssbuch*, p. 203; Fabri, *Evagatorium* III, p. 178f; Paulus Walther v. Gugglingen, *Itinerarium* (Tübingen 1892), p. 241; E. Adler, *Jewish travellers* (London 1930), p. 222; A. v. Harff, *Pilgrimage* (tr. M. Letts) (London 1946), p. 93; *Voyage de Jean Thenaud* (ed. Schefer) (Paris 1884), pp. 173, 207ff; *al-Khitat* II, pp. 28, 35f, 53, 77, 130, 131, 161, 197, 269, 346f, 425, 444; A. Darrag, *L'Egypte sous le règne de Barsbay* (Damascus 1961), p. 84.

38. M. Clerget, *Le Caire* I, p. 240; O. L. Barkan, 'Essai sur les données statistiques des registres de recensement dans l'Empire ottoman aux XVᵉ et XVIᵉ siècles', *JESHO* I (1958), pp. 20, 27.

39. *Le Traité des famines de Maqrizi* trad. G. Wiet, p. 69ff; E. Ashtor, *Les métaux précieux*, p. 56f.

40. al-Makrizi, *op. cit.*, p. 45ff; Abdalbasit, *Nail*, MS. Bodl. 803, f. 195b, 196b, 199a, 202a.

41. *al-Khitat* I, p. 96.

42. Alexandria: al-Djazari, *Djawahir as-suluk*, MS. Paris 6739, f. 171b and see below note 45; the figures given by Piloti (80,000) are exaggerated, see *Traité d'Emmanuel Piloti sur le Passage en Terre Sainte* (ed. Dopp), p. 90. Damascus–Hims: M. Gaudefroy–Demombynes, *La Syrie à l'époque des Mamlouks*, p. 76; L. Frescobaldi–S. Sigoli, *Viaggi in Terra Santa* (Florence 1944), p. 226; B. Krekić, *Dubrovnik (Raguse) et le Levant au moyen âge*, no. 427.

43. *al-Khitat* II, pp. 61, 231, 369; A. Heers, 'Il commercio nel Mediterraneo alla fine del sec. XIV e nei primi anni del XV', *Archivio Storico Italiano* 113 (1955), pp. 161f, 168, 171, 172, 174, 175, 185, 186; *Histoire du commerce de Marseille* II, p. 248; *as-Suluk* I, p. 383f; E. Ashtor, *Histoire des prix et des salaires*, p. 317.

44. soap: ad-Dimishki, *Nukhbat ad-dahr* (ed. Mehren), p. 200; Ibn Battuta I, p. 145; Lapidus, *op. cit.*, p. 33; paper: *al-Khitat* I, p. 367; Ashtor in *JESHO* IV, p. 35; *Subh* II, p. 476; glass: Heyd, *Histoire du commerce du Levant* II, p. 710; C. J. Lamm, *Mittelalterliche Gläser u. Steinschnittarbeiten aus dem Nahen Osten* (Berlin 1930), p. 249ff.

45. *al-Khitat* II, pp. 32, 98, 99, 167, 228; *Traité des famines*, p. 75; an-Nudjum az-zahira VI, p. 714; Ibn Dukmak, *al-Intisar* IV, p. 41ff (cf. *al-Khitat* I, p. 342); al-Adfuwi, *at-Tali as-said* (Cairo 1966), pp. 13, 18, 39 (cf. *al-Khitat* I, p. 232).

46. Y. al-Ishsh, 'Mudhakkarat', etc. *Rev. Acad. Arabe* 18 (1943), p. 152; Ibn Tulun, *Mufakahat al-khillan* I, p. 146; Piloti, p. 136; Krekić, no. 629, 636, 950; *as-Suluk* IV, p. 1211.

47. as-Sakhawi, *ad-Dau al-lami* III, p. 208[11] (the mill was probably called

'Persian' because there were such mills in Adherbeidjan and in neighbouring countries, see Wiedemann, *Aufsätze* I, p. 214ff); Thenaud, p. 209; Lynn White, p. 87; *al-Khitat* I, p. 239, II, pp. 32, 98ff; *Subh al-asha* IV, p. 183; on tiraz in Alexandria in the fourteenth century see *as-Suluk* II, p. 285, price of safran see *Histoire des prix et des salaires*, pp. 343, 432, and cf. A. Petino, 'Lo zafferano nell'economia del medioevo', *Studi di economia e statistica* (Univ. di Catania) I (1950–1), pp. 173, 176f; innovations: Lynn White, p. 119; E. Lipson, *The history of the woollen and worsted industry* (London 1921), p. 132; Cl. Carrère, *Barcelone* (Paris 1967) I, p. 438; monopolies, abolition of tiraz: M. Sobernheim, 'Das Zuckermonopol unter Sultan Barsbai', *Zeitschrift f. Assyriologie* 27, p. 75ff; E. Ashtor, *The Jews under the Mamluks* III, p. 149ff; Ibn Khaldun, *Prolegomena* (tr. Rosenthal) II, p. 66f; cf. E. Ashtor, 'Les lainages dans l'Orient médiéval', *Atti della 2a Settimana di storia economica* (Prato 1970), 29f id., 'Levantine sugar industry in the late Middle Ages', (in) *Proceedings of the Conference on Economic history of the Near East* (Princeton 1974).

48. *Prolegomena* (tr. Rosenthal) II, p. 46; Lapidus, *op. cit.*, p. 33; Salih b. Yahya, *Tarikh Beirut* (Beirut 1927), p. 107f; import of glass: Santo Brasca, *Viaggio in Terra Santa 1480* (Milano 1966), p. 63; G. Wiet, *Précis de l'histoire d'Egypte* II, p. 265; import of paper: *Marino Sanuto* III, col. 1188, 1199; 11, col. 95; soap: J. Heers, *Gênes au XVᵉ siècle* (Paris 1961), p. 377; porcelain: George T. Scanlon, 'Egypt and China, trade and imitation', in D. S. Richards (ed.) *Islam and the trade of Asia*, p. 91.

49. Quatremère, *Histoire des sultans mamlouks* I, 1, p. 252; Marino Sanuto, 'Secreta fidelium crucis', in Bongars, *Gesta Dei per Francos* II, p. 25; Frescobaldi, p. 48; *Hist. du comm. de Marseille*, p. 245f; Carrère II, pp. 502, 525f; Piloti, p. 107; Stephan v. Gumppenberg, in *Reyssbuch* I, p. 451; Giovanni da Uzzano, 'La pratica della mercatura', in Pagnini, *Della decima* (Lisbon–Lucca 1766) IV, p. 114; *Libro di mercatantie* (ed. Borlandi) (Turin 1936), p. 73; Pietro Casola, *Pilgrimage to Jerusalem in the year 1494* (Manchester 1907), p. 231; J. Wansbrough, 'Venice and Florence in the Mamluk commercial privileges', *BSOAS* 28 (1965), pp. 487, 499, tr. p. 511; id., 'A Mamluk letter of 877/1473', *BSOAS* 24 (1961), p. 200ff; id., 'A Mamluk commercial treaty concluded with the republic of Florence', (in) *Documents from Islamic chanceries* (ed. S. M. Stern) (Oxford 1965), p. 53, tr. p. 62; Marino Sanuto III, col. 942, 1198, 1572.

50. See *Histoire des prix et des salaires*, pp. 287ff, 296ff; Abdalbasit, *Nail*, MS. Bodl. 812, f. 245a; as-Sakhawi, *Dhail*, MS. Bodl. 853, f. 207a. As far as possible, the table includes one datum referring to the spring and one to the autumn or winter.

51. MS. Br. Mus., Or. 6854, f. 397a.

52. *Histoire des prix et des salaires*, pp. 311ff, 401f.

53. *Op. cit.*, pp. 308ff, 316f, 399ff, 404f; E. Ashtor, 'L'évolution des prix dans le Proche-Orient à la basse-époque', *JESHO* IV (1961), p. 24ff.

54. ad-Dimishki, p. 109; Abdalbasit, *Nail*, MS. Bodl. 803, f. 31a, 119b; *as-Suluk* II, p. 843; *al-Khitat* I, p. 61; *an-Nudjum az-zahira* VI, p. 272; *Hawadith*, p. 108; Darrag, p. 65; Ibn Iyas IV, pp. 104, 291, 428; *ad-Dau al-lami* V, p. 266; Ibn Kathir, *al-Bidaya* 14, p. 273; MS. Vaticana, Arab. 273, f. 47a; repairs of irrigation system: al-Yunini III, p. 258; Ibn Iyas I, p. 159, IV, pp. 104, 228, 291, 329; Darrag, p. 63f; Abdalbasit, MS. Bodl. 812, f. 217b, 306b, 364a, 400b.

55. Mantran–Sauvaget, p. 77, cf. p. 34; Poliak, *Feudalism*, pp. 64, 69; an-Nuwairi, *Nihayat al-arab* VIII, p. 298; as-Subki, *Muid an-nizam* (Leiden 1908), p. 48; Ibn Iyas IV, pp. 262f, 428, V, p. 30.

56. *as-Suluk* I, p. 564, II, pp. 110, 231, 541; al-Yunini III, p. 251; Baibars al-Mansuri, *Zubdat al-fikra*, MS. Br. Mus. 1233, f. 139b f., cf. *as-Suluk* I, p. 712; Abu 'l-Fida, *Mukhtasar* IV, p. 33; id., *Géographie* (tr.) II, pt. 1, p. 49; Ibn Taghribirdi, *al-Manhal as-safi*, MS. Paris 2068, f. 161a; al-Kutubi, *Uyun at-tawarikh*, MS. Cambridge 699, f. 155b ff.

57. as-Sakhawi, *ad-Dau al-lami* VI, pp. 39[20], 142f, 232, VII, pp. 90[14], 286, VIII, p. 203; al-Yunini IV, p. 200; *as-Suluk* I, p. 735f; *al-Manhal as-safi* (ed. Nadjati) (Cairo 1956) I, p. 366f; Ibn ash-Shihna, *ad-Durr al-muntakhab*, pp. 128, 168, 174; al-Kutubi, f. 169b.

58. *as-Suluk* II, p. 807; Ibn al-Furat IX, p. 382; Krekić, no. 378; Marino Sanuto IV, col. 209, V, col. 31f, 40; 11, col. 646; Heyd II, p. 612f; Abdalbasit, *ar-Raud al-basim*, MS. Vaticana 729, f. 39a; cf. E. Ashtor, 'Quelques problèmes que soulève l'histoire des prix dans l'Orient médiéval', in *Mémorial Gaston Wiet* (Jerusalem 1976).

59. *ad-Dau al-lami* III, p. 208; *as-Suluk* II, p. 112; on the cotton plantations see beside the texts quoted by Heyd 1. c. B. Lewis, 'An Arabic account of the province of Safed', *BSOAS* 15, p. 483; Pietro Casola, p. 239.

60. al-Yunini III, p. 252, cf. IV, p. 152; Ibn Dukmak, *al-Djauhar ath-thamin*, MS. Bodl. 648, f. 137b, 144b; Abdalbasit, MS. Bodl. 812, f. 222a, cf. 361a; the dhura is probably sorghum, see Lewis in *Arabic and Islamic Studies in honour of Gibb*, p. 423; Ibn Tulun I, pp. 228, 239, 315, 329, 354, 370; B. Lewis, 'Studies in the Ottoman archives I', *BSOAS* 16, p. 489f; id., 'Jaffa in the sixteenth century, according to the Ottoman tahrir', *Necati Lugal Armagani* (Ankara 1969), p. 436ff.

61. Krekić, no. 476, 698, 706; *Hist. du comm. de Marseille*, p. 246; Carrère I, p. 315.

62. W. M. Brinner, 'The significance of the harafish and their "sultan",' *JESHO* VI (1963), pp. 190ff, 201; E. Ashtor, 'Essai sur l'alimentation des diverses classes sociales dans l'Orient médiéval', *Annales E.S.C.*, pp. 1032, 1035, cf. *Histoire des prix et des salaires*, pp. 372f, 466.

63. Darrag, pp. 152ff, 157; Mudjir ad-din, *al-Uns al-djalil* (Cairo 1283), pp. 686f, 694, 702; Ibn Tulun I, pp. 41, 44, 45, 213, 249, 292; Ibn al-Wardi, *Tarikh* (Cairo 1325), p. 144; Havliyat dimishkiya, ed. H. Habashi (Cairo 1968), f. 138b; *as-Suluk* II, p. 855.

64. On the 'corn shore', see *al-Khitat* I, p. 88; *Hawadith*, p. 89; Ibn Iyas II, p. 49.

65. Against Lapidus, p. 126f; (on state monopoly of spice trade) see M. Amari, *I diplomi arabi del R. archivio fiorentino*, pp. 348, 364; Krekić, no. 989; Wansbrough in *Documents from Islamic chanceries*, p. 65, X; on traders in various branches see W. M. Brinner, 'The murder of Ibn an-Nasu', *JAOS* 77 (1957), p. 207ff; I. M. Lapidus, 'The grain economy of Mamluk Egypt', *JESHO* 12 (1969), pp. 7, 9ff; Ibn Tulun I, pp. 49, 109; Abdalbasit, MS. Bodl. 812, f. 268a; trade with Turkey, Ibn Tulun I, pp. 146, 268; Abdalbasit f. 235a.

66. Ibn Tulun I, p. 125; Abdalbasit f. 104a, 111a, 202a; Van Berchem, *Matériaux pour un Corpus Inscriptionum Arabicarum* I, p. 446f; Lapidus, appendix E.

67. On families of theologians: K. S. Salibi, 'The Banu Jamaa, a dynasty of Shafiite jurists', *SI* 9 (1958), pp. 97–109; W. M. Brinner, 'The Banu Sasra', *Arabica* VII (1960), pp. 167–95; E. Ashtor, 'Jerusalem in the later Middle Ages', *Jerusalem* V (1955), p. 98ff.

68. Ibn Tulun I, pp. 183, 185, 259, 262, 269, 280, 283, 289, 295, 300, 309, 316, 330, 342; Abdalbasit, f. 363b; Lapidus, p. 173ff.

69. Lapidus, p. 143ff; Ibn Tulun I, pp. 124^{21}, 250 ultima.

70. V. W. Mück, *Der Mansfelder Kupferschieferbergbau* (Eisleben 1910) I, p. 57; J. Strieder, *Studien zur Geschichte kapitalistischer Organisationsformen*, 2nd ed. (Munich–Leipzig 1925), p. 9; J. U. Nef, 'Silver production in Central Europe', *Journal of Political Economy* 49 (1941), p. 586ff.

71. 'Navigationi di Messer Alvise de Ca da Mosto', *Ramusio* I (Venice 1550), f. 108b; E. Ashtor, 'Le taux d'intérêt dans l'Orient médiéval', in *Miscellanea Franco Borlandi* (Naples 1975).

72. E. Ashtor, *Les métaux précieux*, etc. p. 106; Abdalbasit, f. 157b, 167a, 262b, 274a, 294a, 309b, 317b, 363a; Ibn Iyas III, p. 18; Ibn Tulun I, pp. 63, 129, 281; as-Sakhawi, *Dhail*, MS. Bodl. 853, f. 109b.

73. Amari, p. 184ff; Wansbrough, 'Venice and Florence', etc. *BSOAS* 28, pp. 487ff, 497ff; id., 'A Mamluk commercial treaty', etc. *Documents from Islamic chanceries*, p. 39ff; on Genoa see Heyd II, pp. 432, 461f; Heers, 'Il commercio nel Mediterraneo', etc. *Archivio Storico Italiano* 113, p. 170ff; on Ancona see E. Spadolini, *Il commercio, le arti e la loggia de' mercanti in Ancona* (Portocivitanova 1904), p. 10; ASV, Notai, Ba 211, Nicolo Turiano, fasc. V, f. 19a, 41b, 70b ff.; on Naples see *ibid.*, fasc. IV, f. 47b; on the trade of the Catalans see Carrère II, pp. 644, 851ff; on the French trade with the Levant see *Hist. du comm. de Marseille*, pp. 229ff, 339ff; further, Krekić, no. 379, 585, 649, 660, 779, 790, 818, 980, 1015, 1239, 1246, and see index, p. 411, s. v. Alexandria; on the Venetian navigation see A. Tenenti–C. Vivante, 'Les galères marchandes vénitiennes XIVe–XVIe siècles', *Annales E.S.C.* 16 (1961), p. 83ff. See also E. Ashtor, 'The Venetian supremacy in the Levantine trade – monopoly or recolonialism?' *Journal of European Economic History* III (1974), p. 5ff.

74. *Les métaux précieux*, p. 66f.

75. *Op. cit.*, p. 83.

76. For the sources and the method of the calculations see *op. cit.*, pp. 74ff, 123f, and see Priuli I, p. 59f; ASV Proc. S. Marco, Comm. miste Ba 181, fasc. 23; further, E. Ashtor, 'La découverte de la voie maritime aux Indes et les prix des épices', *Mélanges F. Braudel* (Toulouse 1973) I, p. 46.

77. *Les métaux précieux*, p. 104f; Ibn Tulun I, p. 269.

78. *Les métaux précieux*, p. 108; Abdalbasit, f. 205b ff.; Ibn Tulun I, pp. 314, 316; *Djawahir as-suluk*, MS. Br. Mus., Or. 6854, f. 404a.

79. See Aubin in *JA* 241 (1953), p. 126, note 2.

Subject Index

Geographical Index